Using

MICROSOFT®

Visual Basic 5

que®

Using

Using

MICROSOFT®

Visual Basic 5

que®

Bob Reselman

Using Visual Basic

Library of Congress Catalog No.: 97-69810

ISBN: 0-7897-1453-1

99 98 97   6 5 4 3 2 1

Interpretation of the printing code: the rightmost double-digit number is the year of the book's printing; the rightmost single-digit number, the number of the book's printing. For example, a printing code of 96-1 shows that the first printing of the book occurred in 1996.

All terms mentioned in this book that are known to be trademarks or service marks have been appropriately capitalized. Que cannot attest to the accuracy of this information. Use of a term in this book should not be regarded as affecting the validity of any trademark or service mark.

Screen reproductions in this book were created using Collage Plus from Inner Media, Inc., Hollis, NH.

Contents at a Glance

V | Appendixes

Table of Contents

II Visual Basic Programming Fundamentals

6 Using Data Types, Constants, and Variables   89

16   Using Dialog Boxes   251

17   Working with Graphics   273

V | Appendixes

A   Glossary   403

B   What's on the CD-ROM?   417

Index   421

Credits

PRESIDENT
Roland Elgey

SENIOR VICE PRESIDENT/PUBLISHING
Don Fowley

GENERAL MANAGER
Joe Muldoon

MANAGER OF PUBLISHING OPERATIONS
Linda H. Buehler

EXECUTIVE EDITOR
Brad Jones

EDITORIAL SERVICES DIRECTOR
Carla Hall

MANAGING EDITOR
Jodi Jensen

ACQUISITIONS DIRECTOR
Cheryl D. Willoughby

ACQUISITIONS EDITOR
Kelly Marshall

PRODUCTION EDITOR
Sherri L. Fugit

EDITOR
Geneil Breeze

COORDINATOR OF EDITORIAL SERVICES
Debra Frisby

PRODUCT MARKETING MANAGER
Kourtnaye Sturgeon

ASSISTANT PRODUCT MARKETING MANAGER
Gretchen Schlesinger

TECHNICAL EDITOR
Mark Hurst

WEB MASTER
Thomas H. Bennett

SOFTWARE COORDINATOR
Andrea Duvall

TECHNICAL SUPPORT SPECIALIST
Nadeem Muhammed

ACQUISITIONS COORDINATOR
Carmen Krikorian

SOFTWARE RELATIONS COORDINATOR
Susan D. Gallagher

EDITORIAL ASSISTANT
Jennifer Chisholm

BOOK DESIGNER
Ruth Harvey
Kim Scott

COVER DESIGNER
Sandra Schroeder

INDEXER
Craig Small

Composed in *Century Old Style* and *ITC Franklin Gothic* by Que Corporation.

I dedicate this book to my cousin, Agnes—a kindred spirit in every sense of the word.

About the Author

Bob Reselman is a software developer. He lives in Sioux City, IA. When not making, teaching, reading or writing about software, he keeps himself busy with his other interests, which include music, philosophy, and pondering the implications of technology on the average citizen, particularly little kids.

He can be reached at **reselbob@pionet.net**. He invites all interested parties to visit his personal Web Page at: **http://www.pionet.net/~reselbob**. He is always interested in doing interesting projects with interesting people.

Acknowledgements

As far as acknowledgments go, there are three sets of people that deserve recognition and appreciation with regard to this book.

First, I want to thank Eric Dafforn, Sherri Fugit, Brad Jones and Geneil Breeze from Que for their valuable input during the production of this book. Also, I cannot thank enough the most excellent technical editor, Mark Hurst, for his thorough, critical, conscientious guidance and correction through the Author Review process.

I particularly want to acknowledge Kelly Marshall, the best Acquisitions Editor a guy could ask for. Her wisdom, encouragement, and guidance made the most difficult times so much easier. Without her support, this book would not have happened.

Second, I want to acknowledge Gateway 2000. Without the opportunities the company provided, I could not do the sort of things that I do. It is a unique place in which to work.

Lastly and most importantly, I want to acknowledge my wife Dorothy Lifka, the kindest, most tolerant, most intelligent woman I have ever known. Her beauty is without comparison, on the inside and on the outside. Also, I want to acknowledge the patience of my daughters, Geneviève and Alexandra, who had to share me all summer long with this project. They make life a joyous and wonderful experience. I can only trust that I do half as much for them as they do for me. I love them beyond words.

We'd Like to Hear from You!

As part of our continuing effort to produce books of the highest possible quality, Que would like to hear your comments. To stay competitive, we *really* want you, as a computer book reader and user, to let us know what you like or dislike most about this book or other Que products.

You can mail comments, ideas, or suggestions for improving future editions to the address below, or send us a fax at (317) 581-4663. The address of our Internet site is **http://www.mcp.com** (World Wide Web).

Thanks in advance—your comments will help us to continue publishing the best books available on computer topics in today's market.

The Programming and Database Team
Que Corporation
201 W. 103rd Street
Indianapolis, Indiana 46290
USA

Introduction

Learning about the fundamentals of computer programming with Visual Basic Version 5 is what this book offers. This book does not require that you have any prior knowledge of computer programming, although it does assume that you have access to a facility with Windows 95 or Windows NT 4.0. You should feel comfortable using the standard Windows elements—buttons, dialog boxes, check boxes, option buttons, and so on. If you've been using a Windows application such as Word or Excel for some time, you probably have enough experience to get the full benefit of this book. If you are coming to this book with programming experience in a non-Windows environment using languages such as COBOL or CICS, you'll find the "Basic-ness" of Visual Basic to be familiar. However, if you find yourself getting lost, you might want to brush up on your general Windows skills. After all, Visual Basic and Windows go hand-in-hand. ■

How to Use This Book

Doing things with Visual Basic and creating the programs you want is what this book is about. All the concepts and techniques this book presents in are done within the context of example programs that are on the CD-ROM that accompanies this book. All of the programs are completely and professionally commented. As you read through the book, you might find it useful to follow along with the code. In this case, a wise saying to remember is, "One code example is worth a hundred pages of a programming book."

How This Book Is Organized

The linear organization of this book is perfect for learning. To get you started on the path to success, this book starts with the basics and fundamentals, progressing all the way to advanced topics. This book is divided into the following four sections:

Part I: Real Apps, Real Fast: The Basis of Visual Basic Programming

Shows you how to build a simple application. It also covers the basics of Visual Basic programming—ActiveX controls, properties, methods, events, and the structure of the Visual Basic programming environment.

Chapter 1, "Your First Application," shows you an overview of how to make an application with all of Visual Basic 5's features. It's especially helpful for getting the fundamentals.

Chapter 2, "Customizing and Navigating the Visual Basic Programming Environment," describes the Visual Basic 5.0 Integrated Development Environment (IDE). The VB IDE is the workbench upon which you make your Visual Basic programs.

Chapter 3, "Using the Standard Tools," demonstrates how to use the ActiveX controls in the Visual Basic Toolbox to build a program.

Chapter 4, "The Structure of a Visual Basic Project," shows you how to work with forms and modules within the structure of a project. Also, this chapter covers how to work with multiple projects.

Chapter 5, "Working with Properties, Methods, and Events," gives you the programming essentials that you need to master in order to work effectively with objects and controls in Visual Basic.

Part II: Visual Basic Programming Fundamentals

Presents the fundamental concepts and techniques that are general to computer programming overall but are implemented using Visual Basic. The topics that you will cover are variables, conditional statements, loops, statements, and arrays.

Chapter 6, "Using Data Types, Constants, and Variables," demonstrates how to accommodate data and information, whether it is known data or unknown data.

Chapter 7, "Making Statements in a Program," shows you how to write programming instructions in Visual Basic. This chapter demonstrates how to do arithmetic operations and how to display strings.

Chapter 8, "Making Choices with Conditional Statements," covers the decision making features of Visual Basic. In this chapter you learn about `For...If...Then` statement and `Select Case` statement.

Chapter 9, "Working with Loops," demonstrates how to work with and control continuously recurring statements. This chapter shows you how to use `For...Next` and `Do...While` loops.

Chapter 10, "Working with Arrays," shows you how to work with groups and collections of data in order to program efficiently and effectively.

Part III: The Elements of Visual Basic Programming

Deals with items that are specific to Visual Basic programming. You learn how to work with user input, how to handle time, how to work with menus and dialog boxes, and how to use the graphical features of Visual Basic. You also learn how to debug your program and deploy it for others to use.

Chapter 11, "Working with Time and Timers," shows you how to use the `Timer` control to make programs that keep and use time. This chapter shows you how to use the `Date` data type and the various time and date functions that are part of Visual Basic.

Chapter 12, "Designing Windows Applications," discusses the ins and outs of designing and implementing effective Windows applications. In this chapter you learn how to design principles that you can apply throughout your programming efforts.

Chapter 13, "Working with Menus," shows you how to use the Visual Basic Menu Editor to make proper, easy to use menus for your programs.

Chapter 14, "Handling Keyboard and Mouse Input," is where you learn how to accommodate user input from the mouse and keyboard. In this chapter you learn how to work with the various event procedures that pertain to mouse and keyboard devices.

Chapter 15, "Working with Multiple Forms," demonstrates how to use the Multiple Document Interface to make programs that have many forms within a common window.

Chapter 16, "Using Dialog Boxes," shows you how to work with Message Boxes and the Common Dialog Control. In addition, you learn how to make custom dialog boxes from scratch.

Chapter 17, "Working with Graphics," illustrates how to add images and pictures to your programs to make them truly visual applications. Also, this chapter shows you how to use the `PictureBox` and `Image` control.

Chapter 18, "Deploying Your Application," shows you how to use the Application Setup Wizard to distribute your programs on disk, CD-ROM or over the Internet.

Chapter 19, "Finding and Fixing Errors," introduces you to the Visual Basic 5.0 debugging tools. This chapter shows you techniques that you can use to prevent or quickly fix problems that might exist in your program.

Part IV: Advanced Programming Topics

You are introduced to the more complex aspects of Visual Basic programming. You learn how to save and retrieve information from a disk, and you learn how to work with databases. Additionally, you learn about user-defined functions and user-defined data types. Then, you build on what you have learned to explore the fundamentals of building objects and ActiveX controls in Visual Basic.

Chapter 20, "Working with User-Defined Subs and Functions," shows you how to write custom procedures that make your programming efforts more orderly. Learning how to work with user-defined subs and functions allows you to write code that is reusable among the many different applications that you write.

Chapter 21, "Working with Strings and Typecasting," demonstrates how to control and manipulate data in a more precise manner than you have previously. This chapter covers the various string functions that allow you to concatenate and truncate strings. In addition, you learn how to use the various data type conversion functions, such as CStr() and CInt().

Chapter 22, "Working with Control Arrays," shows you how to program controls that are part of a common group. In this chapter you learn how to create controls dynamically at runtime.

Chapter 23, "Saving and Retrieving Information," covers the techniques, statements and functions that you need to know to be able to save and retrieve data to a hard disk.

Chapter 24, "Programming with Databases," introduces you to the fundamentals of writing database applications using the Data control. In this chapter you learn about the different types of databases and the basic concepts of database design.

Chapter 25, "Adding Help to Your Applications," shows you how to write the Help component of your program. Good Help is a sign of a good program. This chapter covers how to use the Help Compiler and the compiler's tagging system.

These pages cover a lot of material. Hopefully, you'll use this book as a reference to which you will continuously return throughout your programming activities. However, be advised that this book is only a tool to help you learn Visual Basic programming. Ultimately, the best way to learn computer programming is to do computer programming. There is no substitute for the challenges you undergo and the learning you get from sitting in front of a computer and making a program from nothing more than the logic, creativity, and perseverance of your own thinking.

Real Apps, Real Fast: The Basis of Visual Basic Programming

Your First Application

The best way to learn programming is to do programming. This chapter shows you how to make a simple Visual Basic program by walking you through all the necessary steps. Later, as you go on through this book, the how's and why's of what you've done in this chapter will fall into place. ■

Learn to install Visual Basic

Get step-by-step instructions for installing Visual Basic 5.0.

See how you can make a simple application

Program your first Visual Basic application using the Integrated Development Environment (IDE).

Master the *CommandButton* controls

Use buttons in your applications to present data to an end user. Get a working introduction to the programming workbench—the Visual Basic IDE.

Learn about *TextBoxes*

Display text using one of the fundamental Visual Basic components.

Installing Visual Basic 5

Before you begin installing Visual Basic, make sure that your system meets the necessary requirements. The minimum configuration requirements that your computer needs to run Visual Basic 5 are the following:

- Windows 95 or Windows NT 3.51 or later as your operating system
- An Intel 80486 microprocessor or higher
- A VGA monitor or one with higher screen resolution
- 16 M of RAM
- 50 M of hard disk space

For the best performance, the recommended system configuration is:

- Windows 95 or Windows NT 3.51 or later as your operating system
- A Pentium class processor
- A VGA monitor or one with higher screen resolution
- 32 M of RAM
- 50 M of hard disk space

To install Visual Basic 5.0 on your system, do the following steps:

1. Put the Visual Basic CD in your CD-ROM drive. (If your system is running on Windows NT 3.51 or if the Autoplay feature of Windows 95 or Windows NT 4.0 is disabled, do Steps two and three. Otherwise skip to Step 4.
2. Open Windows Explorer and select your CD-ROM drive.
3. Double-click the SETUP.EXE file. This starts the Visual Basic setup program.
4. Select "Install Visual Basic 5.0"on the introduction screen (see Figure 1.1).

FIG. 1.1

The Visual Basic introduction screen offers you more than access to the setup program for Visual Basic 5.0.

Part
I

Ch
1

5. The copyright dialog box is the first screen you see after the Introduction screen. Click Continue.

6. Type your personal information in the Name and Organization Information dialog box and press Continue to confirm the information when prompted.

7. Enter the CD Key number in the CD Key dialog box. The CD Key is on the cover of the packaging in which the Visual Basic CD came (see Figure 1.2).

FIG. 1.2

If you don't have a CD Key number you cannot install Visual Basic. Do not loose the key; you must have it should you need to reinstall.

8. Click the OK button in the Product ID confirmation dialog box (see Figure 1.3).

FIG. 1.3

If you enter the CD Key number properly you will be shown a Product ID confirmation screen.

9. The setup program shows you a dialog box that asks you to confirm the installation directory for Visual Basic 5.0. Click the OK button in this confirmation dialog box (see Figure 1.4).

FIG. 1.4

It's best to install Visual Basic 5.0 into the recommended installation directory.

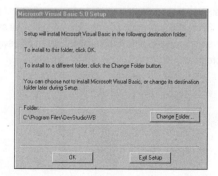

10. Click the I Agree button on the License Agreement dialog box.

11. Click the <u>T</u>ypical installation picture button (see Figure 1.5).

FIG. 1.5

The <u>T</u>ypical installation button installs all the necessary Visual Basic files and many example projects.

The Typical installation button

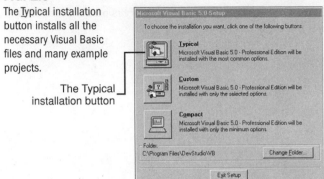

12. Click the <u>C</u>ontinue button in the Choose Program Group dialog box. The setup program checks to make sure that you have all the necessary disk space that a Typical Visual Basic installation requires. If there is enough space, the installation process begins. If there is not enough space, the installation process terminates.

13. After the setup program installs all of the Visual Basic files, you will have to restart your computer. Click the Restart Windows button on the Restart Windows dialog box.

Launching Visual Basic 5

Before you can create your first application (sometimes abbreviated as *app*), you must start Visual Basic. To launch Visual Basic, do the following:

1. Go to the Windows Taskbar and click the Start button to bring up the Start menu.

2. From the Start menu, Select Programs, then select Microsoft Visual Basic 5.0.

3. From the Microsoft Visual Basic 5.0 menu, click Visual Basic 5.0 (see Figure 1.6).

N O T E   In this writing, we are assuming that you've installed Visual Basic 5.0 using the default settings. Things might be different if you made changes during the initial setup. If you put the Visual Basic programs in another program group during installation, you must navigate the Start menu to the correct location of the programs. ▪

FIG. 1.6
Click the Visual Basic
5.0 icon in the
Microsoft Visual Basic
menu item in the
Program menu to
invoke the language.

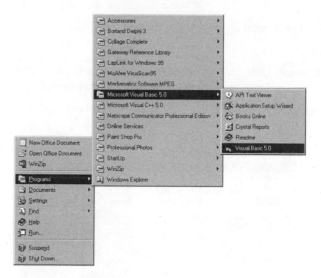

Creating the Application

After you have launched Visual Basic, the New Project dialog box appears. This dialog box enables you to select the type of project you want to create (see Table 1.1). Double-click the icon labeled Standard EXE (see Figure 1.7).

Table 1.1   Visual Basic 5.0 Project Types

Project Type	Description
Standard EXE	Creates a standard Visual Basic program.
ActiveX EXE	Creates an ActiveX program that can share its functionality with other programs.
ActiveX DLL	Creates an ActiveX Dynamic Link Library that can be used by other programs.
ActiveX Control	Creates a custom ActiveX control.
VB Application Wizard	Opens a wizard that creates a project template.
VB Professional Edition Controls	Opens a project with all the Professional ActiveX controls in the Toolbox.
Add-in	Opens a VB Addin project. (An *Add-in* is a custom created tool that lets you work within the VB IDE more easily.)

continues

Table 1.1 Continued

Project Type	Description
ActiveX Document DLL	Creates a special Dynamic Link Library that is to be used with Internet Explorer.
ActiveX Document EXE	Creates a special executable file that is to be used with Internet Explorer.

FIG. 1.7
You select your project type from one of nine New Project icons.

The Standard EXE is the icon you'll most often choose when creating VB projects. Selecting it presents the Visual Basic (*IDE*), or *Integrated Development Environment* (see Figure 1.8). The IDE is where you do the actual programming.

FIG. 1.8
The Integrated Development Environment (IDE) is where you do your programming.

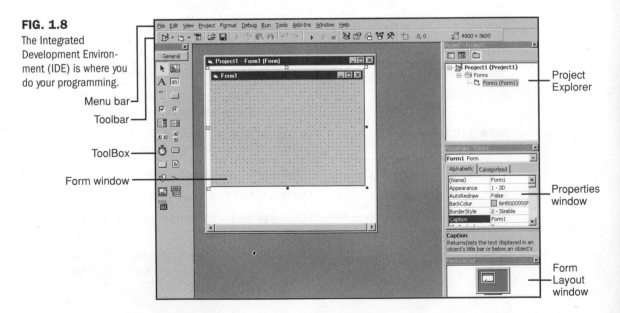

In the middle of the Visual Basic IDE is the Form window. A *form* is the foundation of a Visual Basic program. It's the window upon which you will build your program.

On the left side of the IDE is the Toolbox, which holds the graphical elements that make up your Visual Basic program (see Figure 1.9). The icons in the Toolbox represent *controls.* You place controls on a form to make up the graphical portion of your program. The graphical portion of a program is called the *Graphical User Interface* or *GUI* for short.

FIG. 1.9
The standard tools you use to make a Windows program.

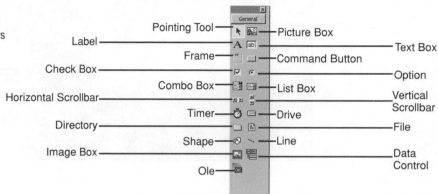

Creating the GUI

The following sections describe an application with two CommandButtons and a TextBox, but you can modify the instructions to make the program fit your needs. To make the GUI for your app, perform the following steps:

1. If you aren't sure which is the CommandButton control, notice that Visual Basic prompts you with small ToolTips window as you move your mouse pointer over the toolbox.

2. Double-click the CommandButton icon in the toolbox. Notice that a CommandButton appears on the form in the Form window (see Figure 1.10).

3. Move your mouse cursor to the form window. Hold down your primary mouse button when the cursor is over the command button on the form window and drag the command button to where you want it on the form (see Figure 1.11). (Usually the *primary* mouse button is the *left* mouse button.)

4. To add a second CommandButton, go back to the Toolbox and double-click the CommandButton icon again. Another CommandButton appears on the form. Before you do this, make sure that you moved the first button away from the center of the form, or you won't see the new one!

5. Move the second CommandButton to where you want it to appear on the form (see Figure 1.12).

6. To add a text box to the form, double-click the TextBox icon in the Toolbox. The TextBox appears near the center of the form, just as the CommandButtons did (see Figure 1.13).

FIG. 1.10
When you double-click a tool, it automatically appears on a form.

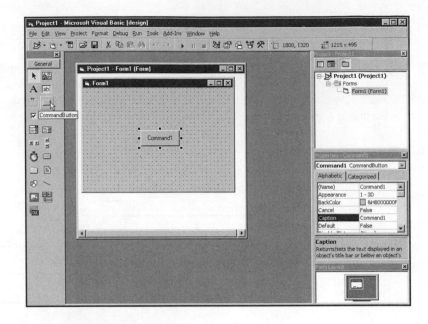

FIG. 1.11
You can move buttons on a form by dragging them.

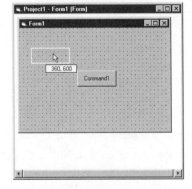

FIG. 1.12
You have many instances of the same type of control on a given form.

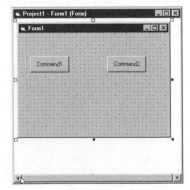

FIG. 1.13
Little boxes around
a TextBox or
CommandButton
mean that it is
selected.

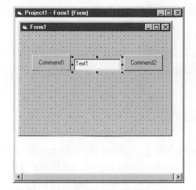

7. Drag the TextBox, just as you did with the CommandButton, to where you want it on the form (see Figure 1.14).

FIG. 1.14
The GUI for your first
application reflects your
control choices on your
form.

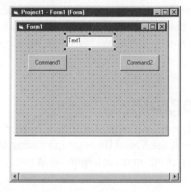

You've just created your first Graphical User Interface. It may not seem like a lot, but much of your programming work already is done.

Running the Program

To run your program, select Start from the Run menu or press the F5 key.

Several of the IDE elements disappear when your program is running. In the title bar of the Visual Basic IDE, the word *run* appears, which indicates that your program is in run mode. Also, notice that when you click either of the buttons, they press in and out. And if you click in the TextBox, a blinking cursor appears (see Figure 1.15).

FIG. 1.15

The controls on your form have full operational behavior at runtime.

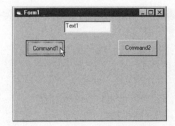

To stop your program from running, select <u>E</u>nd from the <u>R</u>un menu or click the "x" in the upper-right corner of your program's window (not the Visual Basic IDE window).

Strictly speaking, you have a real Windows program, but it won't do much until you add code to your controls.

When you are doing the actual activities of Visual Basic programming such as putting controls on a form or putting code behind those controls, you are in *design time*. When you run your program, you are in *runtime*. You can do some things in design time that you cannot do in runtime and vice versa. For example, a CommandBbutton only goes up and down when clicked at runtime. You can change the position of a control by using your mouse to move it around only at design time.

Adding Code to the Program

To make your program more useful, you have to put some code behind the controls. *Code* is the list of instructions that you write in the Visual Basic programming language. These instructions tell your program what to do. In programming jargon, what your program does is called the program's *behavior*.

For this exercise, the behavior of your program is this: When the user clicks the CommandButton on the left, certain words appear in the TextBox. When the user clicks the CommandButton on the right, a different set of words appears in the TextBox.

> **CAUTION**
>
> When you add code to your program, make sure that you are in design mode and that the program is not running. If the word *design* appears in the title bar, you are in design mode.
>
> To put your program into run mode from the <u>R</u>un menu, select the <u>S</u>tart menu item or press the F5 key. To stop your program from running in order to go back into design mode select <u>E</u>nd from the <u>R</u>un menu.

To add this behavior to your program, follow these steps:

1. Go to the first CommandButton and double-click it. The Code window appears (see Figure 1.16).

FIG. 1.16
The Code window is
where you type Visual
Basic code.

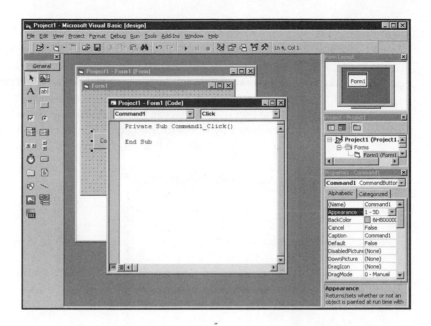

2. In the Code window, type **Text1.Text =** plus the text that you want to associate with the first CommandButton. To match the example shown in Figure 1.17, you can type **Text1.Text = "Hello World."** Make sure that you type the characters exactly where they appear in Figure 1.17 and that you include the quotation marks around the text.

FIG. 1.17
Type the code within
the code blocks, and
remember to add
quotation marks.

Click the "X" to close
the code window

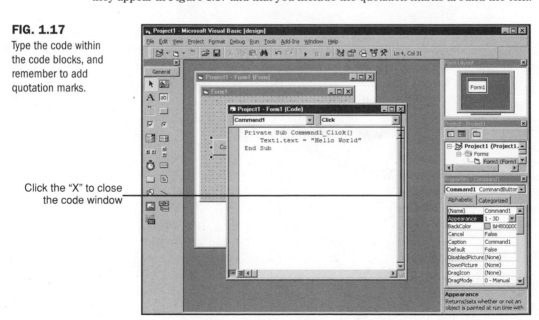

3. Click the "x" to close the Code window.

4. Double-click the second CommandButton on the form. This opens the Code window for that button.

5. In this Code window type the same code as you did in Step 2, but replace the text portion with the text you want to associate with the second CommandButton. To match the example shown in Figure 1.18, you can type **Text1.Text = "Goodbye World."** Again, type the characters exactly where they appear in Figure 1.18 and remember to include the quotation marks around the text that you associate with the second CommandButton.

FIG. 1.18

You should indent your code as you type it in the body of code.

6. Close the Code window by clicking the "x" in the upper-right corner of Code window.

7. Put your program in run mode by selecting <u>S</u>tart from the <u>R</u>un menu or by striking the F5 key.

While your program is in run mode, click the first CommandButton. Notice the words that appear in the TextBox (see Figure 1.19). Now click the second CommandButton. The words that you associated with the second CommandButton should appear in the TextBox, in place of the text of the first button (see Figure 1.20). Stop your program by clicking the "x" in the upper-right corner of the program's window.

FIG. 1.19

Clicking the first CommandButton shows the text that you associated with that button.

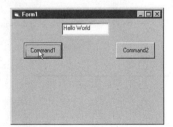

FIG. 1.20
Clicking the second
CommandButton
shows the text
associated with that
button.

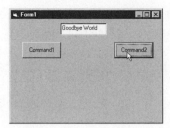

One of the good things about Visual Basic is that it does a lot of the difficult Windows programming for you. Making windows and buttons and then adding functionality to them is a very difficult chore in other languages such as C and C++. Visual Basic lessens the burden by automating many of the common activities of Windows programming.

Cleaning Up Your Program's Interface

Figure 1.21 is similar to how your program looks when it first starts up, before you click any buttons. Notice that the text in the first CommandButton is Command1 and the text in the other CommandButton is Command2. Lastly, notice that the text in the TextBox is Text1. This is confusing and irrelevant to the nature of the program; your users will have no idea what the CommandButtons and the TextBox are supposed to do.

FIG. 1.21
The state of the
program before you
do anything with it is
called the *default state*.

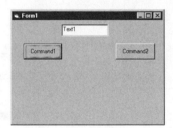

Your program would make more sense if the captions of the respective command buttons indicated their functions.

To change the captions of the CommandButtons, follow these steps:

1. Make sure your program is in design mode. If necessary, select the End menu item from the Run menu. Click CommandButton whose caption you want to change. Notice that a set of eight small boxes appears around the CommandButton after you click it. This means that the control is selected (see Figure 1.22).

CAUTION
Remember, double-clicking a control causes the control's code window to be selected. Single-clicking a control causes the control to be selected.

2. Go to the properties window. Make sure the tab labeled Alphabetic is selected. In the left side of the Properties Window, find the Caption property.

3. Next to the word Caption is the control's current caption (in this case, Command1). Double-click the caption name to highlight it (see Figure 1.22).

FIG. 1.22

You change a property's setting in the Properties window.

Property Window

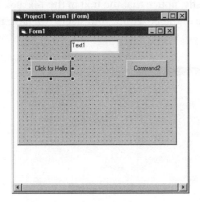

Property Name

Property Setting

4. When the Caption is highlighted in the Properties Window, type the words that you want to be the new caption. Notice the Caption of the CommandButton now changes to what you have just typed (see Figure 1.23).

FIG. 1.23

You change the caption of a CommandButton in the Properties window.

Repeat these steps for any controls whose captions you want to change. If the caption is longer than usual (see Figure 1.24), Visual Basic wraps the text so that all of it fits on the button's face.

To change the default text in the TextBox, select the text box as you did with the CommandButton. However, instead of going to the Caption property, go to the Text property and double-click the setting next to the property name. Change the current text to the text that you want in the TextBox (see Figure 1.25).

FIG. 1.24
If there is too much text for one line, a `CommandButton` automatically "wraps" its caption.

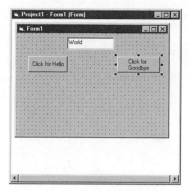

FIG. 1.25
The user can change the setting of the `Text` property of a `TextBox` at runtime by typing new text directly into the `TextBox`.

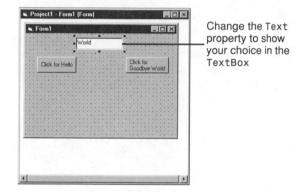

Change the `Text` property to show your choice in the `TextBox`

Run your program by selecting <u>S</u>tart from the <u>R</u>un menu or by striking the F5 key.

You have just cleaned up your first program to make it more comprehensive for the user. Notice that in Figure 1.26 the captions of the `CommandButtons` reflect what the buttons do and that the text in the `TextBox` gives an indication of the relationship between the `TextBox` and the buttons.

FIG. 1.26
A well designed Visual Basic application.

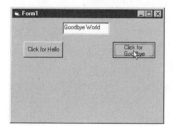

CHAPTER 2

Customizing and Navigating the Visual Basic Programming Environment

Find out about the Visual Basic 5 IDE

Learn about the different parts of the Visual Basic Integrated Development Environment (IDE) and how to manage them.

Control the way you use and view the IDE

Use menus and toolbars and learn how to view the IDE in either Multiple Document or Single Document mode.

The Visual Basic 5 Integrated Development Environment (IDE) is the workbench upon which you make your Visual Basic programs. The Visual Basic IDE enables you to lay out the Graphical User Interface (GUI) for your program, add and debug code, and manage your projects. In addition, the VB5 IDE has features that automate many of the more mundane aspects of designing and implementing your program. The following sections introduce you to the IDE, show you how to work in it, and demonstrate how to custom configure the IDE to your work style. ■

Understanding the Parts of the IDE

The Visual Basic IDE is a collection of menus, toolbars, and windows that make up your programming workbench (see Figure 2.1). Each part of the IDE has features that affect different aspects of your programming activity. The Menu bar enables you to direct the overall activity and management of your programming. The Toolbar enables you to access much of the functionality of the menu bar through the Toolbar's buttons. Forms, the basic building blocks of Visual Basic programs, are presented in a Form window; you use the Toolbox to add controls to the forms of your project. The Project Explorer displays the projects upon which you are working and the different parts of each of those projects. You browse and set a control, form, or module's properties within the Properties window. Finally, you position and view a form or forms on the screen within the Form Layout window.

Learning the ins and outs of the IDE is time well spent. The more you know about the IDE, the more productive you will be. Now that you have an overview, let's take a more in-depth look at the members of the Visual Basic 5 IDE.

FIG. 2.1

The Visual Basic IDE is the programmer's workbench.

Menu bar

Toolbar

Project Explorer

Form window

Properties window

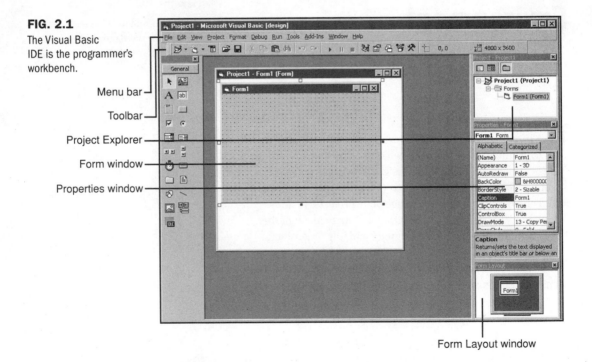

Form Layout window

Adding and Removing Toolbars in the Visual Basic IDE

Toolbars are collections of small iconic buttons that reside in a bar underneath the menu bar. These buttons offer access to functionality that you have in the Visual Basic menu structure. Toolbars are useful because instead of having to negotiate menus and submenus to do what you want, you simply click a specific button in the Toolbar to call a specific functionality in the Visual Basic IDE.

Toolbars usually reside under the menu. They can be grouped together into a single bar. You also can drag the Toolbar onto the IDE's code and form windows to have them "float," for more convenient access.

To add or remove a toolbar to the IDE, perform the following steps:

1. Right-click the Menu bar anywhere. The Toolbar pop-up menu appears, as shown in Figure 2.2.

FIG. 2.2
You select a predefined Toolbar type from the Toolbar pop-up menu.

2. Select the type of standard toolbar that you want from the pop-up menu. If a check is to the left of a toolbar type, that toolbar already is visible.

ToolTips

ToolTips are little windows that appear when you hold the mouse cursor over a control or toolbar button for a few seconds. Inside these windows is some text that tells you what the control or toolbar button is about. Notice that Figure 2.3 shows the Start ToolTip on the right side of the Debug toolbar.

Using the Debug Toolbar

You use the Debug Toolbar to test your program and resolve errors that might occur. When you debug a program, you do things such as run the code a line at a time, examine the values of variables, and stop the code at certain critical points or under certain conditions (see Figure 2.3). For an in-depth discussion of debugging, take a look at Chapter 19, "Finding and Fixing Errors."

Start
Break
End
Toggle Breakpoint
Step Into
Step Over

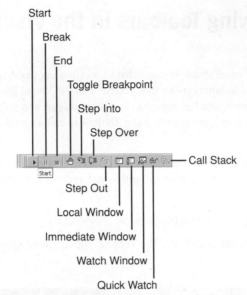

FIG. 2.3
The Debug toolbar enables you to access the debugging functions of the Visual Basic IDE.

Step Out
Local Window
Immediate Window
Watch Window
Quick Watch

Call Stack

Using the Edit Toolbar

You use the Edit Toolbar when you are working with code. The features of the Edit Toolbar are similar to those of the Edit menu. You can Cut and Paste text. You can manipulate the layout of your code and do text selection, searches, and replacement. In addition, you also can use the automatic coding features such as Quick Info (see Figure 2.4).

List Properties/Methods
List Constants
Quick Info
Parameter Info
Complete Word
Indent
Outdent

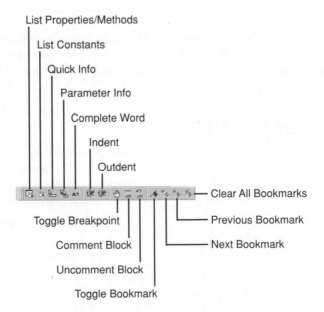

FIG. 2.4
You can access the extended Edit menu and some Debug menu functions from the Edit Toolbar.

Toggle Breakpoint
Comment Block
Uncomment Block
Toggle Bookmark

Clear All Bookmarks
Previous Bookmark
Next Bookmark

Using the Form Editor Toolbar

You use the Form Editor Toolbar to size, move, and align controls on a form. The Form Toolbar has the same set of features as the Format menu (see Figure 2.5). To learn more about how to use controls on a form, read Chapter 12, "Designing Windows Applications."

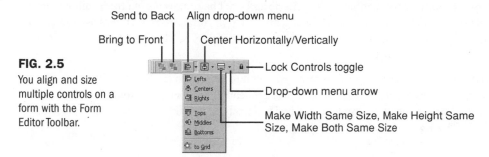

FIG. 2.5
You align and size multiple controls on a form with the Form Editor Toolbar.

Notice that there are small downward-facing arrows to the right of the Align, Center, and Make toolbar buttons. These arrows indicate that a drop-down menu will appear when you select that toolbar button.

Using the Standard Toolbar

The Standard Toolbar is the central toolbar in the Visual Basic IDE. The Standard Toolbar offers many of the features found in the File, Project, Debug, and Run menus (see Figure 2.6).

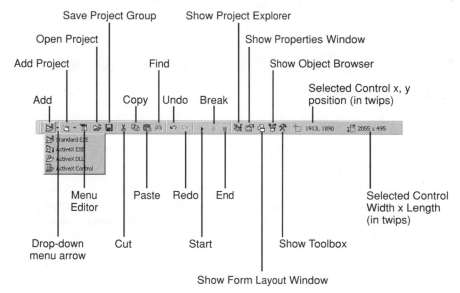

FIG. 2.6
The Standard toolbar allows you fast access to often used functionality and information.

Adding Controls with the Toolbox

The *Controls* are the building blocks from which you assemble your Visual Basic program. The *Toolbox* is a palette of controls, and you build your user interface by selecting controls from the Toolbox and placing them on your forms (see Figure 2.7).

Some of the controls are built into Visual Basic and can't be removed from the Toolbox; these controls reside within Visual Basic itself and are called *intrinsic controls*. Others live outside of Visual Basic and reside in files that end with the extension OCX. These controls can be added and removed from the Toolbox.

No matter what ToolBox control you want, adding it to your form takes only a few steps, as shown with the command buttons in your first application in Chapter 1, "Your First Application." A full discussion of the Toolbox, intrinsic controls, and ActiveX controls takes place in Chapter 3, "Using the Standard Tools."

FIG. 2.7

The Toolbox holds both intrinsic and ActiveX controls, the building blocks of Visual Basic programming.

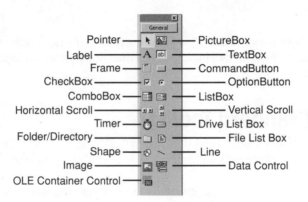

Navigating Through the Form Window and Code Window

Just as controls are the building blocks that you use to assemble your Visual Basic program, a Visual Basic form is the foundation that you build with those blocks. Forms reside in the Form Designer window (see Figure 2.8). You work in the Form Designer window to add controls to your form.

For each Form Designer window, you also can open a code window. Code windows are where you work with the Visual Basic code that you write "behind" your form (refer to Figure 2.9). The Code window has a few graphical features—called *window elements*—that you need to be aware of, as follows:

- The Object box lists the controls on the form and the form itself. You can use the Object box to access controls quickly that you want to code.

FIG. 2.8

The Form window looks like a form in a window in the Multiple Document Interface view.

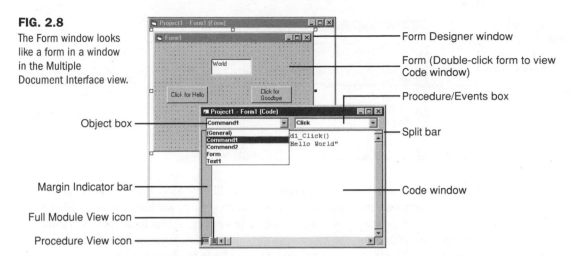

Form Designer window

Form (Double-click form to view Code window)

Procedure/Events box

Object box

Split bar

Margin Indicator bar

Code window

Full Module View icon

Procedure View icon

Part

I

Ch

2

- The Procedure/Events box lists the events associated with a given control. It also lists procedures for a form, if the form has one. (You learn about events in Chapter 5, "Working with Properties, Methods, and Events," and procedures in Chapter 20, "Working with User-Defined Subs and Functions.") You use this element to access your form's events and procedures quickly.

- The split bar divides the Code window into two separate scrollable "panes." This enables you to look at different parts of your code simultaneously.

- The margin indicator bar is the gray area on the side of the Code window where Visual Basic displays bookmarks and breakpoints.

- When you click the Procedure View icon, your code is displayed in the Code window one procedure or event at a time. All you can see is the code for what you select from the procedure/events box (see Figure 2.9).

FIG. 2.9

The Procedure view helps you focus on an event or procedure.

- When you toggle the Full Module View icon, the whole body of your code for the form is displayed, as shown in Figure 2.10. By default, events and procedures are separated from one another by a thin horizontal line between each event or procedure. If you want to reset the Code window back to the original Procedure View state, toggle the icon again.

FIG. 2.10
Full Module view gives
you a sense of your
code in its entirety.

If you have more than one form in your program, you will have more than one Form window. However, not all windows are visible at all times. Sometimes you will have the Form window for a given form open; sometimes you will have the Code window for that form open; and sometimes you will have both open. You can access the Code window from your form's Form window or through the View menu. You can view a form's Code window through the Form window by double-clicking with your mouse directly on the form in the Form window. If you want to view a form's Code window by using the menu bar, go to the View menu and select Code.

Managing Applications with the Project Explorer

The Project Explorer is a new tool added to Visual Basic 5.0 that helps you manage and navigate multiple projects. In previous versions of Visual Basic, it was possible to have only one project at a time in a Visual Basic session. Therefore, if you had any interrelated projects and you wanted to work between them, you had to invoke an instance of Visual Basic for each project.

To accommodate the management of multiple projects, Visual Basic allows you to organize multiple projects into groups called *Project Groups*. You can save the collection of projects in your Visual Basic session into a Project Group file. Project Group files end with the extension VBG.

The Project Explorer is a hierarchical tree-branch structure. Projects are at the top of the tree, and the projects' parts (forms, modules, and so on) descend from the tree. If you want to work on a particular part, you double-click the part to display it. If you want to see the part in a particular view—say a form in a Code window—you select the form by clicking it once. Then click the Code View icon at the top of the Project Explorer Window (see Figure 2.11).

As you become more adept as a programmer and the scope and size of your programs grow, you'll find the Project Explorer to be an extremely useful tool for doing large-scale programming.

View Object shows the Designer for the selected item, where appropriate

FIG. 2.11
You manage and navigate multiple Visual Basic projects with the Project Explorer.

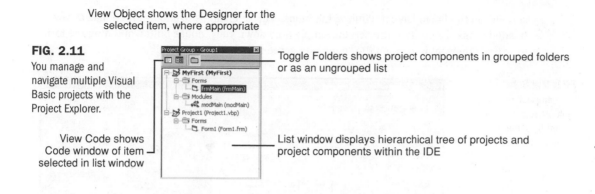

Toggle Folders shows project components in grouped folders or as an ungrouped list

View Code shows Code window of item selected in list window

List window displays hierarchical tree of projects and project components within the IDE

Controlling Settings with the Properties Window

In the Properties window, you read, configure, and control the initial settings of the ActiveX controls in your program. (The programming jargon for a property's setting is a property's *value*.) As you become more familiar with Visual Basic programming, a good portion of your time is going to be spent learning, setting, and manipulating the properties of controls. Because controls are the building blocks of Visual Basic programs, the Properties window is an *essential* tool to master. Figure 2.12 shows you the structure of the Properties window.

FIG. 2.12
The Properties window is a key Visual Basic programming tool.

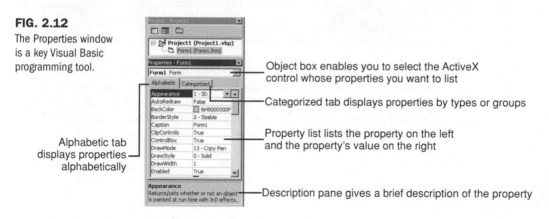

Object box enables you to select the ActiveX control whose properties you want to list

Categorized tab displays properties by types or groups

Property list lists the property on the left and the property's value on the right

Alphabetic tab displays properties alphabetically

Description pane gives a brief description of the property

Often, most of a control's properties can be set at design time.

Setting Forms' Positions with the Form Layout Window

The Form Layout window enables you to set the *runtime* position of one or more forms on a screen. The Form Layout window is a feature new to Visual Basic Version 5.0.

You position a form by moving its representation on the "computer screen" in the Form Layout window with your mouse. As you move the cursor over the small form on the "computer screen" on the Form Layout window, the mouse cursor changes to a four-directional, arrow-headed cross. To position the screen, simply hold down your mouse button and drag the form to where you want it to be on the "computer screen" (see Figure 2.13).

FIG. 2.13

You can position multiple forms on a screen by using the Form Layout window.

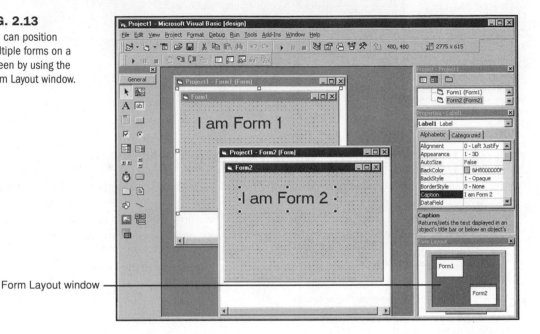

Form Layout window

The Form Layout window is a little tricky to use. Remember, the forms that you place on the Form Layout window's "computer screen" at design time affect the screen position of your program's forms only when the program is actually running, as shown in Figure 2.14. Moving the Form window (as distinct from its image in the Form Layout window) around the IDE at design time does not affect the runtime position of the form if you have the Visual Basic IDE set to SDI mode.

Viewing the IDE

There are two ways to view the Visual Basic IDE: with the *Multiple Document Interface* (MDI) or the *Single Document Interface* (SDI). Multiple Document Interface view shows all the distinct windows of the Visual Basic IDE as member windows within one large IDE window (see Figure 2.15).

In the Single Document Interface view (shown in Figure 2.16), each distinct window of the Visual Basic IDE exists independently of one another. There is no IDE window to live within. Some people who have worked with previous versions of Visual Basic might find working in the IDE in SDI view a little easier in that it is similar to the prior versions' environment. Others find the unified layout of the MDI environment more appealing. There is no better or worse way. It's all a matter of work style.

FIG. 2.14
The positioning of forms in the Form Layout window only takes effect when the program is running.

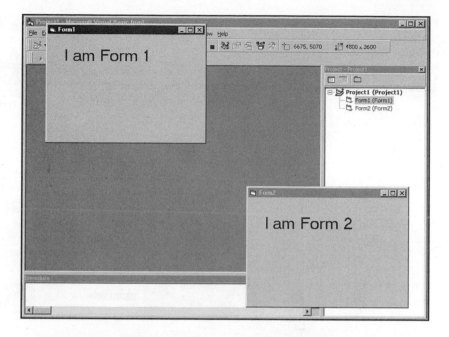

FIG. 2.15
In the MDI view, all windows are part of the Visual Basic IDE window.

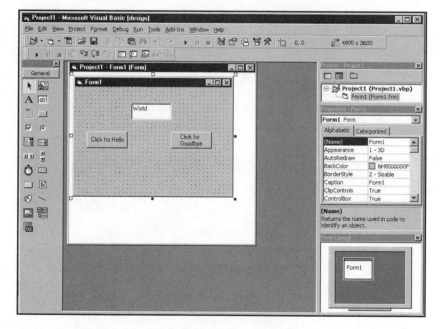

FIG. 2.16

The SDI view is the way the Visual Basic IDE looked prior to version 5.0.

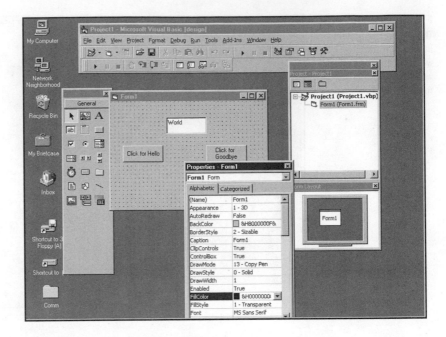

To change from MDI view to SDI view, do the following:

1. Select Options from the Tools menu. The Options tabbed dialog box appears.

2. Click the Advanced tab at the top of the Options tabbed dialog box.

3. Check the SDI Development Environment CheckBox; then click OK at the bottom of the Options tabbed dialog box. You are informed that your environment will change the next time you start Visual Basic, as shown in Figure 2.17.

4. Click OK; then terminate and restart Visual Basic.

FIG. 2.17

You have to restart Visual Basic for changes in the IDE view to take effect.

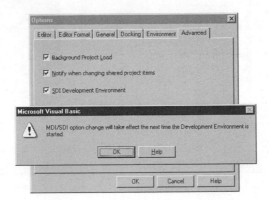

CHAPTER 3

Using the Standard Tools

Before you get into the details of programming in the Visual Basic forms and controls paradigm, you really need to understand at a very fundamental level what a computer program is. A *computer program* is simply a set of instructions that tells the computer how to perform a specific task.

Computers need instructions for every task they perform. They even need instructions for the simplest tasks, such as how to get a keystroke, how to place a letter on the screen, or how to store information to a disk. Fortunately, many of these instructions are contained on the processor chip or are built into the operating system, so you don't have to worry about them. Instead, you can concentrate on providing instructions for the tasks, such as calculating employee payroll, creating the mailing list for your neighborhood, or formatting text to display the information in the latest annual report.

While you read instructions in English, the computer must have its instructions in *binary code,* a series of on or off switches (known as *bits*) in the computer's memory and processors. There are languages such as Assembler that enable you to write this type of code directly. However, it is very difficult and time consuming to write a program this way. Visual Basic, on the other hand, is

Find out about programs

See what a computer program is and how it applies to Visual Basic.

Know what the Standard Controls are

Learn the conceptual fundamentals of Visual Basic programming using controls.

Learn how to use forms

Sample the different methods of sizing and positioning a form.

Master the Standard Controls

Find out about various controls that are standard features with Visual Basic. Learn the various methods of sizing and placing a Standard Control on a form.

Adding ActiveX controls to the Toolbox

Get an introduction to using ActiveX Controls with Visual Basic.

considered a higher level language. The Visual Basic programming language enables you to write your instructions using statements and commands that look more like the language you speak every day. The Visual Basic compiler, a software tool built into the Visual Basic IDE, then takes what you have written out in the Visual Basic language and turns it into "binary language" instructions that the innards of the computer can understand. This compiler output is usually a file that ends with the file extension .EXE, which is known as your program's executable file. ■

Controlling Form Size

Forms are not "one size fits all." To make them look good, you should size them to fit the purpose and amount of information in them, unlike the example in Figure 3.1.

FIG. 3.1

Unlike this example, making a form the appropriate size for its function is a good programming skill.

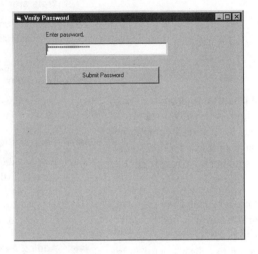

There are three ways to size a form at design time. One way is to do it graphically in the form's Form Window. The second way is to change the value of the form's Width and Height property in the Properties window. The last way is to write some code. Right now you'll learn to change a form's size in the Form Window and through the Properties window. Later, you'll take a look at how to control a form's size through code in Chapter 5, "Working with Properties, Methods, and Events."

Sizing a Form in the Form Window

You size a form in the Form Window by using your mouse to drag the sizing handles that surround the form in the Form window. The sizing handles, also known as *edit nodes*, are illustrated in Figure 3.2. Be advised that the sizing handles only appear on forms when the IDE is in MDI mode. (For an in-depth discussion of MDI versus SDI mode, see Chapter 2, "Customizing and Navigating the Visual Basic Programming Environment.") However, sizing handles appear on any control you select, regardless of the configuration of the IDE. The technique that you are learning to graphically size a form in the Form Designer window can be used in an SDI environment with only slight modification of the technique.

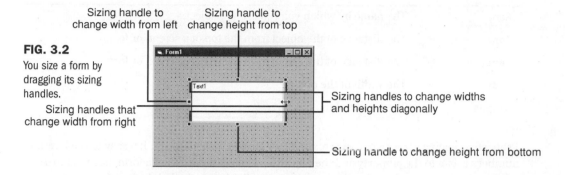

FIG. 3.2
You size a form by dragging its sizing handles.

1. Bring your mouse cursor to the edit node sizing handle on the right, middle edge of the form. Notice that the cursor turns to a horizontal line with an arrowhead on each end.

2. When you see the double-arrowhead line, press your left mouse button and drag the edge of the form to the left. (This same technique also works going left to right.)

To change the height of a form in a Form window, follow these steps:

1. Bring your mouse cursor to the sizing handle on the bottom, middle edge of the form. Notice that the cursor turns to a vertical line with an arrowhead on each end.

2. When you see the double-arrowhead line, press your left mouse button and drag the lower edge of the form up. (This same technique works going top to bottom.)

Sizing a Form Using the Properties Window

To size a form using the Properties window, it helps if you really understand what the term *properties* is all about and how it relates to things called *objects*. A *property* is a quantifiable attribute of an *object*. In Visual Basic, an object is, for now, a Microsoft Windows element.

If you've been using the Windows operating system for any amount of time, you are undoubtedly familiar with the standard Windows elements. You have windows through which you view things, buttons you click to make things happen, text boxes into which you enter data, and lots of other elements that are part of the Windows operating system. These Windows elements also are called objects or *controls*.

In Visual Basic programming a form is just another name for a Windows window. When you create a form in Visual Basic you really are making a window. It's a fine point now, but it will have some significant implications as you become a more advanced Visual Basic programmer.

You can describe a form in terms of its *attributes*. Again, in Visual Basic, attributes are called *properties*.

Table 3.1 shows some of the common properties shared among the various Visual Basic objects, such as a form, button, and TextBox.

Table 3.1 Some Visual Basic Object Properties

Property	Description
Name	The name by which you refer to the object.
Top	The distance of the object from the top of a screen or form.
Left	The distance of the object from the left of a screen or form.
Width	The width of the object.
Height	The height of the object.

Properties, such as length and width, can be described with numbers. It's easy to see how the numbers relate to the property and the object. To change the width of a form using numbers, you change the value of the form's Width property. To change the height for a form, you change the value of the form's Height property.

You can view and edit the properties of a form through the Properties widow (see Figure 3.3).

FIG. 3.3
Select the form from the Object drop-down list.

To change the Width of a form using the Properties window, do the following:

1. Go to the Properties window and select the form (see Figure 3.3).
2. After the Object drop-down list retracts, select the Alphabetic tab from the view tabs underneath the Object drop-down list, at the top of the Properties window.
3. Scroll down to the Width or Height property.
4. Double-click the value to the right of the word Width or Height (see Figure 3.4).

FIG. 3.4
You can view properties alphabetically or by category in the Property window.

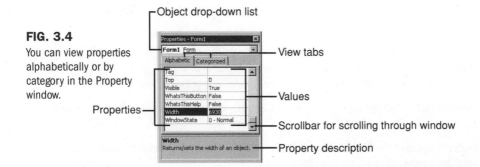

5. Change the value to the new size. (The default unit of measurement in a form is a *twip*. See the "Defining and Calculating Twips" for an explanation of twips.) The new value takes affect when you press the Enter key or click away from the field you edited (see Figure 3.5).

FIG. 3.5
Setting the width of a form in the Properties window is a much more accurate way to size a form.

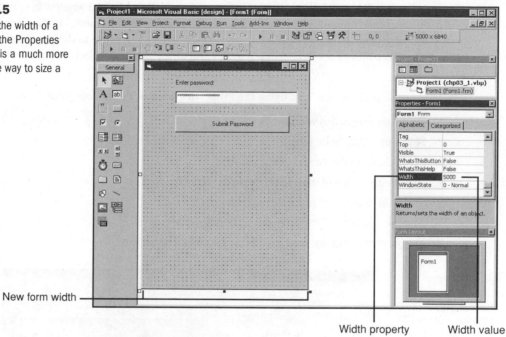

New form width

Width property   Width value

Part
I

Ch
3

Defining and Calculating Twips

Visual Basic uses twips to measure control dimensions. A *twip* is an absolute measurement equivalent to 1/20th of a printer's point, which means there are 1,440 twips per inch. How these dimensions are represented on your monitor depends on the resolution you are working in, but one *pixel*, the smallest dot your monitor can display, generally is between about 12 and 15 twips wide.

To find out how many twips there are per pixel in the resolution you are working in (for which your video card is set), use the Screen object's TwipsPerPixelX and TwipsPerPixelY properties.

For example:

```
x = Screen.TwipsPerPixelX

y = Screen.TwipsPerPixelY
```

To change the height of a form using the Properties window, do the preceding steps, only change the Height property.

Controlling a Form's Position

You change the position of a form in much the same way you change the size of a form. You can do it through the Properties Window. You can write some code. To change the position of a form graphically by using your mouse instead of using the Form Window, you use the Form Layout Window. You saw how to position a form using the Form Layout window in Chapter 2, "Customizing and Navigating the Visual Basic Programming Environment," in the Form Layout Window section. Now you can learn how to position a form relative to the upper-left corner of your screen by using the Properties Window and changing the Top and Left properties of the form.

To change the position of a form using the Properties window, do the following steps:

1. Go to the Properties window.
2. Select the Alphabetic tab.
3. Scroll down to the Top property.
4. Change the value of the Top property to 0 (zero).
5. Scroll up to the Left property.
6. Change the value of the Left property to 0 (zero).
7. Run your program by pressing the F5 key (see Figure 3.6).

FIG. 3.6

Setting the value of a form's Top property to 0 and the value of its Height property to 0 puts the form in the upper-left corner of the screen.

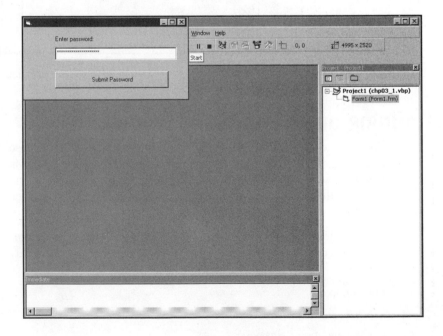

Controlling a Form's Style

Look at the resized form in Figure 3.6. The window is just the right size for the functionality and the placement is not too bad either. Now look at Figure 3.7. This is the same form. The only difference is that the user clicked the maximize button on the upper-right corner of the password form's title bar. There is no way that the user should have been allowed to maximize this form. This could have been prevented by changing the form's BorderStyle.

FIG. 3.7

It is important to set the value of a form's BorderStyle to one that is appropriate for the form's function.

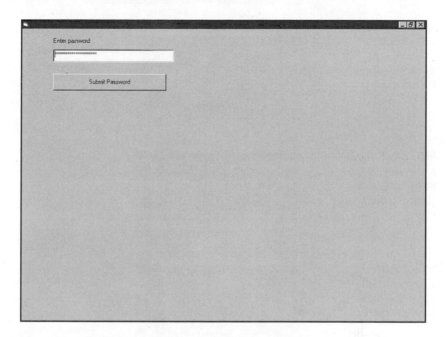

Part
I

Ch
3

You can set Visual Basic forms to have any one of six styles. (see Figures 3.8 to 3.13).

FIG. 3.8

A form with the BorderStyle set to 0, None.

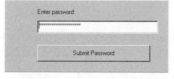

FIG. 3.9

A form with the BorderStyle set to 1, Fixed Single.

FIG. 3.10
A form with the BorderStyle set to 2, Sizable (default). In Visual Basic, the default BorderStyle setting for a new form is 2, Sizable.

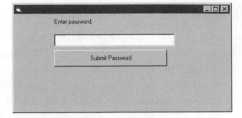

FIG. 3.11
A form with the BorderStyle set to 3, Fixed Dialog.

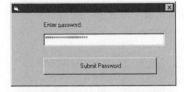

FIG. 3.12
A form with the BorderStyle set to 4, Fixed Window.

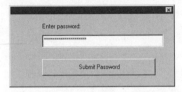

FIG. 3.13
A form with the BorderStyle set to 5, Sizable Window.

Properly setting your form's BorderStyle is an easy way to make your forms look more professional. Table 3.2 describes the different values that you can choose for your form's BorderStyle property.

Table 3.2 BorderStyles for Forms

Number	Style	Description	Example
0	None	No borders, no title bar, not movable.	Backdrop for a splash screen.
1	Fixed Single	Not sizable by dragging borders, but can have minimize and maximize buttons.	A fixed-size window that you want to reside in the taskbar.

Number	Style	Description	Example
2	Sizable	Sizable	Standard window.
3	Fixed Dialog	Not sizable, no minimize or maximize functionality.	Password form, dialog box.
4	Fixed	Similar to fixed ToolWindow dialog, but title bar is shorter and title bar fonts are smaller.	Visual Basic and MS Office floating toolbar.
5	Sizable	Similar to a Fixed ToolWindow but is sizable by dragging on the window's borders.	Visual Basic Properties window.

You set a form's BorderStyle property in the Properties window (see Figure 3.14).

Part
I
Ch
3

FIG. 3.14
You set the value for a form's BorderStyle property from a drop-down list in the Properties window.

Understanding Controls and ActiveX

Controls are the building blocks that you use to assemble your Visual Basic program. You saw this in previous chapters. It's worth repeating, because the notion of programming with controls is what makes the Visual Basic programming experience so unique.

In the previous section, you learned to consider controls as another way to think of Windows elements, but Visual Basic also can be extended by the addition of ActiveX controls. While this is useful for now, it's helpful to understand that controls are really much more. ActiveX controls, formerly called OLE controls or Custom Controls, are discreet small, programs that you can use to add functionality to your program. Controls come in many flavors and can do many things. Most controls have their own *Graphical User Interface (GUI)* that you can program. Some controls are GUI-less; you only can program them by controlling the Properties Window or with code.

Microsoft planned the Visual Basic programming paradigm to be one in which more experienced, low-level programmers could make task-specific controls for other programmers to use. The paradigm has been highly successful. There are thousands of ActiveX controls out there. Making ActiveX controls for Visual Basic programmers is an industry in itself. You can have controls for making charts, sending a fax, doing low-level Windows programming, interacting with mainframe computers, even analyzing radar signals! If you can imagine a need for a control and you have the programming skills, the world is your oyster.

Prior to Visual Basic 5.0, the only way that you could make a ActiveX control for other programmers to use was with a more low-level language such as C(++) or Object Pascal. However, now you also can make controls in Visual Basic as of version 5.0. One of the other good things about ActiveX controls is that you can use them when you are programming in languages other than Visual Basic. It is not at all unusual to use a ActiveX control when you are programming in Visual C++ or Delphi. Controls are *language independent*.

ActiveX controls also are having a great influence in the realm of developing for the Internet. ActiveX controls can be embedded in a Web Page and run in a Web Browser such as Internet Explorer by using a subset of a the Visual Basic language called *VBScript*.

ActiveX is important, no question about it. Right now, don't get too concerned about the particulars—the important thing is that you understand that controls as Windows elements are only a small part of the much bigger picture, which is that Visual Basic programming is based around using ActiveX controls and that there are a lot of controls out there for you to use.

When you buy Visual Basic, a lot of controls "ship in the box" (see Figure 3.15). However, when you install VB, you don't see them all in the toolbox. You only see the Standard controls. Those extra controls are there, you just need to bring them into the toolbox. You learn how to do this in the section, "Adding ActiveX Controls to the Toolbox."

FIG. 3.15

Visual Basic ships with many ActiveX controls that you can use to make very powerful programs!

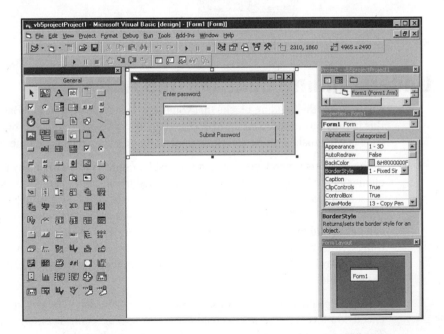

The Standard Controls

The *Standard Controls* are the most commonly used controls in Visual Basic programming. Some are the Windows elements that you have been using for years—buttons, text boxes, labels, scrollbars, check boxes, option buttons, and so on. Others are "system level" controls you need in order to get around your hard disk, do stuff in real time, and do simple work with databases. All editions of Visual Basic 5.0, Standard, Professional, and Enterprise ship with the Standard Controls.

The Standard Controls are accessed through the Toolbox. The binary code for the Standard Controls lives in the Visual Basic runtime *dynamic link libraries* (DLLs). When a user installs your Visual Basic program, all the Standard Controls are there. There is no need to ship any additional files other than the ones you need to run any Visual Basic program. (For more details on shipping your application, see Chapter 18, "Deploying Your Application.")

Table 3.3 lists the Standard Controls. Figure 3.16 shows the icons for the Standard Controls in the Toolbox.

When you make a Visual Basic program, a lot of the code you use is not in your program. It is in another set of files called the Visual Basic *runtime DLLS*.

The Standard Controls and most-often used functions that you use in your programming reside in these Visual Basic runtime file(s).

FIG. 3.16
You can do a lot of programming with just the Standard Controls!

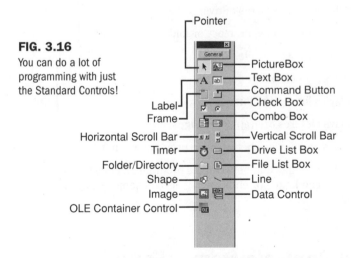

Part
I
Ch
3

Table 3.3 The Standard Controls in Visual Basic

Control Name	Description
PictureBox	Displays graphical images. Also serves as a container for other controls.
Label	Displays text.

continues

Table 3.3   Continued

Control Name	Description
TextBox	Displays text and enables the user to enter and edit text.
Frame	Serves as a container for other controls.
CommandButton	Lets the user initiate actions by clicking the button.
Check Box	Lets the user make true/false choices.
Option Button	A group of option buttons lets the user choose one of a group of items.
Combo Box	Lets the user choose from a drop-down list of items or enter a new value.
List Box	Lets the user choose from a scrollable list of items.
Horizontal Scroll Bar	Lets the user scroll through data in another control form horizontally. Also can be used to select data values (advanced).
Vertical Scroll Bar	Same as Horizontal Scroll Bar only with vertical orientation.
Timer	Lets the program perform functions in real time in the background.
Drive List Box	Lets the user select a disk drive.
Directory List Box	Lets the user select a directory or folder.
File List Box	Lets the user select a file.
Shape	Displays a shape on the form.
Line	Displays a line on the form.
Image	Displays pictures or graphical images.
Data Control	Provides an interface between the program and a database.
OLE Container Control	Provides a connection between the program and an OLE server. Lets you add linked or embedded insertable objects to your forms.

Adding and Removing Controls from a Form

There are two ways to add a control to a form. One way is to double-click the control's icon in the toolbox. The other way is to select and drag. In Chapter 1, "Your First Application," you learned how to double-click a control onto a form in the section, "Creating the GUI."

If you want to follow along, the code discussed in this section is in the project password.vbp, which is in the directory \Chp_3\password\ on the CD-ROM that accompanies this book.

To put a control on a form using select and drag is different, although not at all difficult.

To add a control, just follow these steps:

1. Click the control's icon in the toolbox. (Make sure that you only click once!)
2. Bring your mouse cursor over to the left side of the form, just to the left of the command button. Notice that the mouse cursor has the shape of a crosshair.
3. Holding down your left mouse button, drag diagonally from the upper left to the lower right.
4. Release the mouse button. The control appears (see Figure 3.17).

FIG. 3.17
At design time, all controls have sizing handles on their borders when selected.

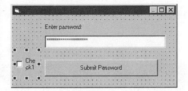

Naming Controls

The capability to name a control properly is the sign of a competent, thoughtful programmer. When you look at the name of a control, you should be able to discern what type of control it is *and* what its functionality is about. Following a naming convention consistently counts! It makes your code easier to read and maintain.

Before we go into naming conventions, let's review the fundamentals of a controls, namely properties. All controls have names. Controls also have types: TextBox, CommandButton, Label, and so on.When you create a control, Visual Basic gives the control a default name. If the control is a TextBox, it gets a default name, Text1. The default name is useful for keeping track of controls as you make them, but it really doesn't give you a good idea of what the control is or what it is about. A good naming convention helps you out with this type of identification.

Wouldn't it be more informative to change the name of the text box from Text1 to txtPassword (see Figure 3.18)? Think about it. The function of the control is to take the user's password. The type of control you use to receive the password input is a TextBox. In this case, consider the characters "txt" to be a prefix that you tack on the beginning of the "functionality name" to denote the control being used is a TextBox.

Control name   Control type

FIG. 3.18
You set the value of a
control's name in the
Properties window.

TextBox control

Name property for
TextBox control

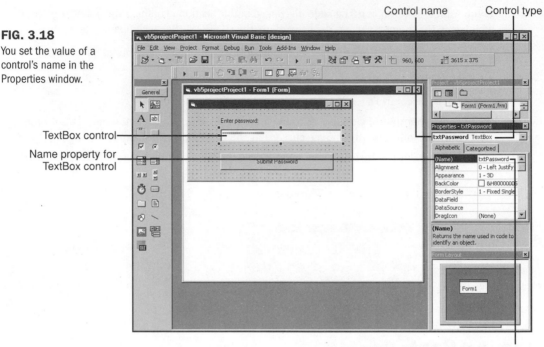

Value of Name property for TextBox control

What you see here is the structure of the naming convention that most Visual Basic programmers use to identify controls. The naming convention is as follows:

    ctlName

where

    ctl is the prefix denoting the control being named

and

    Name is the friendly and functional name of the control.

Thus, by this logic, a form that is designed to take data could be named: frmData. A TextBox that is made to take the first name of someone could be named txtFirstName and a CommandButton that is made to enter data upon clicking it could be named cmdEnter.

Notice that the first character of the friendly-name portion of the naming syntax is uppercase, and that the first character of each word in a friendly name is uppercase. This is done to make the naming easier to read. By making that first character upper case, you implicitly separate it from the prefix and from other words. You don't have to spend an inordinate amount of time trying to figure out what the friendly name and the prefix are. Also, be advised that control name prefixes usually begin with a *lowercase* character.

Visual Basic programmers over time have developed a very rich set of prefixes that are used to identify controls within the standard control naming convention. Table 3.4 shows you some examples of these prefixes. The Programmer's Guide that ships with Visual Basic includes an appendix on naming and other coding conventions.

CAUTION

Name your controls as you make them. Going back and renaming controls after you have used them is an invitation for disaster! Visual Basic will not be able to reapply the new names to code blocks that you already have programmed under the control's older name.

Table 3.4   Prefixes that Identify Visual Basic Controls

Control	Prefix
CheckBox	chk
ComboBox	cbo
Command Button	cmd
Common Dialog	cdl
Data Control	dat
Data Bound ComboBox	dbc
Data Bound Grid	dbg
Data Bound ListBox	dbl
Directory ListBox	dir
Drive ListBox	drv
File ListBox	fil
Form	frm
Frame	fra
Grid	grd
Horizontal ScrollBar	hsb
Image	img
Label	lbl
Line	lin
ListBox	lst
Menu	mnu

Part

I

Ch

3

continues

Table 3.4   Continued

Control	Prefix
OLE Container	ole
Option Button	opt
Picture Box	pic
Shape	shp
TextBox	txt
Timer	tmr
Vertical ScrollBar	vsb

Again, the naming convention and style is important. Programmers take this seriously. So should you.

Sizing and Positioning Controls

You size a control the same way that you size a form, either by dragging its sizing handles, changing the values of its width and height property, or writing some code.

Positioning a control is slightly different than positioning a form. You can still alter the value of the Top and Left property of the control in question in the Properties Window, and you can still write some code (as in Chapter 5, "Working with Properties, Methods, and Events"). However, to move a control's position graphically on a form at design time, you do the following:

1. Select the pointer tool from the Toolbox. (Note that the pointer tool usually is already selected by default.)
2. Place it on the control that you want to move.
3. Hold down the left mouse button. Wait a moment. Notice that a ToolTips window appears. In the ToolTips, there are two numbers separated by a command. These numbers represent the present location of the control. The first number is the value of the control's Left property, and the second number is the location of the control's Top property.
4. Holding the left mouse button down, drag the control to the new location. Notice that the numbers in the ToolTip change as you move the control (see Figure 3.19).

FIG. 3.19

You can create controls on a form by selecting and dragging.

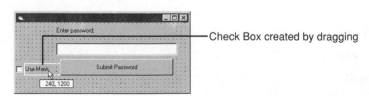

Check Box created by dragging

Understanding Controls

A very important concept to understand when using controls is the relationship of a Container control to a Contained control(s).

A *Container control* is any control or object that contains another control. A Child control is something that is contained. For example, when you paste a command button directly onto a Frame control, the button is contained by the frame. Containment is a conceptual parent-child relationship: In this example, the button is clipped by the edges of the frame, it moves with the frame when the frame is moved, and its Top and Left properties are specified relative to the frame (see Figure 3.20). When you delete a container control, you also delete any controls it contains.

When you create a Form, the Form that you create is considered to be a Child control con tained by the Screen Object.

Part

I

Ch

3

Where this concept really comes into play is with position coordinates. If you make a Form named frmMain and you set the value of the Top property of frmMain to 1000 and the value of the Left property to 1000, frmMain is positioned near the upper left corner of the screen at runtime. However, if you make a CommandButton named cmdExit, place it on frmMain, and then set the value of the Top property of cmdExit to 500 and the value of the Left property of cmdExit to 0, cmdExit is at the left side of the form. Wait—shouldn't the CommandButton be positioned at the left side of the screen? After all, the value of the Left property is set to 0.

The reason that the CommandButton sets itself to the left edge of the Form is because cmdExit is a child contained by frmMain. The CommandButton exists only with frmMain. Therefore, the 0 (zero) left coordinate for the command button, the beginning of its "world" horizontally, so to speak, is the left edge of the Form (see Figure 3.20).

FIG. 3.20
A CommandButton is a Child control contained by the Form.

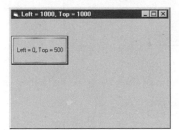

Adding ActiveX Controls to the Toolbox

As in Figure 3.21, you get a lot of ActiveX controls when you buy Visual Basic. However, not all of those controls appear in the toolbox when you first install Visual Basic. To add an ActiveX control to the toolbox, you need to do the following:

1. Click the Project menu and select Components, as shown in Figure 3.21.
2. Click the Controls tab.

3. If the Selected Items Only check box is checked, *uncheck it*.

4. The Components tabbed dialog box presents, among other things, a list of all the ActiveX controls that are registered on your computer. Select the component that you want to add to the ToolBox by checking the box to the left of the desired control. (In this case, Figure 3.22 shows you how to add a Microsoft Chart Control.)

FIG. 3.21

Go to the Components dialog box to add ActiveX controls to the ToolBox.

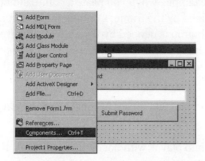

FIG. 3.22

Check an ActiveX control in the Components list to have it appear in the Toolbox.

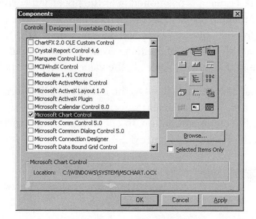

5. Click the OK button and the bottom of the Components tabbed dialog box.

6. The added control appears in the Toolbox.

CHAPTER 4

The Structure of a Visual Basic Project

Visual Basic project structure

Learn about the different parts of a Visual Basic project and how to control them within the Visual Basic Integrated Development Environment.

Using forms and modules

Get the most out of the forms and modules you make.

Managing projects

Use the Project Explorer to manage one or more projects easily.

A Visual Basic project is the "ingredient" of your program as it appears on your programming workbench (the IDE). No matter what type of program you write, you develop them within the framework of a project.

Many beginning programmers have trouble working with projects. However, many common oversights such as misplacing files, losing previously saved projects, and being unable to replicate a project's structure on several different computers can be prevented if you have a good understanding of what the overall structure of a Visual Basic project is and how to work with one. ■

Understanding Projects and Project Files

A Visual Basic program is a collection of forms and modules that get compiled into a binary file. This binary file of the program ends with the file extension .EXE if the program is a Standard EXE or ActiveX EXE, .DLL if the program is an ActiveX DLL, or .OCX if the program is an ActiveX control. A Visual Basic Project consists of these precompiled ingredients: the form(s), modules, and controls that make up that program. The way Visual Basic keeps track of what is in a particular project is by means of a *project file*. A project file ends with the extension .VBP.

A *project file* is a detailed list of the parts of the project. Listing 4.1 shows a text version of project file for a Visual Basic project. There are references to forms and modules, the name of the project ("MyProject"), and so on. Near the end of the listing are a few entries where a line of text is set to equal 0 or 1. These settings instruct Visual Basic how to configure the IDE for this particular project.

The important thing to consider is not the particulars about the project file but that the project file is a list of the contents of a particular project. The project file does *not* contain the parts of the project. It only lists the parts of a project.

Listing 4.1   MYPROJ.VBP—Text Read Out of a Visual Basic Project File

```
Type=Exe
Form=MyForm1.frm
Reference=*\G{00020430-0000-0000-C000-
000000000046}#2.0#0#..\..\..\..\..\WINDOWS\SYSTEM\StdOle2.tlb#OLE Automation
Form=MyForm2.frm
Form=MyForm3.frm
Module=MyModule1; MyModule1.bas
Module=MyModule2; MyModule2.bas
Object={F9043C88-F6F2-101A-A3C9-08002B2F49FB}#1.1#0; COMDLG32.OCX
Object={E7DFBDC4-A859-11D0-BBF4-00A024A734D5}#3.0#0; CCDICE.ocx
Startup="MyForm1"
Command32=""
Name="MyProject"
HelpContextID="0"
CompatibleMode="0"
MajorVer=1
MinorVer=0
RevisionVer=0
AutoIncrementVer=0
ServerSupportFiles=0
VersionCompanyName="AnyUser"
CompilationType=0
OptimizationType=0
FavorPentiumPro(tm)=0
CodeViewDebugInfo=0
NoAliasing=0
BoundsCheck=0
OverflowCheck=0
FlPointCheck=0
FDIVCheck=0
```

```
UnroundedFP=0
StartMode=0
Unattended=0
ThreadPerObject=0
MaxNumberOfThreads=1
```

A Project's Structure

Projects are made up of forms and modules (projects also may contain other kinds of files, but don't worry about that for now). A *module* is a file that contains Visual Basic code that is not attached to any form or control. Modules contain pure programming instructions. You use modules for declaring variables, defining constant values, and making user-defined functions and subroutines.

▶ **See** Chapter 20, "Working with User-Defined Subs and Functions," for more information about modules, **p. 313**

Every form and module you create is saved to disk in its own file. The file name for an individual form ends with the extension .FRM, and the file name for an individual module ends with the extension .BAS. Figure 4.1 shows the parts and relationships of a Visual Basic Project.

Part

I

Ch

4

FIG. 4.1
A simple Visual Basic project is made up of forms, modules, and ActiveX Controls.

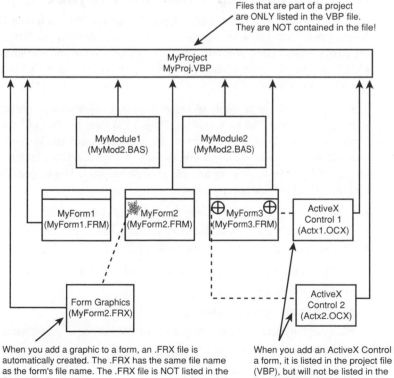

Files that are part of a project are ONLY listed in the VBP file. They are NOT contained in the file!

MyProject
MyProj.VBP

MyModule1
(MyMod2.BAS)

MyModule2
(MyMod2.BAS)

MyForm1
(MyForm1.FRM)

MyForm2
(MyForm2.FRM)

MyForm3
(MyForm3.FRM)

ActiveX
Control 1
(Actx1.OCX)

Form Graphics
(MyForm2.FRX)

ActiveX
Control 2
(Actx2.OCX)

When you add a graphic to a form, an .FRX file is automatically created. The .FRX has the same file name as the form's file name. The .FRX file is NOT listed in the Project Explorer.

When you add an ActiveX Control to a form, it is listed in the project file (VBP), but will not be listed in the Project Explorer window.

Notice that the diagram of MyForm2 (MyForm2.FRM) in Figure 4.1 has a picture in the upper-left corner. This represents a form with a graphic. If you have a form with a graphic embedded in it, or if you have a picture or image control on the form, Visual Basic creates a file with the same file name but with the extension .FRX. Thus, the file Myform2.FRX is generated by Visual Basic. An .FRX file contains information about binary data associated with the graphics for that form (often, but not exclusively, graphical data). Visual Basic associates .FRX files to .FRM files by the file name, MyForm2—such as .FRM to MyForm2.FRX, for example. Don't override Visual Basic's naming convention of generated .FRX files by renaming files; your form may not be able to find its graphic or pictures.

The MyForm3 (MyForm3.FRM) on the middle right of Figure 4.1 contains two ActiveX Controls (symbolized by a cross surrounded by a circle) on the form. If you put ActiveX controls on your form, the addition of the controls is recorded to create a file. As a matter of fact, all of the ActiveX Controls that you presently have installed in the Toolbox, with the exception of the Standard Controls, are listed in the .VBP file for the project. The .OCX files for ActiveX controls usually are installed in the system directory of the Windows directory; for example, C:\Windows\System. Lastly, notice that all the .FRM and .BAS files are listed in the .VBP file, the Visual Basic Project file.

Organizing Projects with the Project Explorer

As you start writing bigger programs, you might find that you have a difficult time moving from form to form and keeping track of the various files that you have in your project. To make life easier, Visual Basic provides a tool for getting around and working within your project. It's called the *Project Explorer.* The Project Explorer is the window that is found on the right side of the IDE, (see Figure 4.2).

The Project Explorer presents an organized way to view your project and to access the members of that project. You looked at the Project Explorer briefly in Chapter 2, "Customizing and Navigating the Visual Basic Programming Environment." You learned that you could organize your view by folder groups; that you could view individual files by form view, if the file is a form; and by code window for any file, module, or form. The Project Explorer also has a context menu feature that is very handy.

Go to the list window in the Project Explorer and right-click a file within it. The context menu for that file within the Project Explorer appears. The Context menu shown in Figure 4.3 enables you to carry out the following tasks:

- View a file by either form window or code window
- View the properties of a file
- Add forms or modules to your project
- Save the current file as either its current name or as a new name
- Delete forms or modules from the project
- Print file

- Choose between making the Project Explorer a floating window or docking it to the IDE
- Hiding the Project Explorer

Toggle Folders Shows projects' components in grouped folders or as ungrouped list

View Object Shows Form window, if possible

View Form Shows the Form Window for the object (e.g. a form) currently selected in the Project Explorer

FIG. 4.2
You select a file to view by clicking it in the Project Explorer.

List window Displays hierarchical tree of projects and project components within the IDE

A selected form in Form View

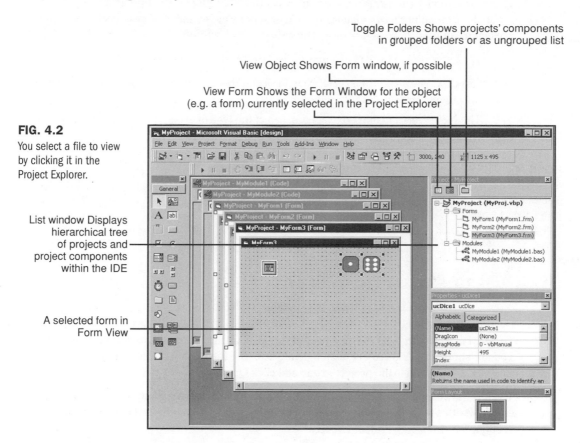

Part I
Ch
4

Because of its quick accessibility and multiple functions, the Project Explorer makes your programming activity a lot easier.

FIG. 4.3
The Project Explorer's List window context menu gives you a fast way to view and print forms and modules.

Creating New Projects

There are two ways to create a project in Visual Basic 5.0. One way is to start a new project group, thus creating a new default project. The other way is to add a new project to an existing project group.

To create a new project as part of a new project group, do the following:

1. Click the File menu then select New Project. (You may be prompted to save changes to the current project.)

2. The New Project dialog box appears. Select the type of project that you want and click Open (see Figure 4.4).

FIG. 4.4
Visual Basic 5.0 enables you to make many different types of programs.

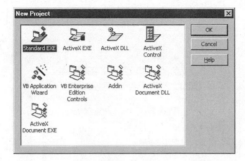

To add a new project to an existing project group, click the File menu, then click Add Project. You are shown the Add Project tabbed dialog box (see Figure 4.5). Select the type of project that you want to add to the project group and click Open.

You'll work with multiple projects within the Project Explorer when you make custom ActiveX controls with Visual Basic. This topic is covered in more detail at the end of this chapter in the section, "Working with Project Groups."

FIG. 4.5
The Add Project dialog box enables you to select a new project type, browse your hard disk for an existing project, or select a project from a list of recent projects.

The Difference Between Projects and Applications

Although a project is all the "ingredients" that you use to make an application, it is *not* the application. (An *application* is another name for a program.) In order to have an application, you must compile your project. When you compile your project, you produce a *binary file*. A binary file sends "machine language" instructions in binary code to the computer's main processor (CPU).

On the other hand, the files that you write for forms and modules that make up your project are text files that contain the Visual Basic programming language.

In summary, you create the form (.FRM) and module (.BAS) files of your program as text files and save them as part of the project using Visual Basic. You compile all the text files in your project into a binary code file, which is the *application*.

Setting a Project's Properties

The most fundamental property that a project has is its Name property. There are others. You can set the title of the project's application. You can set version numbers for each time you compile an application. You can assign help files to use with your application. You can assign an icon to symbolize your application in the Windows Explorer. You can offer a short description of your application. All of these items here are properties of the project.

Part
I

Ch
4

You set and read a project's properties through the Project Properties tabbed dialog box. To access the Project Properties tabbed dialog box, click the Projects menu and select *[Project_Name]* Properties... from the menu drop-down list. The Project Properties tabbed dialog box appears.

Another way to access the Project Properties dialog box is to go to the Project Explorer, right-click the project's .VBP file and select *[Project_Name]* Properties... from the Project Explorer context menu. (see Figure 4.6).

FIG. 4.6
The Project Explorer context menu also enables you to access the Project Properties dialog box.

To name a project, do this: Name an application, set a startup form, describe the application and associate a help file with that application, and use the tabbed Project Properties dialog box. (see Figures 4.7 and 4.8).

FIG. 4.7

You set a project's type, name, help file, and description under the General tab of the Project Properties dialog box.

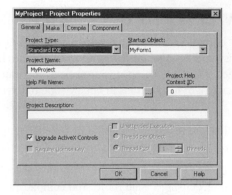

FIG. 4.8

You set an application's version number, title, icon, and descriptive details in the Make tab of the Project Properties dialog box.

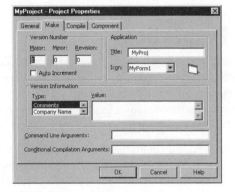

Saving and Naming Your Projects

To save a project, click the File menu, then select Save Project. Saving a project also saves all unsaved files that belong to the project.

When you save a project, if it has not been saved previously, Visual Basic asks you to save all forms and modules that you created for that project to individual files. Visual Basic assigns the file name for each form and module to be the value of the Name property of that form or module, plus the appropriate file extension.

For example, if you are saving a form where the value of the property is Name = frmMain, then Visual Basic by default names the file for that form, frmMain.frm. If you have a module where the property is Name = modMain, Visual Basic names the file for that module, modMain.bas. These file names are suggestions only. You can change them to whatever you want, provided the file name presently is not being used. Be careful, however, that you choose names that are relevant to the file and that won't be confusing to you later. Also, you can reuse a file name—it will overwrite the existing file (but you will be prompted).

After you name all of the form and module files, Visual Basic asks you to name the project's .VBP file. Visual Basic then suggests that you use the project's name as the file name, but again, you can name the project file whatever you want (see Figure 4.9).

FIG. 4.9
Using default naming can be limiting when saving a project. You should assign your own.

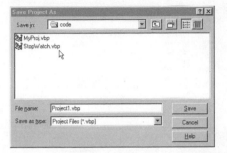

> **CAUTION**
>
> Remember where you save files! If you start Visual Basic from the Start Menu when you save a file, Visual Basic by default, tries to save the file to the Visual Basic directory. Saving a file there isn't recommended.
>
> Before you begin a project, make a directory for it on your hard drive. Then when it is time to save the project file and the forms and modules that are part of the project, just browse to that directory.

Opening Existing Projects

To retrieve an existing project that you recently worked on, look at the bottom of the File menu, which shows a list of up to four projects. These are the last projects that you worked on. Visual Basic automatically keeps track of the last projects with which you worked. To open one, simply select the project from the File menu.

Also, you can click the File menu and select Open Project. Doing this brings up the Open Project tabbed dialog box, as seen in Figure 4.10. You can either browse through your hard drive to find an existing project or you can select a project from the list of projects from which you last were involved by selecting the Recent tab at the top of the Open Project dialog box.

Adding New Files, Forms, and Modules to a Project

Sometimes you have a project that needs to have more than one form or module. For example, you might need to show an About dialog box or a Password dialog box. To meet this requirement, it is necessary that you add a new form to your project.

There are two ways to add a new form or module to a project. The first way is to click the Project menu and select Add Form or Add Module, depending which you want to add (see Figure 4.11).

FIG. 4.10

Selecting the Existing tab from the Open Project dialog box enables you to browse your hard drive for projects. Selecting the Recent tab enables you to choose from a list.

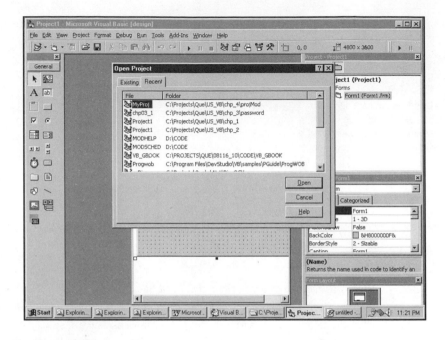

FIG. 4.11

In addition to Forms and Modules, you also can add MDI forms, Class modules, User control, or a Property Page using the Project menu.

Another way to add a form or module is to go to the Project Explorer and right-click the project's .VBP file in the List Window. The Project Explorer's context menu appears. Select Add from the context menu, then from the submenu, select Form to add a form or Module to add a module (see Figure 4.12).

FIG. 4.12
You also can add forms and modules from the Context menu of the Project Explorer.

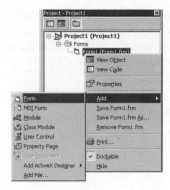

Adding Existing Files, Forms, and Modules to a Project

Sometimes you may want to add a form or a module that you used in another project to one on which you are presently working. To add an existing form or module to your project, you add the file for that form or module. You can add a file in a number of ways: you can click the Project menu and select Add Form Add Module or Add File…, or go to the Project Explorer, right-click the List Window, select Add from the context menu, and select Form, Module or Add File from the pop-up submenu (see Figure 4.13). If you select Add Form or Add Module, you can then pick a previous file from the Existing tab of the Add Form or Add Module dialog box. You can browse for unlisted files within the Add Form or Add Module dialog box.

Part
I
Ch
4

FIG. 4.13
When you select Add File, the Add File dialog box appears.

When the Add File dialog box appears, you can use it to navigate through the drives on your computer or even to navigate onto a network to locate an existing form, module, or other file (see Figure 4.14). You click the Open button on the lower right of the dialog box to bring the file into the Project Explorer. Once the form or module is in the IDE, if you save the project, the added file will be saved as part of the project.

FIG. 4.14

By default, Visual Basic shows you only Visual Basic files in the Add File dialog box. You can see any file type by selecting the appropriate mask in the Files of type: ComboBox.

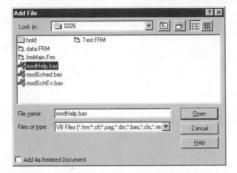

The location of the file has not changed. You did not move it; you only referenced the added file. This is sometimes a tricky point for beginning programmers. Many times a novice programmer adds a file to a project and thinks that the file moved to the project's working directory. If you want to have a copy of the added file reside in the working directory of your project, add the file to the project and choose "Save As" in the working directory. Then, save the project. The relocated file will be added to the project, replacing the referenced file (see Figure 4.15).

FIG. 4.15

You make a new copy of a file using Save As.

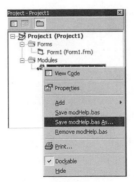

Removing Files, Forms, or Modules from a Project

Sometimes you might find that you accidentally have added a form to a project or made one that is not quite what you had in mind. If you don't want that form or any other VB file in your project, you must formally remove it. Otherwise, it will be included in your program when you compile the project. If you want to remove a form or module file from a project, here are the following steps:

1. In the Project Explorer, right-click the file that you want to remove.
2. From the Project Explorer's context menu, select Remove *[filename]* from the context menu.

Working with Project Groups

One of the new features of Visual Basic 5 is that you have to launch Visual Basic only once to work on many projects. In previous versions, each time you wanted to work on a separate project, you had to launch another instance of Visual Basic. This new feature becomes useful when it is time for you to learn how to make ActiveX controls in Visual Basic. To develop ActiveX controls, you need to be able to run multiple projects at once.

In order to manage and save multiple files, Visual Basic introduced the Project Group. A Project Group is a collection of Visual Basic projects. You save Project Group information in files that end with the extension .VBG. Figure 4.16 shows the project group MyGroup.VBG within the Project Explorer.

Project Group Name (in title bar)

FIG. 4.16
If, within a project group, a project name is in bold type, it means that it will be the project that runs when you strike the F5 key to run the program.

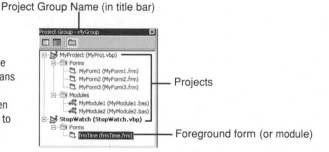

Projects

Foreground form (or module)

Working with project groups can get complex—adding files, adding projects, removing projects, and developing ActiveX controls, and so on. The usefulness of project groups becomes paramount when you are making ActiveX controls in Visual Basic.

For now, the important thing to know is that you can have multiple projects in the Visual Basic IDE within any given programming session and that you can keep a list of the projects presently within the IDE in a Project Group file. A Project Group file ends with the extension VBG.

Later in this book, when you begin to make ActiveX controls using Visual Basic, you'll see how you use program groups to create and test your custom ActiveX control. ●

CHAPTER 5

Working with Properties, Methods, and Events

Learn how to program using properties

Find out what properties are and how to program them to work in your applications.

Use methods

Use methods to affect the behavior of your programs.

Write event-driven programs

Learn about event driven programming and how it applies to Visual Basic.

Properties, methods and events are key elements of object-oriented programming. You use properties to describe an object. You use methods to have an object carry out a task. You respond to an object's behavior by programming events.

Programming with Visual Basic *is* about programming with properties, methods, and events. With a clear understanding of them, you easily can write programs of any depth or significance. ■

Working with Common Properties

While each object in Visual Basic has its own set of properties (some objects have more properties than others), several properties are common to almost all objects. The most important of these common properties are shown in Table 5.1.

Table 5.1 Properties Common to the Visual Basic Standard Controls

Property	Value Type	Description
Left	Integer	Position of the control measured from the Left side of the Form or Frame.
Top	Integer	Position of the control measured from the Top side of the Form or Frame.
Height	Integer	Height of control.
Width	Integer	Width of control.
Name	String	Name by which you refer to the control in your program. Read Only at runtime.
Enabled	Boolean (True/False)	Describes if the control is operational.
Visible	Boolean (True/False)	Describes if the control can be seen at runtime.
Index	Integer	If a control is grouped in a control array, the subscript number of that control. Read Only at runtime.

▶ **See** Chapter 10, "Working with Arrays," for more details about control arrays, **p. 143**

The Visible property and the Enabled property both have settings of either True or False. These properties determine whether an object can be seen by the user and whether the user can interact with the object. If the Visible property is set to False, the object is not shown, and the user won't know that the object is even there. Setting Visible to True allows the object to be displayed. If the Enabled property is set to False, the object is visible (provided that the Visible property is True), but the user cannot interact with the object. Typically, if an object is disabled, it is shown on the screen in a grayed out or dimmed mode. This provides a visual indication to the user that the object is unavailable.

Understanding Methods Object-Oriented Programming

An object-oriented programming language is one that enables you to program using *polym orphism*, *inheritance*, and *encapsulation*. These three elements are considered the pillars of object-oriented programming.

Polymorphism is the capability of having things share the same name and yet have them behave differently depending on the way and situation in which they are used. For example, you might have a command named PRINT. When you apply PRINT to a black and white laser printer, you get a document that has black type. When you apply PRINT to a color printer, you get a document that has typefaces of different colors.

Inheritance is the capability to derive properties, methods and events from one object and apply them to another object, sometimes with special enhancements. For example, suppose you want to make a button that makes a "beeping" sound whenever you click it. Using inheritance, you could make a special button called BeepButton, instead of having to specially program each command button every time you need one. To make the button, you would inherit all the properties, methods, and events of a CommandButton onto BeepButton. But, for BeepButton, you would program it so that whenever it was clicked it would beep. Now, the beep is "built" into the button. To have a button that beeps, all you need to do is use an instance of BeepButton.

Encapsulation is the capability to control the way data is accessed or viewed. For example, when you look at your wristwatch, all you see are the hands of the watch (or digital numerals) reporting the time. The only data you can "set" is the present time (or alarm time, your wristwatch has an alarm). You do not see the inner workings of the watch, nor is it necessary that you do. All you care is that you can get the time and that you can set the time. For all intentions and purposes, the wristwatch is encapsulated. The time and the capability to set the time are exposed to you. By comparison, they are the Public data and methods. The inner parts are Private to the wristwatch and are used only by the wristwatch.

Encapsulation is very powerful because it creates a high degree of code reusability for the programmer. Going back to the wristwatch example, if the inner mechanism of one watch is different from another, it is of no real interest to you. You can still tell and set the time regardless of whether the inner mechanism of the wristwatch is gears and sprockets or a small computer chip. The Public data and methods are still the same, regardless of the inner workings.

The same holds true for code. If code is well encapsulated, a programmer can use the Public data and methods the same way she or he always has, even if the Private code has been changed.

Programming objects work the same way as a wristwatch. When you use a CommandButton, you don't see everything that makes the button go up and down when you click it. All you see are the properties in the Properties Window. The properties of the CommandButton are considered Public— data everyone can see and use. The programming data and code used "inside" the CommandButton are Private. Only the CommandButton can see the inside data and code.

For the most part, Visual Basic is an object-oriented programming language. It enables you to program with objects. And, as your VB programming skills progress, you will be able to create custom objects in Visual Basic that you can use with other languages such as Visual C++ or Delphi. However, lack of language features to support inheritance disqualifies it as a true object-oriented programming language. Other languages such as C++, Delphi (Object Pascal), and Java, are considered genuine object-oriented programming languages. For more details on using object-oriented programming principles read the chapters entitled "Working with Objects and Classes" and "Making ActiveX Controls" on the CD-ROM.

Part
I

Ch
5

Understanding Methods

Forms and controls in Visual Basic are not just idle components that sit and look pretty. These objects are capable of performing tasks. Just as properties of an object define how it looks and behaves, *methods* of an object define the tasks that it can perform. The tasks can be simple—moving the object to another location—or they can be more complex, such as updating information in b9database.

A method is really just a segment of program code that is embedded in the object. Using the embedded method, the object knows how to perform the task; you don't have to provide any additional instructions. This is like starting your car. When you start your car, you invoke the "start method" by turning the key. You don't have to specify to the car (if it's a recent model) that it needs to start fuel flow to the engine, engage the starter gear, provide power to the spark plugs, and so on. Your car already "knows" to do all these things, because they were part of the the car's design.

As with properties, each type of object can have different methods and different numbers of methods. A simple object such as a `label` will have a minimum set of methods. Complex objects such as a `form` or a `data` control may have a dozen or more methods.

While there are different methods for different objects, many objects have the following methods in common:

- `Drag`   Handles the operation of the user's dragging and dropping the object within its container.
- `Move`   Responds to requests by the program to change the position of an object.
- `SetFocus`   Gives focus to the control specified in the method call.
- `ZOrder`   Determines whether an object appears in front of or behind other objects in its container.

Understanding Events and Event-Driven Programming

In addition to performing tasks, the objects in your program can respond to user actions or other external actions. These actions are handled through the use of *events*.

An event occurs whenever the user performs some action on a control, such as clicking a `CommandButton` or changing the contents of a `TextBox`. Events also occur when the user exits a form or switches to another program. You write code to respond to events.

To illustrate events, suppose you are driving and the traffic light turns red. A "turned red" event is generated. You have choices as to how you are going to respond to that event, such as stopping, turning right, or ignoring the red light. You have no control over when or how the light will change. The only control you have is *how* you will respond to the light change event.

It works the same way in VB programming. You have little control over how a user uses the application you wrote. The only thing you can ever know is how your program is going to respond to a button when the user clicks it.

Whenever something "happens" in your program, an event is generated. Particular objects generate events that are particular to the object. Only a form can generate and offer a response to an UnLoad event(we are discounting user-defined events here, which are an advanced feature of Visual Basic). However, some events—the Click event, for example—are common to more than one kind of control. When you click the form, your program can respond to that click by changing the color of the form. When you click a CommandButton on that form, the Click event for the CommandButton can be programmed to close the form and terminate your program. Both objects have the same type of event. However, a form's Click event is distinct from a CommandButton's Click event.

Integrating Properties and Methods

By now, you know that objects have properties to define their appearance and behavior, methods that let them perform tasks, and events that let them respond to user actions. You might think that all these things happen independently of one another, but that is not always the case. Sometimes the properties and methods of an object are related. That is, as you invoke a method of an object, the properties of the object are changed. Also, most times that you use the methods of an object or change its properties with code, you do so in response to an event.

N O T E Some property changes can trigger events. For example, changing the Height or Width property of a form in code triggers the Resize event of the form. ■

You can see one example of the interdependence of methods and properties of an object when the Move method is used and the Left and Top properties are set. You can cause an object to change position either by using the Move method or by setting the Left and Top properties to new values. For example, the following code segment in Listing 5.1 shows two ways to accomplish the same task. The first way sets the Left and Top properties to position the TextBox, txtMove. The other way invokes the Move method to position the control.

Part

I

Ch

5

**Listing 5.1   F_LIST01.TXT—Moving a *TextBox* Using the *Left* and *Top*
Properties or the *Move* Method**

```
'********************************************
'Move the text box by setting the properties
'********************************************
txtMove.Left = 100
txtMove.Top = 100
'**************************************
'Move the text box using the Move method
'**************************************
txtMove.Move 100, 100
```

Additionally, optional arguments of the Move method can change the size of an object. This has the same effect as setting the Height and Width properties to new values.

The following code in Listing 5.2 takes what you saw in the previous code segment and enhances it to position and size the control.

Listing 5.2   F_LIST02.TXT—Moving and Resizing a *TextBox* Using the *Left*, *Top*, *Width*, and *Height* Properties or the *Move* Method

```
'Move and size the text box by setting the properties
'*********************************************
txtMove.Width = 300
txtMove.Height = 120

txtMove.Left = 100
txtMove.Top = 100
'*****************************************
'Move and size the text box using the Move method
'*****************************************
txtMove.Move 100, 100, 300, 120
```

Similarly, the Show and Hide methods of a form have the same effect as changing the form's Visible property. When you invoke the Hide method, the effect is the same as setting the Visible property to False. (The effect, of course, is that the form disappears from the screen.) Likewise, the Show method produces the same effect as setting the Visible property to True.

Determining When an Event Has Occurred

Windows automatically detects events. When Windows senses an event taking place, it attempts to tell your running program about the event. Windows sends your running program a *message*. Your program must interpret that message, determine which event the message stands for, and then act accordingly. The messages sent by Windows are received and processed by the form(s) and controls that make up the interface of your program. As a Visual Basic programmer, you don't have to worry about intercepting and responding to each Windows message; VB does it for you.

Each Visual Basic control or form can raise a particular set of events, but your program doesn't have to handle all the events. If you don't write code for an event, the event is ignored. To write some code to handle a particular event generated by a particular control, you select the object and its event in the Code Window for the form upon which the control resides. You make your selections through the drop-down lists at the top of the code window: Select the object (usually a control) from the left-hand list, and then select the event you're interested in from the right-hand list. Visual Basic now displays an empty procedure for this control/event combination, and this is where you type your code. The procedure that you have selected is formally called an event procedure. Figure 5.1 shows an event procedure written for a CommandButton's Click event. The process of writing event procedures is covered in more detail later in this chapter.

FIG. 5.1
Visual Basic responds
to an event only if you
write code for it.

Beginning line of
the code block

Object selection
drop-down

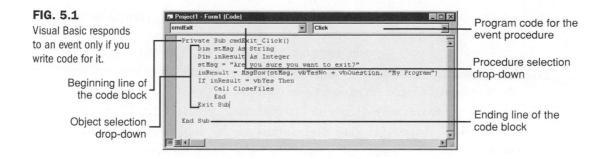

Program code for the
event procedure

Procedure selection
drop-down

Ending line of the
code block

Using User-Initiated Events

Two basic types of events can occur in your Visual Basic program—*user-initiated events* and *system-initiated events*. Most often, you will program for the user-initiated events. These events let your users control the direction of the program. That is, your users can take a specific action whenever they want, which gives them almost complete control over your program. (You can, of course, limit the actions that a user may take by hiding or disabling controls when you don't want the user to have access to them.)

User-initiated events occur because of an action taken by the user. These events include keystrokes and mouse clicks, but there also are other events caused by the user, either directly or indirectly. For example, when the user clicks a TextBox to start editing the information in the box, a Click event is fired for the TextBox. What you may not realize is that several other events also are fired. One is the GotFocus event for the TextBox. This event occurs every time the user moves to the TextBox, either by clicking the mouse or using the Tab key. Also, if the TextBox gets the program's focus, another control must lose the focus. This causes a LostFocus event to fire for the other control. The GotFocus and LostFocus events are caused by the user's action, just as the Click event is. Multiple events can occur for each action a user may take. The order in which the events occur can be important.

Here are some of the main user actions that trigger events in a program:

- Starting the program
- Pressing a key
- Clicking the mouse
- Moving the mouse
- Closing the program

While there are a number of events to which forms and controls can respond, many controls have several events in common as follows:

- Change   Occurs when the user modifies the text in a text box or combo box.
- Click   Occurs when the user clicks an object with the primary mouse button (usually, the left button).

Part

I

Ch

5

- **DblClick**   Occurs when the user double-clicks an object with the primary mouse button.
- **DragDrop**   Occurs when the user drags a control to another location.
- **DragOver**   Occurs when an object is dragged over a control.
- **GotFocus**   Occurs when an object receives the focus.
- **KeyDown**   Occurs when a key is pressed while an object has the focus.
- **KeyPress**   Occurs when a key is pressed and released while an object has the focus.
- **KeyUp**   Occurs when a key is released while an object has the focus.
- **LostFocus**   Occurs just before the focus leaves an object.
- **MouseDown**   Occurs when a mouse button pressed while an object has the mouse pointer over the object.
- **MouseMove**   Occurs when the mouse cursor is moved over an object.
- **MouseUp**   Occurs when a mouse button is released while the mouse pointer is over the object.

You may have noticed that several of the events seem to correspond to the same user action. For example, the Click, MouseDown, and MouseUp events all occur when the user clicks the mouse button. Although some of the differences between the events are obvious—for example, the MouseDown event occurs when you press the mouse button—there are other differences between the events. In the case of pressing a mouse button, the Click event is fired only if the left mouse button is pressed; it does not respond to the click of any other mouse button. The MouseDown and MouseUp events not only respond to any mouse button, but the event also can report which button was pressed, so your program can take appropriate action.

The KeyDown, KeyPress, and KeyUp events work in a similar manner. KeyPress only reports ANSI keystrokes, while the KeyDown and KeyUp events report any code-generating key on the keyboard (including Function keys, for example), along with the state of the Control, Shift and Alt keys. The KeyPress event only tells you which key was pressed, not whether a Shift or Ctrl key was held down when the key was pressed. If you need that information, you need to use the KeyDown or KeyUp events.

Defining Procedures

A *procedure* is a set of VB programming statements that exist with the following body code. Procedures have the following format:

```
[Public ¦ Private] [Static] Sub¦Function¦Property NAME [(arglist)] [As type]
[statements]
Function Name = ReturnValue
```

(You return a value from a function by assigning the return value to the function's NAME.)

```
End Sub¦Function¦Property
```

where the first line of the procedure is the beginning of the body of code and the last line is the body of code.

In Visual Basic 5.0 there are three types of procedures: Sub, Function, and Property. You'll learn a lot more about these in the upcoming chapters. The important thing to understand here is that a procedure is a set of statements and that these statements exist within a formal structure.

N O T E If you enter a Code window by double-clicking an object, the Code window automatically selects that object's most commonly-used event procedure. For example, if you double-click a CommandButton at design time, the Code window is opened to that CommandButton's Click event procedure. ■

Writing Event Procedures

With all these events going on, how do you make your code respond to any of the events? And how do you filter out the events that you don't want? The answer to both questions is the same. To respond to any event for any object, you write program code specifically for that event happening to that object. The place in the program where you write code to respond to an event is the *event procedure*.

To write code, you first need to access the code-editing window. Do this by double-clicking a control on your form. Then click the View Code button in the Project window by selecting the Code item from the View menu or just press F7.

In the Code window, you select the object and event for which you want to write code. When you make a selection, Visual Basic automatically generates an event procedure code block, which is a skeleton of a procedure with the procedure name and the End Sub statement. Notice that the procedure name for an Event procedure uses a naming convention that contains the name of the object and the name of the event with an underscored character connecting them. Figure 5.1 shows how this works with the event procedure named cmdExit_Click(). The cmdExit is the name of the object from which the event is being generated and Click is the event in question.

At this point, now that you've had Visual Basic generate a framework for an event procedure, you can write program statements to take any actions you want for the event. The following code shows how the program displays a second form in response to the user clicking a CommandButton:

```
Private Sub cmdShowDetail_Click()
    frmDetail.Show
End Sub
```

N O T E The GotFocus and LostFocus events are related to just about everything else. Because these events occur whenever the focus moves from one control to another, any action that can change the focus will trigger these events. Therefore, you can use the LostFocus event as a place to do *data validation*, making sure the data the user put in a control is the data you want. However, you need to be careful. Improperly programming `GotFocus` and `LostFocus` can trigger an endless cascade of events that causes your program to stop responding. ■

Using Properties, Methods, and Events in a Sample Program

Now that you have established a good footing on the rudiments properties, methods, and event procedures, this section discusses writing a sample program that takes advantage of what you have just learned.

The program in this section is called MoveMe. `MoveMe` is a form with four buttons (see Figure 5.2). Each button is placed by one of the four corners of the form. When you click the button, the form moves to the place on the screen where the button is on the form. For example, if you click the button at the lower-right side of the form, the form moves to the lower-right side of the screen. Also, to make things interesting, you will build in some notification messages. The form also reports some mouse movement and which control has the focus.

If you want to follow along, the code for this section is in the project, MoveMe.vbp which is in the directory, .\Chp_5\MoveMe, on the CD-ROM that accompanies this book.

As with other sample programs in the book, the instructions and results of the MoveMe program are very specific, but you can tailor them to your needs. The point of this example is to give you an opportunity to use the concepts in the chapter to create a program that is useful for you. Feel free to take liberties with control names, locations of controls on the forms, and so on.

FIG. 5.2

The MoveMe program gives you a good idea of how to program using properties, methods, and event procedures.

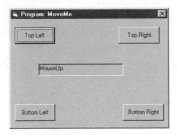

Making the Interface

The first thing that you do is make the Graphical User Interface (GUI) for this program. You should be familiar with how to create a New Project using the File menu. Also, you should be familiar with how to add CommandButtons and other controls from the `ToolBox` to a form. If you are not, you might want to review Chapter 1, "Your First Application," and Chapter 3, "Using the Standard Tools."

To make the GUI for MoveMe do the following:

1. Create a New Project from the File menu. Select Standard EXE from the New Project dialog box.

2. In the Properties window, change the name of the project's default form from Form1 to whatever you want to call it. (This example names it frmMain, as shown in Figure 5.3.) Set the value of the form's BorderStyle property to 1- Fixed Single.

FIG. 5.3

You can set the Name property of an object only at design time. You cannot change it at runtime.

3. Add buttons to frmMain and place them in the form, as shown in Figure 5.4.

FIG. 5.4

You can add a CommandButton to a form by double-clicking the CommandButton icon in the ToolBox.

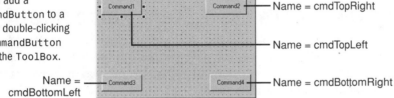

Name = cmdTopRight

Name = cmdTopLeft

Name = cmdBottomLeft

Name = cmdBottomRight

4. Change the values of the Name property for the buttons as shown in Figure 5.4. to cmdTopLeft, cmdTopRight, cmdBottomLeft and cmdBottomRight (Figure 5.4 illustrates this for the cmdTopLeft button).

5. Add a Label to frmMain. Give it a new Name value, such as lblStatus. Set the values of the Width and Height property (the example uses 2535 and 360, respectively). Set the value of the label's BorderStyle property to, 1 - Fixed Single.

6. Position the Label control where you want it on the form, as shown in Figure 5.5.

FIG. 5.5

Setting a Label control's BorderStyle to Fixed Single gives it that chiseled-in look.

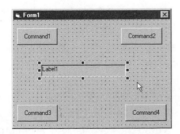

7. Save the form and project with different file names, such as frmMain.frm for the form and MoveMe.vbp for the project, as seen in Figure 5.6.

Part

I

Ch

5

FIG. 5.6

You can make a new directory from within the Save Project As dialog box by clicking the button with a picture of a small folder with a star on the upper right, near the directory drop-down box.

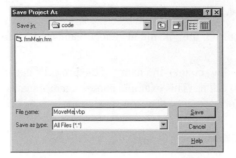

That's all that there is to do right now. You haven't yet set the `Caption` property of the CommandButtons to reflect more adequately what will happen when the user clicks one. You'll do this in an alternative way, by instructing the program to set the `Caption` property of the various CommandButtons at runtime when the form loads itself to be shown. This section also shows you how to clear out the default text from the `lblStatus.Caption` property and set the text in the title bar of the form to have the title of the application.

Programming the Form's *Load* Event Procedure

When a program's form is brought into the memory of your computer, just before the form appears, a Load event is fired. You can respond to the Load event through the `Form_Load()` event procedure. The `Form_Load()` event procedure is Visual Basic's way of saying, "Is there anything that you want to do when I load the form?"

In the case of your sample program, you can set the values of the `Caption` property for the CommandButtons in the `Form_Load` event procedure. Doing this gives the user a better idea of what the CommandButtons are about. Also, you can clear out the default text from the status label's `Caption` property and set the form's `Caption` property (which is really the text in the form's title bar) to report the application's title.

Form_Load Event-Procedure Naming

Earlier in this chapter, you learned that the naming convention Visual Basic uses for an event procedure is to take the name of the object generating the event and couple it to the event with an underscore character. This is true for every object's event procedure except those pertaining to a Form object. With a form, Visual Basic used the generic name, Form.

For example, even if you have a form where the value of the Name property is frmData, the event procedure for the Load event will be named Form_Load().

To code the `Form_Load()` event procedure, double-click anywhere on frmMain, except the form's title bar. This brings up the form's Code Window. After you have the Code Window up, enter the code that you see in Listing 5.3 in to the `Form_Load()` event procedure code. You can modify the code if you have named or positioned your buttons differently or made other changes to the example program.

Listing 5.3   F-LIST03.TXT—The *Form_Load()* Event Procedure for the *MoveMe* Application

```
'Set the captions of the CommandButtons
cmdTopLeft.Caption = "Top Left"
cmdBottomLeft.Caption = "Bottom Left"
cmdTopRight.Caption = "Top Right"
cmdBottomRight.Caption = "Bottom Right"

'Clear out the Status Label's Caption
lblStatus.Caption = ""

'Set the form's title bar text to be the
'name of the application
frmMain.Caption = "Program: MoveMe"
```

Figure 5.7 shows you what the code looks like once you've entered it into the Code Window.

When you set "starting" values for an object's properties, you are initializing the values. The process of setting starting values is called *initialization*.

FIG. 5.7
Visual Basic generates the framework for the Form_Load() event procedure. You provide the code.

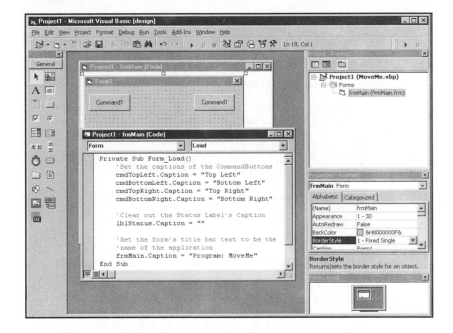

Programming the *Click* Event Procedure

Now that you have initialized the values for the Caption property of the CommandButtons, Label and Form, it's time to put in the code that will move the form around the screen. This code will be added to the Click event procedures of each CommandButton.

Listing 5.4 shows you the Click event procedures for all four CommandButtons. Double-click each CommandButton to bring up the Click event procedure for that CommandButton. Put the associated code within the event procedure code block for the particular button in question. For example, the body of code between Private Sub cmdBottomLeft_Click() and End Sub is put in the cmdButtonLeft_Click() event procedure.

The Screen Object

As you add the code for the CommandButton's Click event procedure in the MoveMe project, you might notice a reference to an object called Screen. The Screen object refers to your monitor screen.

For a detailed description of the Screen properties, read the online documentation that comes with Visual Basic.

Listing 5.4 F_LIST04.TXT—The *Click* Event Procedures for the Four CommandButtons in the MoveMe Project

```
Private Sub cmdBottomLeft_Click()

    'Set the value of the form's TOP property
    'to the most bottom of the screen but bring
    'it up the height of the screen so that the
    'bottom of the form is on the bottom of
    'the screen
    frmMain.Top = Screen.Height - frmMain.Height

    'Set the value of the form's LEFT property
    'to the left  most of the screen.
    frmMain.Left = 0
End Sub

Private Sub cmdBottomRight_Click()

    'Set the value for form's TOP property to the
    'bottom most of the screen, but bring the TOP
    'up the HEIGHT of the form so that the bottom
    'of the form is on the bottom of the screen.
    frmMain.Top = Screen.Height - frmMain.Height
```

```
        'Set the value of the form's LEFT property to
        'the most right of the screen but bring it across
        'the screen, the width of the form so that the
        'right side of the form is on the right
        'side of the screen
        frmMain.Left = Screen.Width - frmMain.Width
    End Sub

    Private Sub cmdTopLeft_Click()

        'Set the value of the form's TOP property
        'to the top most of the screen.
        frmMain.Top = 0

        'Set the value of the form's LEFT property
        'to the left  most of the screen.
        frmMain.Left = 0
    End Sub

    Private Sub cmdTopRight_Click()

        'Set the value of the form's TOP property
        'to the top most of the screen.
        frmMain.Top = 0

        'Set the value of the form's LEFT property to
        'the most right of the screen but bring it across
        'the screen, the width of the form so that the
        'right side of the form is on the right
        'side of the screen
        frmMain.Left = Screen.Width - frmMain.Width
    End Sub
```

The way the code works is straightforward. The top of your monitor always is the value 0 (zero) for the form's Top property. The left of your screen always is the value 0 (zero) for the form's Left property. Thus, to send the form to the top or left of the screen, you set the value of either the Top or Left property to 0.

Getting the form to line up on the right side or bottom of the screen is a little trickier. Remember, there is not a Right or Bottom property for a Form object. To set a form to the right side of the screen, you must set the Left property of the form to the value of the Width property of the Screen object minus the value of the Width of the form . This value of the screen's Width property would be the same coordinate value of the Right property of the Screen, *if there were one!* The same technique is used to determine the bottom of the screen.

If you were to just set the value of the form's Top property to the value of the Screen's Height property, the form would be off the screen, just below the bottom of the screen. This isn't going to work. To set the bottom of the form to the bottom of the screen, you subtract the value of the form's Height property from the value of the Screen's Height property. This effectively "lifts" the form up so you can see it (see Figure 5.8).

> **CAUTION**
>
> Beginning Visual Basic programmers often look for a `Right` or `Bottom` property when trying to set the position for a form.
>
> There are *no* `Right` or `Bottom` values for the form object or any object in Visual Basic!

FIG. 5.8

Placing forms to the right side and the bottom of the screen can be tricky. If you are not careful, you can place a form "off" of the screen.

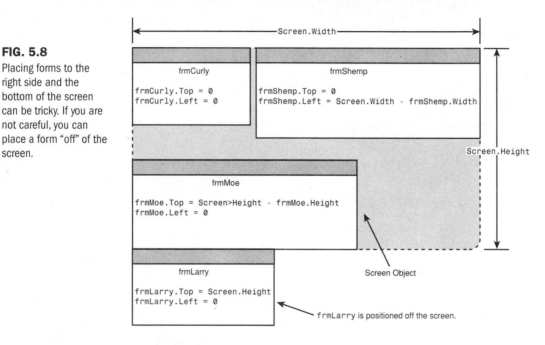

Adding Event Notification

The last thing to do is to put some code in the program that notifies the user when certain events have taken place.

You want to notify the user that a MouseUp and MouseDown event for the form has taken place as well as the GotFocus event for each CommandButton. This means that when the user presses the mouse button on a form or when she lets up on the mouse button, you want to put some text in the lblStatus control that informs the user the event has happened. You want the same thing to happen when the user uses the TAB key to move from CommandButton-to-Command Button, which changes the focus from one button to another.

Doing this requires you to write code in three types of event procedures: the MouseUp event procedure, the MouseDown event procedure, and the GotFocus event procedure.

Listing 5.5 shows the code that you could write in the MouseUp and MouseDown event procedures for frmMain.

Listing 5.5 FLIST05.TXT—The Code for the *MouseUp* and *MouseDown* Event Procedures Reports When the User Presses Down and Lets Up on the Mouse or When the Mouse Cursor Is over the Form

```
Private Sub Form_MouseDown(Button As Integer, Shift As Integer, X _
                          As Single, Y As Single)
    lblStatus.Caption = "MouseDown"
End Sub

Private Sub Form_MouseUp(Button As Integer, Shift As Integer, X _
                        As Single, Y As Single)
    lblStatus.Caption = "MouseUp"
End Sub
```

To bring up the Code window for the MouseDown event procedure, double-click the form. This brings up the Code window for the Form object. Then, select MouseDown from the event procedures drop-down list (see Figure 5.9).

FIG. 5.9

You select an object's events from the event procedure's drop-down list.

Once you are in the Code window for the form's MouseDown event, add the code in Listing 5.5 to the event procedure's code block. In order to program the form's MouseUp event procedure, repeat this process, but select the MouseUp event procedure for the form's event procedure drop-down list.

After this code is in, if your mouse is over the form (not the CommandButton!) and you press your mouse button, the text "MouseDown" appears in the lblStatus control. When you release your mouse button, the text "MouseUp" appears.

Now you need to put in the code that tells the user when a CommandButton gets the focus. Listing 5.6 shows the GotFocus event procedure code for each CommandButton.

Part

I

Ch

5

Listing 5.6   F_LIST06.TXT—When the User Uses the Tab Key to Move Between Command Buttons, This Code Causes a Notification Message to Appear in the *lblStatus*'s Caption

```
Private Sub cmdTopRight_GotFocus()
    lblStatus.Caption = "cmdTopRight GotFocus"
End Sub


Private Sub cmdTopLeft_GotFocus()
    lblStatus.Caption = "cmdTopLeft GotFocus"
End Sub


Private Sub cmdBottomRight_GotFocus()
    lblStatus.Caption = "cmdBottomRight GotFocus"
End Sub


Private Sub cmdBottomLeft_GotFocus()
    lblStatus.Caption = "cmdBottomLeft GotFocus"
End Sub
```

To get to the Code window for a CommandButton, go to that CommandButton, cmdTopLeft for example, double-click it and select GotFocus from the event procedure's drop-down list of the resulting Code window (see Figure 5.10). Put the appropriate code from the preceding listing into the event procedure for the corresponding CommandButton. Do this for each CommandButton on the form.

FIG. 5.10

Be careful when accessing the GotFocus event procedure for a CommandButton. Remember, the Click event procedure is the default.

To run the program, press the F5 key (see Figure 5.11).

FIG. 5.11
Clicking a
CommandButton also
gives it the focus, as
you can see from the
message in the
lblStatus control.

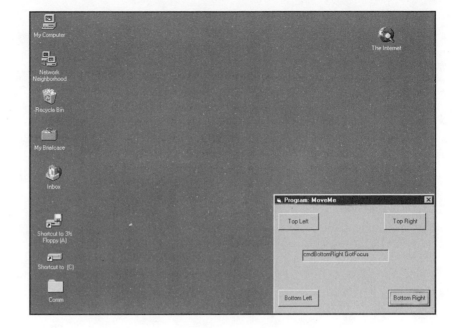

II

Visual Basic Programming Fundamentals

CHAPTER 6

Using Data Types, Constants, and Variables

Variables

Find out how to create and to use variables for storing and retrieving information within your program.

Data Types

Learn how to use the different types of variables to accurately report information.

Constants

Create and use constants to make your programs easier to read and maintain.

Scope

Expose variables in such a way so that you can use the same variable names within your program without compromising the integrity of their value.

Naming Convention

Create variables that are easy to read and understand.

Previous chapters discussed specific aspects of the Visual Basic programming language and development environment, including forms, controls, modules, projects, the Visual Basic IDE, and so on. This chapter discusses the concepts and practices that are more general to the discipline of computer programming, including how to use variables, constants, and data types. ∎

Storing Information in Variables

Figure 6.1 shows a simple addition program, AddNum.EXE, from the project Addnum.prj, in the directory chp_5\AddNum\ on the CD-ROM which accompanies this book.

FIG. 6.1

A simple addition program created in Visual Basic.

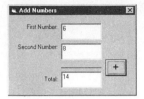

The program enables the user to enter two numbers, and when he or she clicks the "+" button, the program processes the total, which is then displayed in the third text box. This program raises an interesting question: What do you do with the data while it is being processed in your program? The answer is that you temporarily store the information in *variables*.

A *variable* is a placeholder for a value. Think of a variable as a cup that can hold a different amount of jelly beans. You never know how many jelly beans are in the cup at any given time unless you look in the cup.

The same is true for a variable. A variable can hold a different value at different times. You programmatically "look" into it to find out its value.

Use variables if you know that you will have to deal with a quantity at some point but you don't know what the value of it is right now, such as the balance of your checking account. You know the account's balance today, but you have no idea what the balance will be in a week.

N O T E   The properties of a control also are treated like variables in a Visual Basic program. ▨

Declaring Variables

You create (or declare) a variable by using the following form:

```
Dim VarName As DataType
```

Where:

- ▨ Dim is the keyword that tells Visual Basic that you want to declare a variable.
- ▨ VarName is the name of the variable.
- ▨ As is the keyword that tells Visual Basic that you are defining the data type for the variable.
- ▨ DataType is the data type of the variable.

Keyword

A keyword, also known as a *reserved word*, is a word that is reserved for the exclusive use of Visual Basic. *You cannot use keywords for your own programming needs.* Words such as `Dim`, `As`, `New`, `ReDim`, `If`, `Then`, `Else`, `Loop`, `While` and `End` are all Visual Basic keywords.

By default, Visual Basic uses a blue font color to show all keywords that you type in a Code window.

Visual Basic has a lot of keywords. Look in the online documentation that comes with Visual Basic to get a detailed list and explanation of them all.

Listing 6.1 shows the event procedure for the `click` event of the cmdAdd button. Three variables, x, y, and z, are declared. These variables are of type `Integer`. (Data types are discussed later in the chapter. For now, realize that you made variables that will accommodate numbers.)

Listing 6.1   06LIST01.TXT—The Event Procedure for the *cmdAdd Click* Event

```
Private Sub cmdAdd_Click()
    'Declare a variable for the first number
    Dim x As Integer

    'Declare a variable for the second number
    Dim y As Integer

    'Declare a variable to hold the sum of both numbers
    Dim z As Integer

    'Convert the text inputted into the text box
    'into an integer and assign it to the first variable
    x = CInt(txtNumOne.Text)

    'Convert the text inputted into the text box
    'into an integer and assign it to the second variable
    y = CInt(txtNumTwo.Text)

    'Add the first two variables together and assign
    'the result to the third variable
    z = x + y

    'Convert the third variable (which is an integer)
    'to text and assign it to the text property of the
    'TextBox for the result.
    txtTotal.Text = CStr(z)
End Sub
```

Part

II

Ch

6

Some of the code lines in Listing 6.1 have notes within the code that explain the purpose of the code line. This is called *commenting* your code. To comment code, begin a line with the apostrophe character ('). The apostrophe tells Visual Basic that everything on that line or following the apostrophe is not code and thus should be ignored by the compiler.

For example:

```
'This is a commented line.
z = x + y     'The first part of this line is code; the second part is a
comment.
Text1.Text = "This is not a commented line"
```

Naming Variables

When you declare a variable, you must give it a name. Going back to the cup analogy, if you have two cups on a table that hold different amounts of jelly beans, you must be able to distinguish between the cups in order to work with them. Naming makes each variable distinct and easy to identify.

When naming a variable, you have a tremendous amount of flexibility. Variable names can be simple, or they can be descriptive of the information they contain. For example, you may want to name a counter variable I; or you may want to use a more descriptive name, such as NumberOfRedJellyBeansForBob or NumberOfJellyBeansForDorothy. While you are allowed great latitude in naming, there are a few restrictions, as follows:

- The name must start with a letter, not a number or other character.
- The name cannot contain a period.
- The name must be unique within the current procedure or module (this restriction depends on the *scope* of the name, which you learn about a little later).
- The name can be no longer than 255 characters.

For example, the following variable names do *not* work:

1Week (You cannot begin a variable with a number.)

Earnings.To.Data (You cannot use periods.)

Number One (You cannot have spaces between characters.)

The following variable names do work:

MyNum&

i

iNumOne

strInputValue

Number2#

TIP Make your variable names descriptive of the task in order to make your code easy to read, but also keep the names short in order to make the code easy to type. Many programmers use prefixes on their variables to indicate the type of data stored and the scope of the variable. For example, a prefix of g_int - would indicate a global or program-level variable that stores an integer.

Choosing the Correct Variable Type

You can store almost anything in a variable. A variable can hold a number, a string of text, or an instance of an object, including forms, controls, and database objects. This chapter looks specifically at using variables to store numbers, strings, and logical values. You can use a variable to hold any type of information, but different types of variables are designed to work efficiently with different types of information.

Let's go back to our cup example in the previous section. You might want to have a type of cup that can hold only jelly beans, or only cherries, or only nails. What the cup is supposed to hold greatly influences how the cup is constructed. A cup that holds cherries might have little holes in the bottom that allow water to pass through. A cup to hold nails might be made of tough material so that the nails don't puncture it. The same is true of variables. The type of variable must match the data it is going to hold.

When you declare a variable to be of a certain type, you are giving instructions to Visual Basic about how to "build" the variable to accommodate the type of data that the variable will have to hold.

Table 6.1 shows the different types of variables available in Visual Basic. The table also shows the range of values that the variable can hold and the amount of memory required to store the information in the variable. (Sort of like the size of the cup.) Understanding memory requirements are important if you want to optimize your code. You should use variables with smaller memory requirements wherever possible to conserve system resources, but don't worry about optimizing code until you're comfortable with the concept of creating and using variables.

Table 6.1 Variables Store Many Types of Information

Type	Stores	Memory Requirement	Range of Values
Integer	Whole numbers	2 bytes	32,768 to 32,767
Long	Whole numbers	4 bytes	(approximately) +/- 2.1E9 approx.
Single	Decimal numbers	4 bytes	-3.402823E38 to -1.401298E-45 for negative values; 1.401298E-45 to 3.402823E38 for positive values.
Double	Decimal numbers	8 bytes	(dbl-prec fltg-pt) -1.79769313486232E308 to -4.94065645841247E-324 for negative values; 4.94065645841247E-324 to 1.79769313486232E308 for positive values.

continues

Part

II

Ch

6

Table 6.1   Continued

Type	Stores	Memory Requirement	Range of Values
Currency	Numbers with up to 15 digits left of the decimal and four digits right of the decimal	8 bytes	922,337,203,685,477.5808 to 922,337,203,685,477.5807
String	Text information	1 byte/character	Up to 65,000 characters for fixed-length string and up to 2 billion characters for dynamic strings.
Byte	Whole numbers	1 byte	0 to 255
Boolean	Logical values	2 bytes	True or False
Date	Date and time information	8 bytes	Jan 1st 100 to December 31st 9999
Object	Pictures and any any object reference	4 bytes	N/A
Variant	Any of the preceding data types	16 bytes + 1 byte/character	N/A

You know how to name a variable and what a variable can store, but how do you tell the program what you want to store? In reality, you do not have to tell Visual Basic what a variable will contain. Unlike other languages, Visual Basic does not require you to specifically declare a variable before it is used. If a variable is not declared, Visual Basic uses a default data type known as a *variant*. A variant can contain any type of information. However, using a variant for general information has two major drawbacks—it can waste memory resources, and the variable type may produce unpredictable default value behaviors, particularly with arrays. It is a good idea to declare your variables before they are used. This saves you time in the long run and makes your code much more reliable.

Making Explicit Declarations

An explicit declaration means that you must use a statement to define a variable. Each of the following statements can be used to declare explicitly a variable's type:

```
Dim VarName [As VarType][, VarName2 [As VarType2]]
Private VarName[As VarType][, VarName2[As VarType2]]
Static VarName[As VarType][, VarName2[As VarType2]]
Public VarName[As VarType][, VarName2[As VarType2]]
```

Here Dim, Private, Static, and Public are Visual Basic keywords that define how and where the variable can be used. The VarName and VarName2 represent the names of the variables that you want to declare. As indicated in the syntax, you can specify multiple variables in the same statement as long as you separate the variables by commas. (Note that the syntax shows only two variables, but you can specify any number.)

VarType and *VarType2* represent the type name of the respective variables. The *type name* is a keyword that tells Visual Basic what kind of information will be stored in the variable. The type can be one of those specified in Table 6.1 or a user-defined type. (User-defined types are covered in the chapter entitled, "Working with Objects and Classes," on the CD-ROM.) As indicated, the variable type is an optional property. If you include the variable type, you must include the keyword As. If you do not include a variable type, the Variant type (which is the default) is used.

The following code shows the use of these declaration statements for actual variables using explicit declaration:

```
Private iNumVal As Integer
Private iAvgVal As Integer, dInputval As Double
Static sCalcAverage As Single
Dim strInputMsg As String
```

 TIP Use the data type Variant only when you really need to. Do not use it as a catch-all variable. They waste memory and may cause type compatibility problems down the road.

Making Implicit Declarations

In Visual Basic, you do not have to use the keyword Dim, Private, Static or Public. In Visual Basic you can just use a variable name such as:

```
MyVal
```

If you were to put this code in your project, you would have made a variable as type Variant, named MyVal. MyVal would have a default value of Empty. Whenever you use implicit declaration, Visual Basic considers that variable as type Variant.

However, using Implicit declaration is not recommended. Making a variable without a formal declaration is really asking for trouble. If you use implicit declaration, any time you make a spelling mistake or syntax error, Visual Basic will think that you are declaring another variable *implicitly*. This can lead to headaches beyond imagination.

You can protect yourself. You can make the Visual Basic IDE force you to declare a variable *explicitly*. All you need to do is enter the keywords Option Explicit in the first line of the General section of your form or module. You also can configure the IDE to do this for you automatically whenever you add a form or module. To do this, follow these steps:

1. Click the Tools menu, then select Options. The Options tabbed dialog box appears.
2. Select the Editor tab, then check the Require Variable Declaration CheckBox, as shown in Figure 6.2.
3. Click the OK button.

Part
II

Ch
6

FIG. 6.2

It always is preferable
to declare explicitly
your variables.

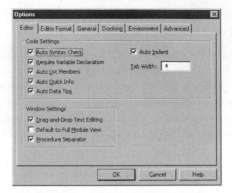

CAUTION

If you set the Require Variable Declaration option after starting to create a program, the option has no effect
on any forms or modules that already have been created. In this case, you need to add the `Option`
`Explicit` statement as the first line of code in any existing forms or modules.

After you have `Option Explicit` set, if you fail to declare a variable, you will receive the message `Variable not defined` when you try to compile your code. The integrated debugger in
Visual Basic (discussed fully in Chapter 19, "Finding and Fixing Errors") highlights the offend-
ing variable and halts the compilation of your program. The benefit of this is that it helps you
avoid errors in your code that might be caused by typographical errors. For example, you
might declare a variable using the following statement:

N O T E By default, VB is set to compile your code every time you run your code. Thus, if you don't
change this setting and you are coding Option Explicit, undeclared variables immediately
appear as errors. If you want to turn this feature off, go to the Options dialog box from the Tools menu
and uncheck the Compile On Demand Checkbox in the General Tab. ▪

```
Dim strMyName As String
```

If, in a later statement, you mistyped the variable name, Visual Basic would catch the error for
you. For example, the following statement would cause an error:

```
strMyNme = "Clark Kent"
```

T I P If you use some capital letters in your variable declarations, then enter your code in all lowercase
letters. Visual Basic automatically sets the capitalization of your variable to match the declaration. This
gives you an immediate visual indication that you typed the name correctly.

Using Type Suffixes with Variables

You saw in the preceding code examples that you use the As keyword to assign a data type to a variable. There is another method that you can use to declare a variable and assign a data type to it. This method uses *data-type suffixes*. With this type of declaration, a special character is used at the end of the variable name when the variable first is assigned a value. Doing this automatically "types" (assigns a type to) the variables. There is no need to use the As keyword. The characters for each variable type are shown in Table 6.2.

Table 6.2   Special Characters at the End of a Variable Name that Can Identify the Type of Data Stored by the Variable

Variable Type	Character
Integer	%
Long	&
Single	!
Double	#
Currency	@
String	$
Byte	None
Boolean	None
Date	None
Object	None
Variant	None

Using type suffixes, the code back in the section "Making Explicit Declarations" could be rewritten as follows:

```
Private NumVal%
Private AvgVal%, Inputval#
Static CalcAverage!
Dim InputMsg$
```

Using suffixes to "type" your variables is a quick, handy way to declare a variable. Also, using a suffix adds a new element of readability to your variable name. For example, now when you run across the variable NumVal% in your code, you know that the variable is of type Integer (from reading the suffix), and that its function is to be a value for a number (from reading the variable name).

Using Strings

A string is a collection of characters. The following are examples of different string values:

```
"Cheese"
"You have made an error!"
"a"
"July 4, 1776"
"75"
```

Notice that each collection of characters is surrounded by a set of quotation marks (""). The quotation marks are very important. In Visual Basic, characters surrounded by quotation marks are understood by Visual Basic to be *string values*. Characters not surrounded by quotation marks are considered to be a variable or a part of the language.

You may be baffled by the string value "75." You might think that it is a value for an integer. It is not. It is a string value. The following example illustrates the string_ness of "75":

```
strNum$ = "7" & "5"
```

Some beginning programmers have trouble with this concept. It takes getting used to. If you take a look at the code in Listing 6.1, you see that the input the user makes into the TextBoxes is treated as numeric string characters that must be converted to integers. You will take a more detailed look at this in Chapter 21, "Working with Strings and Typecasting."

> **CAUTION**
>
> Here, 21 and "21" are not the same thing. One is an integer and the other is a string!

Using Variable-Length and Fixed-Length Strings

Most strings that you use in your programs will be of the type known as *variable-length strings*. These strings can contain any amount of text up to 64,000 characters. As information is stored in the variable, the size of the variable adjusts to accommodate the length of the string. There is, however, a second type of string in Visual Basic—the *fixed-length string*.

As the name implies, a fixed-length string remains the same size, regardless of the information assigned to it. If a fixed-length string variable is assigned an expression shorter than the defined length of the variable, the remaining length of the variable is filled with the space character. If the expression is longer than the variable, only the characters that fit in the variable are stored; the rest are discarded.

A fixed-length string variable may only be declared using an explicit declaration of the form, such as the following:

```
Dim VarName As String * strlength
```

Thus, to make a string called `strMyString` that always is 128 characters long, you would declare it as follows:

```
Dim strMyString as String * 128
```

Notice that this declaration is slightly different from the previous declaration of a string variable. The declaration of a fixed-length string variable contains an asterisk (*) to tell Visual Basic that the string will be a fixed length. The final parameter, `strlength`, tells the program the number of characters that the variable can contain.

N O T E   With fixed-length stings, you can use the `Private` or `Static` keywords in place of `Dim`. ■

In the beginning, you probably won't have a lot of need to use fixed-length strings. As you advance, you will use them, particularly when it's time to program directly to Windows using the Windows API (Application Programming Interface).

Determining Where a Variable Can Be Used

In addition to telling Visual Basic what you want to be able to store in a variable, a `declaration` statement tells Visual Basic where the variable can be used. This area of usage is called the *scope* of the variable. This is analogous to the coverage area of a paging system. When you purchase a pager, you decide whether you want local service, regional service, or national service. This is programmed into your pager when you buy it. If you go outside the service area, your pager does not work. In a similar manner, you can declare variables to work in only one procedure, work in any procedure of a form, or work throughout your program.

By default, a variable declared with the keyword such as `Dim` is local to the procedure in which it is created. Thus, if you declare a variable in the event procedure for a CommandButton's `click` event, it resides and is visible only within that event procedure. Therefore, to create variables that have a scope other than local, you must modify your `declaration` statement.

N O T E   The scope of a variable is determined by not only the type of declaration, but the location as well. For instance, the `Dim` keyword assumes different meanings in different parts of a form's code. You can only use the `Private` keyword on variables in the Declarations section. ■

Creating Variables

In most programs, unless you have only one form and no code modules, you will find that you need some variables that can be accessed from anywhere in the code. These are called `Public` variables. (Other languages may refer to these as `Global` variables.) These variables typically are used to hold information that is used throughout the program. They also may be used to indicate various conditions in the program.

To create a `Public` variable, you place a `declaration` statement with the `Public` keyword in the Declarations section of a module in your program. The following line shows the `Public` declaration of a variable of type Boolean (True/False):

```
Public bIsOpen As Boolean
```

In a form, `Public` keyword has a special meaning. Variables defined as `Public` are considered to be very much like a property of the form and can be "seen" from anywhere in the program. These properties are referenced like the built-in properties of a form or control instead of like a variable. For example, you can have a string variable `strMyName` that was declared `Public` in the form `frmMain`, and you would access the string variable using the following expression:

```
strSomeString = frmMain.strMyName
```

The `Public` properties can be used to pass information between forms and other parts of your program.

If you do not need to access a variable from everywhere in your program, you do not want to use the `Public` keyword in a declaration. Instead, you use the keyword `Dim` within a procedure. When the variable is declared inside a procedure, it only can be used within that procedure. This typically is known as a *local variable*.

The keyword `Private` is used within a form or module's Declaration section to make the variable *only* visible to the form or module within which it is created. This is known typically as *form-* or *module-level variable*.

Keeping a Variable Local

At first glance, you may think that making all variables global is the easiest thing to do, but as your programs grow, the practice won't serve you well in the long run.

You saw in the previous section that each procedure in a VB program can have its own variables. Each procedure can have variable names that might be common across other procedures, but because they are local to that procedure, none of the others "know" about them. Thus, you do not have what are called *name collisions*.

Think of it this way: You might have two procedures, ProcA and ProcB. ProcA creates two variables x% and y% and ProcB also creates two variables x and y%. In ProcA, x% and y% are assigned values that are in turn passed as values to the `Left` and `Top` properties of a `CommandButton`, `Command1`.

In ProcB, the variable y% is assigned a value that is twice the value of x%. Both procedures have variables of the same name. However, because each set of variables was declared local to a distinct procedure, they only are available to the procedures in which they were declared (see Figure 6.3).

FIG. 6.3

Being able to properly scope your variables makes your code more reusable.

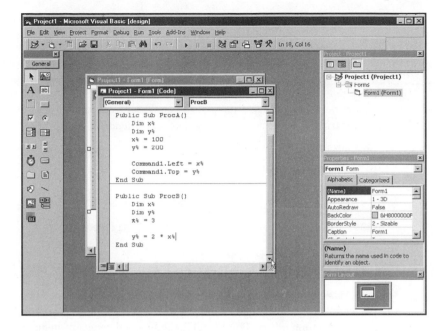

Using Static Variables

Most variables that are created inside a procedure are discarded by Visual Basic when the procedure is finished. There are times, however, when you want to preserve the value of a variable even after the procedure has run. This often is the case when you call the procedure multiple times, and the value of a variable for one call to the procedure is dependent on the value left over from previous calls.

To create a variable that retains its value even after the procedure is through running, you use the `Static` keyword in the variable declaration. This tells Visual Basic that the variable only can be referenced within the procedure, but to hold on to the value because it will be needed again.

NOTE If you use the `Static` keyword to declare a procedure, all variables in the procedure are treated as static. ▪

Static variables commonly are used in Timer events. You'll read more about this in Chapter 11, "Working with Time and Timers."

Using Constants

Variables are just one way of storing information in the memory of a computer. Another way is to use *constants*. Constants in a program are treated a special way. Once you define them (or they are defined for you by Visual Basic), you cannot change them later in the program by

Part

II

Ch

6

using an assignment statement. If you try, Visual Basic generates an error when you run your program.

Constants are most often used to replace a value that is hard to remember, such as the color value for the Windows title bar. It is easier to remember the constant vbActiveTitleBar than the value 2147483646. You also can use a constant to avoid typing long strings if they are used in a number of places. For example, you could set a constant such as ERR_FILE_FOUND containing the string, "The requested file was not found".

Constants also are used a lot for conversion factors, such as 12 inches per foot or 3.3 feet per meter. The following code example shows how constants and variables are used:

```
Const METER_TO_FEET = 3.3
Meters# = CDbl(InputBox("Enter a distance in meters"))
DistFeet# = Meters# * METER_TO_FEET
MsgBox "The distance in feet is: " & CStr(DistFeet#)
```

Using Constants Supplied by Visual Basic

Visual Basic (as of Version 4.0) supplies a number of sets of constants for various activities. There are color-definition constants, data-access constants, keycode constants, and shape constants, among others. The Visual Basic-supplied constants begin with the prefix vb.

The constants that you need for most functions are defined in the Help topic for the function. If you want to know the value of a particular constant, you can use the Object Browser (see Figure 6.4). Access the Object Browser by clicking its icon in the Visual Basic toolbar or striking the F2 key. You can use the list to find the constant that you want. When you select it, its value and function are displayed in the text area at the bottom of the dialog box.

Creating Your Own Constants

While Visual Basic defines a large number of constants for many activities, there will be times when you need to define your own constants. Constants are defined using the Const statement to give the constant a name and a value, as illustrated in the following syntax:

```
Const CONSTANT_NAME [As ConstantType] = value
```

This statement looks similar to the declaration of a variable. As with declaring a variable, you provide a name for the constant and, optionally, specify the type of data it will hold. The Const keyword at the beginning of the statement tells Visual Basic that this statement defines a constant. This distinguishes the statement from one that just assigns a value to a variable. In declaring the type of a constant, you use the same types as you did for defining variables. (These types are defined in Table 6.1.) Finally, to define a constant, you must include the equal sign (=) and the value to be assigned. If you are defining a string, remember to enclose the value in quotes. ("").

FIG. 6.4

Select the appropriate constants from the Classes list to view the constants that are internal to Visual Basic.

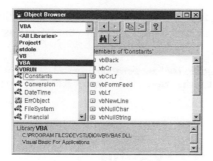

T I P   While you can use the `Const` statement anywhere in a procedure, it is best to define all the necessary constants at the beginning of the procedure.

Also, constants usually are named using all uppercase characters with an underscore character (_) used to separate the characters into words if necessary. However, with Visual Basic it's now conventional to name constants in mixed-case with a lowercase prefix.

Using the *Assignment* Statement

To use variables efficiently, you also need to be able to assign information to the variable and manipulate that information. After setting up a variable, the first thing you need to do to use the variable is to store information in the variable. This is the job of the *assignment statement*. The *assignment statement* is how you specify a variable whose value you want to set. To assign a value to a variable, place an equal sign after the variable name, and then follow this with the expression that represents the value you want stored. The expression can be a literal value, a combination of other variables and constants, or even functions that return a value. There is no limit on the complexity of the expression you use. However, even though Visual Basic attempts to convert mismatching data type automatically, you should try to have the values that you assign to your program's variables be the right type. The following statements illustrate different *assignment* statements:

```
NumStudents% = 25
SumScores% = 2276
AvgScore% = SumScores% / NumStudents%
TopStudent$ = "Janet Simon"
BadStudent$ = txtStudent.Text
```

You can consider most properties of forms and controls as variables. They can be set at design time, but also can be changed at runtime using an assignment statement. You also can use a property on the right side of a statement to assign its value to a variable for further processing.

Part
II

Ch
6

You saw this done in Listing 6.1. After the addition program shown in Figure 6.1 calculates the sum of the two entered numbers, it assigns the result to a third TextBox as shown in the following :

```
Convert the third variable (which is a Double)
'to text and assign it to the text property of the
'textbox for the result.
txtTotal.Text = CStr(z)
```

Revisiting the Addition Program

Now that you've learned more about what variables are about and how to use them, you should have a better sense of what's going on in the code in the addition program shown earlier in the chapter. If you look closely though, you'll see that the programmer made an assumption about user input that will result in a serious error. What would happen if the user did not enter a number into one of the text boxes, but rather another sort of string value? (See Figure 6.5.)

The result is a *crash*. Obviously making sure the right type of data is assigned to the right type of variable (what is referred to as *data validation*) is more than an academic exercise. It is a

FIG. 6.5

Don't assume a user always will do the expected!

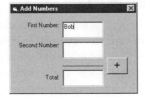

critical programming skill. You will find out how to solve this problem in Chapter 8, "Making Choices with Conditional Statements," Chapter 19, "Finding and Fixing Errors," and Chapter 21, "Working with Strings and Typecasting." ●

Making Statements in a Program

Using *assignment* statements

Use assignment statements to give variables a value.

Using *math* operations

Learn about the various math operations that Visual Basic supports and then use what you've learned to build a calculation utility.

Concatenating strings

Combine various strings into a single string. Also, learn how to continuously extend the value of a single string variable.

Computer programming is more than learning the Visual Basic language. It is about being able to describe and implement your ideas. The way you do this is by making *statements*.

In this chapter you learn how to make statements that assign a value to a variable, do math operations such as addition, multiplication, subtraction, division, and manipulate strings. ■

Using the *Assignment* Statement

You learned previously that you create a variable using the `Dim` keyword. For example:

```
Dim i as Integer
```

However, just because you have created a variable, it does not necessarily follow that that variable has a value that is useful to you. At some point you will have to give that variable an appropriate value. This is the job of the `assignment` *statement*.

To make an assignment statement, you specify a variable whose value you want to set, place an equal sign after the variable name, and then follow this with the expression that represents the value you want stored in that variable. The expression can be a literal value (such as the number 1, or the characters, "Bob"), a combination of other variables and constants, or even functions that return a value. The following statements illustrate different `assignment` statements:

```
i% = 6
SumScores = 2276
AvgScore = SumScores / NumStudents
TopStudent = "Janet Simon"
txtFirstName.Text = FirstName$
```

The last statement assigns the value of a variable, `FirstName$` to the value of a TextBox's `Text` property. This is very common. Most properties of forms and controls are variables. They can be set at design time, but they also can be changed at runtime using an `assignment` statement. You also can use a property on the right side of a statement to assign its value to a variable for further processing. For example, you could change the last of the preceding lines to read a name from a TextBox and assign it to the variable `FirstName$` as shown in the following:

```
FirstName$ = txtFirstName.Text
```

Using Variable Default Values

When you create a variable, Visual Basic assigns a default value to it. The actual default value is dependent upon the variable's data type, as shown in Table 7.1.

Table 7.1   Default Values for a Variable

Data Type	Value
Integer	0
Long	0
Single	0
Double	0
String	""
Boolean	False

Data Type	Value
Variant	EMPTY
Date	0
Currency	0

Using *Math* Operators

Math operations are used to determine customer bills, interest due on savings or credit card balances, average scores for a class test, and many other tasks. Visual Basic supports a number of different math operations that can be used in program statements. These operations and the Visual Basic symbol for each operation are summarized in Table 7.2.

Table 7.2   Math Operations and the Corresponding Visual Basic Operator Symbol

Operation	Operator Symbol
Addition	+
Subtraction	–
Multiplication	*
Division	/
Integer division	\
Modulus	mod
Exponentiation	^

Using *Addition* and *Subtraction* Operators

The two simplest math operations are addition and subtraction. If you have ever used a calculator to do addition and subtraction, you already have a good idea how these operations are performed in a line of computer code.

A computer program, however, gives you greater flexibility than a calculator in the operations you can perform. Your programs are not limited to working with literal numbers (for example, 1, 15, 37.63, 105.2). Your program can add or subtract two or more literal numbers, numeric variables, or any functions that return a numeric value. Also, as with a calculator, you can perform addition and subtraction operations in any combination. Now, take a look at exactly how you perform these operations in your program.

Part II
Ch
7

As indicated in Table 7.2, the operator for addition in Visual Basic is the plus sign (+). The general use of this operator is shown in the following syntax line:

```
Result = iNumberOne + iNumberTwo + iNumberThree
```

Result is a variable (or control property) that will contain the sum of the numbers. The equal sign indicates the assignment of a value to the variable. The iNumberOne, iNumberTwo, and iNumberThree are numeric variables. As described previously, you also can add literal numbers or return values from a function with or instead of numeric variables. You can add as many numbers together as you like, but each number pair must be separated by a plus sign.

The operator for subtraction is the minus sign (-). The syntax basically is the same as for addition:

```
Result = NumberOne - NumberTwo [- NumberThree]
```

While the order does not matter with addition, in subtraction, the number to the right of the minus sign is subtracted from the number to the left of the sign. If you have multiple numbers, the second number is subtracted from the first, then the third number is subtracted from that result, and so on, moving from left to right. For example, consider the following equation:

```
Result = 15 - 6 - 3
```

The computer first subtracts 6 from 15 to yield 9. It then subtracts 3 from 9 to yield 6, which is the final answer stored in the variable Result.

You can create assignment statements that consist solely of addition operators or solely of subtraction operators. You also can use the operators in combination with one another or other math operators. The following code lines show a few valid math operations:

```
dValOne = 1.25 + 3.17
dValTwo = 3.21 - 1
dValThree = dValTwo + dValOne
dValFour = dValThree + 3.75 - 2.1 + 12 - 3
dValFour = dValFour + 1
```

If you are not familiar with computer programming, the last line may look a little funny to you. In fact, that line is not allowed in some programming languages. However, in Visual Basic, you can enter a line of code that tells the program to take the current value of a variable, add another number to it, and then store the resulting value back in the same variable. You also can do this with string variables. (You'll see this done later in this chapter in the "Using the Concatenation Operator" section.)

Using the *Multiplication* Operator

You simply use the multiplication operator—the asterisk (*) operator—to multiply two or more numbers. The syntax of a multiplication statement almost is identical to the ones used for addition and subtraction, as follows:

```
Result = iNumberOne * iNumber2Two * iNumberThree
```

As before, Result is the name of a variable used to contain the product of the numbers being multiplied, and iNumberOne, iNumberTwo, and iNumberThree are numeric variables. Again, you also can use literal numbers or a return value from a function.

As a demonstration of how multiplication and division might be used in a program, consider the example of a program to determine the amount of paint needed to paint a room. Such a program could contain a form that lets the painter enter the length and width of the room, the height of the ceiling, and the coverage and cost of a single can of paint. Your program could then calculate the number of gallons of paint required and the cost of the paint. An example of the form for such a program is shown in Figure 7.1. The actual code to perform the calculations is shown in Listing 7.1. The code for this example is in the project called prjPaint.vbp, in the directory Chp_7\prjPaint\, on the CD-ROM that accompanies this book.

FIG. 7.1

It's a good idea to make sure that a string value "looks" like a number and that the string is not empty before you assign it to a numeric variable.

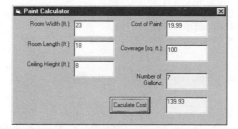

Listing 7.1 AF_ALIST0a.TXT—Cost Estimation Using Multiplication and Division Operators

```
Private Sub cmdCalc_Click()
    Dim RmLength% 'Length of Room
    Dim RmWidth%  'Width of Room
    Dim RmHeight% 'Hieght of Ceiling
    Dim RmPerimeter ' The perimeter of the room
    Dim WallArea%    'The area of a wall
    Dim NumOfGal%    'Number of gallons of paint
    Dim PaintCoverage% 'Square footage each can covers
    Dim dCanCost As Double  'Cost of a can of paint
    Dim dProjectCost As Double 'Total project cost
    Dim Msg$ 'Message variable


    'Make sure the TextBox has not been left blank
    If txtRmLength.Text <> "" Then
        'Check to make sure the text is a numeral then
        'convert the text to the appropriate data type
        'and assign the text to the room dimension
        'variables
        If IsNumeric(txtRmLength.Text) Then
            RmLength% = CInt(txtRmLength.Text)
        End If
    Else
        'If it is blank, send the cursor back to the
```

continues

Part

II

Ch

7

Listing 7.1 Continued

```
                'blank TextBox.

                'Make a message
                Msg$ = "You cannot leave Room Length blank or enter "
                Msg$ = Msg$ & "non-numeric data. Please enter a number"
                'Display the message
                MsgBox Msg$, vbExclamation, "Data entry error"
                'Send the mouse cursor back to the TextBox
                txtRmLength.SetFocus
                'Leave the Sub
                Exit Sub
        End If

        'Make sure the TextBox has not been left blank
        If txtRmHeight.Text <> "" Then
            If IsNumeric(txtRmHeight.Text) Then
                RmHeight% = CInt(txtRmHeight.Text)
            End If
        Else
                'If it is blank, send the cursor back to the
                'blank TextBox.

                'Make a message
                Msg$ = "You cannot leave Ceiling Height blank or enter "
                Msg$ = Msg$ & "non-numeric data. Please enter a number"
                'Display the message
                MsgBox Msg$, vbExclamation, "Data entry error"
                'Send the mouse cursor back to the TextBox
                txtRmHeight.SetFocus
                'Leave the Sub
                Exit Sub
        End If

        'Make sure the TextBox has not been left blank
        If txtRmWidth.Text <> "" Then
            If IsNumeric(txtRmWidth.Text) Then
                RmWidth% = CInt(txtRmWidth.Text)
            End If
        Else
                'If it is blank, send the cursor back to the
                'blank TextBox.

                'Make a message
                Msg$ = "You cannot leave Room Width blank or enter "
                Msg$ = Msg$ & "non-numeric data. Please enter a number"
                'Display the message
                MsgBox Msg$, vbExclamation, "Data entry error"

                'Send the mouse cursor back to the TextBox
                txtRmWidth.SetFocus
                'Leave the Sub
                Exit Sub
        End If
```

```
'Do the same for the paint coveage and cost
'Make sure the TextBox has not been left blank
If txtPaintCover.Text <> "" Then
    If IsNumeric(txtPaintCover.Text) Then
        PaintCoverage% = CInt(txtPaintCover.Text)
    End If
Else
    'If it is blank, send the cursor back to the
    'blank TextBox.

    'Make a message
    Msg$ = "You cannot leave Coverage blank or enter "
    Msg$ = Msg$ & "non-numeric data. Please enter a number"
    'Display the message
    MsgBox Msg$, vbExclamation, "Data entry error"
    'Send the mouse cursor back to the TextBox
    txtPaintCover.SetFocus
    'Leave the Sub
    Exit Sub
End If


'Make sure the TextBox has not been left blank
If txtPaintCost.Text <> "" Then
    If IsNumeric(txtPaintCost.Text) Then
        dCanCost = CDbl(txtPaintCost.Text)
    End If
    Else
    'If it is blank, send the cursor back to the
    'blank TextBox.

    'Make a message
    Msg$ = "You cannot leave Paint Cost blank or enter "
    Msg$ = Msg$ & "non-numeric data. Please enter a number"
    'Display the message
    MsgBox Msg$, vbExclamation, "Data entry error"
    'Send the mouse cursor back to the TextBox
    txtPaintCost.SetFocus
    'Leave the Sub
    Exit Sub
End If


    RmPerimeter = (2 * RmLength%) + (2 * RmWidth%)
    WallArea% = RmPerimeter * RmHeight
    NumOfGal% = WallArea% / PaintCoverage%
    dProjectCost = NumOfGal% * dCanCost
    lblGallons.Caption = CStr(NumOfGal)
    lblTotalCost.Caption = CStr(dProjectCost)
End Sub
```

Using the *Division* Operator

Division in Visual Basic is a little more complicated than multiplication. In Listing 7.1, you saw one type of division used. This division is what you are most familiar with and what you find on your calculator. This type of division returns a number with its decimal portion, if one is present.

However, Visual Basic supports three different ways to divide numbers. These are known as *floating-point division* (the normal type of division, with which you are familiar); *integer division*; and *modulus*, or *remainder division*.

Floating-point division is the typical division that you learned in school. You divide one number by another, and the result is a decimal number. The floating-point division operator is the forward slash (/) as seen in the following:

```
Result = NumberOne / NumberTwo
Result = 2.3 / 2 'The value of Result is 1.15
```

Integer division divides one number into another, and then returns only the integer portion of the result. The operator for integer division is the backward slash (\):

```
Result = NumberOne \ NumberTwo
Result = 2.3 \ 2 'The value of Result is 1
```

Modulus, or remainder division, divides one number into another and returns what is left over after you have obtained the largest integer quotient possible. The modulus operator is the word mod as follows:

```
Result = NumberOne Mod NumberTwo
Result = 11 Mod 3 'The value of Result is 2 (11/3 = 3 with a remainder of 2)
```

As with the case of addition, subtraction, and multiplication, if you divide more than two numbers, each number pair must be separated by a division operator. Also, as with the other operations, multiple operators are handled by reading the equation from left to right.

Using Exponents

Exponents also are known as *powers* of a number. For example, 2 raised to the third power is equivalent to $2 \times 2 \times 2$, or 8. Exponents are used a lot in computer operations, where many things are represented as powers of two. Exponents also are used extensively in scientific and engineering work, where many things are represented as powers of ten or as natural logarithms. Simpler exponents are used in statistics, where many calculations depend on the squares and the square roots of numbers.

To raise a number to a power, you use the *exponential operator*, which is a caret (^). Exponents greater than one indicate a number raised to a power. Fractional exponents indicate a root, and negative exponents indicate a fraction. The following is the syntax for using the exponential operator:

```
Result = NumberOne ^ Exponent
```

The equations in the following table, Table 7.1, show several common uses of exponents. The operation performed by each equation also is indicated:

Table 7.1 Common Uses of Elements	
Sample Exponent	**Function Performed**
3 ^ 2 = 9	This is the square of the number.
9 ^ 0.5 = 3	This is the square root of the number.
2 ^ 2 = 0.25	A fraction is obtained by using a negative exponent.

Setting the Order of Precedence in Statements

Consider the following statement:

```
x% = 9 + 4 * 2
```

Depending on how you look at it, x% could have two values, 26 or 17. If you do the addition of 9 + 4 first and then multiply by 2 you get 26. However, if you multiply 4×2 first and then add 9, it equals 17. The answer you get depends on the order in which things happen. The order in which operations happen is called the *order of precedence*.

In Visual Basic, the default order of precedence is that in a statement that has both multiplication or division operators and addition or subtraction operators, multiplication or division is performed *first*, before the addition or subtraction. In the preceding example, the default answer is 17.

If you want to ensure that arithmetic operations happen in the order you want them to, you can use parentheses to group operations. For example, using the preceding statement, you could group operations as:

```
x% = (9 + 4) * 2 'The value of x% is 26
```

or

```
x% = 9 + (4 * 2) 'The value of x% = 17
```

Experienced programmers usually use parentheses to define the ordering of operations within their programs. Using parentheses to define order of precedence removes ambiguity. You will want to use parentheses in your code. Doing so does not affect the speed of your program and assures the accuracy and clarity of your code.

Using the *Concatenation* Operator

Visual Basic supports only one string operator, the *concatenation operator.* This operator is used to combine two or more strings of text, similar to the way the addition operator is used to combine two or more numbers. The concatenation operator is the ampersand symbol (&). When you combine two strings with the concatenation operator, the second string is added directly to the end of the first string. The result is a longer string containing the full contents of both source strings.

▶ **See** Chapter 6, "Using Data Types, Constants, and Variables," **p. 89** and Chapter 21, "Working with Strings and Typecasting," for more information about Strings, **p. 331**

The concatenation operator is used in an `assignment` statement as follows:

```
NewString$ = strExpressionOne & strExpressionTwo & strExpressionThree
```

In this syntax, `NewString$` represents the variable that will contain the result of the concatenation operation. Here, `strExpressionOne`, `strExpressonTwo`, and `strExpressionThree` all represent string expressions. These can be any valid strings, including string variables, literal expressions (enclosed in quotes), or functions that return a string. The ampersand between a pair of string expressions tells Visual Basic to concatenate the two expressions. The ampersand must be preceded and followed by a space. The syntax shows an optional second ampersand and a third string expression. You can combine any number of strings with a single statement. Just remember to separate each pair of expressions with an ampersand.

N O T E   If you are working on converting programs from an older version of Visual Basic, you may find strings combined using the plus sign operator. This was prevalent in versions of Visual Basic prior to version 4, as well as in older BASIC languages. While Visual Basic still supports the plus sign operator for backward compatability, you should use the ampersand for any work that you do to avoid confusion with the mathematical addition operation. ■

Listing 7.2 shows how the concatenation of strings is used in a simple program to generate mailing labels. The fields from the different text boxes are combined to create the different lines of the mailing label. The form for this program is shown in Figure 7.2. The code for this example is in the project prjName.vbp in the directory Chp_7\prjName\, on the CD-ROM that accompanies this book.

Listing 7.2   6ALIST01—A Good Example of How OptionButtons Are Used to Make Exclusive Choices

```
Private Sub cmdShowName_Click()
  Dim strTitle As String
  Dim strFirst As String
  Dim strLast As String
  Dim strFullName As String

  strFirst = txtFirstName.Text
  strLast = txtLastName.Text
  If optMr.Value Then strTitle$ = "Mr. "
  If optMrs.Value Then strTitle$ = "Mrs. "
  If optMiss.Value Then strTitle$ = "Miss "
  If optMrs.Value Then strTitle$ = "Ms. "
  strFullName = strTitle$ & strFirst$ & " " & strLast$
  lblFullName.Caption = strFullName
End Sub
```

FIG. 7.2

A simple name reporting program illustrates the function of the concatenation operator.

Also, you saw string concatenation used previously in the prjPaint example in Listing 7.1. The statement that's used to build a message for the error MessageBox is:

```
Msg$ = "You cannot leave Room Length blank or enter "
Msg$ = Msg$ & "non-numeric data. Please enter a number"
```

This is an example of concatenating a string onto a single string variable.

Being able to make concise, robust statements is a fundamental skill of computer programming. As your programming skills develop, you'll find that the line count of your code shrinks. You can write well behaved statements that do more with less. However, getting to this point takes time, practice, and experience. Right now, if you can write statements that are clear and accurate, you'll be in good shape. The rest will come with time. ●

Part

II

Ch

7

Making Choices with Conditional Statements

Most computer programs make choices: Can I give this person the amount of money they've asked for? Is this aircraft friend or foe? Is this word spelled correctly? Should I let this user on the network?

Being able to write programs that make choices based on a given condition or a set of conditions is an important skill for you to have. This chapter teaches you how to write programs that make decisions.

Also, this chapter discusses how to use the `OptionButton` Standard Control. The OptionBbuttons and decision-making programs go hand-in-hand, so this is a good way for you to learn how to use them. ■

Learn about *If...Then* statements

Find out how to use `If...Then` statements to analyze data in order to have your programs make decisions.

Learn about multiple line *If...Then* statements

Learn how to write code that can accommodate many different conditions within a given statement.

Learn about *Select Case* statements

Learn to use the `Select Case` statement to write flexible code that can analyze a very large number of conditions and respond with multiple commands.

Making Decisions in Your Program

Most statements in your programs will be assignment statements, but there are other statements that are important for handling more complex tasks. These statements are known collectively as *control statements*. Without control statements, you could not write very flexible programs. Your program would start at the first line of code and would proceed line-by-line until the last line was reached. At that point, the program would stop.

One type of control statement is the *decision statement*. These statements are used to control the execution of parts in your program based on conditions that exist at the time the statement is encountered. There are two main types of decision statements: If...Then statements and Select Case statements. Each one is covered in this chapter.

Understanding the *If* Statement

The logic of a simple If statement is as follows: If a *condition* exists, do *something*. For example, if it is raining, bring an umbrella, or if the water is boiling, make the coffee. You also can extend this logic to include an alternative action: If a *condition* exists, do this, Else do that.

For example:

> If the student answers 65 percent of the questions correctly, pass him or her, Else fail him or her.

You can further extend this logic to handle multiple actions: If a *condition* exists, do this, this, and this, Else do that, that, and that.

For example:

> If the student answers 65 percent of the questions correctly, pass him or her for this test and add the test score to his or her average, Else fail him or her and ask if he or she wants to take the test again.

Lastly, you can extend the logic of the If statement to accommodate multiple conditions and multiple actions: If a condition exists and another condition exists, do this, this, and this, Else do that, that, and that.

For example:

> If it is raining and it is not summer, bring an umbrella and wear a jacket, Else bring an umbrella.

Writing *If* Statements

In Visual Basic, there are two ways that you can write an If statement for handling True conditions—the *single-line* If statement and the *multiline* If statement. Each uses the If statement to check a condition. If the condition is True, the program runs the commands associated with the If statement. If the condition is False, the commands are skipped.

Writing a Single-Line *If* Statement

The single-line If statement is used to perform a single task when the condition in the statement is True. The following is the syntax of the single-line If statement:

```
If condition Then command
```

The condition represents any type of statement or function that evaluates to True. The condition can be any of the following:

- Comparison of a variable to a literal, another variable, or a function.
- A variable that contains a True or False value.
- Any function that returns a True or False value. You learn about functions and subs later in this book.

The command represents the task to be performed if the condition is True. This can be any valid Visual Basic statement other than a variable declaration.

Take a look at the program Simple Calculator shown in Figure 8.1. This source code for this program is the project name simplclc.vbp in the directory Chp_8\simplclc\ on the CD-ROM that comes with this book.

FIG. 8.1

Simple Calculator extends the AddNum application that you saw in Chapter 6, "Using Data Types, Constants, and Variables."

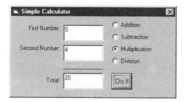

The way the program works is that you enter a number in each of the two upper TextBoxes, select a math operation, and then click the Do it button. The program performs the selected math operation on the numbers and displays the result in a third text box.

The way the program "decides" which math operation to perform is by evaluating the setting of the Value property of the OptionButton assigned to each operation. If the Value property of an OptionButton is set to True, the program does the associated math operation. The following shows the piece of code from the program. This code is a conditional statement that performs the addition if True. The following code snippet is an example of a single line If statement:

```
If optAddition.Value = True Then z = x + y
```

Listing 8.1 shows you the entire code for the event procedure for the click of the cmdOperation CommandButton, the button that the user clicks to perform the selected math operation.

Listing 8.1   07LIST01.TXT—Event Procedure for the *Click* Event of the cmdOperation (Do it) Button Makes Decisions Based on the State of the *OptionsButtons* Value

```
Private Sub cmdOperation_Click()
    'Declare a variable for the first number
    Dim x As Double

    'Declare a variable for the second number
    Dim y As Double

    'Declare a variable to hold the sum of both numbers
    Dim z As Double

    'Convert the text inputted into the text box
    'into an integer and assign it to the first variable
    x = CDbl(txtNumOne.Text)

    'Convert the text imputted into the text box
    'into an integer and assign it to the second variable
    y = CDbl(txtNumTwo.Text)

    'Decide what operation to do based on the
    'value ofselected option button
    If optAddition.Value = True Then z = x + y

    If optSubtraction.Value = True Then z = x - y

    If optMultiplication.Value = True Then z = x * y

    'For division, make sure that the second number is
    'not equal to  zero. You can not divide a number by
    ' zero. Blows up!
    If optDivision.Value = True Then
        If y <> 0 Then
            z = x / y
        Else
            'Report an  error
            MsgBox "Cannot divide by zero", vbCritical, "Error"
        End If
    End If


    'Convert the third variable (which is a Double)

    'to text and assign it to the text property of the
    'textbox for the result.
    txtTotal.Text = CStr(z)
End Sub
```

Executing Multiple Commands in the *Conditional* Statement

If you need to execute more than one command in response to a condition, you can use a block
`If...Then` statement. A block `If...Then` statement bounds a range of statements between the
`If` statement and an `End If` statement. If the condition in the `If` statement is `True`, all the commands between the `If` and `End If` statements are run. If the condition is `False`, the program
skips to the first line after the `End If` statement.

The structure of a multiple command `If` statement is as follows:

```
If condition Then
      Command One
      Command Two
      Command ...n
End If
```

Here `If` and `Then` are the Visual Basic keywords that "bracket" the condition and `End If` are the
keywords that end the code block.

Figure 8.2 shows a small program, Decide.EXE. The Decide.EXE uses two OptionButtons to
offer the user two choices, Nice and Evil. If the user selects the Nice option, the form positions
itself in the upper left corner of the screen and changes the text and color. If the user selects
the Evil option, the form positions itself in the lower right corner of the screen and makes a
different set of color and text changes (see Figure 8.3). If neither option is chosen when the
user clicks the "Decide" button (which really can only happen upon the initial viewing of the
form) the form shows an error message in its title bar.

N O T E If, within a group of OptionButtons, none of the OptionButtons' `Value` property is set to
True in design mode, when the code is run, all the OptionButtons will appear unselected.
However, at runtime, once an OptionButton is selected, from then on, at least one OptionButton within
the group always will be set to True.

FIG. 8.2

OptionButtons
offer exclusive choices
to the user.

Listing 8.2 is a code snippet from the event procedure from the `cmdDecide` click event. This
code shows you how to write a multiline `conditional` statement that analyzes the value of a
group of OptionButtons.

Listing 8.2   07LIST02.TXT—You can Have Multiple Command Statements in an *If...Then* Statement

```
If optNice.Value = True Then
    'Make the form's BackColor blue
    frmDecide.BackColor = vbBlue
    'Make the Nice option's BackColor white
    optNice.BackColor = vbWhite
    'Make the Evil option's BackColor the same
    'color as the form's BackColor
    optEvil.BackColor = frmDecide.BackColor
    'Set the text in the form's title bar to denote the
    'choice
    frmDecide.Caption = "Decision: " & optNice.Caption
    'Position the from at the upper left of the screen
    frmDecide.Move 0, 0
End If
```

This is the code that the program executes if the user selects the OptionButton named optNice. It is an example of a multiple line If...Then statement. Notice that there are multiple statements between an If...End If code block.

FIG. 8.3

You can use conditional statements to position forms.

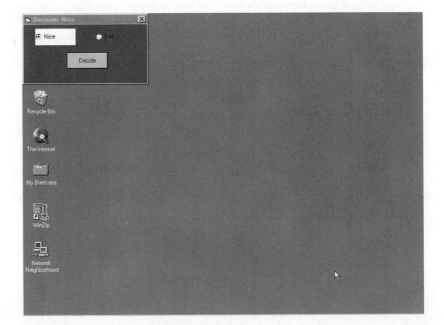

Using *If...Then...Else* Statements

As you learned earlier, sometimes you might have a situation where if one condition exists, you do one set of commands, and if it doesn't, you do another set. If you have money in your checking account, write a check, `Else` transfer funds from your savings account into the checking account, for example.

This is called an `If...Then...Else` statement. An `If...Then...Else` takes the following format:

```
If condition Then
     statements to process if condition is True
Else
     statements to process if condition is False
End If
```

The `If` and `End If` statements of this block are the same as before. The condition still is any logical expression or variable that yields a `True` or `False` value. The key element of this set of statements is the `Else` statement. This statement is placed after the last statement to be executed if the condition is `True`, and before the first statement to be executed if the condition is `False`. For a `True` condition, the program processes the statements up to the `Else` statement and then skips to the first statement after the `End If`. If the condition is `False`, the program skips the statements prior to the `Else` statement and starts processing with the first statement after the `Else`.

You saw the following code snippet at the end of Listing 8.1. This is an excellent example of a simple `If...Then...Else` statement. As follows, if the value of the variable y is greater than 0 (zero), the program does some division; otherwise, the program displays a Windows message box with an error message.

```
If y <> 0 Then
    z = x / y
Else
    'Report an  error
    MsgBox "Cannot divide by zero", vbCritical, "Error"
End If
```

N O T E If you want to execute code for only the `False` portion of the statement, you can just place code statements between the `Else` and `End If` statements. You are not required to place any statements between the `If` and `Else` statements. ▪

Working with Multiple *If* Statements

In the previous sections, you saw the simple block `If` statements, which evaluate one condition and can execute commands for either a `True` or a `False` condition. You also can evaluate multiple conditions with an additional statement in the block. `If...Then...ElseIf` statements let you specify another condition to evaluate whether or not the first condition is `False`. Using the `ElseIf` statement, you can evaluate any number of conditions. Listing 8.3 shows a snippet of code from the program, Grader.EXE that is from project, grader.vbp, in the directory, \chp_8\grader\ on the CD-ROM that comes with this book. The code snippet uses the `ElseIf` conditional structure as a way to determine the grade for a test based on a range of correct answers (see Figure 8.4).

Listing 8.3   07LIST03.TXT—Use *ElseIf* to Evaluate Multiple Conditions

```
If CorrectAnswers% >= 10 Then
     strGrade = "A"
ElseIf CorrectAnswers% = 9 Then
     strGrade = "A-"
ElseIf CorrectAnswers% = 8 Then
     strGrade = "B
ElseIf CorrectAnswers% = 7 Then
     strGrade = "B-"
ElseIf CorrectAnswers% = 6 Then
     strGrade = "C
ElseIf CorrectAnswers% = 5 Then
     strGrade = "C-"
ElseIf CorrectAnswers% = 4 Then
     strGrade = "D"
ElseIf CorrectAnswers% = 3 Then
     strGrade = "D-"
Else
     strGrade = "F"
End If
```

The preceding code works first by evaluating the condition in the If statement. If the condition is True, the statement (or statements) immediately following the If statement is executed, and then the program skips to the first statement after the End If statement.

FIG. 8.4
The Grader
program uses the
If...Then...ElseIf
format for conditional
statements.

If the first condition is False, the program skips to the first ElseIf statement and evaluates its condition. If this condition is True, the statements following the ElseIf are executed, and control again passes to the statement after the End If. This process continues for as many ElseIf statements as are in the block.

If all the conditions are False, the program skips to the Else statement and processes the commands between the Else and the End If statements. The Else statement is not required.

Using Nested *If* Statements

If you need to test for a condition provided another condition is already True, such as If it is 6:30 A.M. and If it is a weekday, for example— use nested If statements. A nested If statement is an If statement enclosed within another If statement. The format for a nested If statement is as follows:

```
If condition Then
    If another_condition Then
        statement
    Else
        statement
    End If
End If
```

The code snippet that follows demonstrates a nested If statement. You originally saw it in the cmdOperation click event procedure.

```
If optDivision.Value = True Then
    If y <> 0 Then
        z = x / y
    Else
        'Report an error
        MsgBox "Cannot divide by zero", vbCritical, "Error"
    End If
End If
```

Using the *Select Case* Statement

Another way to handle decisions in a program is to use the Select Case statement. This enables you to run any of a series of statement groups based on the value of a single variable. The Select Case statement identifies the variable to be evaluated. Then, a series of Case statements specifies the possible values. If the value of the variable matches the value (or values) indicated in the Case statement, the commands after the Case statement are executed. If the value does not match, the program proceeds to the next Case statement. The Select Case structure is similar to a series of If/Then/ElseIf statements. The following lines of code show the syntax of the Select Case block:

```
Select Case TestValue
    Case Value1
        Statement_Group_1
    Case Value2
        Statement_Group_2
End Select
```

The first statement of the Select Case block is the Select Case statement itself. This statement identifies the value to be tested against possible results. This value, represented by the TestValue argument, can be any valid numeric or string expression, including a literal, a variable, a logical expression or a function.

Each conditional group of commands (those that are run if the condition is met) is started by a Case statement. The Case statement identifies the expression to which the TestValue is compared. The Case statement can express a single value or a range of values. If the TestValue is equal to or within range of the expression, the commands after the Case statement are run. The program runs the commands between the current Case statement and the next Case statement or the End Select statement. If the TestValue is not equal to the value expression or does not fall within a range defined for the Case statement, the program proceeds to the next

`Case` statement. Listing 8.4 shows you Select Case Statement tests for equality. It also shows you a Select Case Statement that tests for a range.

Listing 8.4   H_LIST07.TXT—Using Equality in a *Select Case* Statement

```
Select Case x%
    Case 1:
        MsgBox "I am 1"
    Case 2:
        MsgBox "I am 2"
End Select
Listing 8. 5  h_LIST08.TXT—Using a Range in a Case Statement.
Select Case x%
      Case 6 To 9
            MsgBox "I am more than 5 and less than 10"
      Case 101 To 199
            MsgBox "I am more than 100 and less than 200"
      Case Else
            MsgBox "Not in Range"
  End Select
```

The `End Select` statement identifies the end of the `Select Case` block.

N O T E   Only one case in the `Select Case` block is run for a given value of `TestValue`. ▪

CAUTION

The `TestValue` and `Value` expressions must represent the same data type. For example, if the `TestValue` is a number, the values in the `Case` statements also must be numbers.

The simplest form of the `Select Case` block uses only a single value for the comparison expression. Listing 8.5 shows a `Select Case` statement that accomplishes the same thing that the `If...Then...ElseIf` code in Listing 8.3 did. The benefit of using a `Select Case` to accomplish the grading task is that the code is easier to read, and easier to extend.

Listing 8.5   07LIST4.TXT—Using a *Select Case* Statement Sometimes Is a More Controllable Alternative to Writing an Extended *If...Then...ElseIf* Statement

```
Private Sub cmdGrader_Click()
    Dim CorrectAnswers%
    Dim strGrade As String

    'Get the correct answers from the textbox
    CorrectAnswers% = CInt(txtNumberRight.Text)
```

```
        'Assign the grade based on the correct answers
        Select Case CorrectAnswers%
            Case 10
                strGrade = "A"
            Case 9
                strGrade = "A-"
            Case 8
                strGrade = "B"
            Case 7
                strGrade = "B-"
            Case 6
                strGrade = "C"
            Case 5
                strGrade = "C-"
            Case 4
                strGrade = "D"
            Case 3
             strGrade = "D-"
            Case Else
             strGrade = "F"
        End Select
        'Display the grade
        lblGrade.Caption = strGrade
End Sub
```

When it comes time to add another grade level, suppose an "A+" if the student answers eleven correctly in the following example, all you need is to add a new case, Case 11. If you were to use the ElseIf technique you would have to rewrite significant portions of the If...Then...ElseIf code block (see Listing 8.6).

Listing 8.6 07LIST5.TXT—Extending a Select Case Block can be a Straightforward Task

```
Select Case CorrectAnswers%
        'Add a case for 11 correct answers
        Case 11
            strGrade = "A+"
        Case 10
            strGrade = "A"
        Case 9
            strGrade = "A-"
        Case 8
            strGrade = "B"
        Case 7
            strGrade = "B-"
        Case 6
            strGrade = "C"
        Case 5
            strGrade = "C-"
        Case 4
            strGrade = "D"
```

continues

Listing 8.6   Continued

```
        Case 3
          strGrade = "D-"
        Case Else
          strGrade = "F"
End Select
```

Using Relational Operators in *Select Case* Blocks

You also can use relational operators in a Select Case block (see Table 8.1). There may be times that you want to test for cases within a range, say greater than or less than a certain number. To accomplish this with a Select Case block, you must use the Is keyword. To test within a certain range use the To keyword as you saw above in Listing 8.7.

Just as you can check to see if equality exists between two quantities using the "=" sign, you also can check to see if numbers are less than, greater than, or not equal to one another. Table 8.1 shows the relational operators that you can use in your conditional statements.

Table 8.1   Relational Operators

Symbol	Meaning	Example	Result
=	Equal	8 = 9	False
>	Greater than	8 > 9	False
<	Less than	8 < 9	True
>=	Greater than or equal to	8 >= 8	True
<=	Less than or equal to	7 <= 6	False
<>	Not equal to	6 <> 7	True

Pay particular attention the order of characters in the less than and greater than symbols. They must be ordered as shown previously.

Using "=>" or "=<" will produce an error.

Listing 8.7 shows you how to use the Is keyword to create a "greater than" statement within a Select Case block. Notice that the relational operator, ">" is used as follows to make any number of correct answers greater than 11 result in a grade of "A++."

Listing 8.7   07LIST6.TXT—You Can Handle a Range of Numbers Within a
***Select Case* Code Block**

```
Select Case CorrectAnswers%
        'Make any answer greater than 11 an A++
        Case Is > 11
            strGrade = "A++"
        Case 11
            strGrade = "A+"
        Case 10
            strGrade = "A"
        Case 9
            strGrade = "A-"
        Case 8
            strGrade = "B"
        Case 7
            strGrade = "B-"
        Case 6
            strGrade = "C"
        Case 5
            strGrade = "C-"
        Case 4
            strGrade = "D"
        Case 3
         strGrade = "D-"
        Case Else
         strGrade = "F"
   End Select
```

The complete project to which the above code applies is Grader2.vbp in the directory
.\Chp_8\Grader2 which in on the CD-ROM that accompanies this book.

The Select Case statements are a powerful addition to your programming toolkit that take you
to the next level of programming expertise. As you learn more about them, you learn how to
use both If statements and Select Case statements together to make very detailed, extended
decisions within your programs. ●

Working with Loops

A *loop* is a statement or group of statements that your program does over and over until it is told to stop or to do something else. You can use loops to inspect arrays, (see Chapter 10, "Working with Arrays,") to do a set of tasks while a certain condition exists, or even to *not* do anything until a certain condition is met.

Two commonly used types of loops are supported by Visual Basic—counter loops and conditional loops. *Counter loops* are used to perform a task a set number of times. *Conditional loops* are used to perform a task *while* a specified condition exists or *until* a specified condition exists. Each of these loops is discussed in this chapter. Visual Basic also supports collection loops using the For Each...Next statement. However, discussion of this type of loop is outside the scope of this book. ∎

Using the Loops

Learn about the different types of loops that you can use in Visual Basic.

For...Next loop

Learn how to use the For...Next loop to populate a TextBox.

Do...While loop

Learn how to use the Do...While loop to populate a TextBox.

Do...Until loop

Learn how Do...Until loops relate to other types of loops.

Exiting loops

Learn how to exit a loop and break an infinite loop.

Using *For...Next* Loops

A counter loop also is known as a `For` loop, or a `For...Next` loop. They are called `For...Next` loops because the beginning and end of the loop are defined by the `For` statement and the `Next` statement, respectively.

The syntax of a `For...Next` loop is:

```
For CounterVar = StartNum To EndNum [Step StepNum]
    statements
Next [CounterVar]
```

Where:

>   *For* is the Visual Basic keyword for the start of the `For` loop.
>
>   *CounterVar* is a user-defined variable that the loop uses as a counter.
>
>   *StartNum* is the number from which the loop starts.
>
>   *To* is the Visual Basic keyword that separates the `StartNum` from the `EndNum`.
>
>   *EndNum* is the number at which the loop stops.
>
>   *Step* is the Visual Basic keyword that indicates that the loop should step. It is an optional argument.
>
>   *StepNum* is the number that indicates what the size of the step increment (or decrement) should be. It can be negative.
>
>   *Next* is the Visual Basic keyword that completes the `For...Next` statement.
>
>   *CounterVar*, as previously indicated, is the counter used with the `For` keyword. It is optional to use it with the `Next` keyword.

At the beginning of a `For...Next` loop, you define a counter variable as well as the beginning and end points of the variable's value. The first time the loop is run, the counter variable is set to the value of the beginning point. Then each time the program runs through the loop, the value of the counter increments. If the `Step` keyword is used, the counter variable increments as dictated by the number following the `Step` keyword. For example:

```
For i% = 0 To 10 Step 2
```

`i%` increments by 2.

As the counter variable increments, it is checked against the value of the end point. If the counter is larger than the end point, the program skips out of the loop and onto the first statement following the loop.

> **CAUTION**
>
> If the beginning value of the loop is greater than the ending value, the loop won't execute at all, as shown in the first example. The exception is if you set up the loop to count backwards, as shown in the second example.

For example:

```
For i% = 9 To 0 'This is an error!!!
    MsgBox "This is loop number: " & Cstr(i%)
Next i%
```

causes an error because the start boundary of the loop, 9, is greater than the end boundary, 0.

However,

```
For i% = 9 To 0 Step -1
    MsgBox "This is loop number: " & Cstr(i%)
Next i%
```

does *not* cause an error because the loop uses the Step keyword to decrement backward -1, from 9 to 0.

The counter variable is changed each time the loop reaches the Next statement. Unless otherwise specified using the Step keyword, the counter is increased by one for each loop.

Listing 9.1, the event handler for the For...=Next button click event (see Figure 8.1), shows a For...Next loop that exposes the counter variable within a larger string that is displayed in a TextBox. As the loop progresses, the counter variable is converted to a string and inserted within the strings BeginMsg$ and EndMsg$. Those strings are concatenated onto a master "holding" string, DisplayMsg$, which grows with each trip through the loop. A line break character is added to DisplayMsg$ at the end of the loop. After leaving the loop, the master string DisplayMsg$ then is assigned to the Text property of txtDisplay.

N O T E You *concatenate* a string when you add another string onto a string. For example:

```
        FullName$ = FullName$ & FirstName$
FullName$ = FullName$ & " "
FullName$ = FullName$ & LastName$
```

concatenates three strings onto one string. ■

Listing 9.1   08LIST01.TXT—You May Use a *For...Next* Loop to Concatenate Strings

```
Private Sub cmdForNext_Click()
    Dim i%
    Dim BeginMsg$
    Dim EndMsg$
    Dim DisplayMsg$
    'Make a phrase for the beginning of a line
    BeginMsg$ = "This is line: "

    'Make a phrase for the end of a aline
    EndMsg$ = " of a For...Next loop"

    'Do a For...Next Loop that
    For i% = 0 To 20
        'Puts the beginning of the line in place
        DisplayMsg$ = DisplayMsg$ & BeginMsg$
```

continues

Listing 9.1   Continued

```
            'Convert the counter integer to a string
            'and place it in the middle of the string
            'that is being constructed
            DisplayMsg$ = DisplayMsg$ & CStr(i%)

            'Add the end of the message
            DisplayMsg$ = DisplayMsg$ & EndMsg$

            'Put in a line break constant
            DisplayMsg$ = DisplayMsg$ & vbCrLf
    Next i%

        'Display the resulting string in the textbox
        txtDisplay.Text = DisplayMsg$

End Sub
```

FIG. 9.1

When you set a TextBox
MultiLine property to
True, make sure that
you set the TextBox
ScrollBars property
accordingly. Otherwise,
you may not be able to
see all the text.

 T I P For reading your program easily, it is good practice to include the variable name in the Next statement. This is especially important in nested loops.

CAUTION

Although you can use any numeric variable for the counter, you need to be aware of the limits of variable types. For example, trying to run a loop 40,000 times using an integer variable causes an error during execution because an integer has a maximum value of 32,767.

CAUTION

Never reset the value of the counter variable inside a For...Next loop. Doing so may cause an infinite loop.

For example:

```
For i% = 0 to 4
     i% = 0 ' This will cause an infinite loop
Next i%
```

causes an infinite loop.

Terminating the *For...Next* Loop Early

Typically, your `For...Next` loop should run through all the values of the counter variable. However, there may be times when you want the loop to terminate early. To do this, simply place an `Exit For` statement at the point in your loop where you want the loop to stop. The `Exit For` statement typically is associated within an `If...Then` statement.

Listing 9.2 shows an enhancement to the code listed in Listing 9.1. This code shows an added `If...Then` statement at the beginning of the `For...Next` loop. When the loop begins, the code enters the `If...Then` statement to take a look at the value of the `CheckBox` on the form. If the `CheckBox` on the form is checked, this indicates to the program that the loop needs to terminate when the value of the counting variable exceeds the quantity 10 (see Figure 9.2). Therefore, if this condition exists (the `CheckBox` is checked), the `Exit For` statement contained in the `If...Then` statement nested within the first `If...Then` statement forces the program out of the `For...Next` loop.

Part
II

Ch
9

Listing 9.2 08LIST02.TXT—You Can Set Many Alternative Actions Within a
***For...Next* Loop**

```
.
.
.
    'Do a For...Next Loop that
    For i% = 0 To 20

        'Take a look to see if the CheckBox
        'on the form is checked
        If chkLimit.Value = 1 Then
            'if it is, then Exit the For statement
            'when i% is greater than 10
            If i% > 10 Then Exit For
        End If

        'Put the beginning of the line in place
        DisplayMsg$ = DisplayMsg$ & BeginMsg$

        'Convert the counter integer to a string
        'and place it in the middle of the string
        'that is being constructed
        DisplayMsg$ = DisplayMsg$ & CStr(i%)

        'Add the end of the message
        DisplayMsg$ = DisplayMsg$ & EndMsg$

        'Put in a line break constant
        DisplayMsg$ = DisplayMsg$ & vbCrLf
    Next i%
.
.
.
```

FIG. 9.2

CheckBoxes are good controls to use when you need to set or clear a condition.

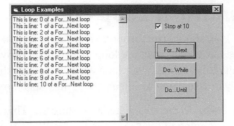

Using *Do...Loop* Statements

A Do...Loop is a conditional loop. A *conditional loop* is in force as long or until a condition exists. The key feature of a conditional loop is, of course, the *condition*. The condition is any expression that can return either a True or a False value. This True/False value can be a return value from a function (Chapter 20, "Working with User-Defined Subs and Functions," discusses functions fully); the value of a property, such as the Value property of an OptionButton; or an expression, such as NumVal < 15. The two basic types of conditional loops are Do...While, which repeats while the condition is True, and Do...Until loop, which repeats until the condition is True.

Using *Do...While* Loops

A Do...While loop works pretty much as the name implies: Do something while a certain condition is true. For example: To keep adding one to a number, MyNum While MyNum is less than twenty, as follows:

```
Do While MyNum <20
      MyNum = MyNum + 1
Loop
```

The keyword While in the Do...While statement tells the program that the loop will be repeated while the condition expression is true. When the condition in a Do...While loop becomes false, the program moves out of the loop and onto the next statement after the Loop statement.

The syntax for a Do...While loop is:

```
Do While condition
    statement(s)
Loop
```

Where

> *Do* is the Visual Basic keyword that denotes the beginning of the Do loop.
>
> *While* is the Visual Basic keyword that denotes the loop is a While loop.
>
> *condition* is the state that *must* exist. For example: x = 10, MyVal <> True or y < x.
>
> *statement(s)* is the Visual Basic statement(s) to execute while the loop is in force.
>
> *Loop* is the Visual Basic keyword that indicates the end of the loop block.

Or, you can use this equally valid syntax:

```
Do
    statement(s)
Loop While condition
```

As you can see in this example, the `Do...While` loop has two forms. The difference between the two is the placement of the condition—either at the beginning of the loop or at the end.

Listing 9.3 looks similar to the `For...Next` loop code in Listing 9.2. But when you take a close look, you'll notice that where before there was a `For...Next` loop, there is now a `Do...While` loop that runs while the value of `i%` is less than or equal to 20 (see Figure 9.3).

Part

II

Ch

9

CAUTION

When using a `Do...While` loop, do not forget to increment the counting variable in your code! Also, it's good practice to initialize the loop variable instead of relying on the default.

For example:

```
Dim i%
i% = 0
txtMessage.Text = ""
Do While i% < 10
    txtMessage.Text = txtMessage.Text _
                   & CStr(i%)
Loop
```

goes on infinitely.

```
Dim i%
i% = 0
txtMessage.Text = ""
Do While i% < 10
    txtMessage.Text = txtMessage.Text _
                   & CStr(i%)
    i% = i% + 1
Loop
```

loops, terminates, and displays the TextBox's text just fine.

Listing 9.3   08LIST03.TXT—Operationally, a *Do...While* Loop Can Do the Same Things a *For...Next* Loop Does

```
Private Sub cmdDoWhile_Click()
    Dim i%
    Dim BeginMsg$
    Dim EndMsg$
    Dim DisplayMsg$
    'Make a phrase for the beginning of a line
    BeginMsg$ = "This is line: "

    'Make a phrase for the end of a a line
```

continues

Listing 9.3   Continued

```
EndMsg$ = " of a Do...While loop"

'Make a Do..While loop
Do While i% <= 20

    'Take a look to see if the checkbox
    'on the form is checked
    If chkLimit.Value = 1 Then
        'if it is, then Exit the Do statement
        'when i% is greater than 10
        If i% > 10 Then Exit Do
    End If

    'Put the beginning of the line in place
    DisplayMsg$ = DisplayMsg$ & BeginMsg$

    'Convert the counter integer to a string
    'and place it in the middle of the string
    'that is being constructed
    DisplayMsg$ = DisplayMsg$ & CStr(i%)

    'Add the end of the message
    DisplayMsg$ = DisplayMsg$ & EndMsg$

    'Put in a line break constant
    DisplayMsg$ = DisplayMsg$ & vbCrLf

    i% = i% + 1
Loop


    'Display the resulting string in the TextBox
    txtDisplay.Text = DisplayMsg$

End Sub
```

FIG. 9.3

Looping while i% is less than or equal to 20, using a Do...While loop.

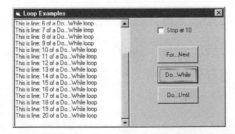

By placing the While condition clause in the Do statement, you tell the program that you want to evaluate the condition *before* you run any statements inside the loop. If the condition is True, the repetitive statements between the Do statement and the Loop statement are run. Then the program returns to the `Do` statement to evaluate the condition again. As soon as the condition is `False`, the program moves to the statement following the `Loop` statement. Both the `Do` and the `Loop` statements must be present.

With the form of the loop where the `While` keyword is with the `Do` keyword, the statements inside the loop may never be run. If the condition is `False` before the loop is run the first time, the program just proceeds to the statements after the loop.

To run the `Do...While` loop at least once, use the second form of the `Do...While` loop. This form of the loop places the condition in the `Loop` statement. For example:

```
Do
    Text1.Text = Text1.Text & CStr(i%)
    i% = i% + 1
Loop While i% < 10
```

This tells the program that you want the loop to run at least once and then to evaluate the condition to determine whether to repeat the loop.

> **CAUTION**
>
> Do not put the `While` condition clause in both the `Do` and the `Loop` statements because this causes an error when you try to run your program.

N O T E If you are working on code developed by someone else, you may find a loop that starts with a `While` statement and ends with a `Wend` statement. This type of loop works the same way as a `Do...While` loop with the `While` clause in the `Do` statement. Visual Basic still supports a `While...Wend` loop, but I recommend that you use the `Do...While` loop because it is more flexible. ■

Using *Do...Until* Statements

The `Do...Until` loop basically is the same as the `Do...While` loop except that the statements inside a `Do...Until` loop are run only as long as the condition is false—in other words, as long as the condition is *not* met. When the condition becomes true, the loop terminates. There are two forms of syntax for the `Do...Until` loop (just as there are two forms of syntax for the `Do...While` loop)—one with the condition in the `Do` statement and one with the condition in the `Loop` statement. If you place the condition in the same line as the `Do` keyword, the condition is evaluated before the statements in the loop are executed. If you place the condition in the same line as the `Loop` keyword, the loop is run at least once before the condition is evaluated.

Listing 9.4 shows the event procedure for the `cmdDoUntil` button's `Click` event (see Figure 9.4). Within the event procedure is a `Do...Until` loop. The loop runs until the counter variable `i%` is greater than 20, or if the Limit to 10 `CheckBox` is checked. This code is similar to the code for the `cmdDoWhile_Click()` event procedure. The only difference is that the `Do...While` loop from the `cmdDoWhile` click was changed to a `Do...Until` loop in the `cmdDoUntil` click event. Also, the `EndMsg$` string was changed from, "`Do...While` loop" to "`Do...Until` loop."

As you can see, Do...While loops and Do...Until loops are closely related. Generally, which one you use is a matter of personal style.

TIP Indenting your code inside a loop or other structure (such as an If statement) makes the code easier to read.

Listing 9.4 08LIST04.TXT—*Do...Until* Loops Are Similar to *Do...While* Loops Except When the Condition Is True—Then Loop Terminates

```
Private Sub cmdDoUntil_Click()
    Dim i%
    Dim BeginMsg$
    Dim EndMsg$
    Dim DisplayMsg$
    'Make a phrase for the beginning of a line
    BeginMsg$ = "This is line: "

    'Make a phrase for the end of a a line
    EndMsg$ = " of a Do...Until loop"

    'Make a Do..Until loop
    Do Until i% > 20

        'Take a look to see if the checkbox
        'on the form is checked
        If chkLimit.Value = 1 Then
            'if it is, then Exit the Do statement
            'when i% is greater than 10
            If i% > 10 Then Exit Do
        End If

        'Put the beginning of the line in place
        DisplayMsg$ = DisplayMsg$ & BeginMsg$

        'Convert the counter integer to a string
        'and place it in the middle of the string
        'that is being constructed
        DisplayMsg$ = DisplayMsg$ & CStr(i%)

        'Add the end of the message
        DisplayMsg$ = DisplayMsg$ & EndMsg$

        'Put in a line break constant
        DisplayMsg$ = DisplayMsg$ & vbCrLf

        i% = i% + 1
    Loop

    'Display the resulting string in the TextBox
    txtDisplay.Text = DisplayMsg$

End Sub
```

FIG. 9.4
The Do...Until code still checks the value of the CheckBox.

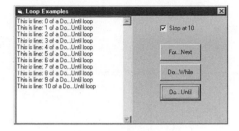

Breaking an *Infinite* Loop

Getting comfortable using loops takes time. The more you use them, the better you'll get at identifying situations in which to use them. Loops can be a powerful programming tool, but they can cause enormous headaches if not properly programmed.

Listing 9.5 shows a programmer's worst nightmare, the `infinite` loop. The logic of the code tells the program to go on *forever*. When your code enters this loop, it locks everything else out of your program, allowing nothing else to happen. If you run your program within the Visual Basic IDE, most of the time *infinite* loops also lock it up.

> **Listing 9.5   08LIST05.TXT—Example of *Infinite* Loop that Goes on Forever and Locks Up Your Program**

```
Dim i%
Do While i% = 0
    i% = 0

Loop
```

Fortunately, you *can* terminate endless loops. If your program is running within the Visual Basic IDE, to terminate an infinite loop, press the Ctrl+Break keys on your keyboard. When you press these keys, the loop breaks at a line of code within the `infinite` loop. If your program is not running within the IDE, the only way to terminate it is to end the program from within the Windows Task Manager. (For detailed information about the Task Manager, read the online documentation that comes with Windows.) ●

Part
II

Ch
9

CHAPTER 10

Working with Arrays

Programming a large amount of data or data that is categorically related means that at some point you will have to deal with arrays. Arrays can be tricky. However, if you get a strong conceptual understanding of them and learn the ins and outs of their syntax, you'll be using them like a pro in no time. Also, as you begin to master arrays, you'll find that they go hand-in-hand with Visual Basic's ListBox and ComboBox Standard Controls. ■

Arrays

Learn what arrays are and how to use them effectively.

Sizing arrays

Create arrays of different types with varying size.

Multidimensional arrays

Extend your use of arrays to accommodate multiple layers of elements.

Using loops with arrays

Use loops to find out all the values in an array.

List boxes and combo boxes

Learn about list boxes and combo boxes and how to use them with arrays.

Understanding and Declaring Arrays

An *array* is a collection of variables of the same name and same type. You may recall that Chapter 6 compared a variable to a cup that holds an unknown value or a value that always is changing (see Figure 10.1.)

FIG. 10.1

A variable is a placeholder for a value of a certain type.

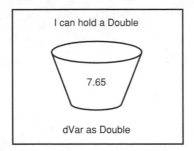

I can hold a Double

7.65

dVar as Double

Think of an array as a collection of cups. Each cup in the collection can hold the same type of data, and all cups in the collection have the same name. Each cup is an *element* of the collection and has a number assigned to its element position. The first element of an array usually has a position number of 0 (zero).

Arrays can be different sizes (see Figure 10.2). One array might have four elements, another array might have 27 elements, and it is even possible for an array to have *no* elements at all—just the possibility of having elements that are created at a later time.

You declare an array in much the same way that you declare a variable:

`Dim¦Public¦Private ArrayName(Subscript) As DataType`

Where:

`Dim¦Public¦Private` is the Visual Basic keyword that declares the array and scope of the array. The array can be declared with `Dim`, making it private to the procedure in which it is made; `Public`, making it visible from all points in the program; or `Private` within the `General` section of a form or Module, which makes the variable visible only within a given form or module. Using `Dim` at the module level defaults to `Public`.

`ArrayName` is the name of the array.

`Subscript` is the subscript for the highest element in the array (if you use three as the number, then there are four elements). Remember, element positions start with the number 0 (zero). Thus, if you declare an array where `NumOfElementPos = 6`, you actually will have seven element positions and thus seven elements. (You'll read more about this in the following sections.)

`As` is the Visual Basic keyword that denotes an impending type declaration.

`DataType` is any valid Visual Basic data type.

FIG. 10.2
You declare an array in much the same way that you declare a variable.

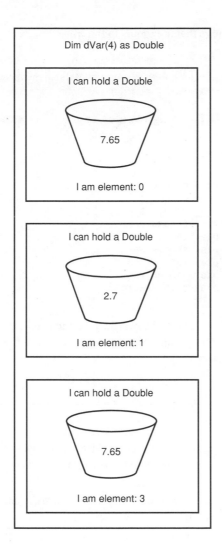

Thus, to declare an array of integers with five elements in it, the declaration is as follows:

```
Dim iMyIntArray(4) As Integer
```

To assign a value to each element in the array, iMyIntArray, you would do this:

```
iMyIntArray(0) = 9
iMyIntArray(1) = 342
iMyIntArray(2) = 2746
iMyIntArray(3) = 0
iMyIntArray(4) = 8901
```

To change the value of the fourth element of the array iMyIntArray from 0 (zero) to 45, you do the following:

```
iMyIntArray(3) = 45
```

Part
II
Ch
10

To declare an array of nine strings that are global to the whole program, you would do this:

```
Public strMyStringArray(8) As String
```

Listing 10.1 shows how to assign values to the elements of the array dimensioned above.

Listing 10.1 10LIST01.TXT—Assign Values to the Elements of an Array as You Would to a Variable

```
Public strMyStringArray(8) As String

strMyStringArray(0) = "I am a pitcher"
strMyStringArray(1) = "I am a catcher"
strMyStringArray(2) = "I play first base"
strMyStringArray(3) = "I play second base"
strMyStringArray(4) = "I play third base"
strMyStringArray(5) = "I play shortstop"
strMyStringArray(6) = "I play left field"
strMyStringArray(7) = "I play center field"
strMyStringArray(8) = "I play right field"
```

You can also declare an array using the To keyword within the subscript syntax. For example, if you wanted to create an array of 5 variables of type, Integer in which the lower subscript is 1 and the upper subscript is 5, you write:

```
Dim MyInt(1 To 5) as Integer.
```

Option Base

When you declare an array, the first element of the array is AnyArrayElement(0), (zero). If this is confusing, you can make it so that when you declare an array, the first element is referenced as AnyArrayElement(1). To do this, insert the statement Option Base 1 in the General section of a module within your project.

Because the default "first element" of an array is 0 (zero), you only have to use Option Base 1 when you want the "first element" to be 1.

Changing the Number of Elements in an Array

Although you can determine the number of elements in an array when you declare it (also known as *dimensioning an array*), you might need to alter the size of the array later. Changing the number of elements in an array is called *redimensioning* an array. Use the ReDim keyword to change the number of elements in an existing array. To change the number of elements in any array, use the following syntax:

```
ReDim [Preserve] ArrayName(Subscript) As DataType
```

Where:

ReDim is the Visual Basic keyword that denotes that the array is being redimensioned.

Preserve is the optional Visual Basic keyword that makes it so that all preexisting elements in the array hold their value. If you do not use the Preserve keyword when you redimension the array, the value of all the elements goes to zero for numeric data types, empty strings for strings, and EMPTY for variants.

ArrayName is the name of the array.

Subscript is the subscript for the highest element in the array.

As is the Visual Basic keyword that denotes impending type declaration.

DataType is any valid Visual Basic data type.

Listing 10.2 shows how to redimension the array strMyStringArray to contain ten elements.

Listing 10.2   10LIST02.TXT—Use the Keyword Preserve to Have the Preexisting Elements in the Array Maintain Their Value

```
ReDim Preserve strMyStringArray(9)

strMyStringArray(9) = "I am the designated hitter"
```

Notice that the ReDim statement does not use the type declaration portion of its syntax. The As type portion of the ReDim statement is optional. Omitting it does not compromise the integrity of the statement.

However, before you go on, be advised that the actual implementation of the ReDim statement is different than the conceptual illustration presented above.

If you plan to create an array that you plan to ReDim, you *cannot* hard code the element size of the array on initial declaration. Thus, Listing 10.1 as an extension of Listing 10.2 is erroneous code.

To create an array that will be resized, you must first create the array without any elements. Listing 10.3 shows the proper, complete way to create an array for eventual redimensioning.

Listing 10.3   10LIST03.TXT—You Must First *Dim* an Array Without Any Elements Before You Can *ReDim* It

```
'Create an array without any elements
Dim strMyStringArray() as String

'Dimension the array for 9 elements
ReDim strMyStringArray(8)

'Assign values to the array elements
strMyStringArray(0) = "I am a pitcher"
strMyStringArray(1) = "I am a catcher"
strMyStringArray(2) = "I play first base"
strMyStringArray(3) = "I play second base"
strMyStringArray(4) = "I play third base"
```

continues

Part

II

Ch

10

Listing 10.3   Continued

```
strMyStringArray(5) = "I play shortstop"
strMyStringArray(6) = "I play left field"
strMyStringArray(7) = "I play center field"
strMyStringArray(8) = "I play right field"

'Add an element and make it so all the values
'of the previous elements are kept intact
ReDim Preserve strMyStringArray(9)

'Assign a value to the new array element
strMyStringArray(9) = "I am the designated hitter"
```

Notice in Listing 10.3 that the first ReDim statement does not use the Preserve keyword. This is permissible because initially there are no values in the newly resized array to preserve. However, in the second ReDim statement, the Preserve keyword is very much required. The preexisting elements have values assigned to them that you do not want to lose. If you did *not* use the Preserve keyword in the second ReDim statement after the value assignment to the new element, the array strMyStringArray would have the following values:

```
strMyStringArray(0) = ""
strMyStringArray(1) = ""
strMyStringArray(2) = ""
strMyStringArray(3) = ""
strMyStringArray(4) = ""
strMyStringArray(5) = ""
strMyStringArray(6) = ""
strMyStringArray(7) = ""
strMyStringArray(8) = ""
strMyStringArray(9) = "I am the designated hitter"
```

Be careful. Remember, arrays are tricky!

Multidimensional Arrays

So far you have been working with one-dimensional arrays—arrays that are a "one row" collection of variables (refer to Figure 10.2). In Visual Basic, you also can make arrays that have up to 60 dimensions. Programmers usually don't need to make an array of more than three dimensions, and two-dimensional arrays usually suffice for most introductory programming projects.

Think of a two-dimensional array as a tic-tac-toe board—columns and rows that intersect to form a grid. Each grid cell has a definable location that takes the form Column_Number, Row_Number. Figure 10.3 is a conceptual illustration of a two-dimensional array of Integers, iVar(2,4). Notice that each element is defined by the coordinates of the column position and the row position. For example, the array element, iVar(0, 0) = 5 and iVar(2,2) = 49.

To make two-dimensional array, use the following syntax:

```
Dim|Public|Private ArrayName(SubscriptOfCols, SubscriptOfRows) As DataType
```

FIG. 10.3

Think of two-dimensional arrays as a collection of cups arranged in columns and rows.

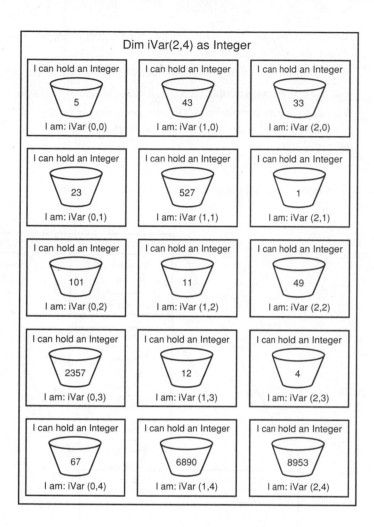

Dim iVar(2,4) as Integer

I can hold an Integer	I can hold an Integer	I can hold an Integer
5	43	33
I am: iVar (0,0)	I am: iVar (1,0)	I am: iVar (2,0)
23	527	1
I am: iVar (0,1)	I am: iVar (1,1)	I am: iVar (2,1)
101	11	49
I am: iVar (0,2)	I am: iVar (1,2)	I am: iVar (2,2)
2357	12	4
I am: iVar (0,3)	I am: iVar (1,3)	I am: iVar (2,3)
67	6890	8953
I am: iVar (0,4)	I am: iVar (1,4)	I am: iVar (2,4)

Part
II

Ch
10

Where:

Dim¦Public¦Private is the Visual Basic keyword that declares the array and scope of the array. The array can be declared with Dim, making it private to the procedure in which it is made; Public, making it visible from all points in the program; or Private within the General section of a form or module, which makes the variable visible only within a given form or module. Using Dim at the module level defaults to Public.

ArrayName is the name of the array.

SubscriptOfCols is the number of "columns" of the array.

SubscriptOfRows is the number of element "rows" in the array.

As is the Visual Basic keyword that denotes type declaration.

DataType is any valid Visual Basic data type.

Be advised, you also can use the To keyword syntax when declaring the subscript range of each dimension in an array.

Thus, to declare the array shown in Figure 10.3, you would use the syntax:

```
Dim iVar(2,4) as Integer
```

Whereas you can consider a two-dimensional array to be a rectangle, you can consider a three-dimensional array as a rectangular block. A three-dimensional array is declared as follows:

```
Dim iVar(1,2,1) as Integer
```

Figure 10.4 is a conceptual illustration of a the three-dimensional array defined in the preceding line.

FIG. 10.4

A three-dimensional array (1,2,1) has twelve elements.

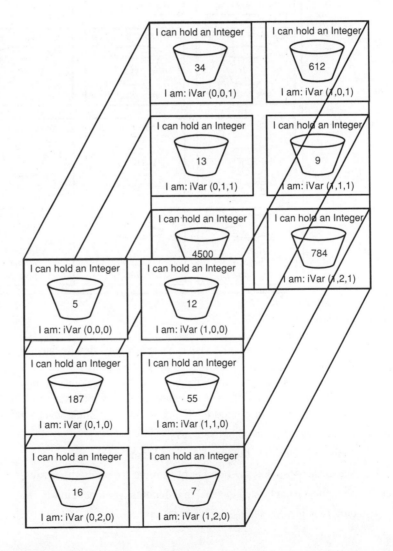

In the array iVar, the value assigned to each element, as depicted in Figure 10.4, is as follows:

```
iVar(0,0,0) = 5
iVar(0,1,0) = 187
iVar(0,2,0) = 16
iVar(1,0,0) = 12
iVar(1,1,0) = 55
iVar(1,2,0) = 7
iVar(0,0,1) =  34
iVar(0,1,1) = 13
iVar(0,2,1) = 4500
iVar(1,0,1) = 612
iVar(1,1,1) = 9
iVar(1,2,1) = 784
```

Using Loops to Traverse an Array

You can use the For...Next loop that you learned about in Chapter 9, "Working with Loops," to walk through or *traverse* an array.

Here's how it works: A For...Next loop increments its counting variable as it loops. That being the case, you assign the counting variable of the For...Next loop to the syntactical element position of the array and then set the lower bound of the array in question to the syntactical start point of the For...Loop and the upper bound of the array to the syntactical end point of the For...Next loop. You then run the loop. Every time you go through the loop, you will be at an element of the array.

Listing 10.4 shows a code example of using a For...Next loop to traverse an array. The listing is the event procedure for a button click. In the event procedure, an array of 20 elements is created. A For...Next loop is used two times—once to assign values to every element in the array and a second time to find the value assigned to every element—and then make a string that reports the value of that element (see Figure 10.5).

Listing 10.4   10LIST04.TXT—*For...Next* Loops Are a Good Tool for Traversing an Array

```
Private Sub cmdTraverse_Click()
    Dim i%
    Dim iMyArray(19) As Integer
    Dim BeginMsg$
    Dim MidMsg$
    Dim LoopMsg$
    Dim FullMsg$

    'Assign a value to each element in the array
    'by using a loop to traverse to each element
    'in the array.
    For i% = 0 To 19
        'Make the value of the element to be
        'twice the value of i%
```

continues

Listing 10.4   Continued

```
        iMyArray(i%) = i% * 2
    Next i%

    'Create the BeginMsg$ string
    BeginMsg$ = "The element is: "
    MidMsg$ = ", The value is: "
    'Go through the array again and make
    'a string to display
    For i% = 0 To 19
        LoopMsg$ = LoopMsg$ & BeginMsg$ & CStr(i%)
        LoopMsg$ = LoopMsg$ & MidMsg$ & iMyArray(i%)

        'Concatenate the loop message to the
        'full message. Also add a line break
        FullMsg$ = FullMsg$ & LoopMsg$ & vbCrLf

        'Clean out the loop message so that
        'new value next time through the loop
        LoopMsg$ = ""
    Next i%

    txtTraverse.Text = FullMsg$
End Sub
```

FIG. 10.5

This program adds a value to every element in a 20-element array of integers, the value of which is twice the position number of the element.

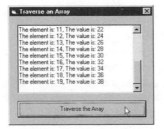

Working with *ListBoxes* and *ComboBoxes*

Of all the standard controls, the ListBox and ComboBox are best suited for categorizing and listing information from which the user can make choices and selections. The ListBox control and the ComboBox control are closely related. The manner in which you manipulate them is almost identical: the difference is that the ComboBox combines a ListBox control with a TextBox (hence the name), and allows selection from a list or by typing.

Both the ListBox and ComboBox handle lists. A *list*, in Visual Basic parlance, is an array of strings formally referred to as the List property. The List property is the list of strings in the control. (The List property is common to both the ListBox and ComboBox control.) Most work that you do with ListBoxes and ComboBoxes involves adding and removing strings from the ListBox or ComboBox's List property. Visual Basic allows two ways to add strings to the List property of the ListBox and ComboBox. One way is to do it at design time. The other way is at runtime.

Adding Strings to a *ListBox* at Design Time

To add strings to a ListBox List at design time, do the following:

1. Add a List control to the form.
2. Select the List control on the form.
3. Go to the Properties window in the Visual Basic IDE.
4. Select the List property from the Properties window. When you click the List property, a down arrow appears to the right of the value line of the List property (see Figure 10.6).

FIG. 10.6
You can add strings to a ListBox or ComboBox at design time by entering values in the List property drop-down list.

ListBox control ⟶

ComboBox control ⟶

ListBox control ⟶

List property ⟶

List drop-down list ⟶

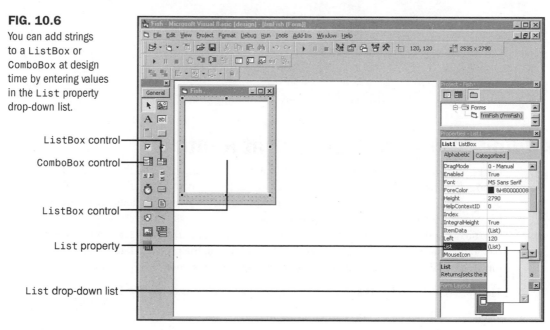

5. Click the down arrow in the List property value line.
6. A drop-down box appears. Type the strings for the List in the drop-down box.
7. To type in multiple lines to the List, press Ctrl+Enter to add a new line to the List property (see Figure 10.7).
8. The strings of the List property appear at design time in the ListBox on the form (see Figure 10.8).

FIG. 10.7
To add multiple lines to the `ListBox` control at design time, press Ctrl+Enter.

FIG. 10.8
You can view a `ListBox`'s list at design time.

Adding Strings to a *ListBox* at Runtime

`ListBoxes` and `ComboBoxes` are dynamic by nature. Their contents can change a lot. Therefore, although using the design time method that you just read about to populate the `List` property of the controls might be useful when your program starts up, over the long term, you need to be able to add and remove strings to and from the control's `List` property as it is running. `ListBoxes` and `ComboBoxes` make extensive use of the `AddItem`, `RemoveItem`, and `Clear` methods to do this. The code for the following examples are in the project, Heroes.vbp in the directory Chp_10\Heroes on the CD-ROM that accompanies this book.

The `AddItem` method adds a string to the `List` of a `Listbox` or `ComboBox`. Its syntax is:

```
Object.AddItem StringToAdd
```

Where:

> *Object* is the `Name` property of the `ListBox` or `ComboBox`.
>
> *AddItem* is the Visual Basic keyword for the method.
>
> *StringToAdd* is the string that you want to add to the control.

CAUTION

You cannot assign a value to a method. You can only pass a value to a method. Therefore, the following causes an error:

MyList.AddItem = "Apples"

The correct way to use the AddItem method is as follows:

MyList.AddItem "Apples"

Listing 10.5 shows you how to use the AddItem method within a form's Load event to add strings to the List of a ListBox.

Listing 10.5   10LIST05.TXT—The *AddItem* Method Addresses the Dynamic Nature of the *ListBox* Control

```
Private Sub Form_Load()
    lstHero.AddItem "Superman"
    lstHero.AddItem "Batman"
    lstHero.AddItem "Green Lantern"
    lstHero.AddItem "Aquaman"
    lstHero.AddItem "SpiderMan"
    lstHero.AddItem "Daredevil"
    lstHero.AddItem "Hulk"
End Sub
```

Figure 10.9 shows the result of the form's Load event.

FIG. 10.9

The AddItem method can be used in a form's Load event to initialize the value for the ListBox control.

Selecting Items from a *List*

To understand how Visual Basic determines the value of a string selected in the List of a ListBox or ComboBox, you need to be clear about this notion that the List is an array of strings. As you learned earlier in this chapter, an array is declared as follows:

ArrayName(Subscript)

Therefore, if you declared MyArray(3), you would notate the elements in that array as follows:

```
MyArray(0)
MyArray(1)
MyArray(2)
MyArray(3)
```

If you wanted to find out what value was assigned to the second element, you could say:

```
MyValue = MyArray(1).
```

Don't forget, the default for the first element is `MyArray(0)`.

`ListBoxes` and `ComboBoxes` use a similar format. However, the property `List` is the general term that Visual Basic uses to refer to the "array of strings" in a `ListBox`. And the position number of an item in a `List`, within a `ListBox` or `ComboBox`, is the `ListIndex` property. Thus, to find the value of the second string in the `ListBox`, `lstHero`, as shown in Listing 10.5, the statement would be as follows:

```
SecondString$ = lstHero.List(1)
```

The value of `SecondString$` is `Batman`.

When you click a string in a `ListBox`, Visual Basic assigns the position number of that string to the `ListIndex` property of the control. Therefore, to find out the value of the string that is selected in a `ListBox`, use the following statement:

```
SelectedString$ =  MyListBox.List(MyListBox.ListIndex)
```

N O T E   A fast way to find out the value of the string a user selects in a `ListBox` or `ComboBox` is to use the `Text` property.

For example:

```
Dim strMyStr as String
strMyStr = List1.Text
```

or

```
strMyStr - Combo1.Text
```

Listing 10.6 shows code that reports back the value of a string that a user selected from a `ListBox`.

Listing 10.6   10LIST06.TXT—Don't Forget that *List* and *ListIndex* Are Both Properties of an Object—Object Name Must Be Present with Property

```
Private Sub lstHero_Click()
    lblHero.Caption = lstHero.List(lstHero.ListIndex)
End Sub
```

Listing 10.6 is the event procedure for the `Click` event of the `ListBox` control, `lstHero`. When the user clicks a string in the `ListBox`, the code executes and reports back the value of the selection within the `Caption` property of the `Label`, `lblHero`. Figure 10.10 shows the what happens after the user selects a string.

FIG. 10.10

You can program the `Click`, `MouseUp`, or `MouseDown` events of a `ListBox` to find the value of a user's selection.

Take time to study the code provided here to get a good sense of what is going on. You might also want to study the documentation that comes with your copy of Visual Basic.

Removing Items from a List

You remove a string from a `List` in a `ListBox` or `ComboBox` by using the `RemoveItem` method. The syntax for the `RemoveItem` method is as follows:

```
Object.RemoveItem Index
```

Where:

> *Object* is the `Name` property of the `ListBox` or `ComboBox`.
>
> *RemoveItem* is the Visual Basic keyword for the method.
>
> *Index* is the position in the `List` property of the string that you want to remove from the control. To remove a selected item from a list, use the `ListIndex` property of the control.

Figure 10.11 shows an enhancement to the program shown in Figure 10.10. A button has been added to remove the string that the user selects from the `ListBox`. Listing 10.7 shows the `RemoveItem` method used in code.

FIG. 10.11

Make sure that you clear the text from the `Caption` property of the `Label` control, `lblHero`. If you don't, the user will remove the string from the `ListBox`, but the removed string will still appear in the `Label` control.

Listing 10.7   10LIST07.TXT—Code for Removing a String from a *ListBox*

```
Private Sub cmdRemove_Click()
    lstHero.RemoveItem (lstHero.ListIndex)
    lblHero.Caption = ""
End Sub
```

Clearing a List

If you want to remove *all* the strings in a ListBox or ComboBox, use the Clear method. The syntax for the Clear method is straightforward.

`Object.Clear`

Where:

> *Object* is the Name property of the ListBox or ComboBox.
>
> *Clear* is the Visual Basic keyword for the method.

The code that clears all the strings in the ListBox of the program shown in Figure 10.11 is as follows:

`lstHero.Clear`

Understanding *ComboBox* Styles

The ListBox and ComboBox are practically identical controls. They do have much in common, but each has a distinct use. ListBoxes take up more room than ComboBoxes. Also, when you are making a choice in a ListBox, you cannot select or input data that is not listed.

As a control, the ComboBox offers a bit more flexibility and economic use of a form's space.

ComboBoxes have a Style property that enables you to select the operational characteristics and appearance of the control. The code in the project, ListCbo.vbp in the directory Chp_10\ListCbo, which is on the CD-ROM that accompanies this book, demonstrates the different styles of a ComboBox. Table 10.1 describes these styles. Figure 10.12 shows the ComboBox styles applied to a form.

Table 10.1   ComboBox Styles

Number	Style	Description
0	Drop-down Combo	This style shows a drop-down list. However, the user also can enter data not listed in the ComboBox by inputting text directly into the TextBox portion of the ComboBox.

Number	Style	Description
1	Simple Combo	A combination of a `TextBox` and a `ListBox`, which doesn't drop down. You can select data from the `ListBox` or type in new data in a `TextBox`. The size of a simple `ComboBox` includes both the edit and list portions. When you first apply the `ComboBox` to a form, ComboBox is sized so that none of the `ListBox` is displayed. Increase the `Height` property to display more of the `ListBox`.
2	Drop-down List	This style shows a drop-down list from which the user can select data. The user cannot enter data into the control. The control is read-only.

FIG. 10.12
Notice that with a drop-down `ComboBox` style, you can add data to the control at runtime that is not on the drop-down list.

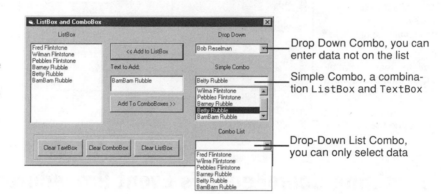

Drop Down Combo, you can enter data not on the list

Simple Combo, a combination `ListBox` and `TextBox`

Drop-Down List Combo, you can only select data

Part II
Ch 10

The most common styles that you will see used are the drop-down Combo and drop-down `List`. As mentioned earlier, you use a drop-down `ComboBox` style when you want to allow the user to add data that is not in the `ComboBox`'s list. You use the drop-down `List` style when you want the user to choose from data that is *only* in the drop-down list of the `ComboBox`.

▶ **See** the section "Choosing Between *ListBoxes* and *ComboBoxes*" in Chapter 12, "Designing Windows Applications," for more information about using the `ListBox` and `ComboBox` controls **p. 191**

Using the Baseball ScoreKeeper Program

Now that you have a conceptual understanding of arrays, `ListBoxes`, and `ComboBoxes`, it's time to take a look at an application that makes extensive use of them.

The Baseball ScoreKeeper program that comes on the CD-ROM that accompanies this book (Chp_10\BaseBall\prjBaseball.vbp) uses many of the array's features that you have just learned about. It uses arrays to keep track of each inning's score throughout the game. It uses `For...Next` loops to traverse arrays to set and get particular values of an array's element. Also, the program uses arrays in conjunction with a `ListBox` to list a team's roster and to display which play is presently at bat.

To use the program, the user picks a team that presently is at bat by clicking the `OptionButton` at the left of the form for a particular team. Then the user can select the current player at bat from the `ListBox` that lists the players of the team. At the end of an inning, the user enters the inning number in the Inning `TextBox` at the lower mid-left of the form. She or he then enters the runs scored in the Runs Scored `TextBox` at the lower right of the form. Finally, the user clicks the Add Runs button. The runs scored are shown in the appropriate scoreboard `Label` for the team along with a total of all the runs scored in the game in a separate `Label` control (see Figure 10.13).

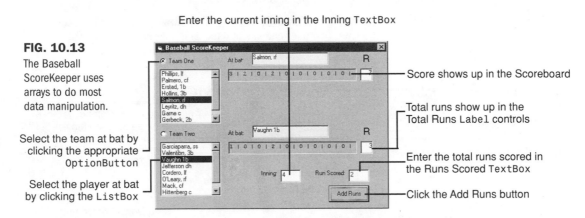

FIG. 10.13

The Baseball ScoreKeeper uses arrays to do most data manipulation.

Examining ScoreKeeper's Event Procedures

The bulk of the work in the Baseball ScoreKeeper program takes place within the code of two event procedures, the `Form_Load` and the `cmdAddRun_Click`. First, the `Form_Load` initializes the program by following four tasks:

1. Declare local variables for score keeping and a "scoreboard string." In addition, declare two arrays—one for each team's roster. Finally, redimension the two global scorekeeping arrays (one for each team) to nine elements. Each element will hold the score for each inning.

2. Use a `For...Next` loop to traverse each element in the Team One scorekeeping array, `gTeamOneInnings()`. Within each loop, take the value in each element and add it to the variable (`TotalScore%`) that holds the total score for the all the innings. Also, convert the value in each element to a character using the `CStr()` function (you'll learn more about these in Chapter 21, "Working With Strings and Typecasting"). Combine this converted character with the "¦" character, and combine all this to a larger scorekeeping string variable, `InningString$`. Assign the value of the `InningString$` variable to the scoreboard `Label` Caption. Then assign the value of the `TotalScore%` variable to the total runs `Label` Caption. Reset the `TotalScore%` and `InningString$` variables and perform the whole process in Step 2 again for Team Two.

3. Redimension the team roster arrays for both teams to have nine elements. Then add the names and playing positions of each player to the element that corresponds to the player's position in the batting order.

4. Use a For...Next loop in conjunction with the AddItem method of each team's Listbox to traverse the roster arrays of each team and add the value of each element in the array (player name and playing position) to the respective ListBox.

Listing 10.8 shows these steps within the code of the Form_Load event procedure.

Listing 10.8   01LIST08.TXT—The *Form_Load()* Event Procedure Initializes the Main Form of the Baseball Scorekeeper Application

```
Private Sub Form_Load()
    '=====================STEP ONE====================
    Dim i% 'Counter variable
    Dim TotalScore%
    Dim InningsString$ 'String to display score for each inning
    Dim TeamOneRoster$() 'Array to hold players' names
    Dim TeamTwoRoster$() 'Array to hold players' names
    'Redimension the global score arrays
    'DEFAULT_INNINGS is a constant declared in the module,
    'modBaseBall
    ReDim gTeamOneInnings(DEFAULT_INNINGS - 1)
    ReDim gTeamTwoInnings(DEFAULT_INNINGS - 1)

    '=====================STEP TWO====================
    'Initialize the default score for Team One

    TotalScore% = 0
    For i% = 0 To DEFAULT_INNINGS - 1

        InningsString$ = InningsString$ & CStr(gTeamOneInnings(i%)) _
            & " ¦ "
    Next i%

    'Display the concatenated string in the score label
    lblTeamOne.Caption = InningsString$
    'Display the total score for Team One
    lblTeamOneScore.Caption = CStr(TotalScore%)

    'Clean out score string for new trip through Team Two's score
    InningsString$ = ""


    'Initialize the default score for Team Two
    For i% = 0 To DEFAULT_INNINGS - 1
    InningsString$ = InningsString$ & CStr(gTeamTwoInnings(i%)) _
        & " ¦ "
    Next i%
    'Display the concatenated string in the score label
    lblTeamTwo.Caption = InningsString$
    'Display the total score for Team Two
```

continues

Part
II

Ch
10

Listing 10.8 Continued

```
lblTeamTwoScore.Caption = CStr(TotalScore%)
'======================STEP THREE=====================
'Make room in the roster arrays for 9 players
ReDim TeamOneRoster$(8) 'Remember arrays elements begin at zero
ReDim TeamTwoRoster$(8)

'Add the players for Team One to the roster array
TeamOneRoster$(0) = "Phillips, lf"
TeamOneRoster$(1) = "Palmero, cf"
TeamOneRoster$(2) = "Erstad, 1b"
TeamOneRoster$(3) = "Hollins, 3b"
TeamOneRoster$(4) = "Salmon, rf"
TeamOneRoster$(5) = "Leyritz, dh"
TeamOneRoster$(6) = "Garne c"
TeamOneRoster$(7) = "Gerbeck, 2b"
TeamOneRoster$(8) = "DiScensa, ss"

'Add the players for Team Two to the roster array
TeamTwoRoster$(0) = "Garciaparra, ss"
TeamTwoRoster$(1) = "Valentibn, 3b"
TeamTwoRoster$(2) = "Vaughn 1b"
TeamTwoRoster$(3) = "Jefferson dh"
TeamTwoRoster$(4) = "Cordero, lf"
TeamTwoRoster$(5) = "O'Leary, rf"
TeamTwoRoster$(6) = "Mack, cf"
TeamTwoRoster$(7) = "Hittenberg c"
TeamTwoRoster$(8) = "Frey, 2b"

'======================STEP FOUR=====================
'Traverse the roster arrays and add the contents
'the the roster listboxes.
For i% = 0 To 8
    lstTeamOne.AddItem (TeamOneRoster(i%))
    lstTeamTwo.AddItem (TeamTwoRoster(i%))
Next i%


End Sub
```

The Add Runs button does the work of adding the runs scored in a given inning to the "scoreboard." The cmdAddRun_Click() event procedure is the code that does this. It too requires four tasks:

1. Create variables that reflect the current inning and current score. Make a counter variable. Also create a variable that holds the total score and the "scoreboard string."

2. Take the text that was entered in the Inning TextBox; inspect it to make sure that it is a number using the IsNumeric() functions. The (IsNumeric() is a Visual Basic function that checks a string number to see if it "looks" like a number. (Check the Visual Basic online documentation for details.) Also make sure that the user did not enter a number higher than the number of innings in the game so far. If everything is okay, assign that value to the current inning variable, CurrentInning%. Do the same sort of IsNumeric()

check on the text in the runs scored TextBox, txtRuns. If everything is okay, assign that value to the current score variable, CurrentScore%.

3. Check the value of the OptionButton for Team One. If that OptionButton is selected, its value will be True. Assign the value in the current score variable, CurrentScore%, to an element in the global array that holds the values for every inning's score, gTeamOneInnings(). The element position to which to assign the current score is one less than the value of the current inning variable, CurrentInning%. Remember, in this case, the first element in the gTeamOneInnings array is zero. If the OptionButton for Team One is false, then the OptionButton for Team Two must have been selected. Do this step in terms of Team Two.

4. Traverse the global arrays that hold the value of every inning's score for each team and determine the total runs scored for each team. Also, construct the "scoreboard string." Assign the results to the appropriate controls. (This is an exact repeat of the work that you did in the fourth step of the Form_Load() event procedure.)

Listing 10.9 shows the even procedure for the cmdAddRuns_Click event.

Listing 10.9   10LIST09.TXT—The Add Runs Button Determines the Team and Inning to Which the Scored Runs Apply

```
Private Sub cmdAddRun_Click()
    '=====================STEP One====================
    Dim CurrentInning%
    Dim CurrentScore%
    Dim i%
    Dim TotalScore%
    Dim InningsString$


    '=====================STEP TWO====================
    'Convert the text in the txtInning to an Integer if
    'indeed the text looks like a number
    If IsNumeric(txtInning.Text) Then
        CurrentInning% = CInt(txtInning.Text)
    Else
        CurrentInning% = 1
    End If


    'Make sure the inning number is not more than 9
    If CurrentInning% > DEFAULT_INNINGS Then
        CurrentInning% = DEFAULT_INNINGS
    End If


    'Convert the text in the txtRuns to an Integer if
    'indeed the text looks like a number
    If IsNumeric(txtRuns.Text) Then
        CurrentScore% = CInt(txtRuns.Text)
    Else
        CurrentScore% = 0
    End If
    '=====================STEP THREE====================
```

continues

Listing 10.9 Continued

```
'Set the score to the designated inning for the team
'identified by the check option box.
If opTeamOne.Value = True Then
    gTeamOneInnings(CurrentInning% - 1) = CurrentScore%
Else
    'If TeamOne.Value is not true then TeamTwo.Value must
    'be True. It's a logic thing!
    gTeamTwoInnings(CurrentInning% - 1) = CurrentScore%
End If

'Set the new score for Team One
For i% = 0 To DEFAULT_INNINGS - 1
    TotalScore% = TotalScore% + gTeamOneInnings(i%)
    InningsString$ = InningsString$ & CStr(gTeamOneInnings(i%)) _
        & " ¦ "
Next i%
    '=====================STEP FOUR====================
'Display the concatenated string in the score label
lblTeamOne.Caption = InningsString$
'Display the total score for Team One
lblTeamOneScore.Caption = CStr(TotalScore%)

'Clean out score string for new trip through Team Two's score
InningsString$ = ""
'Clean out the total score integer variable
TotalScore% = 0

'Set the new score for Team Two
For i% = 0 To DEFAULT_INNINGS - 1
    TotalScore% = TotalScore% + gTeamTwoInnings(i%)
    InningsString$ = InningsString$ & CStr(gTeamTwoInnings(i%)) _
        & " ¦ "
Next i%

'Display the concatenated string in the score label
lblTeamTwo.Caption = InningsString$
'Display the total score for Team One
lblTeamTwoScore.Caption = CStr(TotalScore%)


End Sub
```

The last thing that the program does is report who is at bat. This is done when the user selects the name of a player from a team's roster ListBox. The event procedure for the Click event of each ListBox handles this chore.

Listing 10.10 shows the code for Team One's ListBox Click event procedure. This code uses the List and ListIndex properties that you learned about in the section "Selecting Items from a List."

Listing 10.10   10LIST10.TXT—Code for *lstTeamOne_Click* Procedure Is Practically Identical to the Code for the *lstTeamTwo_Click()* Event Procedure

```
Private Sub lstTeamOne_Click()
    'Have the name that the user clicks appear in the
    'at bat label
    lblTeamOneAtBat.Caption = lstTeamOne.List(lstTeamOne.ListIndex)
End Sub
```

The only difference in the code for the `lstTeamOne_Click()` event procedure and the code for the `lstTeamTwo_Click()` event procedure is that the first references the Team One "at bat" `Label` and `ListBox`, whereas the other references the Team Two "at bat" `Label` and `ListBox`.

You might notice that some potential problems need to be addressed. What happens if the user enters a letter character such as "a" in the Runs Scored or Inning TextBox? What happens if this game goes into extra innings? How do you remind the user to change the player at bat if he or she forgets? What if the user forgets to change the team up at bat?

These are not insurmountable problems. For the most part, you now have the tools that you need to address these issues head on. All that is required is a little thought and experimentation. ●

Part

II

Ch

10

The Elements of Visual Basic Programming

Working with Time and Timers

At some point in your programming activities with Visual Basic, you'll need to be able to measure time. You might want to write a program that keeps track of how many hours an employee works or one that only runs during certain hours of the day. Or, you might need to do something at a precise interval of time such as check the price of a stock or bond every minute. The tools and functions that you need to meet these programming needs come with Visual Basic. This chapter shows you what they are and how to use them. ■

Working with the Date data type

Learn how to use the Date data type to measure and manipulate time in your programs.

Using the *Timer* control

Build a clock program with the Timer control that has realtime functionality.

Using the *Format()* function

Learn how to use the Format function to custom display date values.

Using the *WindowState* Property

Use WindowState property to give your programs custom display behaviors.

Using the *DateDiff()* Function

Write a robust program with the DateDiff() function that reports the user's age in seconds, days, or years.

Understanding Serial Time

Before you can work with time, you need to understand how Visual Basic measures time. Visual Basics deals with time differently than you probably are accustomed to thinking about it. Visual Basic uses the Date data type to manipulate time values. With regard to the Date type, the basic unit of time is the day. A day has a numeric value of 1. An hour is 1/24 of a day. Twelve hours is .5 days, thirty hours is 1.25 days, or simply 1.25, and so on.

In Julian time, Day 1, AD is January 1, 0000. The Date data type treats things differently. Day 1 in Visual Basic is January 1, 100. Day 2 is January 2, 100. Thus June 12, 1968 is Day 25001, or simply 25001—the 25001st day from 12/31/1899. The serial date 25001.5 translates to noon, June 12, 1968. The Date data type displays dates according to the date format recognized by your computer. The Date data type displays time according to how your computer's time format is set, either by 12 hour or 24 hour format.

You can assign date literals to Date variables by enclosing the literal within a pair of number signs (#). For example:

```
Dim MyDate as Date
MyDate = #August 13, 1997#
```

Also, the Date data type can be converted to any other numeric data type. Figure 11.1 shows the date, August 4, 1997, 10:56 P.M., as a Double.

FIG. 11.1

If you convert a Date value to another numeric type, the value to the left of the decimal represents the day. The value to the right of the decimal represents the time.

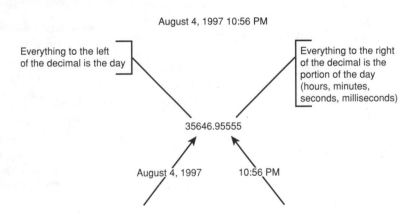

August 4, 1997 10:56 PM

Everything to the left of the decimal is the day

Everything to the right of the decimal is the portion of the day (hours, minutes, seconds, milliseconds)

35646.95555

August 4, 1997   10:56 PM

Understanding the *Timer* Control

Visual Basic provides a control that enables you to track time. The control is called the Timer control (see Figure 11.2). Think of the Timer control as a little clock that once turned on, fires a programmable event at a prescribed interval of time.

The event that the Timer fires is called a Timer event, and the event procedure that you program is TimerName_Timer() where TimerName is the value of the Name property of the Timer control. You can make the period of time between which the Timer event is fired as small as once every thousandth of a second or as large as your program requires. However, to be practical, the best resolution is only 55ms because the system clock only ticks 18 times per second. You set this period of time by assigning a value to the `Timer` control's Interval property. The unit of measure for the Interval property is a millisecond. The following code snippet shows the value of `Timer` control's Interval property if you want the `Timer` event to fire every half second.

```
Timer1.Interval = 500
```

FIG. 11.2

The `Timer` control is an invisible control. You do not see it at runtime.

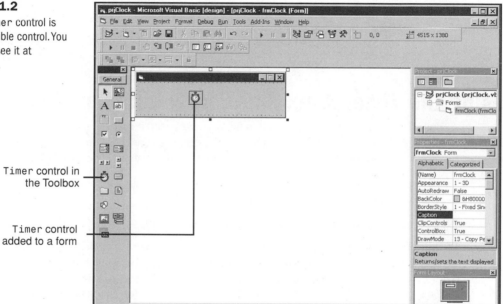

Timer control in the Toolbox

Timer control added to a form

Because all the `Timer` control really does is fire a `Timer` event, the control does not have many properties (see Table 11.1).

Table 11.1 *Timer* Control Properties

Property	Description	Comment
Name	Name of the `Timer`	Defaults to Timer1 if you have one Timer control, Timer2 if you have two Timer controls, and so on.
Enabled	Turns `Timer` off and on	Default: True.
Index	Reports position with `control array`	Advanced use.
Interval	Determines when a `Timer` event should fire	1 second = 1000.

continues

Table 11.1   Continued

Property	Description	Comment
Left	Position of `Timer` on form	Irrelevant, Timer is invisible at runtime.
Tag	User defined value	The `Tag` property is like having a variable built right into the control. It is a "catch all" property to which you can assign any data that is necessary to your program and that you want to persist throughout the life of your program.
Top	Position of `Timer`	Irrelevant, `Timer` is on form invisible at runtime.

Using the *Time*, *Date*, and *Now* Functions

Although a `Timer` can be programmed to fire a Timer event, it really doesn't know what time it is at any given point during its operation. For the `Timer` to report the time of day, it must check the computer's system clock and report back the time the system clock passes to it.

To access the computer's system clock, you use the `Time` function to get the system time. To get the system date, you use the `Date` function.

If you want to find out the time *and* date on the system clock, you can use the `Now` function.

Listing 11.1 shows the click event procedures for three `CommandButtons`, `cmdTime`, `cmdDate`, and `cmdNow`. These buttons are associated with the `Time`, `Date`, and `Now` functions, respectively. Figure 11.3 shows the data that each function returns. The full code for this program is in the project, DateTime.vbp, in the directory, Chp_11\datetime, on the CD-ROM that comes with this book.

Listing 11.1   11LIST01—Event Procedures That Use the *Time*, *Date*, and *Now* Functions

```
Private Sub cmdTime_Click()
    'Get the time and convert it to a string
    cmdTime.Caption = CStr(Time)
End Sub

Private Sub cmdDate_Click()
    'Get the date and convert it to a string
    cmdDate.Caption = CStr(Date)
End Sub

Private Sub cmdNow_Click()
    'Get the date and time. Convert them to a string
    cmdNow.Caption = CStr(Now)
End Sub
```

FIG. 11.3

The `Time`, `Date`, and Now functions return a variant (Date) data type. Convert this data to a string using the `CStr()` function if you are going to assign the return to a string.

Using a *Timer* to Build a Clock Program

Look at the project prjClock.vbp, which is on the CD-ROM that comes with this book in the directory Chp_11\clock. The program shows the running time on the form's client area and the current date in the form's title bar. When you minimize the form, the running time appears in the form's caption on the Taskbar.

To build a Clock program, do the following steps. Keep in mind that you can customize the settings to your specifications.

1. Start a New Project and size the default form to your specifications, such as those shown previously in Figure 11.2.

2. Place a `Label` control and `Timer` control on the form, examples of which are shown in Figure 11.2.

3. Set the form's `Name` property to frmClock. Set the Label's `Name` property to TimeDisplay. Leave the `Timer`'s `Name` property as the default, `Timer1`.

4. Set the value of the `BorderStyle` property of the form to `1-Fixed Single`. Set the value of the `MinButton` property of the form to `True`.

5. In Listing 11.2 add the code between the lines, `Private Sub Form_Load()` and `End Sub`, to the `Form_Load()` event procedure.

Listing 11.2   11LIST02.TXT—The *Form_Load()* Event Procedure

```
Private Sub Form_Load()
    'Set the position and size of the Label control
    'to the form's client area.
    lblTimeDisplay.Top = ScaleTop
    lblTimeDisplay.Left = ScaleLeft
     lblTimeDisplay.Width = ScaleWidth
    lblTimeDisplay.Height = ScaleHeight
End Sub
```

6. Set the value of the `Timer`'s `Interval` property to 500. Set the value of the `Timer`'s `Enabled` property to `True`.

7. Insert the body of code between the lines `Private Sub Timer1_Timer()` and `End Sub` in Listing 11.3 into the `Timer` event procedure.

Listing 11.3   11FIG03—The *Timer1_Timer()* Event Procedure

```
Private Sub Timer1_Timer()
    'If the form is diplayed as a window, show
    'the time in the client area and the date
    'in the window's title bar.
    If frmClock.WindowState = vbNormal Then
        lblTimeDisplay.Caption = CStr(Time)
        frmClock.Caption = Format(Date, "Long Date")
    Else
        'If the form is minimized into the Task Bar,
        'set the caption to show the time. This will
        'make the time appear in the Task Bar.
        frmClock.Caption = CStr(Time)
    End If
End Sub
```

8. Save and run the code (see Figure 11.4).

FIG. 11.4

Setting the form's MaxButton property to False disables it.

The Clock program uses a few things that you haven't seen before. It uses the Format() function to set the string that displays the date to show the complete day, month, and year. A detailed discussion of the Format() function takes place in the following section. Also, you set the form's MinButton property to True to enable the minimize button on the title bar, thus allowing the form to be minimized to the Taskbar.

Forms have three properties that affect the three buttons on the right side of the title bar. They are the MinButton, MaxButton, and ControlBox properties. Table 11.2 shows you the various settings that you can use.

Table 11.2   Title Bar Button Properties

Property	Compatible BorderStyle	Comment
MinButton	1 - Fixed Single 2 - Sizable	ControlBox property must be set to True.
MaxButton	1 - Fixed Single 2 - Sizable	ControlBox property must be set to True.
ControlBox	All	Overrides MinButton and MaxButton settings.

The program also checks the value of the form's WindowState property to determine whether the form is minimized . The WindowState property has three values:

      0 - Normal (vbNormal)

      1 - Minimized (vbMinimized)

      2 - Maximized (vbMaximized)

You can read the value of the `WindowState` property to determine whether a window is sized regular, full screen, or in the Taskbar. You set the value of the `WindowState` property to make a window normal, full screen, or in the Taskbar. Be careful when you set these properties. You may run into a situation where you accidentally set the `BorderStyle` to be `Fixed Single` and the `WindowState` to be `Maximized`. This will result in a non-sizable, splash screen type of window that the user will be unable to control.

Using the *Format()* Function

The `Format()` function is a powerful Visual Basic function that allows you to control the way strings present themselves. The function is primarily used to display time/date values and numbers, although you can use it to give string values a consistent look.

The `Format()` function takes the following syntax:

```
MyString$ = Format(Expression, Format_String, FirstDayofWeek, FirstWeekOfYear)
```

Where:

    MyString$ is the return value.

    Format is the name of the function.

    Expression is any expression that returns a string, date, or numeric value.

    Format_String is the string template that tells the function how you want the result string to appear.

    FirstDayOfWeek is a constant that sets the first day of the week, optional. The default is Sunday, but if you want Saturday to be considered the first day of the week, you reset this argument.

    FirstWeekOfYear is a constant expression that specifies the first week of the year, optional. The week in which January 1 falls is the first week of the year, by default. However, you can have other settings — the first full week, for example. (If you want more details about these last two arguments, read the on-line documentation that comes with Visual Basic.)

The `Format()` function has many levels of complexity. You can use its intrinsic settings, or you can make up your own user-defined settings.

The key to working with the `Format()` function is getting a grasp of the `Format_String` parameter. The `Format_String` parameter "tells" the value as described in the Expression parameter how to appear as a string. Table 11.3 shows you how to use the settings that come built into the `Format()` function to manipulate the appearance of time and date strings.

Table 11.3   Using the *Format()* Function for Time and Date

Format_String	Example	Result
"Long Date"	Format(36000, "Long Date")	"Friday, July 24, 1998"
"Medium Date"	Format(36000, "Medium Date")	"24-Jul-98"
"Short Date"	Format(36000, "Short Date")	"7/24/98"
"Long Time"	Format(0.874, "Long Time")	"8:58:34 PM"
"Medium Time"	Format(0.874, "Medium Time")	"08:58 PM"
"Short Time"	Format(0.874, "Short Time")	"20:58"

Table 11.4 shows you how to use the Format() function to manipulate numeric values into a desired string display.

Table 11.4   Using the *Format()* Function for Numbers

Format_String	Example	Result
"General Number"	Format(36000, "General Number")	"36000"
"Currency"	Format(36000, "Currency")	"$36,000.00"
"Fixed"	Format(36000, "Fixed")	"36000.00"
"Standard"	Format(36000, "Standard")	"36,000.00"
"Percent"	Format(36000, "Percent")	"3600000.00%"
"Scientific"	Format(36000, "Scientific")	"3.60E+04"
"Yes/No"	Format(36000, "Yes/No")	"Yes"
"True/False"	Format(36000, "True/False")	"True"
"On/Off"	Format(36000, "On/Off")	"On"

There is a common difficulty that many people experience when learning to use the Format() function. Sometimes they forget to put the Format_String parameter between quotation marks. The function is looking for the literal string. If you do not put that parameter between quotes, the function fails.

```
MyString$ = Format(.50, Percent) 'This will generate an error
MyString$ = Format(.50, "Percent") 'This will work
```

Calculating Date Differences

If you need to write a program that tells you the amount of time between two dates, use the DateDiff() function. The DateDiff() function has the following syntax:

```
MyLong = DateDiff(Interval, Start_Date, End_Date, FirstDayOfWeek,
FirstWeekOfYear):
```

Where:

> *MyLong* is the return value of type, Long.
>
> *DateDiff* is the function name.
>
> *Interval* is a string describing the interval of time by which the date difference will be measured (see Table 11.5).
>
> *Start_Date* is the date from which to start measuring (of data type, Date).
>
> *End_Date* is the date from which to end measuring (of data type, Date).
>
> *FirstDayOfWeek* is a constant that sets the first day of the week, optional (similar to the parameter used in the Format() function).
>
> *FirstWeekOfYear* is a constant expression that specifies the first week of the year, optional (similar to the parameter used in the Format() function).

Table 11.5   The Different Values for the *DateDiff()* Interval Parameter

Value	Interval	Usage	Return Value
"yyyy"	Year	DateDiff("yyyy", "7/4/76", "7/4/86")	10
"q"	Quarter	DateDiff("q", "7/4/76", "7/4/86")	40
"m"	Month	DateDiff("m", "7/4/76", "7/4/86")	120
"y"	Day of year	DateDiff("y", "7/4/76", "7/4/86")	3652
"d"	Day	DateDiff("d", "7/4/76", "7/4/86")	3652
"w"	Weekday	DateDiff("w", "7/4/76", "7/4/86")	521
"ww"	Week	DateDiff("ww", "7/4/76", "7/4/86")	521
"h"	Hour	DateDiff("h", "7/4/76", "7/4/86")	87648
"n"	Minute	DateDiff("n", "7/4/76", "7/4/86")	5258880
"s"	Second	DateDiff("s", "7/4/76", "7/4/86")	315532800

Part

III

Ch

11

N O T E   For a detailed discussion of the difference between the Week and Weekday intervals and the Day of year and Day interval, see the online documentation that comes with Visual Basic.

The DateDiff() function works by taking the first date, represented by parameter Start_Date and subtracting it from the second date, represented by parameter End_Date. After the subtraction takes place, the function returns a number of type Long, which is the difference in dates. The unit of measure by which the difference is reported is dictated by the string value of the Interval parameter (see Table 11.5).

On the CD-ROM that comes with this book, the project DateDff.vbp in the directory Chp_11\DateDiff illustrates how to use the DateDiff() function to report the age of a person both in days and in years.

The program works by having the user enter his or her birthday in the TextBox at the upper part of the form. To start the program, the user clicks the Start counting button. Within the click event procedure for that button, the code verifies that the entry "looks" like a valid date string using the IsDate() function. If the string is indeed valid, the birthday text is converted to a date, assigned to a global date variable, gf_dtBirthday (gf is a prefix that denotes the variable is global to the form), and the Timer is enabled. If the string is not valid, an error message is shown. After the user closes the message box, the code sets the cursor back to the TextBox, highlights the problematic text, and exits the event procedure.

Within the Timer1_Timer() event procedure, which will be in force every half second (Interval = 500), the Timer control looks at the system date and time using the Now function. The event procedure uses the DateDiff() function twice—once to measure the difference between the instantaneous time and the birthday time (as assigned to the global birthday variable) in terms of days, and once to measure the difference in dates in terms of years. The different return values are assigned to their respective local variables, lYourAgeInDays and lYourAgeInYears. Listing 11.4 shows the click event procedure and Timer event procedure from the code. Figure 11.5 shows the program displaying calculated values.

Listing 11.4 11LIST04.TXT—Source Code That Uses *DateDiff()*

```
Private Sub cmdStart_Click()

    'Check to make sure that the string "looks"
    'like a date.
    If IsDate(txtBDate.Text) Then
        'If it is a date, convert the text to a date data type
        'and assign it to the global birthday date variable
        gf_dtBirthday = CDate(txtBDate.Text)
    Else
        'If it isn't, then report an error
        MsgBox "You must enter a proper date!", vbCritical, "Data error"
        'Set the cursor back to the textbox
        txtBDate.SetFocus
        'Set the cursor to the beginning of the textbox
        txtBDate.SelStart = 0
        'Highlight the erroneous text
        txtBDate.SelLength = Len(txtBDate.Text)
        'Leave the sub
        Exit Sub
    End If

    'Turn on the timer
    Timer1.Enabled = True
End Sub

Private Sub Timer1_Timer()
```

```
        Dim lYourAgeInSecs As Long
        Dim lYourAgeInDays As Long
        Dim lYourAgeInYears As Long

        'Calculate the date difference in seconds
        lYourAgeInSecs = DateDiff("s", gf_dtBirthday, Now)

        'Calculate the date difference in days
        lYourAgeInDays = DateDiff("d", gf_dtBirthday, Now)

        'Calculate the date difference in years
        lYourAgeInYears = DateDiff("yyyy", gf_dtBirthday, Now)


        'Report the date differences
        lblAgeSecs.Caption = CStr(lYourAgeInSecs)
        lblAgeDays.Caption = CStr(lYourAgeInDays)
        lblAgeYears.Caption = CStr(lYourAgeInYears)
End Sub
```

Using Static Variables with a *Timer*

Part III
Ch
11

You might need to keep track of the number of times a Timer control has fired a Timer event. For example, you might need to write a program that attempts to do an activity every half second for no more than ten tries. If you create a counter variable that is local to the Timer event, every time the Timer event procedure terminates, the variable would go out of scope and reset its value to 0, (zero). Clearly this method will not allow you to accomplish what you need to. However, there are two alternative ways.

You can set a global variable that you increment and against which you check the value within the Timer event. Listing 11.5 shows the code that would do this.

Listing 11.5   11List05.TXT—Using a Global Variable to Keep Track of *Timer* Events

```
Sub Timer1_Timer()
    If g_TimeLimit% > 10 Then
        MsgBox "Attempts exceeded!"
    Else
    'Attempt to do something
    End if

    g_TimeLimit% = g_TimeLimit% + 1

End Sub
```

Although this would work, it is not really optimal code. When you make a global variable to keep track of the number of times the Timer event executes, you create a dependency that is external to the Timer control. If you decide to eliminate the Timer from the code for some reason, this global variable would still be hanging around with no real purpose. At some point, this would come back to haunt you.

FIG. 11.5
Using the *Format()* function would make the days and seconds values easier to read.

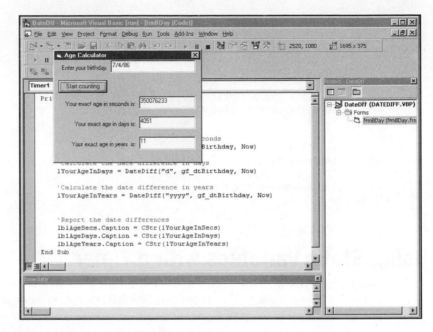

A better strategy for keeping track of the number of times the `Timer` event procedure executes is to declare a counter variable using the `Static` keyword (see Listing 11.6).

Listing 11.6   11List06.TXT—Using a Static Variable to Keep Track of *Timer* Events

```
Private Sub Timer1_Timer()
    'Make a static variable that will retain value even
    'after the event procedure terminates
    Static i%

    'Report the present value of i%
    frmMain.Caption = "Present value of i%: " & CStr(i%)

    'Report the running time
    lblTime.Caption = Format(Time, "Long Time")

    'Check to see if the counter has exceeded 10 loops
    If i% >= 10 Then
        'If the counter is exceeded, send a notice
        lblLimitNotice.Caption = "Limit Exceeded!"
    Else
        'If not, keep the reporting label blank
        lblLimitNotice.Caption = ""
```

```
    End If

    'Increment the counter
    i% = i% + 1
End Sub
```

When you make a variable that is Static, it keeps its value even after the procedure in which it is declared goes out of scope. The advantage of doing this is that the variable is *encapsulated* within the control on which it is dependent. The value of the variable persists, regardless of the state of the procedure in which it was made.

Figure 11.6 shows you a program that uses a static variable. It is in the project, StatVar.vbp on the CD-ROM that comes with this book, in the directory Chp_11\statvar.

FIG. 11.6

Static variables allow values to persist.

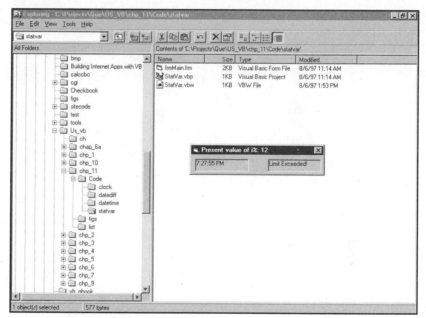

Part

III

Ch

11

Using Static variables does not mean that you should abandon declaring global variables within the General section of a form or module. Quite the contrary, you should be judicious in your use of Static variables. Nothing is more frustrating than discovering that you have a bug in your program that might be caused by a misbehaving global value and then having to search all your code to determine whether a misassigned Static variable is the culprit. If you need to have a variable, the value of which is shared among many areas of your code, you should declare them as Public or Private variables in the General section. ●

CHAPTER 12

Designing Windows Applications

Although Visual Basic makes programming easier, it does not necessarily make you a better programmer. Being an effective software developer means having a clear idea of *what* program you want to write, *whom* you want to write it for, and *how* you want to do it. As you write more production-level code, you'll find that the ease of use of your programs determines the long-term success of your code.

Understanding the activities and dynamics of each phase is important to the overall efficiency of your development effort and the quality of your end product. ◼

User-centered software

Design programs that put the user first.

Production cycles

Learn about the three phases of software development.

Make effective GUIs

Learn how to make an easy-to-use graphical user interface.

Giving your users choices

Offer your users choices using List Boxes, ComboBoxes, Option Buttons, and CheckBoxes.

Good programming practices

Learn how to write code that is easy to read and maintain.

The Pre-Production Phase

In the pre-production phase of developing a Windows application, your product is defined and specified. In pre-production, you draw the blueprint upon which your product will be built. In this phase, you decide on the purpose of the product, what its features are, and of those determined features, which version of your product will implement a given feature set.

The process of software development can be broken up into three phases as listed in Table 12.1.

Table 12.1 The Three Phases of Software Development

Phase	Activity
Pre-production	Determine user
	Analyze user needs and usage style
	Determine features set
	Prioritize features
	Create specification
	Create schematic of program
Production	Divide work among programming group
	Code and build
	Debug
	Perform usability tests
	Correct bugs and address usability issues
Post-production	Prepare online help and end-user manuals
	Document program for future maintenance
	Prepare program for deployment
	Evaluate program and process for future versions

You create a user profile in pre-production. For instance, you determine whether your intended users are comfortable with Windows, thus requiring little elementary support. If your users have never used a computer before, your program will require a good deal of on-screen instruction.

Localization issues are also identified during this phase. Will your product be released in United States English? Will it require United Kingdom English as well? Will you eventually be releasing it in French, Japanese, or Arabic? These important issues must be considered, and you should address them at the beginning of the development process where change is cheap rather than at the end of the process where change is very, very expensive.

 TIP It is always most cost effective to correct a mistake or make a change to a program feature in the pre-production phase. If your client decides that he or she wants to add an alarm feature into the clock program that you're building, adding the alarm will be a fairly simple, inexpensive modification if it's done at this point. All you need to do is change the specification. But if your client decides to have the alarm feature added while the project is in post-production, such a change is costly in terms of time and money. The program must be respecified, recoded, retested, and redocumented.

The Production Phase

During the production phase of the development process, you take the product specification prepared in pre-production and turn it into code. In addition, you create media and other resources that your code may require. In this phase, you determine the optimal language in which to code. (Even though this is a book on Visual Basic, remember that Visual Basic might not always be the best language. Even VB has its limitations and misapplications.) If you are working within a group of programmers, production is where you divide the work and do build control. (*Build control* is the process of integrating the various pieces of code developed among a group of programmers into one distinct, verifiable version.)

Two schools of thought concerning production methodology are worth mentioning here. One method is called the *waterfall* method (see Figure 12.1). In the waterfall method, each production activity is discrete and nonrepetitive. The testing process is separate from the programming part of the software development process. Within the waterfall method, you consider design, coding, testing, and deployment to be a "one shot" deal. You design the code, write the code, test it, fix it, and deploy it.

The other method is called the *iterative* method (see Figure 12.2). An iterative production methodology assumes that your application will be a continuously evolving product. As each piece of code is designed, a test is written for it, and documentation is anticipated. Testers, technical writers, and programmers work hand-in-hand. From the beginning, the iterative production process is one of continual improvement. The goal is to get the product "good enough" to ship. After the application is deployed, you review its shortcomings and improve it for deployment with another version number.

Part III
Ch 12

FIG. 12.1
The waterfall method requires that most testing take place as a one time, independent activity.

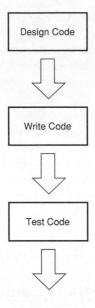

FIG. 12.2
The iterative production method requires that testing take place throughout the production phase.

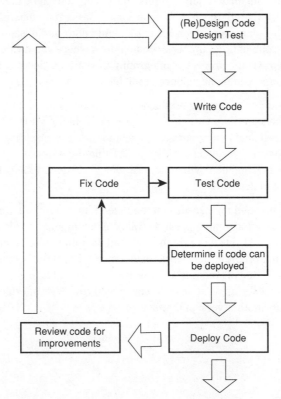

The Post-Production Phase

In the post-production phase of software development, the built software is documented, prepared for deployment, and evaluated for future version releases.

After your code is acceptably bug free and compliant to specification, you must write the documentation for it. The scope of the documentation includes not only the online help and manuals for the end-user but also the "blood and guts" manuals for the people who will be maintaining your code in following versions.

As your program is being documented, you also can prepare it for deployment. *Deployment* is the act of distributing your program to others. Whether the deployment be a modest activity, such as a floppy disk in an envelope, or a more extravagant shrink wrap release, you want to put as much effort into your deployment as you did with your programming. (You'll take a detailed look at deployment in Chapter 18, "Deploying Your Application.") At the end of every software development process, look over what you have done to determine how to do it better on the next version.

Most software is developed under strict time constraints. No person or enterprise can take forever to produce a functional application. As a result, it is often not possible to implement every specified feature into a given release. Therefore, planning to implement features over progressive versions is a viable development strategy.

The evaluation of "real-life use" of your code happens in the post-production period. The true test of a software product's effectiveness and usability is the test of time. No laboratory condition can ever adequately anticipate every nuance of user interaction. It is only by deploying your program, supporting your program, and eliciting the end-user's responses and suggestions for future improvements that you can realistically and accurately evaluate what works and what doesn't.

Designing Forms

Although the Windows operating system has many Graphical User Interface (GUI) design issues, many Windows programs still use Windows components (menus, buttons, list boxes, combo boxes, and so on) very unpredictably. Inconsistency defeats the fundamental purpose of the GUI paradigm—to make operating a computer a more productive, enjoyable, less frustrating experience for the user.

Making a good form is more than inserting controls and programming events. To make a well-designed form, you should understand the function(s) of a particular form, how it is going to be used, when it is going to be used, and how it relates to the other forms within a given program.

Take a look at the form frmSettings (frmESet.frm) in Figure 12.3. This form is in the project EvilJot.vbp, which is in the directory, Chp_12\Pads\, that comes on the CD-ROM accompanying this book. The purpose of this form is to set the display attributes for another form. This form suffers from a number of poor design choices that prevent it from effectively achieving its full functionality.

FIG. 12.3

This is an example of a poorly designed Display Settings form.

Lack of descriptive labeling

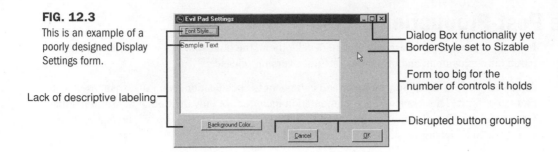

Dialog Box functionality yet BorderStyle set to Sizable

Form too big for the number of controls it holds

Disrupted button grouping

The first item for correction is the choice of setting the form's BorderStyle to Sizable. Should the user resize the form either by intention or mistake (double-clicking the title bar is *not* an uncommon accident), the form will not resize or reposition the controls to accommodate the new form size. Forms that are sizable are generally used in instances where the user needs a window of varying size to accomplish something; for example, Word's documents window or Paint's drawing window. The correction to this problem is to set the form's BorderStyle to Fixed Single or Fixed Dialog.

Notice the initial size and location of the form. It completely covers the form whose attributes are to be set. This could easily confuse the user. To remedy this flaw, the form should be repositioned so that when it appears, the portion of the form that's affected is showing.

Notice, too, that the form suffers from poor, almost nonexistent descriptive labeling. The designer is assuming that the user will intuitively know what this form is about, what the function of the label control is, and how each button will affect the overall program.

Probably the bigger cause for concern with regard to this form's design is the almost arbitrary use of space and the inconsistent placement of buttons and labels on the form. When it comes to the size of a fixed size form (such as a dialog box), the rule of thumb is "less is best." You want to allow the form to take up no more real estate than it needs, but not to make it so small that controls are congested and control text and captions are illegible.

You should also organize the placement of controls according to functionality. In the frmSettings form, separating the Font Style and Background Color buttons is confusing and causes extra mouse movement activity that really is not necessary. Positioning the Font Style and Background Color buttons together in one group and the OK and Cancel buttons in another creates distinct areas of functionality that the user will find more organized and memorable.

Figure 12.4 illustrates the improved form, frmSettngs (frmSet.frm), which is part of the Visual Basic project, goodjot.vbp. Notice the reduced size of the form, the change of the form's BorderStyle, the reorganization of the form's buttons, and the inclusion of a frame to provide a sense of functional unity and descriptive labeling.

FIG. 12.4
A logical and concise design improves the Display Settings form.

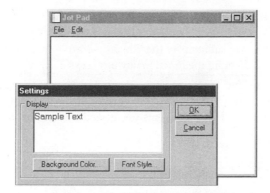

Designing Menus with the User in Mind

Consistent, effective menus make your programs easier and faster to use. The following high-level guidelines and suggestions enable you to make professional-looking menus that meet the user's expectations.

■ *Follow standard Windows layout conventions.* The large installed base of Windows users has developed a certain expectation about how Windows applications should work and look. One of the areas where user expectation is extremely strong is the layout of the menu bar. In Figure 12.5, the menu designer has chosen to breach standard Windows menu bar layout conventions. Conventional expectation is that the menu bar item File comes first in a menu bar, followed by Edit. This change forces the user to relearn a habitual menu navigation method. The unconventional ordering of the menu bar will cause the user initial confusion. In this case, not conforming to the de facto Windows convention accomplishes little and possibly will have a negative impact on the program.

Part
III

Ch
12

FIG. 12.5
Reordering the standard Window menu bar is not always a good idea.

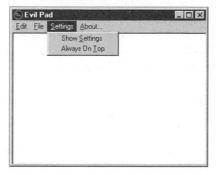

■ *Group menu items logically and concisely.* Referring to Figure 12.5, notice that the illustrated menu bar item Settings has only two subitems, Show Settings and Always on Top. Moving these two subitems to the File drop-down menu condenses the overall menu bar without affecting the functionality or accessibility of the moved items.

■ *Use separator bars.* After the Show Settings and Always on Top drop-down menu items have been moved to the File menu (see Figure 12.6), group them together by putting a separator bar before and after the items (discussed fully in Chapter 13, "Working With Menus").

FIG. 12.6

The File menu with the Setting and Always on Top menu items consolidated into it. Notice the use of separator bars to group the functionality.

Separator bars group the Setting and Always on Top functionality

■ *Avoid redundant menu entries.* Although it always is a good idea to offer the user multiple ways of performing the same behavior within your program (such as a choice between mouse clicks and key combinations), don't have a particular functionality appear in more than one place in your program's menu. Also avoid having the same menu captions appear in more than one place in your program that do two entirely different actions. In Figure 12.7, notice that the caption Settings appears both in the File menu and as a menu bar entry, Settings. When you click the Settings menu item in the File menu, the Setting *dialog box* appears. When you click the Settings menu bar item, the Settings *drop-down menu* appears. This is bad business. Not only will having the caption, Settings, in two different areas of the program's menu confuse the user, having two different behaviors attached to the Settings caption will absolutely confound them.

■ *Avoid menu bar items without drop-down menus.* If you have a menu bar item without any subitems, you should rethink your design decisions (see Figure 12.8). An orphan menu bar item has the behavior of a button. If you want that behavior, use a button control instead. A better solution is to move the orphan menu bar item to be a subitem of another menu bar item that groups a similar set of functions (such as the grouping shown earlier in Figure 12.6).

FIG. 12.7
Notice that the Se_t_tings menu item appears in the _F_ile drop-down menu and on the menu bar. This is a confusing design choice. Avoid redundant menu items.

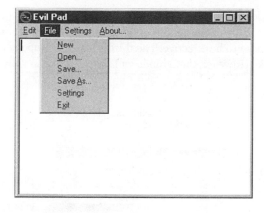

FIG. 12.8
Menu bar items should not invoke dialog boxes. They should invoke drop-down menus.

■ *Remember to use the ellipsis(...)*. When an ellipsis appears next to an item in a drop-down menu, it means that clicking that menu item makes a dialog box appear. Many people unfamiliar with designing Windows applications for general or enterprise-wide use frequently forget to use it. Using the ellipsis in the correct situation adds professionalism to your application.

Part
III

Ch
12

Choosing Between *ListBoxes* and *ComboBoxes*

As described in Chapter 10, "Working with Arrays," Visual Basic provides two powerful control types for selecting and entering data: the ListBox and the ComboBox.

A ListBox enables the user to view a list of all available choices before, during, and after the selection is made. A ListBox allows no user input. The user can input data only by selecting from a list. This can be a drawback should the user need to input data that the program does not provide. Another drawback of the ListBox is that it requires a good deal of window space to be useful. A ListBox that shows only two or three items can appear cramped and awkward.

Sometimes using a ComboBox when window space is at a premium is a better design choice. The ComboBox has three styles, Dropdown Combo, Simple Combo, and Dropdown List (see Figure 12.9). Dropdown Combo displays a Dropdown List that also permits typed-in user input.

The Simple Combo style shows an input box above a list, almost like a ListBox with TextBox above it. The drawback of using the Simple Combo style is that like a ListBox, it requires a good deal of window space to be effective. The third style, the Dropdown List style, is similar to the Simple Combo style. However, the Dropdown List does not allow the user to type in any input.

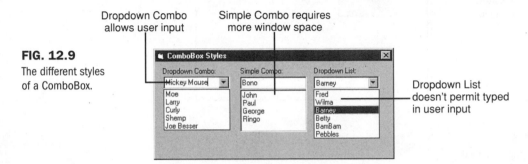

FIG. 12.9
The different styles of a ComboBox.

Overusing ListBoxes and ComboBoxes also can harm an application's performance. If a ListBox or ComboBox lists too many items, the control can increase the load time of the form to which the control belongs. You can reduce the number of items in a list by finding out what the actual limits are. Does a user need all the states in the United States, or only the ten with which the company normally does business? Does the user need to see all the names in the list? Or will an alphabetic portion of the list suffice?

Choosing Between *OptionButtons* and *CheckBoxes*

To present a fixed number of choices, use the CheckBox and OptionButton controls. A CheckBox gives the user two choices only: on or off, implemented or not implemented. For example, the View tab of Windows Explorer's Options dialog box uses the check box to indicate whether to Display the full MS-DOS path in the title bar (see Figure 12.10). An OptionButton presents the user with a fixed list of exclusive choices. For example, the Background tab of Windows Display Properties uses an OptionButton to set a screen's wallpaper to the exclusive states of Tile or Center (see Figure 12.11).

Writing Readable Code Using Visual Basic Constants

Regardless of whether you are a member of a team of programmers or a one-person shop, your code must be maintained either by you or others. Figuring out code is difficult enough as you write it, but it's much more difficult to figure out six months later when you try to improve and enhance it. If you take certain precautions and use a certain amount of foresight, though, code maintenance can be relatively painless.

FIG. 12.10
The Display the full MS-DOS path in the title bar CheckBox gives you just one choice— yes or no.

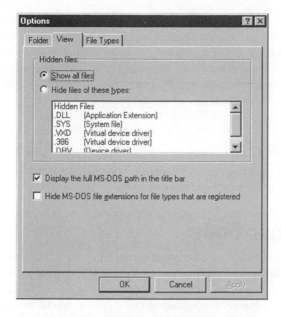

FIG. 12.11
This Windows Display Properties tab uses an OptionButton to set a screen's wallpaper to the exclusive states of Tile or Center. You cannot choose both.

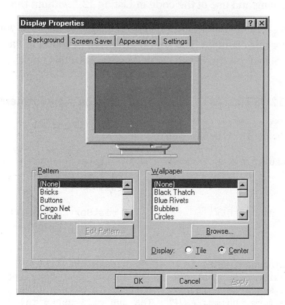

Part
III
Ch
12

Visual Basic enables you to write code with numeric values to specify how an object should behave. This capability makes writing code easier, but makes reading the code more difficult afterwards. The solution is to use global constants that represent these values. Code that uses constants is much easier to read.

Some programmers are proud that they can read code without the help of constants. Unfortunately, not all programmers can do so, including some who may need to maintain your code. By using the Visual Basic global constants, you make your code more readable to all programmers, even those who cannot read code as easily. Using constants still makes your code easier to read, especially if you tend to forget what you have done and why. For example, which of the following code lines is more readily understandable?

```
frmMain.Show 1
```

```
frmMain.Show vbModal
```

When you read code that uses the constants, you do not have to remember what each value means. It is evident in the naming of the constant.

Commenting Your Code

Writing commented code is a pain, but reading uncommented code, even code that you wrote just yesterday, can be agony. Figuring out the logic of a piece code is time consuming. Taking the time to put in comments, on the other hand, saves you time in the long run. There's an old saying among programmers, "You can never comment too much!" Imagine trying to read and understand the meaning and use of the code in Listing 12.1 without the comments.

If you want to get a sense of context for the code listed in Listing 12.1, you can view the complete source code for this example. The source code can be found in the project vbSched.vbp, in the directory \vbSched\ on the CD-ROM that comes with this book.

Listing 12.1   12LIST01.TXT—Code that Sets an Appointment Calendar

```
'****************************************************
'Sub/Function Name: InitAppointments
'
'Arguments: Granularity as Integer      An Integer representing
'                                        the time partition of the
'                                        appointment list.
'
'
'           lst as ListBox              A ListBox containing the
'                                        daily appointments.
'Return: None
'
'Remarks:    InitAppointments is used to create the list of
'            appointments that get added to the list box, lst
'            The sub creates strings that begin with a time stamp of
'            the form, hh:mm: AM/PM. The sub will query the
'            appointments table for all existing appointments for that
'            day. If it finds an appointment it will be added to the
'            appointment list, at the appropriate time.
'
'
'            After all appointments have been entered and all times
'            listed for a 24 hours a day, the sub, sets the top of the list
'            to be 08:00 AM.
```

```vb
'
'
'Progammer/Creator: Bob Reselman
'Copyright ©1997 Macmillian Publishing
'*************************************************'
Public Sub InitAppointments(Granularity As Integer, _
                    lst As ListBox)
    Dim h%
    Dim m%
    Dim hr$
    Dim entry$
    Dim g%
    'Set the granularity to a local variable
    g% = Granularity
    'Clear the list box
    lst.Clear
    'Go through the morning hours
    For h% = 0 To 12
        'Go through the minutes by the steps as defined
        'the granularity variable, g.
        For m% = 0 To 45 Step g%
            'If the length of the hour is less than 2 digits (i.e., 9)
            'then add a zero to the left of the single digit
            If Len(CStr(h%)) = 1 Then
                'Oh, yes make it a string
                hr$ = "0" & CStr(h%)
            Else
                'even if it is two digits
                hr$ = CStr(h%)
            End If
            'Add the "AM" part to the string
            If h% <> 12 Then
                If m% = 0 Then
                    'Add double zeros to the hour, in addition
                    'to the "AM"
                    entry$ = hr$ & ":" & "00 AM:"
                Else
                    'If it is not right on the hour, just add
                    'the "AM" to the end of the string
                    entry$ = hr$ & ":" & CStr(m%) & " AM:"
                End If
            Else
                'If it is the twelfth hour it is really a "PM"
                If m% = 0 Then
                    'Right on the hour, add a double zero and the "PM"
                    entry$ = hr$ & ":" & "00 PM:"
                Else
                    'Off the hour, just "PM"
                    entry$ = hr$ & ":" & CStr(m%) & " PM:"
                End If
            End If
            'Make the entry string
            entry$ = entry$ & GetGutter(COLUMN_GUTTER) & gOpenApptLine$
```

continues

Listing 12.1   Continued

```
                'Add the string to list
                lst.AddItem entry$
        Next m%
    Next h%
    'Now do the evening hours the same as you did the morning
    For h% = 1 To 11
            For m% = 0 To 45 Step g%
                If Len(CStr(h%)) = 1 Then
                    hr$ = "0" & CStr(h%)
                Else
                    hr$ = CStr(h%)
                End If

                If m% = 0 Then
                    entry$ = hr$ & ":" & "00 PM:"
                Else
                    entry$ = hr$ & ":" & CStr(m%) & " PM:"
                End If
               entry$ = entry$ & GetGutter(COLUMN_GUTTER) & gOpenApptLine$
                lst.AddItem entry$
            Next m%
        Next h%
    'Set the top to 8 AM
    Dim strLook$
    Dim strLookFor$
    Dim i%
    strLookFor$ = "08:00 AM:"

    'Take a look at every item in the list
    For i% = 0 To lst.ListCount - 1
        strLook$ = lst.List(i%)
        'If it matches the time to look for, set that line
        'as the top line.
        If InStr(strLook$, strLookFor$) <> 0 Then
            lst.TopIndex = i%
        End If
    Next i%
    'Set the time increment semaphore. You'll need it to
    'figure out how to make end times.
    gAppointmentDelta% = g%
End Sub
```

Using Descriptive Naming

Visual Basic enables you to use up to 255 characters to name a variable, sub, or function and 40 characters for a control. You can take advantage of this feature to make your code easier to understand by giving your variables, functions, and controls names that reflect their identity, purpose, function, or position. Listing 12.2 shows an example of using descriptive naming to make your code more readable. For example, you can use the prefix "gf" (global to form; omit quotes) with a variable which has form visibility, while you can use the prefix, "g" (global; omit quotes) for variables that have visibility throughout the application.

Also, you can use data type suffixes such as, %,&, !, #, and $ (Integer, Long, Single, Double, and String, respectively) as shorthand to declare not only a variables type but to communicate also the type of the variable when it is used later within the body of code.

▶ **See** the section, "Using Type Suffixes with Variables," in Chapter 6, "Using Data Types, Constants, and Variables," for a review of data type suffixes, **p. 97**

Listing 12.2   L-LIST0a.TXT—An Example of Using Descriptive Naming for Variables and Controls

```
Private Sub cmdChoices_MouseDown(Index As Integer, Button As Integer, Shift As
Integer, X As Single, Y As Single)
    Dim i%
    'The pressed button typeface will be set according to the
    'option, optFontFace value set
    'Set the old font (the gf_ prefix denotes global to form)
    'so it can reset on MouseUp
    gf_OldFontFace$ = cmdChoices(Index).Font

    'Adjust for the new font setting
    If optFontFace(0) = True Then
        cmdChoices(Index).Font = optFontFace(0).Caption
    Else
        cmdChoices(Index).Font = optFontFace(1).Caption
    End If

    'Query to option buttons and set the Caption case
    'for the button depressed
    For i% = 0 To 2
        Select Case i%
        Case 0
            If optFontCase(i%).Value = True Then _
                cmdChoices(Index).Caption = _
                    UCase(cmdChoices(Index).Caption)
        Case 1
            If optFontCase(i%).Value = True Then _
                cmdChoices(Index).Caption = _
                    LCase(cmdChoices(Index).Caption)
        Case 2
            If optFontCase(i%).Value = True Then _
                cmdChoices(Index).Caption = _
                    gf_OldFontCase$(Index)
        End Select
    Next i%
End Sub
```

Part
III

Ch
12

CHAPTER 13

Working with Menus

When you create a program, you provide many functions for your users. Many programs have file functions that let the user create and save files. You also may have edit functions and additional functions that are specific to your program, giving the user many possible things to do.

One of the most important things in any program is enabling the user to access easily all the functions of the program. Users are accustomed to accessing most functions with a single click of the mouse—or at most, two clicks. And, most users want all the functions located conveniently in one place. You handle this expectation of your programs by using *menus*. ∎

Make menus

Use the Menu Editor to make menus for your programs.

Menus as controls

Program using a menu's properties and methods.

Designing menus

You can design an effective menu.

Accelerator keys

Learn how to add accelerator keys to your menus.

Shortcut keys

Add shortcut keys to your programs.

Using Visual Basic's Menu Editor

Visual Basic simplifies much of the low-level programming difficulty of designing and constructing menus by providing you with a tool that automates the process. The tool is the *Menu Editor*. With the Menu Editor, you create menu bars located at the top of a form with associated drop-down submenus or pop-up menus that the user typically accesses by clicking the right mouse button. To make a simple menu, do the following:

1. Open a New Project. Name the project and Save the project with its new file name. Rename the default form (with a name such as frmMenu) and save it to a new file name, such as frmMenu.frm.

2. Open the Menu Editor. There are three ways to open the Menu Editor: click the Menu Editor button on the Standard toolbar, click the Tools menu and select Menu Editor, or press Ctrl+E. Figure 13.1 shows you how to access the Menu Editor using the Standard toolbar.

FIG. 13.1

Make sure that the form in question has the focus when you want to select the Menu Editor from the Standard toolbar. If the form is not showing and does not have the focus, the Menu Editor icon is grayed out.

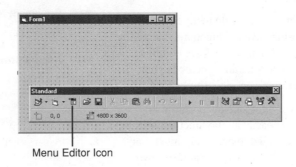

Menu Editor Icon

3. Type **&File** in the Caption field of the Menu Editor dialog box. (Do *not* include quotation marks.)

4. Type **mnuFile** in the Name field. (Again, no quotes. See Figure 13.2.)

5. Click the Next button.

FIG. 13.2

Do not press Enter when you are finished entering data in the various fields of the Menu Editor. This causes the Menu Editor to create a new menu item. Rather, use the Tab key or the mouse to move between fields.

6. Click the button with the arrow pointing to the right. This is the indent button.

7. Type **E&xit** in the Caption field and **itmExit** in the Name field. (Make sure that you include the ampersands. The ampersand forces the character that comes after it to be underlined when it appears in the menu.)

8. Click OK in the upper-right corner of the Menu Editor (see Figure 13.3).

FIG. 13.3

The arrow buttons allow you to indent and rearrange items in the menu list.

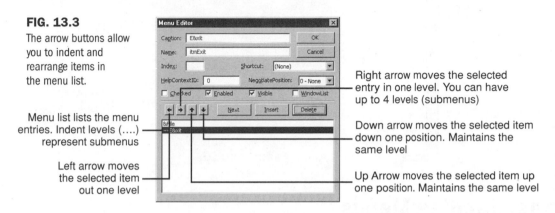

Right arrow moves the selected entry in one level. You can have up to 4 levels (submenus)

Menu list lists the menu entries. Indent levels (....) represent submenus

Down arrow moves the selected item down one position. Maintains the same level

Left arrow moves the selected item out one level

Up Arrow moves the selected item up one position. Maintains the same level

9. The menu you've just created is embedded in the form. Single-click the Exit item in the File drop-down menu that you've just created (see Figure 13.4). The code window for the `itmExit_Click()` event procedure appears.

FIG. 13.4

An entry item in a menu is just like any other Visual Basic control. It has properties and one event, the `Click` event.

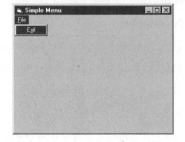

10. Add the `End` statement to the `itmExit_Click ( )` event procedure, as shown in Figure 13.5.

11. Press the F5 key to run the code.

Granted, this is a simple exercise, but it demonstrates the fundamental techniques for making a menu using the Menu Editor. What you've done is you've added a File menu to the main form. The menu has a submenu item called Exit that enables the user to terminate the program when she or he clicks it. You accomplished the program's termination by putting the `End` statement in the event procedure for the Exit menu items `Click` event.

FIG. 13.5

You write code in menu item event procedures as you would for any other Visual Basic control.

Understanding Menus

As mentioned earlier, a menu is a control with its own set of properties and one event, the Click event. Table 13.1 shows the most commonly used properties for a Menu object.

Table 13.1   Commonly Used Properties of the Menu Object

Property	Value/Type	Description
Caption	string	The string that appears in the menu.
Checked	Boolean	Makes check appear before the Caption string.
Enabled	Boolean	Makes the Caption string not ghosted if True.
Name	String	Name of object. Available only at design time.
Shortcut	N/A	Key combination that allows you to access the menu item's functionality. You choose this setting from a list that appears in the Shortcut drop-down list in the Menu Editor. Available only at design time.
WindowList	Boolean	Used to make a "top" level menu in an MDI form display a list of windows open in that MDI form. Available only at design time.

As with any control, you assign a value to the Name property when you create a menu or menu item. Failing to set the Name value results in an error.

Another common mistake is to leave the value of the Caption property set to NULL (""). This results in a functional menu item that shows up in the menu bar as a blank line.

Adding Access Keys to Menu Items

In addition to clicking a menu item to perform a task, you can also access a menu item's functionality by using *access keys* and *accelerator keys*. An access key is denoted by an underlined character in a menu item's Caption. For example, in Figure 13.4, the menu item, mnuFile's Caption has an underline under the character, "F" in File. Thus, when you hold down the Alt key and press F, you get the same result as if you had clicked the File menu. This is how access works. As you saw earlier, you denote an access character by putting an ampersand before the given character you want to use.

Access keys are grouped according to menus. You can have different access keys with the same letter, Save and Paste Special for instance, as long as they appear in different menus. (In MS Word, these would appear under the menus File and Edit, respectively.) If two access keys with the same letter appear in the same menu, the first key in the hierarchy is the only one executed.

Adding Accelerator (Shortcut) Keys to Menu Items

Using accelerator keys (also known as *shortcut keys*) is another way of performing menu functions from the keyboard. You set an accelerator key or key combination by choosing a combination from within the Menu Editor's Shortcut field drop-down list.

Accelerator keys are functional throughout the scope of the entire program, regardless of whether the menu item is visible. Therefore, you can assign only one shortcut key or key combination per item. Redundancies are not accepted by the Visual Basic IDE.

Figure 13.6 shows the Shortcut Ctrl+X assigned to the menu item mnuExit in the Menu Editor.

FIG. 13.6
Each application can have only one instance of an accelerator key combination. If you use Ctrl+X for Cut, you can not use Ctrl+X for Exit too.

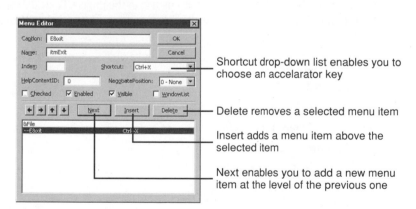

Shortcut drop-down list enables you to choose an accelerator key

Delete removes a selected menu item

Insert adds a menu item above the selected item

Next enables you to add a new menu item at the level of the previous one

Part
III

Ch
13

Creating Pop-up Menus

There are two types of menus: menu bars and pop-up menus. A *menu bar* is the type that you made in the preceding section—a series of menus embedded in a form. A *pop-up menu* is, as the name implies, a menu that "pops up" from somewhere on a form. For example, when you right-click the Windows Explorer, a pop-up menu appears. You can make any menu appear as a pop-up menu by using a form's `PopupMenu` method:

`PopupMenu mnuFile`

Where:

> `PopupMenu` is the method.
>
> `mnuFile` is a valid menu object.

A menu object can exist both within a menu bar and as a pop-up menu as well (see Figure 13.7).

FIG. 13.7
When you use the PopupMenu method as shown in the right dialog box, only the submenu items of a menu will appear.

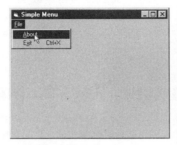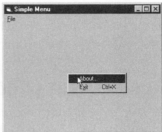

Creating Complex Menus

Now that you have an overview of how to use the Menu Editor to make a menu, the following example makes a menu system for a simple text editor.

The Amazing Text Editor, the code for which is in the project TextEdit.vbp in the Chp_13\ TextEdit\directory on the CD-ROM that accompanies this book, can do the following tasks:

- Create a new file
- Open an existing file
- Save a file
- Reverse the editor's font and background color setting
- Provide copyright notification
- Exit the program
- Undo the preceding action
- Cut, copy, and paste text
- Select all text

Before you start coding, take some time to review the program's features to make a properly designed and categorized menu system. Most menu bars begin with a File menu and are followed by an Edit menu. This is a convention that has evolved over the years. Unless your program has a dramatically unusual feature set, try to adhere to this convention.

▶ **See** Chapter 12, "Designing Windows Applications," for more information about proper menu design **p. 183**

Table 13.2 shows a viable menu categorization for the feature set of the Amazing Text Editor.

Table 13.2   Menu and Submenu Categories for the Amazing Text Editor

File	Edit
New	Undo
Open	Cut
Save	Copy
Settings	Paste
About	Select All
Exit	

Now that you have a categorized menu system, you can implement it in the Menu Editor. Table 13.3 shows the menu hierarchy and Name and Caption properties as well as accelerator and shortcut keys for each menu object. Be advised that the shortcut keys used in the table adhere to the established convention that Windows programmers use for menu items with the demonstrated functionality.

Table 13.3   Menu Objects for the Amazing Text Editor

Name	Caption	Level	Shortcut
mnuFile	&File	0	None
itmNew	&New	1	None
itmOpen	&Open	1	None
itmSave	&Save	1	None
sepOne	-	1	None
itmSettings	Se&ttings	1	None
itmBlackOnWhite	Black On White	2	None
itmWhiteOnBlack	White On Black	2	None
itmAbout	&About	1	None
sepTwo	-	1	None
itmExit	E&xit	1	Ctrl+X
mnuEdit	&Edit	0	None

continues

Table 13.3   Continued

Name	Caption	Level	Shortcut
itmUndo	&Undo	1	Ctrl+Z
sepThree	-	1	None
itmCut	Cu&t	1	Ctrl+X
itmCopy	&Copy	1	Ctrl+C
itmPaste	&Paste	1	Ctrl+V
sepFour	-	1	None
itmSelectAll	Select &All	1	Ctrl+A

Adding Separator Lines to Menus

You add separator lines to a menu by using the dash character (-). Notice that Table 13.3 lists some entries that have a `Caption` value of "-" and begin with the prefix, "sep" in the object `Name`. When you run the program, separator lines appear in the drop-down menus where the dashes are used (see Figure 13.8). The "sep" prefix is a naming convention used by the author of this book to denote that the name of the menu item reflects a separator line. You cannot use separator lines at the 0 (zero) level of a menu's hierarchy. You must be at least one indent level in.

FIG. 13.8
If a submenu item has another submenu associated with it, you will see a right-pointing arrowhead to the right of the submenu item's caption.

Separator lines—

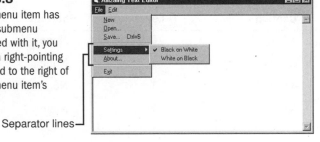

Using the *Checked* Property

You use the `Checked` property of a menu to communicate that some state exists or that a choice has been made. The Amazing Text Editor uses checks in its menu system to communicate the current choice made for font/background color layout. If the user clicks the menu item with the caption "Black on White," the font color will be set to black, and the background client area will be set to white. Choosing "White on Black" creates the opposite scenario. To communicate this choice, a check is placed next to the selection (refer to Figure 13.8).

You can set the value of a menu item's Checked property at runtime or design time. If you want to set its value at design time, you can set it within the Menu Editor, by checking the <u>C</u>hecked check box—checked for True, unchecked for False. You set the value of the Checked property, at design time, within code as follows:

```
MyMenuItem.Checked = True
```

When the value of the a menu item's Checked property is set to True, a check mark appears to the left of the caption of a menu item.

You use this syntax to set the Checked property at runtime. Listing 13.1 shows the event procedure for the itmBlackOnWhite_Click() event. This is an example of how to set the Checked property of a menu item at runtime.

Listing 13.1   13LIST01.TXT—Checked Property Is not Exclusive—You can Set Multiple Checked Events to True

```
Private Sub itmBlackOnWhite_Click()
    'Set the color scheme for Black on White
    txtMain.BackColor = vbWhite
    txtMain.ForeColor = vbBlack

    'Set the menu checks accordingly
    itmBlackOnWhite.Checked = True
    itmWhiteOnBlack.Checked = False
End Sub
```

Cutting, Copying, and Pasting with the *Clipboard* Object

One of the more important features that the Windows operating system brought to computing was the capability to transfer data from one application to another using the Clipboard. The Clipboard is an area of memory reserved by the operating system to which you set and from which you retrieve data. All applications have access to the Clipboard. Over time, the type of data that you can save to the Clipboard has become quite complex. You can save any registered Windows object as well as simple text and numeric values.

Visual Basic allows the applications that you write to access the Windows Clipboard through the Clipboard object. The Clipboard object does not have any properties. However, it does have a number of methods. Table 13.4 shows the various Clipboard methods with a description of each.

Part
III

Ch
13

Table 13.4   Clipboard Object Methods

Method	Description
Clear	Clears all data from the Clipboard
GetData	Returns a graphic from the Clipboard
GetFormat	Returns an integer that references the type of data in the Clipboard
GetText	Retrieves ASCII text from the Clipboard
SetData	Sends a graphic to the Clipboard
SetText	Sends ASCII text to the Clipboard

The Amazing Text Editor's Edit menu Cut, Copy, and Paste items (see Figure 13.9) use the Clipboard to set and retrieve text to and from the Clipboard. Listing 13.2 shows the code for itmCopy_Click(), the event procedure that copies selected text to the Clipboard.

FIG. 13.9

The Edit menu items use the conventional Windows shortcut keys.

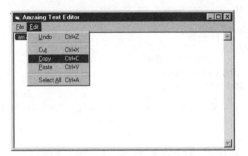

Listing 13.2   13LIST02.TXT—Set Text from the Clipboard Using the *SetText* Method

```
Private Sub itmCopy_Click()
    Clipboard.SetText txtMain.SelText
End Sub
```

The code takes the value of the SelText property of the TextBox and uses the Clipboard's SetText method to send the text to the Clipboard.

Listing 13.3 shows you how to retrieve text from the Clipboard. The listing is a snippet of code from the Paste menu item's Click event procedure.

Listing 13.3   13LIST03.TXT—Retrieve Text from the Clipboard Using the *GetText()* Method

```
Private Sub itmPaste_Click()
    Dim Temp$                    'Text from clipboard
```

```
            Dim strLeft As String    'Variable to hold text from left of cursor
            Dim strRight As String   'Variable to hold text from right of cursor
            Dim strFull As String    'Full text

            'Get the text from the clipboard
            Temp$ = Clipboard.GetText(vbCFText)
          .
          .
          .
        End Sub
```

Selecting Text in a *TextBox*

The Cut and Paste code in the Amazing Text Editor makes extensive use of copying selected text to and from the Clipboard. The code determines which text to copy by using the `SelText` property of the `TextBox`.

The `TextBox` control has many standard Windows text-selection features built right into it. When you double-click a word that has been written into a `TextBox`, it automatically knows enough to highlight the characters of that word. If you drag your mouse cursor across a line of text, that line will be highlighted automatically. When you click a `TextBox`, the mouse cursor automatically is positioned between the characters where you clicked.

The `Textbox` has three "selection" properties—`SelStart`, `SelLength`, and `SelText`. The value of `SelStart` is the string position of the mouse cursor within a `TextBox`'s contents. The value of `SelLength` is the number of characters highlighted during a selection process. The value of `SelText` is characters highlighted during the selection process. Listing 13.4 and Figure 13.10 show how to use the `SelStart` and `SelLength` properties to select a block of text.

Listing 13.4   13LIST04.TXT—You Can Position the Cursor Anywhere Within a String by Setting the *SelStart* Property

```
Private Sub Form_Click()
    Text1.SelStart = 3
    Text1.SelLength = 6
End Sub
```

Part
III

Ch
13

FIG. 13.10

The `SelStart` and `SelLength` properties make the TextBox a powerful control.

Not only can you read these properties, but you also can set them at runtime. SelStart and SelLength are pretty straightforward. However, if you set SelText at runtime, Visual Basic automatically inserts the string value of SelText into the contents of the TextBox at the position of the mouse cursor, moving the existing text to make the accommodation (see Listing 13.5 and Figure 13.11).

FIG. 13.11

SelText is a good property to use if you want to insert text into a TextBox repeatedly.

Listing 13.5   13LIST05.TXT—Use the Value of *SelStart* Property at Runtime Carefully

```
Private Sub Command1_Click()
    Text1.SelText = "Dog "
End Sub
```

As you study the code for the Amazing Text Editor, you'll find some things in it that are new to you. You'll see the Right(), Left(), and Len() functions; the MsgBox statement; and a user-defined function, NoImplement. This code and the concepts are explained in the following chapters as you continue to develop this program. ●

CHAPTER 14

Handling Keyboard and Mouse Input

Most programs are designed with the capability to interact with people. Whether it is a word processor into which you type data on your keyboard or game of Solitaire where you move pictures of cards around the screen with a mouse, accommodating input from users is something most programs are expected to do. In order for users to interact with the programs you write, you must be able to process keyboard and mouse input. Visual Basic makes handling keyboard and mouse input a relatively simple chore. In this chapter, you look at the basic concepts and skills that you need in order to work effectively with keyboard and mouse input. ■

Device Independence

Learn how Windows abstracts hardware devices to make programming easier.

Handle keyboard Input

Use the different Visual Basic event procedures to manipulate keyboard input.

ASCII Characters and VB KeyCodes

Learn about the ASCII character set and the Visual Basic KeyCode constants.

Handle Mouse Input

Work with input from the mouse using Visual Basic mouse movement event procedures.

Understanding Device Input

Windows is a *device independent* operating system. In a device, independent operating system hardware such as the keyboard, mouse, monitor, and printer are *abstracted*. In other words, the programmer never knows the exact type of hardware connected to a given system. All she or he knows is that there is a particular category of hardware out there. The programmer codes to a Printer, not a HP LaserJet™ III. The same is true for the keyboard and mouse. What particular brand of input device is attached to a computer is the business of Windows. As a programmer, all you care about is that there are general categories of hardware devices from which you can accept data and to which you can send data (see Figure 14.1). Device independence enables you to treat hardware devices as nothing more than event generators.

FIG. 14.1

The device independence of Windows frees the Visual Basic programmer from the difficult task of writing code for a particular piece of hardware.

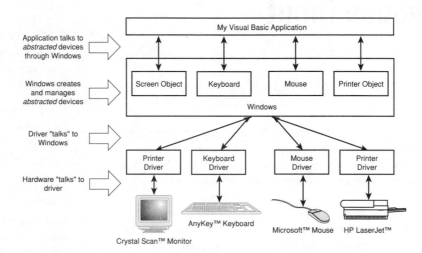

Most Visual Basic controls support three keyboard input events, KeyPress(), KeyUp(), and KeyDown(); and five mouse events, Click() DblClick(), MouseUp(), MouseDown(), and MoveMove().

Working with the *KeyPress* Event

When a user presses down a key within your program, Windows fires a KeyPress event to the form that has the focus and then onto the control that has the focus. The KeyPress event has the following syntax:

```
Private Sub ControlName_KeyPress(KeyAscii as Integer)
```

Where:

>   Private denotes the scope of the event.
>
>   Sub denotes a procedure.
>
>   ControlName is the name of the control from which the event is being fired.

`KeyPress` is the name of the event.

`KeyAscii` is the ASCII code of the character being pressed.

The `KeyPress` is associated with the character of the key being pressed. When the event is fired, Visual Basic passes the ASCII number of the character being input to the `KeyAscii` argument and thus makes it available to the event procedure for use. You might find having a parameter attached to an event handler seems new. If so, you might want to take a minute to think about it. You will be seeing a lot of these in the `KeyPress`, `KeyDown` and `KeyUp` events.

An ASCII code is a number that is assigned, by formal convention, to each letter in the alphabet (separate numbers exist for both upper- and lowercase letters) as well as number characters and punctuation characters. Table 14.1 shows the more often used characters with their associated ASCII numbers.

Table 14.1   The Popular ASCII Characters

Number	Character	Number	Character	Number	Character
32	[space]	64	@	96	`
33	!	65	A	97	a
34	"	66	B	98	b
35	#	67	C	99	c
36	$	68	D	100	d
37	%	69	E	101	e
38	&	70	F	102	f
39	'	71	G	103	g
40	(	72	H	104	h
41	)	73	I	105	i
42	*	74	J	106	j
43	+	75	K	107	k
44	,	76	L	108	l
45	-	77	M	109	m
46	.	78	N	110	n
47	/	79	O	111	o
48	0	80	P	112	p
49	1	81	Q	113	q
50	2	82	R	114	r

Part
III

Ch
14

continues

Table 14.1 Continued

Number	Character	Number	Character	Number	Character
51	3	83	S	115	s
52	4	84	T	116	t
53	5	85	U	117	u
54	6	86	V	118	v
55	7	87	W	119	w
56	8	88	X	120	x
57	9	89	Y	121	y
58	:	90	Z	122	z
59	;	91	[	123	{
60	<	92	\	124		
61	=	93	]	125	}
62	>	94	^	126	~
63	?	95	_		

Figure 14.2 shows you the output from a program that reports the value and the corresponding character of the KeyAscii parameter that is passed during the KeyPress event for a TextBox. Listing 14.1 shows the code for the KeyPress event procedure for the TextBox. In this case, the character "g" was passed to the TextBox.

FIG. 14.2

The KeyPress event is associated with the actual character sent to the control.

ASCII Number: 103, Character: g

Listing 14.1 14LIST01.txt—The *Chr$* Function Converts a Character's ASCII Code to a String

```
Private Sub Text1_KeyPress(KeyAscii As Integer)
    Dim ChrPressed$ 'variable to hold inputted character
    Dim AscNum$   'variable to hold Ascii num
    Dim Msg$      'variable to hold message string

    'Convert KeyAscii to a character
    ChrPressed$ = Chr$(KeyAscii) 'Char$ is a VB function

    'Convert the actual number to a string
    AscNum$ = CStr(KeyAscii)     'CStr is a VB function
```

```
    'Create a display string
    Msg$ = Msg$ & "ASCII Number: " & AscNum$
    Msg$ = Msg$ & ", " & "Character: " & ChrPressed$
    'Show the display string
    MsgBox Msg$
End Sub
```

The code for the preceding example is in the project simplKey.VBP, in the directory Chp_14\simplKey\ that comes on the CD-ROM that accompanies this book.

Working with the *KeyUp/KeyDown* Events

Every time a key on the keyboard is held down, a KeyDown event is fired to the control that has the focus. When the key is released, a KeyUp event is fired.

The important distinction to make between the KeyUp/KeyDown events and the KeyPress event is that the former is associated with characters, while the latter is associated with keys of the keyboard. Remember, most keys can input one of two characters depending on the state of the Shift key ("a" and "A," for example). If it is important to your program to know which character has been input, use the KeyPress event. However, if it is important that you know which *key* has been pressed, use the KeyUp/KeyDown event.

The KeyUp/KeyDown event procedures use the following syntax:

```
Private Sub ControlName_KeyUp(KeyCode as Integer, Shift as Integer)
Private Sub ControlName_KeyDown(KeyCode as Integer, Shift as Integer)
```

Where:

> Private denotes the scope of the event.
>
> Sub denotes a procedure.
>
> ControlName is the name of the control from which the event is being fired.
>
> KeyUp/KeyDown is the name of the event.
>
> KeyCode is an integer that reports the KeyCode constant of the key being pressed up/down.
>
> Shift is an integer that reports if the Shift, Control, and/or Alt keys also are being held down (see Table 14.2).

Table 14.2   The Different Values for the Shift Parameter

Combination [Key(s) Held Down]	Value
Shift	1
Ctrl	2
Alt	4

continues

Table 14.2 Continued

Combination [Key(s) Held Down]	Value
Shift + Ctrl	3
Shift + Alt	5
Ctrl + Alt	6
Shift + Ctrl + Alt	7

The trick to using the KeyUp/KeyDown event handler is working with the KeyCode parameter in conjunction with the Shift parameter. In addition to reporting which alphabetic key has been struck, the KeyCode parameter also can report if the user tapped a function key (F1–F12), a key on the numeric keypad, the arrow keys, or any other key on the keypad. When a key is struck, Visual Basic sends a value to the KeyCode parameter reporting the key in question. The number sent to the KeyCode parameter is represented by a constant value. Table 14.3 shows the KeyCode constants for the various keys on a user's keyboard.

Table 14.3 Visual Basic 5.0 *KeyCode* Constants

Constant	Key
vbKeyLButton	Left mouse button
vbKeyRButton	Right mouse button
vbKeyCancel	CANCEL key
vbKeyMButton	Middle mouse button
vbKeyBack	BACKSPACE key
vbKeyTab	TAB key
vbKeyClear	CLEAR key
vbKeyReturn	ENTER key
vbKeyShift	SHIFT key
vbKeyControl	CTRL key
vbKeyMenu	MENU key
vbKeyPause	PAUSE key
vbKeyCapital	CAPS LOCK key
vbKeyEscape	ESC key
vbKeySpace	SPACEBAR key
vbKeyPageUp	PAGE UP key
vbKeyPageDown	PAGE DOWN key

Constant	Key
vbKeyEnd	END key
vbKeyHome	HOME key
vbKeyLeft	LEFT ARROW key
vbKeyUp	UP ARROW key
vbKeyRight	RIGHT ARROW key
vbKeyDown	DOWN ARROW key
vbKeySelect	SELECT key
vbKeyPrint	PRINT SCREEN key
vbKeyExecute	EXECUTE key
vbKeySnapshot	SNAPSHOT key
vbKeyInsert	INSERT key
vbKeyDelete	DELETE key
vbKeyHelp	HELP key
vbKeyNumlock	NUM LOCK key
vbKeyA	A key
vbKeyB	B key
vbKeyC	C key
vbKeyD	D key
vbKeyE	E key
vbKeyF	F key
vbKeyG	G key
vbKeyH	H key
vbKeyI	I key
vbKeyJ	J key
vbKeyK	K key
vbKeyL	L key
vbKeyM	M key
vbKeyN	N key
vbKeyO	O key
vbKeyP	P key

Part
III

Ch
14

continues

Table 14.3   Continued

Constant	Key
vbKeyQ	Q key
vbKeyR	R key
vbKeyS	S key
vbKeyT	T key
vbKeyU	U key
vbKeyV	V key
vbKeyW	W key
vbKeyX	X key
vbKeyY	Y key
vbKeyZ	Z key
vbKey0	0 key
vbKey1	1 key
vbKey2	2 key
vbKey3	3 key
vbKey4	4 key
vbKey5	5 key
vbKey6	6 key
vbKey7	7 key
vbKey8	8 key
vbKey9	9 key
vbKeyNumpad0	0 key
vbKeyNumpad1	1 key
vbKeyNumpad2	2 key
vbKeyNumpad3	3 key
vbKeyNumpad4	4 key
vbKeyNumpad5	5 key
vbKeyNumpad6	6 key
vbKeyNumpad7	7 key
vbKeyNumpad8	8 key

Constant	Key
vbKeyNumpad9	9 key
vbKeyMultiply	MULTIPLICATION SIGN (*) key
vbKeyAdd	PLUS SIGN (+) key
vbKeySeparator	ENTER key
vbKeySubtract	MINUS SIGN (–) key
vbKeyDecimal	DECIMAL POINT (.) key
vbKeyDivide	DIVISION SIGN (/) key
vbKeyF1	F1 key
vbKeyF2	F2 key
vbKeyF3	F3 key
vbKeyF4	F4 key
vbKeyF5	F5 key
vbKeyF6	F6 key
vbKeyF7	F7 key
vbKeyF8	F8 key
vbKeyF9	F9 key
vbKeyF10	F10 key
vbKeyF11	F11 key
vbKeyF12	F12 key
vbKeyF13	F13 key
vbKeyF14	F14 key
vbKeyF15	F15 key
vbKeyF16	F16 key

Listing 14.2 shows a piece of code from the project KeyEvent.vbp. The project is in the directory Chp_14\KeyEvent\ on the CD-ROM that accompanies this book. This code reports which function key on the user's keyboard has been pressed. It also reports the state of the Shift, Ctrl, and Alt keys. Figure 14.3 shows the code in action.

Part
III

Ch
14

Listing 14.2   n_LIST0a.TXT—Use the *KeyUp/KeyDown* Event Procedure to See If a Function Key Has Been Pressed

```
Private Sub Form_KeyDown(KeyCode As Integer, Shift As Integer)
Dim strKey As String 'variable to hold key string
```

continues

Listing 14.2   Continued

```
'Pass the Keycode parameter through a Case statement.
'If the key up/down is a function key, the Case
'case statement will catch it.
Select Case KeyCode
    Case vbKeyF1
        strKey = "F1"
    Case vbKeyF2
        strKey = "F2"
    Case vbKeyF3
        strKey = "F3"
    Case vbKeyF4
        strKey = "F4"
    Case vbKeyF5
        strKey = "F5"
    Case vbKeyF6
        strKey = "F6"
    Case vbKeyF7
        strKey = "F7"
    Case vbKeyF8
        strKey = "F8"
    Case vbKeyF9
        strKey = "F9"
    Case vbKeyF10
        strKey = "F10"
    Case vbKeyF11
        strKey = "F11"
    Case vbKeyF12
        strKey = "F12"
    Case vbKeyF13
        strKey = "F13"
    Case vbKeyF14
        strKey = "F14"
    Case vbKeyF15
        strKey = "F15"
    Case vbKeyF16
        strKey = "F16"
    Case Else
        strKey = "Some other key"
End Select
'Check to see if the Shift,Ctrl or Alt key is down
Select Case Shift
    Case 0
        Form1.Caption = "No key down"
    Case 1
        Form1.Caption = "Shift down"
    Case 2
        Form1.Caption = "Ctrl down"
    Case 3
        Form1.Caption = "Shift and Ctrl down"
    Case 4
        Form1.Caption = "Alt down"
    Case 5
        Form1.Caption = "Shift and Alt down"
```

```
        Case 6
            Form1.Caption = "Ctrl and Alt down"
        Case 7
            Form1.Caption = "Shift, Ctrl and Alt down"
    End Select
    'Report which key is down
    Label1.Caption = "Key Down, Key: " & strKey
End Sub
```

FIG. 14.3

The KeyUp/KeyDown event procedure enables access to all keys on the keyboard.

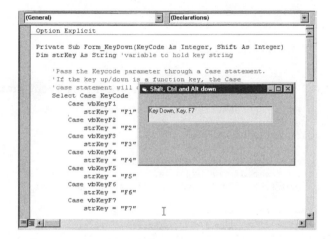

Using the *KeyPreview* Property

There will be times when you will want a form to process keyboard input even if a control on a form has the focus. The form's KeyPreview property enables you to do this.

When you create a form, the default value of the KeyPreview property is False. Thus, any keyboard input that you send to a control on the form (a TextBox, for instance) goes directly to that control. However, if you set the value of KeyPreview property to True, the form intercepts all keyboard input. You can then access the input through the form's keyboard event procedures. Once the form handles the input, it is then passed onto the control with the focus.

On the accompanying CD-ROM is a sample project, KeyPress.vbp, in the directory Chp_14\keypress. In the KeyPress.vbp project, the form's KeyPress() event procedure intercepts all keyboard input headed for a TextBox, manipulates it into a backward string, and ASCII reads it out, as shown in Figure 14.4. It then sends each respective string to its own TextBox control. The reason that the form can intercept and distribute all the keyboard input to the various TextBoxes is because the value of the KeyPreview property is set to True. Listing 14.3 shows the code for the Form_KeyPress() event procedure.

FIG. 14.4
If the value of the form's `KeyPreview` property was set to `False`, only the `Forward` TextBox would receive data.

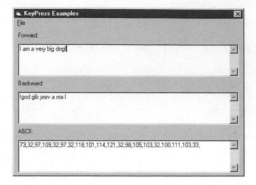

Listing 14.3 14LIST03.TXT—The Form's *KeyPress* Event Procedure

```
Private Sub Form_KeyPress(KeyAscii As Integer)
    'Send the mouse cursor to the first textbox
    txtForward.SetFocus

    'Convert the KeyAscii parameter to a character and
    'put it in front of the existing text
    txtBackward.Text = Chr$(KeyAscii) & txtBackward.Text

    'Turn the KeyAscii value to a numeral and
    'concatenate it to the end of the existing string
    txtAscii.Text = txtAscii.Text & CStr(KeyAscii) & ","
End Sub
```

Understanding Mouse Input

Every time you do something with the mouse, a `mouse` event is fired in your Visual Basic application. If you click the mouse, a `Click` event is fired. When you double-click the mouse, a `DblClick` event if fired. When you press a mouse button down, a `MouseDown` event is fired. Letting the mouse button up causes a `MouseUp` event. Every time the mouse moves, a `MouseMove` event occurs. Where and when a given event occurs depends on the position of the mouse pointer.

Most controls support the event procedures just described. However, some such as the `ComboBox` control have no support for the `MouseDown`/`MouseUp` and `MouseMove` events.

Sometimes one gesture with a mouse fires many events. When you click a mouse, not only is a `Click` event fired, but a `MouseDown` and `MouseUp` event is fired, too. Getting control of the interactions among all the different events takes some getting used to.

Using the *Click* Event

To program a Click event procedure, do the following:

1. Start a New project. Name the project and the form, such as TClick and frmTClick, respectively. Add a TextBox to the form as shown in Figure 14.5.

2. Assign a name to the TextBox, such as txtClick.

FIG. 14.5
The TextBox supports the Click event procedure.

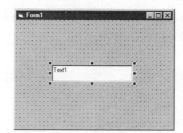

3. Double-click the TextBox to open the code window. Go to the event procedure drop-down list and change the event procedure from the Change event to the Click event, as shown in Figure 14.6.

FIG. 14.6
Be aware that the default event procedure for the TextBox control is the Change event. Some people mistakenly program this event thinking it is the Click event.

4. In the Properties window, clear the value of the Text property for txtClick from "Text1" to an empty string (see Figure 14.7).

5. Add the lines of code between Private Sub txtClick_Click() and End Sub in Listing 14.4 to the txtClick_Click() event procedure.

6. Compile and run the code.

Part
III

Ch

14

FIG. 14.7
Deleting the Text property string value in the Properties Window deletes text from the TextBox.

Listing 14.4   14LIST4.TXT—This Code Displays a Message in the *Textbox* that Reports How Many Times You've Clicked It

```
Private Sub txtClick_Click()
    'make this static so it keeps its
    'value from click to click
    Static i%

    'Make a variable to hold a message string
    Dim Msg$

    'Begin a message
    Msg$ = "This is click number "

    'Convert the counter variable from an
    'integer to a string and concatenate it
    'to the previous string
    Msg$ = Msg$ & CStr(i%) & "."

    'Display the string in the text box
    txtClick.Text = Msg$

    'Increment the counter variable
    i% = i% + 1
End Sub
```

As you can see, the Click event is a simple event procedure to program (see Figure 14.8). As a matter of fact, you can follow the same process to program the DblClick event procedure. However, remember that variables declared in a Click event procedure go out of scope when the procedure is completed. Therefore, if you want to maintain a state or value from click to click, it is best to use a Static variable within the Click event procedure.

FIG. 14.8
Programming the Click event in a TextBox control is an atypical thing to do. Although useful for demonstration purposes, it confuses the user when she or he tries to input text.

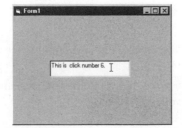

The code for this exercise is in the project TClick.vbp in the directory Chp_14\TClick on the CD-ROM that comes with this book.

Working with *MouseDown/MouseUp* Events

The MouseDown/MouseUp event procedure uses the following syntax:

```
Private Sub ControlName_MouseDown(Button As Integer, Shift As Integer, x As
Single, y As Single)
Private Sub ControlName_MouseUp(Button As Integer, Shift As Integer, x As Single,
y As Single)
```

Where:

Private denotes the scope of the event.

Sub denotes a procedure.

ControlName is the name of the control from which the event is being fired.

MouseUp (MouseDown) is the event procedure.

Button is an integer that reports the mouse button or combination of mouse buttons pressed (see Table 14.4).

Shift is an integer that reports if the Shift, Control, and/or Alt keys also are being held down (see Table 14.2).

x is the horizontal position of the mouse cursor.

y is the vertical position of the mouse cursor.

Table 14.4   Mouse Button Values

Mouse Button(s) Pressed	Button Parameter Value
Left	1
Right	2
Left & Right	3
Middle	4
Left & Middle	5
Right & Middle	6
All	7

In many ways, working with the MouseDown and MouseUp event procedures is very similar to working with the KeyDown and KeyUp procedures. The difference is that the MouseDown/MouseUp event procedure has a few different parameters passed into it. When a MouseDown event is fired, Visual Basic passes information about what mouse button was pressed and if the Shift, Ctrl or Alt key is being held down. Also, VB passes in the location of the mouse cursor within the control that is firing the event. The same is true when working with the MouseUp event. Although you might think the MouseDown and MouseUp events are just a complication of the Click event procedure, you ought to consider them more of an enhancement than a complication.

For instance, you can take advantage of the value of the Shift parameter of the MouseDown event procedure to do things that you cannot do within a Click event procedure. Imagine that you want to have a secret way to display an Easter Egg. (An Easter Egg is a hidden "signature" that a programmer puts in his or her program to verify that she or he indeed wrote it.) Listing 14.5 shows you how to use the Shift parameter with a form's MouseDown event procedure so that only someone holding down the Shift key is able to display a message box when the form is clicked.

You can review this example on the CD-ROM. It is the project MouseBut.VBP in the directory Chp_14\mousebut.

Listing 14.5   14LIST05.TXT—If Shift Parameter Is Equivalent to 1 Then the Shift Key Is Being Held Down

```
Private Sub Form_MouseDown(Button As Integer, Shift As Integer, X As Single, Y
As Single)
    If Shift = 1 Then
        MsgBox "I am a secret Easter Egg"
    End If
End Sub
```

On the CD-ROM that accompanies this book there is a project called Mouse.VBP in the directory Chp_14\mouse. This project demonstrates programming the MouseDown and MouseUp event procedures as well as the Click and DblClick event procedures. The project reports all the mouse activity that takes place within a Frame control, frMouse. When the user presses down on a mouse button, thus firing a MouseDown event, the MouseDown event procedure reports which button and which combination of the Shift, Ctrl, and Alt have been pressed. The event procedure uses two Select Case statements to create a string that reports the status of the Shift and Button parameters. The event procedure also reports the position of the mouse cursor (see Figure 14.9). Listing 14.6 shows the code for the MouseDown and MouseUp event procedures.

Listing 14.6   14LIST06—The *MouseDown* Event Procedure for the Frame Control, *frMouse*

```
Private Sub frMouse_MouseDown(Button As Integer, Shift As Integer, x As Single,
y As Single)
    Dim strButton As String   'holds the converted value of the Button param
    Dim strShift As String    'holds the converted value of the Shift param
    Dim strX As String        'holds the converted value of the X param
    Dim strY As String        'holds the converted value of the Y param

    'Convert the X and Y parameters from integers to a string
```

```
strX = CStr(x)
strY = CStr(y)

'Run the SHIFT parameter through a Select Case statement
'in order to figure out what combination of Shift, Ctrl or
'Alt keys are depressed.

'Assign the result to the Shift string variable
Select Case Shift
    Case 0
        strShift = ""
    Case 1
        strShift = "Shift"
    Case 2
        strShift = "Ctrl"
    Case 3
        strShift = "Shift + Ctrl"
    Case 4
        strShift = "Alt"
    Case 5
        strShift = "Shift + Alt"
    Case 6
        strShift = "Ctrl + Alt"
    Case 7
        strShift = "Shift + Ctrl + Alt"
End Select

'Run the BUTTON parameter through a Select Case statement to
'determine what combination of the Mouse Buttons have been
'pushed. Assign the result to the Button string variable
Select Case Button
    Case 0
        strButton = ""
    Case 1
        strButton = "Left"
    Case 2
        strButton = "Right"
    Case 3
        strButton = "Left + Right"
    Case 4
        strButton = "Middle"
    Case 5
        strButton = "Left + Middle"
    Case 6
        strButton = "Right + Middle"
    Case 7
        strButton = "All"
End Select

'Display the event fired
lblMouse.Caption = "Mouse Down"

'Display the combination of keys pressed
lblShift.Caption = strShift
```

Part

III

Ch

14

continues

Listing 14.6 Continued

```
        'Display the mouse buttons pressed
        lblButton.Caption = strButton
    End Sub


    Private Sub frMouse_MouseUp(Button As Integer, Shift As Integer, x As Single, y
    As Single)
        'Diplay the event fired
        lblMouse.Caption = "Mouse Up"
    End Sub
```

FIG. 14.9

The mouse click
event fires a Click,
MouseDown and
MouseUp event.

You'll notice in Figure 14.9 that the position of the mouse cursor is reported in twips. This number might be confusing at times. If you need to report the position of the mouse in pixels, substitute this code:

```
'Report the X and Y position in pixels by dividing the value
'of X and Y by the TwipsPerPixelX(Y) property of the Screen object.
'Convert the X and Y parameters from integers to a string
    strX = CStr(x/Screen.TwipsPerPixelX)
    strY = CStr(y/Screen.TwipsPerPixely)
```

for the code:

```
'Convert the X and Y parameters from integers to a string
    strX = CStr(x)
    strY = CStr(y)
```

which appears near the beginning of the frMouse_MouseDown() event procedure's body of code. Also, you'll notice that the code for the MouseUp event is minimal compared to the MouseDown event. Doing this was intentional. When the user releases a mouse button both the MouseUp and MouseMove events are fired. If the code in each of the event procedures is trying to affect the same controls, you run into a conflict because you have to make sure that the scope of activity of each event procedure is relatively exclusive. In the Mouse.VBP project, the MouseUp event sets a Label control's caption, while the MouseMove event reports the position of the mouse cursor in another Label control.

Working with the *MouseMove* Event

The syntax for the MouseMove event procedure is as follows:

```
Private Sub ControlName_MouseMove(Button As Integer, Shift As Integer, x As
Single, y As Single)
```

It is identical to the MouseDown and MouseUp event procedures. Whenever you move the mouse, a MouseMove event is fired.

The Mouse.VBP project from the CD-ROM demonstrates programming the MouseMove event. The MouseMove event procedure is programmed to report the location of the mouse within the Frame control (see Figure 14.10).

FIG. 14.10

Most controls support the MouseMove event procedure.

As shown in Listing 14.7, the MouseMove event procedure of the Frame takes the value of the x and y parameters passed to it and displays those values in a Label control. Every time the mouse moves, the new value is reported.

Listing 14.7 14LIST07.TXT—Reporting the Value of the Mouse Cursor Using the *MouseMove* Event Procedure

```
Private Sub frMouse_MouseMove(Button As Integer, Shift As Integer, x As Single,
y As Single)
    Dim strX As String        'holds the converted value of the X param
    Dim strY As String        'holds the converted value of the Y param

    'Convert the X and Y parameters from integers to a string
    strX = CStr(x)
    strY = CStr(y)

    'Display the mouse cursor position
    lblCursor.Caption = "X: " & strX & ", " & "Y: " & strY
End Sub
```

Part

III

Ch

14

When programming with the MouseMove event, remember that the event is fired *every time the mouse moves*. This may sound simplistic, but the implications are important. If the code you write in the MouseMove event handler takes longer to execute than the amount of time until the next MouseMoves is fired, your program will display some very strange, possibly fatal behaviors. For instance, in Listing 14.8, every time the mouse moves, the code creates a new For...Next loop, thus creating a queue of loops waiting to execute. The loops could go on forever. This unanticipated behavior will affect the integrity of your program.

Listing 14.8   14LIST08.TXT—Careful Using the *MouseMove* Event Procedure with Loops

```
Private Sub Form_MouseMove(Button As Integer, Shift As Integer, X As Single, Y
As Single)
    Dim i%
    'This loop could go on forever under certain conditions
    'depending on the frequency of mouse movement.
    For i% = 0 To 10000
        Form1.Caption = CStr(i%)
    Next i%
End Sub
```

Recognizing VB's Limitations with Mouse Input

Visual Basic has two significant shortcomings when it comes to handling mouse input. The first shortcoming is that the mouse event procedures are control specific. In other words, there is no easy way to have a form's mouse-movement event procedures override a contained child control's event procedure. If you have a Frame control on a form and you move the mouse cursor over the Frame from the form, the frame's mouse movement event procedures will be executed upon entering the frame. The form's MouseMove event procedure is ignored.

Also, the X and Y mouse cursor location parameters of the event procedure are relative to the control upon which the mouse cursor is being moved. Going back to the Frame on a form scenario, if you put the mouse pointer in the upper-left corner of the form, the x and y parameters passed to the form's MoveMove() event procedure are 0,0. If you put your mouse pointer in the upper-left corner of the Frame, the x and y parameters passed to the Frame's MoveMove() event procedure also are 0,0. (This assumes that the Frame is not in the upper-left corner of the form.) Even though the Frame is a contained child to the form, it does not report back the coordinates of the form. It reports back coordinates in terms of its own real estate (see Figure 14.11).

The second shortcoming of Visual Basic with regard to mouse input is that Visual Basic cannot report the location of the mouse outside of its application. This means that after the mouse cursor leaves your Visual Basic application, VB has no idea where it is. Thus, if you have to write a program that needs to know the location of the mouse cursor anywhere on the screen, this is going to be a very difficult thing to accomplish. You can use Visual Basic to access functions in the Windows API (Application Programming Interface) that enable you to use an advanced programming technique called *subclassing* in order to accomplish this task. However, this type of API programming is very advanced and very delicate. An error in a Visual Basic application that implements subclassing can cause serious problems not only in the VB application but throughout the entire system.

The upper x, y coordinates reported in the form's MouseMove event procedure are 0,0.

FIG. 14.11

Keeping track of the location of the mouse cursor relative to the form can be difficult.

The upper x, y coordinates reported in the Frame's MouseMove event procedure also are 0,0.

A Visual Basic application cannot detect mouse-movement outside of itself.

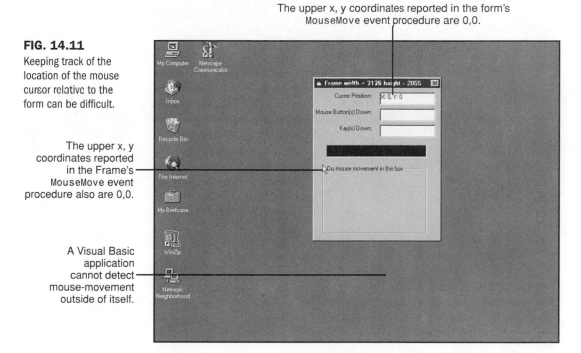

▶ **See** "Making ActiveX Controls" on the CD, for more information about using the Windows API.

CHAPTER 15

Working with Multiple Forms

Forms are much more than containers on which to place your controls. They are the visual glue that binds all of an application's controls together. Users focus on the controls that you show them, but a change in the appearance of a form can create a completely different impression.

The MDI (Multiple Document Interface) is a powerful form technique that enables you to create applications that use hierarchical form relationships. In other words, applications that use MDI enable you to have one form, called a *parent*, that can contain many other forms. These "contained" forms are called *children*.

The are a lot of applications around that use MDI windows, such as Microsoft Word and PaintShop Pro (Figures 15.1 and 15.2). Applications that use MDI forms tend to have a feature set that requires them to show a lot of different data at the same time in different windows yet be unified in a common presentation or control window. ■

Work effectively with MDI Forms

Make an application that enables you to work with multiple forms within a common environment.

Use advanced *MDI Form* properties

Learn how to use the advanced properties of MDI Forms to give them a 3-D appearance and to make MDI child forms automatically visible when loaded.

Dynamically position controls and forms

Size and position forms at runtime.

Use the Windows Registry

Learn how to used the Visual Basic Registry functions to set and retrieve data from the Windows Registry.

FIG. 15.1
The Microsoft Word user interface is an example of the Multiple Document Interface.

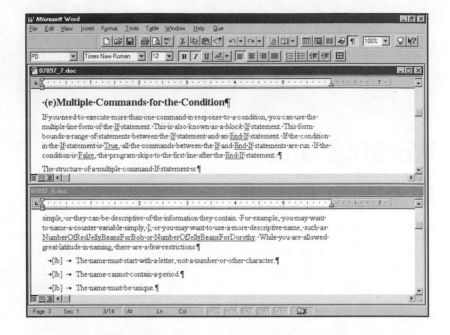

FIG. 15.2
Paint Shop Pro by JASC is another example of the Multiple Document Interface.

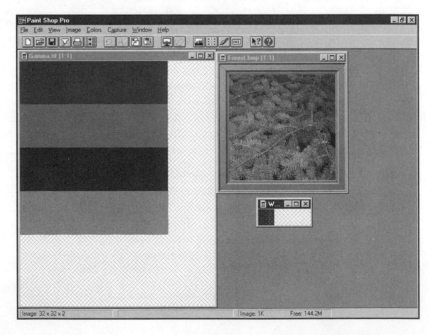

The Structure of an MDI Application

Visual Basic has a defined MDI object called the *MDIForm*. A given VB application can contain *only* one MDIForm object. However, an application may have a multitude of other forms, some of which can be children of the MDIForm object and some of which can be independent, stand-alone windows. The child windows of an MDI Form do not contain a menu of their own. Instead, they are controlled by the menu of their parent MDI form. If you add a menu to an MDI child form, at runtime it will not be visible within the MDI child form. The active child's menu appears on the parent window in place of the parent's menu.

TIP The letters SDI stand for Single Document Interface. MDI stands for Multiple Document Interface. An example of an SDI application is the WordPad program that comes with Windows 95. WordPad enables you to show only one document at a time. Microsoft Word on the other hand is an MDI application. It enables you to show many documents at one time in its main window.

Making a Simple MDI Application

To make a simple MDI application, follow these steps. The forms and other components of the application have suggested names, but you should feel free to experiment and tailor the program to your needs.

1. Open New Project and rename this project as SIMPLMDI.VBP.
2. Rename the project's default form to frmChild. Save the form file with the name FRMCHILD.FRM.
3. Go to the Project menu and click Add MDI Form. This adds an MDI form to your project. Rename the MDI form to mdiMain. Save the form file with the file name MDIMAIN.FRM.
4. Set frmChild's MDIChild property to TRUE. This makes the form a child of mdiMain.
5. Strike the keys Ctrl+E. This brings up the Menu Editor.
6. Create a menu for the form mdiMain as shown in the Figure 15.3. Set the values of the Name and Caption properties of the menu and menu items as shown in Table 15.1. Make sure that you set the WindowList CheckBox for mnuWindow to checked. The WindowList CheckBox is on the mid-right side of the Menu Editor dialog box.

Table 15.1   Menu Object Names for SimplMDI

Caption	Name	Indent Level
&File	mnuFile	0
&Add	itmAdd	1
E&xit	itmExit	1

continues

Table 15.1   Continued

Caption	Name	Indent Level
&Window	mnuWindow	0
&Cascade	itmCascade	1
&Tile	itmTile	1

FIG. 15.3

Using the Menu
Editor, make a menu
for mdiMain.

7. Go to the Project menu, SimplMDI Properties… item (see Figure 15.4). Select the
General tab. In the Startup Object drop-down combo box located at the upper-right of the
dialog box, set the startup form to mdiMain (see Figure 15.5).

FIG. 15.4

The location of the VB
menu item to set
project properties has
changed in Visual
Basic 5.0.

8. Add the body of code between the lines `Private Sub itmAdd_Click()` and `End Sub`, in
Listing 15.1 to the `itmAdd_Click` event of mdiMain's menu.

FIG. 15.5
The Project Properties
dialog box has
become more
comprehensive in
Visual Basic 5.0.

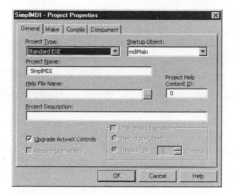

Listing 15.1 16LIST01.TXT— *itmAdd_Click ()* Event Handler for the Form mdiMain Creates and Shows New mdiChild Form—Notice the Event also Serialized the New Form's Caption

```
Private Sub itmAdd_Click()
Dim NewForm As New frmChild ' Declare another new form.
Dim FormNum%
'Add it to the new form
Load NewForm
'Get a number for the new form, less the MDI parent
FormNum% = Forms.Count - 1
' Set its caption
NewForm.Caption = "I am MDI child: " + CStr(FormNum%)
End Sub
```

9. Add the body of code between the lines `Private Sub itmExit_Click()` and `End Sub` in Listing 15.2 to the `itmExit_Click()` event handler.

Listing 15.2 16LIST02.TXT—The *itmExit_Click ()* Event Handler for Form mdiMain

```
Private Sub itmExit_Click()
End
End Sub
```

10. Add the code in Listing 15.3 to the `itmCascade_Click()` event handler.

Listing 15.3 16LIST03.TXT—The *itmCascade_Click ()* Event Handler for Form mdiMain

```
Private Sub itmCascade_Click()
Arrange vbCascade
End Sub
```

11. Add the body of code between the lines `Private Sub itmTile_Click()` and `End Sub` in Listing 15.4 to the `itmTile_Click()` event handler.

12. Compile and run the code.

Listing 15.4   16LIST04.TXT—*The itmTile_Click Event()* Handler for Form mdiMain

```
Private Sub itmTile_Click()
Arrange vbTileHorizontal
End Sub
```

The code for SimplMDI works this way: First you create a standard VB project and do some renaming. Then you add an `MDI form` to the project. You go back to the default form that was created when you originally made the project. You make it a child of the MDI form, mdiMain, by changing its `MDIChild` property to `True`. Then you bring up the Menu Editor and make a menu for the mdiMain form. You check the `WindowsList` CheckBox for mnuWindow. Checking `WindowList` enables the menu to list all the open windows of an `MDI form` object. After the menu is made, you change the startup form. Then you add the event handlers for the menu items. Finally, you compile and run the code. (Figure 15.6.)

FIG. 15.6

The project
SimplMDI.VBP
at runtime.

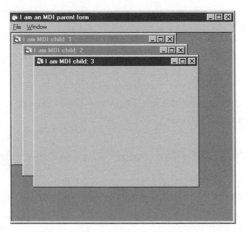

The `itmAdd_Click()` event procedure dynamically creates a new form using the `New` operator. The new form's caption has a number added to the end of the string assigned to it. This number, FormNum%, indicates the order in which the child form was created. FormNum% is determined by polling the application to report all of its forms using the `Forms.Count` property. Once all the forms are determined, 1 is subtracted. This is done because the application can have only one `MDIForm` object. Therefore, within the scope of this application, the resulting number must be the number of child forms the `MDIForm` object contains.

The application uses the `Arrange` method of the `MDIForm` object in the `itmCascade_Click()` and `itmTile_Click()` event handlers. The `Arrange` method automatically positions child windows within an MDI window. The `Arrange` method takes an argument, *arrangement*, that can be set to one of the following (see Table 15.2):

Table 15.2   Window *Arrange* Settings

Constant	Value	Description
vbCascade	0	Cascade all non-minimized MDI child forms
vbTileHorizontal	1	Tile all non-minimized MDI child forms
vbTileVertical	2	Tile all non-minimized MDI child forms vertically
vbArrangeIcons	3	Arrange icons for minimized MDI child forms

Once you have the basic framework for an MDI application in place, you can use the properties specific to the `MDIForm` object to make your application more engaging.

The *Appearance* Property

Users respond positively to forms with a three-dimensional (3-D) look and feel. Visual Basic provides a method for making 3-D forms simply by changing the `Appearance` property to `1 - 3D`.

TIP Be careful how many controls you place on a form. A form with too many controls can begin to look unpleasant. Forms should contain logical groupings of controls. The most common methods for grouping controls are spacing and using frames.

The *AutoShowChildren* Property

By default, the `AutoShowChildren` property is set to `False`. Thus, unless you remember to use the `Show` method in your code to display the form after you load it, the user will have to go through some sort of process to make the form visible. This can be a potential headache for you if you forget to use the `Show` method to display newly loaded form. When you set the `AutoShowChildren` property to `True`, an `MDIchild` form becomes visible when displayed using the `Load` statement. Doing this saves you programming time while also making your code more reliable.

Placing Applications Dynamically at Runtime

Well-designed programs have graphical interfaces that look right no matter what system on which they run. When you design an interface, you really have no idea of the environment in which your program eventually will run. Therefore, applications that you create should position and size their forms and controls correctly regardless of screen size, resolution, or color depth.

Relying on design-time sizing and placement, while good for most of the programs that you write, will not prove 100 percent reliable for all of them. In some cases you must rely on dynamic sizing and placement of your controls at runtime.

Figure 15.7 shows an example of a user interface that was designed and hard coded for an 800 × 600 pixel screen resolution at a twip size of 15, yet this computer has it displayed at a screen resolution of 640 × 480 at a twip per pixel size of 13. Because the design did not account for the 640 × 480, 13 twip display, the interface is distorted and unusable. Using dynamic sizing and placement would have served this programmer well.

FIG. 15.7
Hard coding form size and location can have serious consequences if the system's configuration does not conform to the programmer's expectation.

Centering Forms on the Screen

In most cases, when your program starts, you want your forms to be in the center of the screen as they appear. Visual Basic 5.0 has a new form property that enables you to set the startup position of a form at runtime. The property is StartUpPosition. You can set this property at runtime or at design time. You can choose from the following values of the StartUpPosition property (see Table 15.3) as follows:

Table 15.3   *StartUpPosition* **Property Values**

Constant	Value	Description
vbStartUpManual	0	No setting specified
vbStartUpOwner	1	Center on parent if form is a UserForm (Used with MS Office)
vbStartUpCenter	2	Center on screen
vbStartUpWindowsDefault	3	Position in upper-left corner of screen

Determining Screen Resolution with *ScreenInfo()*

If you want to have your forms display their contents correctly at runtime, you need to be able to elicit certain system properties such as screen width, height, and pixel size. After you know these display settings, you can adjust your controls to accommodate them.

Listing 15.5, the user-defined function ScreenInfo(), returns the width and height of the screen in pixels as well as the pixel size in twips, as set by the video card (see Figure 15.8). (You will cover user defined subs and functions in detail in Chapter 20, "Working with User-Defined Subs and Functions.") A function of this nature is important if you want to make sure that your form's controls are not spaced in such a way that they run off the form or that they are sized so small that all the necessary text is not visible. If you want to see an implementation of this function, take a look at the project SCREENFO.VBP in the CD-ROM that comes with this book. The function, ScreenInfo() is in the module MODSCRN.BAS.

Listing 15.5   16LIST05.TXT—The Function *ScreenInfo* Returns Important Information About the Screen Object

```
Public Function ScreenInfo(ScreenWidth As Integer, ScreenHeight As Integer) As
Integer
'**************************************************
'Function: ScreenInfo
'
'The Function return information about a system's screen
'object
'
'
'Arguments:
    'ScreenWidth As Integer      This integer argument is a pass
    '                            pass back reflecting the Screen.Width
    '                            in pixels
    '
    'ScreenHeight As Integer     This integer argument is a pass
    '                            pass back reflecting the Screen.Height
    '                            in pixels
    '
'Return: An integer reflecting the TwipsPerPixelX value.
    '**************************************************
Dim TwipX%, TwipY%, sw%, sh%
'Get the Twip Values
TwipX% = Screen.TwipsPerPixelX
TwipY% = Screen.TwipsPerPixelY
'Get the Screen width and convert it to pixels
sw% = Screen.Width / TwipX%
'Get the Screen Height and convert it to pixels
sh% = Screen.Height / TwipY%
'Return the Width
ScreenWidth = sw%
'Return the Height
ScreenHeight = sh%
'Return the TwipX
ScreenInfo = TwipX%
End Function
```

FIG. 15.8

The Screen Information program reports back the resolution of your computer's screen.

Dynamically Creating and Placing Controls

Imagine you have a work requirement for a program that you are writing that will not allow you to hard code the location of a control or set of controls. An example of this would be a toolbar in which the user must have the freedom to move and display controls as is appropriate for their need. In order to satisfy this requirement, you must be able to place controls relative to one another at runtime.

The project Dymanic.vbp demonstrates an example of how to dynamically place a control array of buttons either vertically or horizontally at runtime. In addition to placing the buttons, Dymanic.vbp writes the setting (Vertical or Horizontal) to the Windows 95 Registry using the Visual Basic Registry functions. Saving the position setting and later retrieving it from the Registry during the Form_Load event enables the location of the controls to persist from session to session. (If you want to follow along, the complete code for the project Dymanic.vbp is in the directory \Chp_16\Dynamic on the CD-ROM that accompanies this book.)

▶ **See** "Working with Control Arrays," **p. 349** for more information about Control Arrays.

To make Dymanic.vbp, remember that even though example names for forms, modules, and so on are provided, you can name these components according to your program's needs. Follow these steps:

1. Create a new project and rename this project as Dymanic.vbp.

2. Rename the default form to frmDynamic and save the form file with the file name frmDyNam.frm.

3. Set the Caption property of the form to "Dynamic Control."

4. Set the BorderStyle of the form to 3-Fixed Dialog.

5. Add the module ModAlign.bas to the project. This file can be found on the CD-ROM that comes with this book, in the directory Chp_16\Dynamic\.

6. Add a CommandButton to the upper-left corner of the form and leave the name of the button as the default, Command1. Leave the caption of the button as Command1. Set the Index property of the CommandButton equal to 0 to create a CommandButton control array. This is very important!

7. Strike Ctrl+E to bring up the Menu Editor. Create a menu as shown in Figure 15.9. Name the objects as shown in Table 15.4.

Table 15.4 Menu Settings for the Project Dynamic.vbp

Caption	Name	Indents
&File	mnuFile	0
&Layout	itmLayout	1
&Vertical	itmVertical	2
&Horizontal	itmHorizontal	2
•	SepOne	1
E&xit	itmExit	1

FIG. 15.9
Don't forget that the separator dashes must be indented at least one level.

8. Add the code in Listing 15.6 to the Declarations section of frmDynamic.

Listing 15.6   16LIST06.TXT—The Code for the frmDynamic Declarations Section

```
Option Explicit
Public gNumOfButtons%
Public Sub LoadButtons(NumOfButtons As Integer)
    '***************************************************
'Procedure: LoadButtons
    '
'The procedure dynamically loads buttons into a
'conrol array
'Aruguments: NumOfButtons As Integer  , the number of
'buttons you want to have on the form. Not the number
'of buttons to load.
    '
    '***************************************************
Dim i%
For i% = 1 To NumOfButtons
Load Command1(i)
```

continues

Listing 15.6 Continued

```
Next i%
End Sub
Public Sub SetButtonsVert(NumOfButtons As Integer)
    '************************************************
'Procedure: SetButtonsVert
    '
'The procedure dynamically arranges a set of buttons
'from a control array into a vertical line. It
'also saves the alignment to the registry using the
'SaveSetting Registry procedure from Visual Basic
    '
'Arugments: NumOfButtons As Integer
    '
    '
    '************************************************
Dim i%
'Iterate through the control array, doing a value check
'NumOfButtons.
If NumOfButtons > 0 Then
'Iterate through the controls
For i% = 1 To NumOfButtons
'Align the Left of the control to the Left of
'the previous control.
Command1(i%).Left = Command1(i% - 1).Left
'Set the control directly below the previous
'control
Command1(i%).Top = Command1(i% - 1).Top + _
Command1(i% - 1).Height
'Set the control visible to true
Command1(i%).Visible = True
Next i%
'Enable the "Horizontal"menu item
itmHorizontal.Enabled = True
'Disable the "Vertical"menu item"
itmVertical.Enabled = False
'Let the Registry know that the buttons are
'now set vertically ("V"), so if can arrange
'the controls this way on startup.
Call SaveSetting(App.Title, "Orientation", "Buttons", "V")
End If
End Sub
Public Sub SetButtonsHorz(NumOfButtons As Integer)
    '************************************************
'Procedure: SetButtonsHorz
    '
'The procedure dynamically arranges a set of buttons
'from a control array into a horizontal line. It
'also saves the alignment to the registry using the
'SaveSetting Registry procedure from Visual Basic
'Arugments: NumOfButtons As Integer
    '
    '
    '************************************************
Dim i%
```

```
'Iterate through the control array, doing a value check
'NumOfButtons.
If NumOfButtons > 0 Then
For i% = 1 To NumOfButtons
'Set the control to the top of the previous one
Command1(i%).Top = Command1(i% - 1).Top
'Set the control to the direct right of the previous one
Command1(i%).Left = Command1(i% - 1).Left + Command1(i% - 1).Width
'Make it visible
Command1(i%).Visible = True
Next i%
'Disable the "Horizontal"menu item
itmHorizontal.Enabled = False
'Enable the "Vertical"menu item
itmVertical.Enabled = True
'Let the Registry know that the buttons are
'now set horizontally ("H"), so if can arrange
'the controls this way on startup.
Call SaveSetting(App.Title, "Orientation", "Buttons", "H")
End If
End Sub
```

9. Add the body of code between the lines, `Private Sub Form_Load()` and `End Sub`, in Listing 15.7 to the `Form_Load()` event of frmDynamic.

Listing 15.7   16LIST07.TXT—The *Form_Load* Event Handler for the Form frmDynamic

```
Private Sub Form_Load()
Dim Orientation$
'Set how many buttons you want to display
'including the one already on the form.
gNumOfButtons = 5

'Load the buttons
Call LoadButtons(gNumOfButtons)
'Get the orientation setting from the Registry
'using the Visual Basic GettSetting function.
Orientation$ = GetSetting(App.Title, "Orientation", "Buttons", "V")
'Set the orientation of the buttons
If Orientation$ = "V"Then
Call SetButtonsVert(gNumOfButtons)
Else
Call SetButtonsHorz(gNumOfButtons)
End If
'Set the form Caption
frmDynamic.Caption = "Dynamic Control Generation Demo"
'Center the form using a custom function
Call CenterForm(Me)
End Sub
```

10. Add the code in Listing 15.8 to the menu item's Click event procedure.

11. Compile and run the code.

Listing 15.8   16LIST08.TXT—The Menu Item's Click Event Handlers for the Form frmDynamic

```
Private Sub itmHorizontal_Click()
Call SetButtonsHorz(gNumOfButtons)
End Sub
Private Sub itmVertical_Click()
Call SetButtonsVert(gNumOfButtons)
End Sub
Private Sub itmExit_Click()
End
End Sub
```

In this project the work of positioning the `CommandButton` control array is handled by the user defined procedures, `SetButtonsHorz` and `SetButtonsVert`.

▶ **See** Chapter 20, "Working with User-Defined Subs and Functions," for more information about User-Defined Subs and Functions **p. 313**

The key to these procedures is the `For...Next` statement that enables the program to iterate through all the members of the control array. In the case of a horizontal alignment, the `Top` property of the CommandButtons in the array are set to the `Top` of the first array member. Then, the `Left` property is set to be the value of the previous member's `Left` plus the value of the previous member's `Width` property, effectively setting all members next to each other.

In a vertical alignment, which is done by calling the Sub `SetButtonsVert`, the methodology of the iteration is reversed. The `Left` property of all members of the control array are all set to the first member and the `Top` properties are set to the `Top` of the previous member plus the `Height` of the previous member (see Figure 15.10.)

FIG. 15.10

The application, Dynamic Control Generation Demo allows you to create controls on a form, dynamically, at runtime.

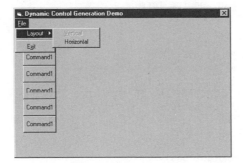

Using the Visual Basic Registry Functions

In the preceding sections you saw that the functions `SetButtonsHorz()` and `SetButtonsVert()` used the some Visual Basic functions to save and retrieve data to the Windows Registry. Let's take a look at these functions in more detail.

Visual Basic comes with four procedures that you can use to access the Windows 95 Registry. These procedures are `DeleteSetting`, `GetSettng`, `GetAllSettings`, and `SaveSetting`. These procedures are easy to use as the following example demonstrates. However, these internal Registry functions have one major drawback: Visual Basic only can get and write data to a specific key in the Registry, `MyComputer\HKEY_CURRENT\USER\Software\VB and VBA Program Settings`. This process is automatic to VB. Visual Basic cannot write to or read from any other keys in the Registry without the aid of the `Win32 API` functions. Figure 15.11 shows the location of the Visual Basic application keys in the Windows 95 Registry.

FIG. 15.11
When you use the Registry functions internal to VB, data is saved in a key dedicated to all VB and VBA applications.

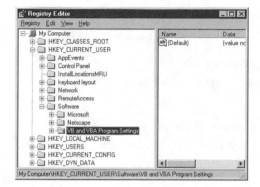

Retrieving Values with *GetSetting()*

You use the `GetSetting()` function to retrieve a value from a particular section in Visual Basic key of the Windows Registry. The syntax for the `GetSetting()` function is:

```
MyString = GetSetting(VBKeyName, Section, Key [,Default]).
```
Where:

> `MyString` is the string value returned by `GetSetting`.
>
> `GetSetting` is the name of the function.
>
> `VBKeyName` is a string value that is the name of the key within the VB/VBA area of the Registry.
>
> `Section` is string value representing the section or sub_key for the specific applications setting.
>
> `Key` is a string value that represents the name of a specific entry within the section. A section can have many keys.

The optional argument `Default` is a string value that represents the value to return if GetSettings fails or encounters an error.

If the function is successful, it returns the string found at the key setting. If it is unsuccessful it returns the string value assigned to the argument `Default`.

Thus the code snippet:

```
Return$ = GetSetting(App.Title, "FormInit", "Left", DefaultLeft$)
```

looks for a Registry entry as shown in Figure 15.12. If it fails, it returns the value assigned to the example string, `DefaultLeft$`.

Saving Values to the Registry with the *SaveSetting* Statement

If you want to save a value to the `MyComputer\HKEY_CURRENT\USER\Software\VB and VBA Program Settings` key in the Registry, you use the `SaveSetting` statement.

The syntax for the `SaveSetting` statement is:

```
SaveSettings VBKeyName, Section, Key, Setting
```

Where:

> `SaveSetting` is the statement name.
>
> `VBKeyName` is a string value that is the name of the key within the VB/VBA area of the Registry.
>
> `Section` is string value representing the section or sub_key for the specific applications setting.
>
> `Key` is a string value that represents the name of a specific entry within the section. A section can have many keys.
>
> `Setting` is a string value that you want to set to a given key.

This procedure relates closely to the `GetSetting()` function. It is the inverse. Where you use `GetSetting()` to retrieve a VB value from a specified key in the Registry, you use `SaveSetting` to set a value to the given VB key. All arguments, except for the last one, are identical.

Thus, the code snippet:

```
SaveSettingApp.Title, "FormInit", "Left", "975"
```

produces the Registry setting shown in the Figure 15.12.

FIG. 15.12

A Registry entry of values for a Visual Basic application.

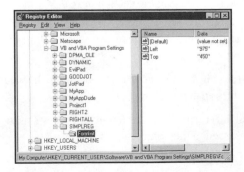

Retrieving an Array of Settings with *GetAllSettings()*

You use the Visual Basic function GetAllSettings() to retrieve an array from the Registry that contains all of the key settings and those key's respective values of a particular section within MyComputer\HKEY_CURRENT\USER\Software\VB and VBA Program Settings. The syntax for GetAllSettings() is:

```
MyVariant = GetAllSettings(VBKeyName, Section)
```

Where:

> MyVariant is an array of values returned by the function, of type, variant.
>
> GetAllSettings is the function name.
>
> VBKeyName is a string value that is the name of the key within the VB/VBA area of the Registry.
>
> Section is the string value representing the section to query.

When you use GetAllSettings(), the function returns a two dimensional array in the form of a variant. To get the values, you transverse the array as you would any other.

▶ **See** Chapter 10, "Working with Arrays," on **p. 143** for more information about how to traverse an array.

Deleting a Key Section with the *DeleteSetting* Statement

If you want to delete an entire section from a Key, you use the DeleteSetting statement. The syntax for the DeleteSetting statement is:

```
DeleteSetting VBKeyName, Section, Key
```

Where:

> DeleteSetting is the statement name.
>
> VBKeyName is a string value that is the name of the key within the VB/VBA of the Registry.
>
> Section is the string value representing the section to delete.
>
> Key is the string value representing a specific subKey to delete. If you do not set this parameter (which is optional), all the subKeys of the section are deleted.

Thus, the code snippet:

```
DeleteSetting App.Title, "FormInit"
```

deletes the Registry setting shown previously in Figure 15.12. ●

CHAPTER 16

Using Dialog Boxes

A dialog box works much as the name implies; it enables the program and the user to communicate briefly about a specific topic. For instance, you might want your program to inform the user that he or she has committed an error. Or, you might want to present the user with a set of choices to make or options to choose from that are specific to a certain operation. You use dialog boxes to do these things.

This chapter shows you the different types of dialog boxes, and it shows you how to make and use each type. ■

Message boxes

Make message boxes using the `MsgBox` statement and `MsgBox()` function.

OptionButtons and *CheckBoxes*

Learn how to use `OptionButtons` and `Checkboxes` to set conditions and make decisions.

Input boxes

Learn how to allow the user to enter data in your program using input boxes.

Common dialog boxes

Learn how to use common dialog boxes to save files, set fonts, and print documents in your program.

Custom dialog boxes

Learn how to make custom dialog boxes to meet special requirements in your programs.

Creating Message Boxes

The *message box* is a simple form that displays a message and at least one CommandButton (see Figure 16.1).

FIG. 16.1

A message box is task modal. This means that the application cannot continue until the message box is closed.

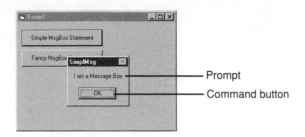

Prompt

Command button

The CommandButton is used to acknowledge the message. Optionally, the message box can display an icon or use multiple buttons to let the user make a decision. Message boxes can be used in either of two ways. You can use the message box to simply display information, or you can use the message box to get a decision from the user.

Listing 16.1 is code for a MsgBox statement that displays a message box as shown in Figure 16.1.

Listing 16.1   16LIST01.TXT—The Code for a Simple Message Box

```
Private Sub Command1_Click()
    MsgBox "I am a Message Box"
End Sub
```

Choosing Between the *MsgBox* Function and the *MsgBox* Statement

You can display a message box using the MsgBox statement or the MsgBox() function. The difference between them is that the function displays the message box and returns a value, but the statement displays only the message box. Also, there is a slight syntactical difference—the use of parentheses and a return value is required for the MsgBox() function.

The syntax for a MsgBox statement is:

```
MsgBox strMessage, Options strTitle, strHelpFile, HelpContextID
```

The syntax for a MsgBox() function is:

```
RetInt = MsgBox (strMessage, Options strTitle, strHelpFile, HelpContextID)
```

Where:

> *RetInt* is an integer that stores the value of the return from the `MsgBox()` function.
>
> *MsgBox* is the statement/function name.
>
> *StrMessage* is a string expression to display in the message area of the message box.
>
> *Options* is an integer constant(s) that determines what button (or combination of buttons) and icons to display in the message box. *Usage is optional*.
>
> *StrTitle* is a string expression to display in the title bar of the message box. *Usage is optional*.
>
> *strHelpFile* is a string that reflects to the path of the Help file that provides additional information that pertains to the topic of the message box. *Usage is optional*.
>
> *HelpContextID* is a help context ID constant that references a topic in the Help file as determined by `strHelpFile`. *Usage is optional*.

The simple message box is acceptable for many types of messages, but you probably will want to dress up your messages a little more. You can specify two optional arguments for the `MsgBox` statement and `MsgBox()` function—the `Options` argument and the `strTitle` argument. The `Options` argument is an integer number that specifies the icon to display in the message box, the CommandButton(s) set to display, and which of the CommandButtons is the default. The `strTitle` argument is a text string that specifies custom text to be shown in the title bar of the message box. Figure 16.2 shows a simple message box that has been enhanced to show an icon and additional buttons. The code that displays the message box is shown in Listing 16.2.

FIG. 16.2

Adding an appropriate icon and additional buttons enhances the utility of the message box.

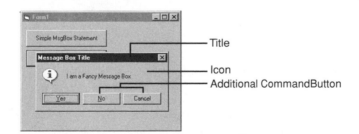

Title
Icon
Additional CommandButton

Listing 16.2   16LIST02.TXT—Combining the *Button* Constant and *Icon* Constant to Create a Value for the *Options* Parameter

```
Private Sub Command2_Click()
    MsgBox "I am a Fancy Message Box", _
           vbInformation + vbYesNoCancel, _
           "Message Box Title"
End Sub
```

Adding Icons to Message Boxes

You have a choice of four icons to display in a message box. These icons and their purposes are summarized in Table 16.1.

Table 16.1   Message Box Icons and Constants

Icon	Constant	Icon Name	Purpose
❌	vbCritical	Critical message	Indicates that a severe error has occurred. Often a program is shut down after this message.
⚠️	vbExclamation	Warning message	Indicates that a program error has occurred that requires user correction or that may lead to undesirable results.
❓	vbQuestion	Query	Indicates that the program requires additional information from the user before processing can continue.
ℹ️	vbInformation	Information Message	Informs the user of the status of the program. Most often used to notify the user of the completion of a task.

If you are wondering how you are going to remember the syntax of the MsgBox statement/function and the constants to be used for the options, don't worry. The new statement completion capabilities of Visual Basic's Code Editor help tremendously. When you type the space after the MsgBox statement/function name in the Code window, a popup appears that shows you the syntax of the command (see Figure 16.3).

After you enter the message to be displayed and enter a comma, Visual Basic pops up a list of constants that can be used to add an icon to the message box, or to specify the button set to be used. You can select one of the constants from the list by pressing Ctrl+Enter or typing it in yourself.

FIG. 16.3

Syntax help bolds the argument to which you are assigning a value.

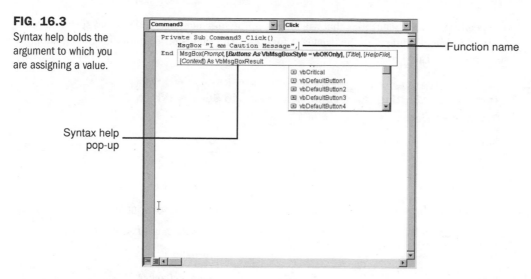

Function name

Syntax help pop-up

Retrieving a Value from the *MsgBox()* Function

The MsgBox statement, as described previously, works fine for informing users of a problem or prompting them to take an action. However, if you need to get a decision from the user, you need to return a value using the MsgBox() function. (The syntax for the function is described earlier.)

You can use six sets of command buttons in the MsgBox() function:

- *OK.* Displays a single button with the caption OK. This simply asks the user to acknowledge receipt of the message before continuing.

- *OK, Cancel.* Displays two buttons in the message box, letting the user choose between accepting the message and requesting a cancellation of the operation.

- *Abort, Retry, Ignore.* Displays three buttons, usually along with an error message. The user can choose to abort the operation, retry it, or ignore the error and continue with program execution.

- *Yes, No, Cancel.* Displays three buttons, typically with a question. The user can answer yes or no to the question, or choose to cancel the operation.

- *Yes, No.* Displays two buttons for a simple yes or no choice.

- *Retry, Cancel.* Displays the two buttons that allow the user to retry the operation or cancel it. A typical use is to indicate that the printer is not responding. The user can either retry or cancel the printout.

To specify the CommandButtons that will appear in the message box, you need to specify a value for the Options argument of the MsgBox() function. The values for each of the command-button sets appear in Table 16.2.

Table 16.2   Setting the Options Argument to Specify Which Set of Buttons to Use

Button Set	Value	Constant
OK	0	vbOKOnly
OK, Cancel	1	vbOKCancel
Abort, Retry, Ignore	2	VBAbortRetryIgnore
Yes, No, Cancel	3	vbYesNoCancel
Yes, No	4	vbYesNo
Retry, Cancel	5	vbRetryCancel

The MsgBox() function is designed so that any combination of the icon constant and the CommandButton constant creates a unique value. This value is then broken down by the function to specify the individual pieces. The code shown earlier in Listing 16.2 combines an icon constant and CommandButton constant to create an information message with three buttons, Yes, No, and Cancel. The results of the code were illustrated in earlier Figure 16.2.

N O T E   When you use the pop-up constants list, you can select a second constant by entering a plus sign (+) after the first constant. ◼

Setting a Default Button on a Message Box

If you are using more than one CommandButton in the message box, you can also specify which button is the default. The *default button* is the one that has focus when the message box is displayed. This button is the one that the user is most likely to choose or that will be clicked if the user just automatically presses Enter.

To specify which button is the default, you need to add another constant to the Options argument of the MsgBox() function. These are identified in the following table:

Default Button	Value	Constant
First	0	vbDefaultButton1
Second	256	vbDefaultButton2
Third	512	vbDefaultButton3
Fourth	768	vbDefaultButton4

You can choose from seven buttons, with the selection depending on the button set used in the message box. Each of these buttons, when clicked, returns a different value to your program (see Table 16.3).

Table 16.3   Return Values Indicate the User's Choice

Button	Value	Constant
OK	1	vbOK
Cancel	2	vbCancel
Abort	3	vbAbort
Retry	4	vbRetry
Ignore	5	vbIgnore
Yes	6	vbYes
No	7	vbNo

After you know which button was selected by the user, you can use the information in your program. Listing 16.3 shows code to confirm the deletion of a file:

Listing 16.3   16LIST03.TXT—Using a Custom Configured Confirmation Message Box

```
Private Sub Command4_Click()
Dim strTextFile As String    'path of file to delete
    Dim Msg$                     'Message box message
    Dim OpVal%                   'Option value variable
    Dim RetVal%                  'variable for return value
    Dim TitleMsg$                'Title message variable

    'Set the file to delete
    strTextFile = "MYDATA.TXT"

    'Create a message for the message box
    Msg$ = "Do you really want to delete file: '"
    Msg$ = Msg$ & strTextFile & "'?"

    'Create a custom value for the Option parameter
    OpVal% = vbExclamation + vbYesNo + vbDefaultButton2

    'Create a title string
    TitleMsg$ = "Delete Confirmation"

    'Display the message box and get a return value
    RetVal% = MsgBox(Msg$, OpVal%, TitleMsg$)

    'If the value is Yes, set the commandButton
    'caption to report that the Kill function as
```

continues

Listing 16.3   Continued

```
'been selected
If RetVal% = vbYes Then
    Command4.Caption = "Kill " & strTextFile
End If


End Sub
```

If you want to see this code in action, the preceding examples can be reviewed in the project SimplMsg.VBP in the directory \Chp_16\SimplMsg\ on the CD-ROM that accompanies this book.

Creating Input Boxes

Many times in a program, you need to get a single piece of information from the user. You might need the user to enter a person's name, the name of a file, or a number for various purposes. Although the message box lets your users make choices, it does not allow them to enter information in response to the message. Therefore, you have to use some other means to get the information. Visual Basic provides a second built-in dialog box for exactly this purpose: the *input box*.

The input box displays a message to tell the user what to enter, a text box where the user can enter the data, and two command buttons—OK and Cancel—that can be used to either accept or abort the input data. A sample input box is shown in Figure 16.4.

FIG. 16.4

Using the InputBox() function is a fast way to get data from the user.

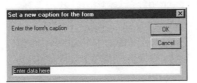

The input box works much like the message box with a return value. You specify a variable to receive the information returned from the input box and then supply the message and (optionally) a title and default value as arguments to the function. The syntax used for the InputBox() function is the following:

```
strRetVal = InputBox(strMessage, strtTitle, strDefaulTitle, xPos, yPos,
strHelpFile, HelpContextID)
```

Where:

strRetVal is a string that stores the value of the return from the InputBox() function.

InputBox is a function name.

strMessage is a string expression to display in the message area of the input box.

strTitle is a string literal or variable to display in the title bar of the input box. *Usage is optional.*

strDefalutTitle is a string literal or variable to display default text in the input area. *Usage is optional.*

xPos is the horizontal position at which to place the input box (in twips). *Usage is optional.*

yPos is the vertical position at which to place the input box (in twips). *Usage is optional.*

strHelpFile is a string that reflects to the path of the Help file that provides additional information that pertains to the topic of the message box. *Usage is optional.*

HelpContextID is a help context ID constant that references a topic in the Help file as determined by strHelpFile. *Usage is optional.*

When you use the input box, the user can enter data in the box and then choose OK or Cancel. If the user chooses OK, the input box returns whatever text is in the input field. If the user chooses Cancel, the input box returns an empty string, regardless of what the user typed.

Listing 16.4 shows code that uses the InputBox() function to set the Caption of a form.

Listing 16.4   16LIST04.TXT—Using an Input Box to Set the Value of a Control Property

```
Private Sub Form_Load()
    Dim Msg$                'variable to message
    Dim TitleMsg$           'variable to hold text for title bar
    Dim DefaultMsg$         'default message for input area
    Dim RetMsg$             'string return value

    'Set the message variable
    Msg$ = "Enter the form's caption"

    'Set the title variable
    TitleMsg$ = "Set a new caption for the form"

    'Set the default text variable
    DefaultMsg$ = "Enter data here"

    'Display the Input box and assign the return
    'to the return variable
    RetMsg$ = InputBox(Msg$, TitleMsg$, DefaultMsg$)

    'Check to make sure that the user did not
    'enter blank text
    If RetMsg$ <> "" Then
        'If it's not blank assign the return
        'to the form's caption
        frmInput.Caption = RetMsg$
    Else
        'If it is blank then assign an internal
        'value to the caption.
        frmInput.Caption = "Input Exercise"
    End If
End Sub
```

The code for the input box examples is in the project `InputStuff.VBP` in the directory `\Chp_16\InputBox`.

Getting User Input from the *CommonDialog* Control

At some point you'll probably want to write a program in which your users will need to be able to specify file names, select fonts and colors, and control the printer. Although you could create your own dialog boxes to handle these tasks, there is no need to do so. Visual Basic provides you with the `CommonDialog` control, which allows you to easily display predefined dialog boxes to obtain information from the user. And although the ease of setup is a great benefit, an even bigger bonus is that these dialog boxes are already familiar to the user. This is because they are the same dialog boxes used by Windows itself.

Using a single `CommonDialog` control, you have access to the following four Windows dialog boxes:

- *File.* Lets the user select a file to open or choose a file name in which to save information.
- *Font.* Lets the user choose a base font and set any font attributes that are desired.
- *Color.* Lets the user choose from a standard color or create a custom color for use in the program.
- *Print.* Lets the user select a printer and set some of the printer parameters.

To access the `CommonDialog` control, you first have to add it to your project by selecting it from the Components dialog box (see Figure 16.5). This dialog box is accessible by clicking the Components form in the Project menu. After the `CommonDialog` control is added to your Toolbox, you can add the control to a form by clicking the control and drawing it on the form just like any other control. The `CommonDialog` control appears on your form as an icon; the control itself is not visible when your application is running.

FIG. 16.5

The `CommonDialog` control is an ActiveX control that comes with Visual Basic 5.0.

Check the `CommonDialog` ActiveX control.

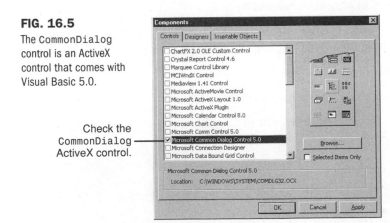

The following sections discusses each type of dialog box that can be accessed with the CommonDialog control. For each of these dialog boxes, you must set the properties of the control. You can do this through the Properties window, or you can use the CommonDialog control's Property Pages dialog box. The Property Pages dialog box provides you easy access to the specific properties that are necessary for each of the common dialog box types (see Figure 16.6). You access the Property Pages dialog box by clicking the ellipsis button in the Custom property of the CommonDialog control in the Properties window.

Part
III

Ch
16

FIG. 16.6
The elements of the CommonDialog ActiveX control.

CommonDialog control

Access the property page from the Custom property in the Properties windows by clicking the ellipsis

CommonDialog icon

Property page

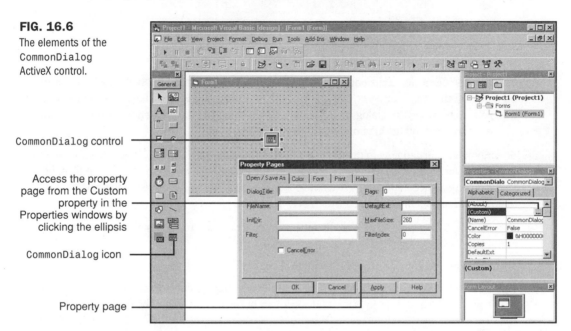

Retrieving File Information with the File Dialog Box

A key use of the CommonDialog control is to obtain file names from the user. The CommonDialog control can be used in either of two modes: file open and file save. The file open mode lets the user specify a file to be retrieved and used by your program. The file save mode lets the user specify a name for a file to be saved. This is the equivalent of the Save As dialog box for many programs.

The dialog boxes for the Open and Save functions are similar. Figure 16.7 shows the dialog box with the major components indicated.

To open an existing file, you use the ShowOpen method of the CommonDialog control. (This method displays the dialog box shown in Figure 16.7.) You use this method by specifying the name of the CommonDialog control and the method name, as shown in the following line of code:

```
CdlGetFile.ShowOpen
```

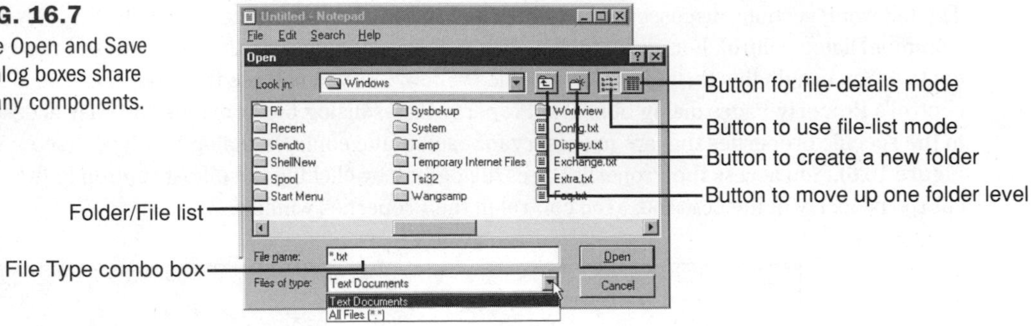

FIG. 16.7
The Open and Save dialog boxes share many components.

Button for file-details mode
Button to use file-list mode
Button to create a new folder
Button to move up one folder level
Folder/File list
File Type combo box

Running the `CommonDialog` control to get a file name to save is essentially the same as for opening a file. In this case, however, the name of the method is `ShowSave`. There are a few subtle differences between the dialog boxes shown for the `Open` and `Save` functions, such as the title of the dialog box and the captions on the command buttons.

So far, you've learned how to display the File dialog boxes with all files shown in a folder. You may, however, want to specify that only certain file types, such as text or document files, be shown. You can accomplish this with the `CommonDialog` control. The file types shown in the dialog box are specified by using the `Filter` property.

You set the `Filter` property either in design mode from the Properties dialog box, or at runtime with an assignment statement as shown here:

```
controlname.Filter = "description¦filtercond"
```

Here, `controlname` is the assigned name of the `CommonDialog` control, and `Filter` is the name of the property. `description` is a text description of the type of files to be shown. Examples of the description are "Text Files," "Word Documents," and "All Files." The vertical line is known as the *pipe symbol*. This symbol must be present. The `filtercond` is the actual filter for the files. You typically express the filter as an asterisk followed by a period and the extension of the files that you want to display. The filters that correspond to the preceding descriptions are `*.txt`, `*.doc`, and `*.*`, respectively.

> **CAUTION**
> Do not include spaces before or after the pipe symbol, or you may not get the file list that you want.

If you specify the `Filter` property with an assignment statement, you must enclose the filter in double quotes. The quotes are omitted if you specify the filter from the Properties dialog box.

You can specify multiple `description¦filtercond` pairs within the `Filter` property. Each pair must be separated from the other pairs by the pipe symbol, as shown in the following example:

```
GetFile.Filter = "Text Documents¦*.txt ¦All Files (*.*)¦*.*"
```

Take a look at the FileType ComboBox in Figure 16.7 to see the preceding code applied to a common dialog box.

Lastly, once all your filtering is set, you use the `FileName` property of the `CommonDialog` control to retrieve the name of the file that the user selected. The syntax for this property is:

`MyFileName$ = GetFile.FileName.`

Selecting Font Information with the Font Dialog Box

Setting up the `CommonDialog` control to show the Font dialog box is just as easy as setting it up for file functions. In fact, you can use the same `CommonDialog` control to handle file, font, color, and printer functions.

The first step in using the `CommonDialog` control to handle font selection is to set a value for the `Flags` property. This property tells the `CommonDialog` control whether you want to show screen fonts, printer fonts, or both. The `Flags` property can be set to one of the three constants listed in the following table:

Font Set	Constant	Value
Screen fonts	`cdlCFScreenFonts`	1
Printer fonts	`cdlCFPrinterFonts`	2
Both sets	`cdlCFBoth`	3

CAUTION

If you do not set a value for the `Flags` property, you get an error message stating that no fonts are installed.

You can set the value of the `Flags` property from the design environment by using the Properties dialog box or from your program by using an assignment statement. After the `Flags` property has been set, you can run the Font dialog box from your code using the `ShowFont` method. This method has the same syntax as the `ShowOpen` method, described earlier. Figure 16.8 shows the Font dialog box presented to the user. This particular dialog box contains only screen fonts.

FIG. 16.8

The Font common dialog box lets the user select fonts.

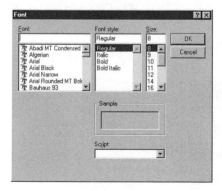

The information about the fonts chosen from the CommonDialog control is contained in the control's properties. Table 16.4 shows the control's properties and the font attributes that each manipulates.

Table 16.4   Control Properties that Store Font Attributes

Property	Attribute
FontName	The name of the base font
FontSize	The height of the font in points
FontBold	Whether boldface was selected
FontItalic	Whether italic was selected
FontUnderline	Whether the font is underlined
FontStrikethru	Whether the font has a line through it

The font information can be used to set the font of any control in your program, or even to set the font for the Printer object. The following code shows how the font information would be retrieved and used to change the fonts in a TextBox:

```
GetFont.ShowFont
txtSample.FontName = GetFont.FontName
txtSample.FontSize = GetFont.FontSize
txtSample.FontBold = GetFont.FontBold
txtSample.FontItalic = GetFont.FontItalic
txtSample.FontUnderline = GetFont.FontUnderline
txtSample.FontStrikethru = GetFont.FontStrikethru
```

Selecting Colors with the Color Dialog Box

The CommonDialog control's Color dialog box lets the user select colors that can be used for the foreground or background colors of your forms or controls (see Figure 16.9). The user has the option of choosing one of the standard colors or creating and selecting a custom color.

FIG. 16.9
The Color common dialog box lets your users choose a color to use in the program.

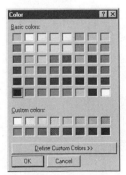

Setting up the CommonDialog control for colors basically is the same as for fonts. You set the Flags property to the constant cdlCCRGBInit and then call the ShowColor method.

When the user selects a color from the dialog box, its color value is stored in the Color property of the control. The following code shows how to change a form's background color using the Color dialog box:

```
GetColor.Flags = cdlCCRGBInit
GetColor.ShowColor
Myform.BackColor = GetColor.Color
```

Setting Printer Options with the Print Dialog Box

The CommonDialog control's Print dialog box lets the user select which printer to use for a printout and specify options for the print process (see Figure 16.10). These options include specifying all pages, a range of pages, or the selection to print. There is also an option to specify the number of copies to be printed, as well as an option to print to a file.

FIG. 16.10

The Print common dialog box lets the user select which printer to use and specify print options.

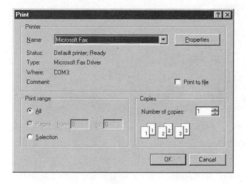

To run the Print dialog box, just call the CommonDialog control's ShowPrinter method. No flags are set prior to the call.

After the Print dialog box is displayed, the user can select the printer from the Name list at the top of the dialog box. This list contains all the printers installed in Windows. Right below the Name list is the Status line, which tells you the current status of the selected printer.

The Print dialog box returns the information from the user in the dialog box's properties. The FromPage and ToPage properties tell you the starting and ending pages of the printout selected by the user. The Copies property tells you how many copies the user wants printed.

This is provided only as information. The Print dialog box does not automatically set up the desired printout. Your program must do that.

The code for the CommonDiaglog control examples is in the project SimpleCD.VBP in the directory \Chp_16\SimplCD.

Creating Your Own Dialog Boxes

Although Visual Basic provides you with a number of dialogs—such as the message box and input box—to use in your programs, sometimes there are things that you need to do that just can't be accomplished with these built-in tools. For instance, you might need a dialog box that displays a ComboBox that contains a list of possible captions for your program's main form.

To make such a dialog box, follow these steps. Remember that names of forms, buttons, and so on are only suggestions and that you can alter them to your taste.

1. Open a New project. Name the project CustDlg. Name the default form frmMain. Set the value of the Caption property to "and empty string," which means no text should be present in the value area of the Caption property in the Properties window.

2. From the Project menu, select Add Form to add an additional form to the project. Name the additional form frmCustDlg. Set the value of the BorderStyle for the form to 3-Fixed Dialog and the value of the StartUpPosition to 2-CenterScreen (see Figure 16.11).

FIG. 16.11
The Add Form menu item shows you an Add Form dialog box from which you can choose many types of predefined forms.

3. Add a ComboBox and two CommandButtons to the form frmCustDialog. Name the ComboBox cboCaptions. Name the CommandButtons cmdOK and cmdCancel, respectively. Set the value of the Style property of the ComboBox to 2-Dropdown ListSet. Set the size and position of the controls as shown in Figure 16.12.

FIG. 16.12
When you set the style of the combo box to 2-Dropdown List, initially, the combo box appears without text.

4. Add a CheckBox to frmCustDlg. Set the value of the Name property of the CheckBox to chkShowTime and the value of the Caption property to "Show Time in Main Form." (Omit the quotes) Set the Value property of chkShowTime to 1-Checked. Set the size and position of the CheckBox as shown in Figure 16.13.

5. Add two `OptionButtons`. Set the value of the `Name` property for one to optTime and set the value of the `Caption` property to "Time Only." (Omit the quotes.) Set the `Value` property of optTime to `True`. Set the size and position of optTime as shown in Figure 16.13.

6. Set the value of the `Name` property of the other `OptionButton` to optTimeDate and set the value of the `Caption` property to "Time and Date." (Omit the quotes.) Set the size and position of optTimedDate as shown in Figure 16.13.

FIG. 16.13

You use a CheckBox to set and clear a condition. You use OptionButtons to choose among exclusive choices.

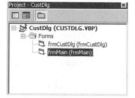

7. Double-click frmMain in the Project Explorer to bring the form into the Designer (see Figure 16.14).

FIG. 16.14

You can use the Project Explorer to move among forms and modules and bring a form or code window into the Designer.

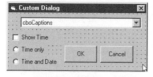

8. Add a `CommandButton` to frmMain. Name the `CommandButton` cmdSettings. Set the value of the `Caption` to "Settings." Size and position the `CommandButton` as shown in Figure 16.15.

FIG. 16.15

An ellipsis (...) means that a dialog box will appear when the button is clicked.

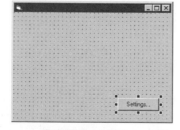

9. Type the code in Listing 16.5 into the `cmdSettings_Click()` event procedure of the CommandButton cmdSettings. (Ignore the code comments, if you want, and make sure that you change the names in the code if you've given your objects different names.)

Listing 16.5 o_LIST0a.TXT—Using the Constant *vbModal*

```
Private Sub cmdSettings_Click()
    Dim Msg$      'Message variable
    Dim TimeMsg$  'Time variable

    'Show the custom dialog task modally.
    'This means that the program cannot continue
    'until the custom form is closed.
    frmCustDlg.Show vbModal

    'Assign the text in the ComboBox to the caption
    'of the Main form.

    'Make sure the return is not an empty string
    If frmCustDlg.cboCaptions.Text <> "" Then
        'Examine the value of the Show Time CheckBox.
        'This indicates if the user wants to show the
        'time. (Remember, if it is zero, that means it is
        'not checked.)
        If frmCustDlg.chkShowTime.Value = 0 Then
            TimeMsg$ = ""
        Else
            'If it is checked, look to see which
            'OptionButton is set
            If frmCustDlg.optTime.Value = True Then
                TimeMsg$ = CDate(Time())
            Else
                'Logic dictates that the optTimeDate
                'OptionButton must be selected.
                TimeMsg$ = CDate(Date) & " " & CDate(Time())
            End If
        End If
        Msg$ = frmCustDlg.cboCaptions.Text & " " & TimeMsg$
    Else
        'If it is, set a default value.
        Msg$ = "Main Form" & TimeMsg$
    End If

    'Assign the value of the message variable to the
    'caption of the main form.
    frmMain.Caption = Msg$
End Sub
```

N O T E You can use the Show method to display a form. When you call the Show method of a form, the form is automatically loaded into memory and displayed. Conversely, when you use the Hide method to make a form invisible, the form remains in memory.

If you use the parameter vbModal (1) after the Show call, the form will appear modal. ∎

10. Go to frmCustDlg by double-clicking the form in the Project Explorer. Add the code in Listing 16.6 to the chkShowTime_Click() event procedure of the form frmCustDlg.

Listing 16.6 o_LIST0b.TXT—Enabling *OptionButtons* by Examining the Setting of the *Value* Property of a *CheckBox* During a *Click* Event.

```
    If chkShowTime.Value = 0 Then
        optTime.Enabled = False
        optTimeDate.Enabled = False
    Else
        optTime.Enabled = True
        optTimeDate.Enabled = True
    End If
End Sub
```

11. Go to frmCustDlg by double-clicking the form in the Project Explorer. Add the code in Listing 16.7 to the Form_Load() event procedure of the form frmCustDlg.

Listing 16.7 16LIST06.TXT—Using the AddItem method to populate the ComboBox.

```
Private Sub Form_Load()
    cboCaptions.AddItem "Great Custom Dialog"
    cboCaptions.AddItem "Very Nice Custom Dialog"
    cboCaptions.AddItem "Extraordinary Custom Dialog"
End Sub
```

12. Add the code in Listing 16.8 to cmdOK_Click() and cmdCancel_Click() event procedures.

Listing 16.8 16LIST07.TXT—Using the Keyword "Me" to Reference Forms

```
Private Sub cmdCancel_Click()
    Me.Hide
End Sub


Private Sub cmdOk_Click()
    Me.Hide
End Sub
```

13. Save, compile, and run the code.

Figure 16.16 shows the code from the preceding steps at runtime. This is the way the custom dialog box works:

■ When the custom dialog box is loaded by clicking the Settings button in the main form, the code populates the ComboBox using the AddItem method of the ComboBox control within the Load event procedure of the custom dialog box form.

■ The custom form, frmCustDlg, is loaded modally, effectively suspending the activity of the program until the custom dialog box form is closed.

- After the form is closed using the Hide method of the custom form, control of the program returns to the `Click` event handler of the Settings button on the main form.
- Within the `Click` event handler, the `CombBox Text` property is examined to make sure that it is not an empty string.
- If it is not an empty string the program looks to see if the CheckBox, chkShowTime is checked. If it is checked, the program looks to see which OptionButton is set to True.
- If it is optTime, it sets the `TimeMsg$` user-defined variable to the current time. If it is optTimeDate the program sets the `TimeMsg$` variable to show both the current time and date.
- Then a `Msg$` variable is assigned the ComboxBox's Text string and the TimeMsg$ string.
- If the `ComboBox` is an empty string, the `Msg$` user-defined variable is assigned the string, "Main Form" and the value of the `TimeMsg$` variable.
- The `Msg$` variable is then assigned to the Caption property of the Main form.

FIG. 16.16
Create a form with modal display behavior by using the `vbModal` constant with the form's `Show` method.

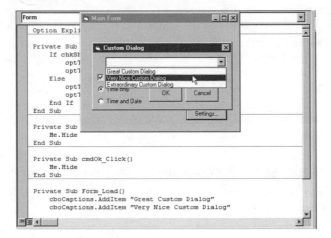

> **CAUTION**
> Make sure that you use the Hide method to close the custom dialog box. If you use the `UnLoad` statement to close the form, you will lose the value that you selected.

The code for the custom dialog box examples is in the project `CustDlg.VBP` in the directory `\Chp_16\CustDlg`.

Using OptionButtons

In the preceding section, you used OptionButtons and CheckBoxes to set states and conditions within your Custom Dialog box. Now let's take a detailed look at each control.

You use the OptionButton control to choose among exclusive choices. An exclusive choice is a choice that once made, it counts out all other choices. For instance, if you want a user to declare his or her gender, you would use a set of two OptionButtons. That way, the user could choose between male and female. By choosing male, the user automatically excludes female and vice versa.

You can have many OptionButtons on a form. But, you can only choose one. If another option button is selected, it automatically clears the previously selected one.

OptionButtons have most of the properties common to the other Intrinsic Controls. The way that you can tell if a particular OptionButton is selected is by the setting of the Value property. If the OptionButton's Value is set to True, then you know that the OptionButton has been selected. If the Value is set to False, you know that the OptionButton is clear.

You can group OptionButtons within the Frame control so that you can have a number of sets of exclusive choices. Figure 16.17 shows two sets of OptionButtons.

Using the two Frame controls enables you to use OptionButtons to select one choice from two different categories.

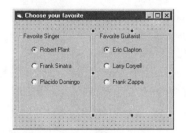

FIG. 16.17
You can group OptionButtons by inserting a Frame control on a form, selecting the inserted Frame, and then placing an OptionButton within the selected Frame.

Using *CheckBoxes*

The CheckBox is the control that you want to use when you want to make a series of inclusive choices or if you want to choose between two states of an item.

The CheckBox has most of the same properties of the other Intrinsic Controls. The CheckBox also has a lot in common with its cousin, the OptionButton. The thing that is special about the CheckBox is that you can check multiple CheckBoxes on a form. Also, the CheckBox's Value property has three settings: 0-Unchecked (default), 1-Checked, and 2-Grayed (dimmed) whereas the OptionButton's Value property has only two settings, 0-Unselected (False) or 1-Selected (True).

As stated previously, you use the CheckBox to indicate inclusive choices. Figure 16.18 shows the Font dialog from Microsoft Word. Notice the way that the CheckBoxes in the lower left corner are used to allow a user to select font effects. The user can check the CheckBox(es), choose some of the effects, all of the effects, or none of the effects.

Also notice that in Figure 16.18 the Superscript and Subscript Checkboxes are grayed. This means that both effects are in force—some characters are set to superscript or subscript and some are not.

FIG. 16.18
Microsoft Word uses
CheckBoxes to offer
users inclusive choices.

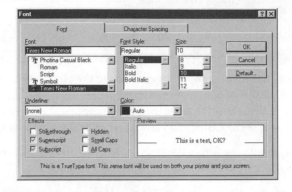

Using Form Templates

If you don't want to go through the hassle of making a new form every time you need customization, you can use the form templates that Microsoft provides. Form templates are prebuilt forms that come with default code that enables you to speed your programming.

You can select a form template by choosing the Project menu and selecting Add Form (see Figure 16.19). Some of the form templates are as follows:

- *About Dialog.*   Used to provide the user with information about your program.
- *Log In Dialog.*   Enables the user to enter a user ID and password.
- *Options Dialog.*   Creates a dialog box similar to Property Pages or the Options dialog boxes of Visual Basic.
- *Tip dialog.*   Can provide a Tip of the Day function for your program.

Once you have selected a form template, you can add custom code to create additional functionality that your program might need.

FIG. 16.19
Microsoft provides a full
selection of form
templates for the most
commonly used dialog
boxes.

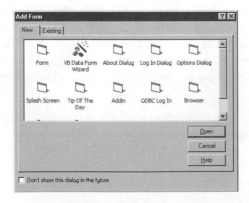

CHAPTER 17

Working with Graphics

Knowing how to work with graphics is an important part of Windows programming. You use graphics to create interest and to communicate. For instance, you can create an icon that uniquely identifies your program in the Start menu or the Windows Explorer. Or, you can report the ongoing status of an operation by using a number of related graphics—a blinking green traffic light to indicate that an operation is in force or a red traffic light to show that an operation has terminated.

For the most part, programming graphics in Visual Basic is handled by two of the Intrinsic Controls—PictureBox and Image. This chapter shows you how to use each and discusses the subtle differences between them. ■

Graphic controls

Find out how to use the PictureBox and Image Controls.

Using the *LoadPicture* function

Load a graphic from disk by using the LoadPicture() function.

Using the File list box

Read the contents of a folder using the FileListBox control.

Making custom buttons

Learn how to use the various properties of the Image control to make a custom button by using the Image control.

Changing the size of pictures

Change the proportions of graphics in a PictureBox and Image control by using the Stretch property.

Adding Graphics to a Form

To add graphics to a form, follow these steps. (Although the projects, forms, and so on have specific names in the chapter's sample programs, feel free to experiment with naming them and other parts of the code to fit your needs.)

1. Open a New Standard EXE project. Name the project SmplGrfx. Name the default form frmMain. Set the value of the form's `Caption` to Simple Graphics.

2. Add a `PictureBox` to the form by either double-clicking the `PictureBox` icon in the `ToolBox` or by selecting the `PictureBox` and then dragging your mouse across the form.

3. Name the `PictureBox` picMain.

4. Add an `Image` control to the form. You can use the same procedures as those described for the `PictureBox`. Name the `Image` control imgMain.

5. Size and place the `PictureBox` and `Image` control where you want them on the form, as shown in Figure 17.1.

FIG. 17.1

The default value for the `BorderStyle` property of the `PictureBox` control is 1- Fixed Single. The default value for the `BorderStyle` property of the `Image` control is 0 - None.

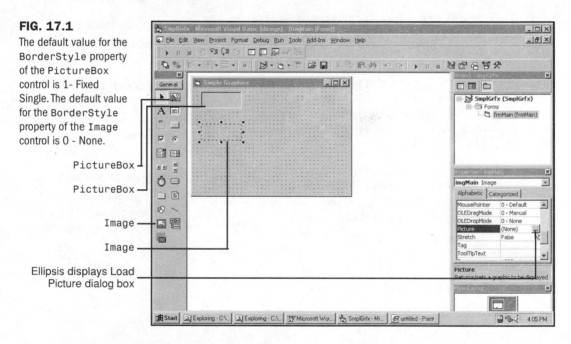

6. Select the `PictureBox` picMain. Go to the `Picture` property in the Properties window. Open the Load Picture dialog box, as shown in Figure 17.2.

7. Go to the Windows directory and select Bubbles.bmp. Click the Open button on the Load Picture dialog box. The bitmap Bubbles.bmp appears in the `PictureBox` (see Figure 17.3).

N O T E Bubbles.bmp is a bitmap that ships with Windows. If by some chance the bitmap is not present in your Windows directory, choose another bitmap. ■

FIG. 17.2
If you scroll through the Windows directory, you will find that the operating system ships with many graphics files of different types.

8. Set the value of the AutoSize property of the PictureBox picMain to True. This enlarges the area of the PictureBox to accommodate the size of the bitmap Bubbles.bmp.

9. Select the Image control and set the value of the Picture property to the bitmap Triangles.bmp. (The bitmap is in the Windows directory.) Use the same operation that you used to set the value of the PictureBox control's Picture property. However, do not try to set an AutoSize property.

10. Save and run your code (see Figure 17.3).

Part
III

Ch
17

FIG. 17.3
The Image control does not support an AutoSize property. It automatically resizes itself to the dimensions of the assigned picture when the graphic is added.

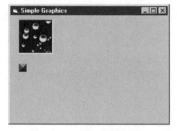

As you can see, adding a picture to a form using the PictureBox or Image control is not a complicated operation.

Changing a Picture at Runtime

You can change the graphic assigned to the Picture property of a PictureBox or Image control at runtime by changing the value of the control's Picture property. To change the value of the control's Picture property at runtime, do the following:

1. Reopen the project SmplGrfx.vbp.

2. Add a CommandButton to the form. Name it cmdChange. Set the value of the Caption property to Change the graphic.

3. Add the following code to the cmdChange_Click() event procedure.

   ```
   picMain.Picture = imgMain.Picture
   ```

4. Save and run the code (see Figure 17.4).

FIG. 17.4

Setting the
`PictureBox` control's
`AutoSize` property to
`True` resizes the
control's area when new
pictures are assigned at
runtime.

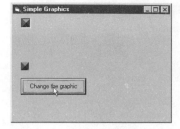

The code for the preceding examples are in the project SmplGrfx.vbp in the directory
Chp_17\SmplGrfx\ on the CD-ROM that accompanies this book.

Making a Custom Button

You can use the process of setting a `Picture` property at runtime to make a custom button that
is operationally identical to a `CommandButton`. To make a custom button, do the following:

1. Open a <u>N</u>ew project and name it CustBut.vbp. Change the name of the default form to
   frmCust and set the value of the form's `Caption` to Custom Button.

2. Add three `Image` controls to the form. Set the value of the property name of one `imgMain`.
   Set the value of the `Name` property of another `imgUp`, and set the value of the `Name`
   property of the last `imgDown`.

3. Assign the icon files listed in the following table to the respective `Image` controls. The
   icon files are in the directory 17\CustBut\ that is on the CD-ROM that accompanies this
   book.

Control	Icon File
imgMain	none
imgUp	cdUp.ico
imgDown	cdDown.ico

4. Place the `Image` controls on the form, such as those shown in Figure 17.5.

FIG. 17.5

Icon files (.ico) can have
transparent regions.

5. Add the event procedure code shown in Listing 17.1 for the Form_Load(), imgMain_MouseDown(), and imgMain_MouseUp() event procedures to the General section of frmCust.

Listing 17.1   17LIST01.TXT—Settings for the Custom Button *Image* Control

```
Private Sub Form_Load()
    imgMain.Picture = imgUp.Picture
End Sub


Private Sub imgMain_MouseDown(Button As Integer, _
                Shift As Integer, X As Single, Y As Single)
    imgMain.Picture = imgDown.Picture
End Sub


Private Sub imgMain_MouseUp(Button As Integer, _
                Shift As Integer, X As Single, Y As Single)
    imgMain.Picture = imgUp.Picture
End Sub
```

6. Set the value of the Visible property for the Image controls imgDown and imgUp to False.

7. Set the following code in the Click event of the Image control imgMain.

   MsgBox "I am a custom button!"

8. Save and run the code (see Figure 17.6).

FIG. 17.6

The custom button, imgMain, can still reference the Picture property of the imgDown and imgUp controls even though the value of the Visible property is set to False.

When you run the code in the project CustBut.vbp, the Image control imgMain is now a custom button with an associated Click event procedure. The key to the construction of the custom button is to have the Image control's MouseDown and MouseUp behavior be identifiable with general "button down" and "button up" graphical behaviors of a CommandButton. When you click a CommandButton, you'll see that the CommandButton shows a different picture when the mouse is down than when the mouse is up. The custom button you just made does the same thing (see Figure 17.7). By the same token, you can program the Click event procedure of the Image control "custom button" without interfering with other mouse behaviors, because the imaging behavior of that control is relegated to the MouseDown and MouseUp event procedures only.

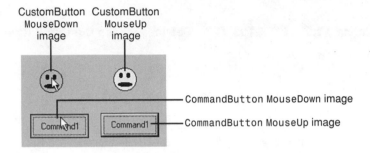

FIG. 17.7
MouseDown and MouseUp images are slightly different to give the impression of state changes.

Adding Graphics to Forms with *LoadPicture()*

At times, you might have a graphic file on your hard disk that you want to load into a PictureBox or Image control. You do this using the LoadPicture() function.

The syntax for the LoadPicture() function is:

MyPicture = LoadPicture(strFilePath)

Where:

MyPicture is a picture for a PictureBox or Image control.

LoadPicture is the function name.

strFilePath is a string that references the exact location on the hard disk of the graphics file that you want to load.

To load a file from disk, do the following:

1. Open a New Standard EXE project. Name the project LoadPrj.vbp. Rename the default form frmLoad. Set the value of the form's Caption property to Load File.
2. Add a PictureBox to the form. Name the PictureBox picLoad. Set the value of the AutoSize property of the PictureBox to True.
3. Add a CommandButton to the form. Name the CommandButton cmdLoad. Set the value of the Caption property of the CommandButton cmdLoad to Load from File.
4. Size and place the controls on the form, as shown in Figure 17.8.
5. Add the following code to the Click event procedure of the CommandButton cmdLoad. (This code assumes that the bitmap circles.bmp is in the Windows directory.

```
picLoad.Picture = LoadPicture("c:\windows\circles.bmp")
```

6. Save and run the code.

Figure 17.9 shows the program in run mode. The code for this example can be found in the directory \Chp_17\LoadFile\.

FIG. 17.8

Make sure that when you set the value of a `PictureBox`'s `AutoSize` property to `True` you leave enough room for the `PictureBox` to expand to accommodate a large picture.

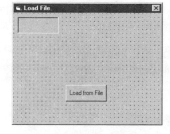

FIG. 17.9

To clear a `PictureBox` or `Image` control, call `LoadPicture` without any arguments: picLoad.Picture = LoadPicture.

Making a Form Icon

Windows programs commonly have an icon embedded within the executable file (EXE) that graphically represents the given program. When you make your program, Visual Basic automatically assigns one of your form's icons to your executable. Unless you change it, this will be Visual Basic's default form icon (see Figure 17.10).

FIG. 17.10

You set the unique properties of your program within the Project Properties dialog box.

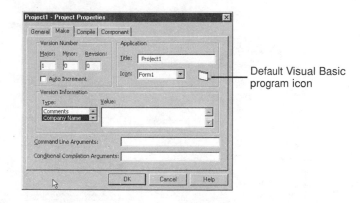

Default Visual Basic program icon

You can, however, embed a custom icon into your program's executable file. To do this, you first need to create an icon. You cannot create an icon within Visual Basic or with the MS Paint program that ships with Windows. However, the Visual Basic 5.0 CD-ROM contains a handy program for making icons. It is called the Microsoft Image Editor (imagedit.exe) and it is in the directory \TOOLS\IMAGEDIT.

After you have made an icon, you assign it to the Icon property of a form in your project. To assign your custom icon to a form, do the following:

1. Select the Icon property of the form. An ellipsis appears in the value area.

2. Click the ellipsis to display the Load Icon dialog box. Browse for your custom icon (see Figure 17.11).

FIG. 17.11

In the Windows Explorer, icon files show the image of each icon file in all Views.

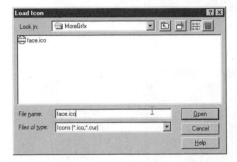

3. Click the Open button. This adds the icon to the form.

After you've added your custom icon to the form, if the form in question is the only form in the project, the icon assigned to the Icon property of the form will be assigned as the icon for the program. If you have multiple forms, select the form with the icon that you want to be the program's icon from the Icon drop-down list in the Project Properties dialog box Make tab (see Figure 17.12).

FIG. 17.12

Visual Basic 5.0 has greatly enhanced the properties of an application. You can set many of them in the Project Properties dialog box.

Form's icon

Icon drop-down list

Application Icon

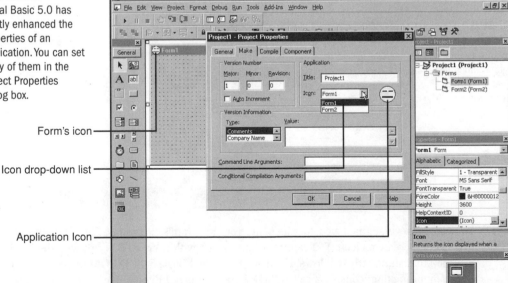

Loading Files Using a File *ListBox*

Look at the project MoreGrfx.vbp in the directory \Chp_17\MoreGrfx\ on the CD-ROM that comes with this book. This program is a summarization of all the techniques that you have learned to display graphics thus far (see Figure 17.13).

FIG. 17.13

The application More Graphics uses `OptionsBoxes` to determine which technique the program should use to display images.

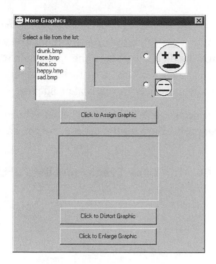

The program allows you to display icon or bitmap images embedded in the form into a `PictureBox`. Also, the application enables you to select a file from disk to display in the main `PictureBox` control picDisplay.

The application uses a `FileListBox` to display the graphic files available to display. The `FileListBox` is similar to the `ListBox`. However, where the `ListBox` must be programmed to load string values to display, the `FileListBox` automatically displays strings that reflect the files of a specific directory. All you need to do is "tell" the `FileListBox` from which directory it should read files. You do this by setting the value of the `Path` property of the `FileListBox` to the exact location of the directory in which the files you want to display reside.

▶ **See** the section, "Working with *ListBoxes* and *ComboBoxes*," in Chapter 10, "Working with Arrays," for more information about *ListBoxes*, **p. 152**

Listing 17.2 shows the `Form_Load()` event procedure for the project MoreGrfx.vbp. This event procedure is where the value of the `Path` property for the `FileListBox` File1 is set.

Listing 17.2 17LIST02.TXT—Using the *Filter* Property of the *FileListBox*

```
Private Sub Form_Load()
    'Set the path of the FileListbox to be the
    'directory in which the application resides.
    File1.Path = App.Path
```

continues

Listing 17.2   Continued

```
        'Make it so the FileListbox only displays
        'bitmap and icon files.
        File1.Pattern = "*.bmp;*.ico"
End Sub
```

Notice that the value of the FileListBox's Path property is set to the value of App object's Path property. The App object holds information about your application. The value of the Path property of the App object reports back the directory where the application executable file resides. Thus, setting the value of the Path property of the FileListBox like this tells the FileListBox to display the files in the directory from which the application started.

After a file is selected in the FileListBox, File1, the user clicks the CommandButton cmdAssign. Listing 17.3 shows the Click event procedure for the CommandButton named cmdAssign.

Listing 17.3   17LIST03.TXT—The *Click* Event Procedure of the *CommandButton*

```
Private Sub cmdAssign_Click()
    Dim strFilePath As String

    'Query the option buttons to see which one
    'has been checked.
    If opBitmap.Value = True Then
        'Show the bitmap graphic
        picDisplay.Picture = picBitmap.Picture
    ElseIf opIcon.Value = True Then
        'Show the icon graphic
        picDisplay.Picture = picIcon.Picture
    ElseIf opList.Value = True Then
        'Assign the exact path of the graphic in the file list box to
        'the the filepath string variable. Don't forget, to get the
        'string in a list box you must identify the Listindex
        'selected within a List Control's List array.
        strFilePath = File1.Path & "\" & File1.List(File1.ListIndex)
        'Load the picture from disk and assign it to the picture
        'property of the Picture control.
        picDisplay.Picture = LoadPicture(strFilePath)

    End If
End Sub
```

As shown in Listing 17.3, if the OptionButton opList is checked, the application loads the selected file from disk into the PictureBox, picDisplay, using the LoadPicture() function. Study this code closely; many of its nuances can be fully understood only by working directly with the program and looking at the entire code.

Creating Special Effects with Graphics

In the project MoreGrfx.vbp, after the user assigns a picture to the PictureBox picDisplay, he or she can decide to distort the picture by clicking the CommandButton cmdDistort. When the button is clicked, the picture in the PictureBox is assigned to the Picture property of the Image control imgDistort using the following statement:

```
imgDistort.Width = picDisplay.Width * 1.5
imgDistort.Picture = picDisplay.Picture
```

The Image control distorts the picture because the value of the Stretch property of imgDistort is set to True and the value of the Width property of the Image control is modified to make its dimensions irregular relative to the PictureBox, picDispay. The PictureBox must have the value of its AutoSize property set to True to resize itself to accommodate the area of pictures assigned to it. The Image control, however, resizes itself by default to accommodate the area of assigned pictures. However, when the value of the Image control's Stretch property is set to True, Visual Basic *resizes the assigned picture* to the dimensions of the Image control, regardless of the size of the Image control. This can make for some unusual distortions (see Figure 17.14).

FIG. 17.14
You can use the Stretch property of the Image control to distort pictures. To enlarge a picture, just size the Image control to the same ratio as the original picture.

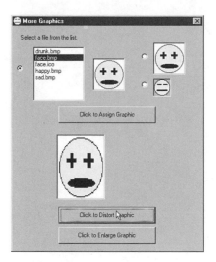

However, you can use the Stretch property to enlarge a picture within an Image control. Listing 17.4 shows the code for the cmdEnlarge_Click() event procedure. The cmdEnlarge CommandButton enables the user to enlarge the picture displayed in the smaller PictureBox picDisplay. The trick to enlarging a picture is to maintain the picture's width-to-height ratio when sizing the Image control to which the newly assigned picture will be stretched. The code in the listing determines the ratio of the PictureBox picDisplay by calculating the control's width over its height. Then the code applies that ratio to the Height of the Image control imgEnlarge. As a result, the value of imgEnlarge.Width is reset. Thus, the ratio is maintained.

Listing 17.4   17LIST04.TXT—The Code to Enlarge a Picture

```
Private Sub cmdEnlage_Click()
    Dim dSizeRatio As Double
    'Figure out the ratio
    dSizeRatio = picDisplay.Width / picDisplay.Height

    'Apply the ratio to Image control's Height to
    'get the new Width
     imgDistort.Width = imgDistort.Height * dSizeRatio
End Sub
```

CHAPTER 18

Deploying Your Application

Detail your application with the _App_ object

Learn how to use the App object to describe and verify your application.

Compile your code

Learn how to compile your code into a stand-alone executable.

Use the Application Setup Wizard

Use the Application Setup Wizard to deploy your application by floppy disk, CD-ROM, or over a network.

The days of deploying your application as a single executable file on a floppy disk are long gone. Today, your Windows program written in Visual Basic is made up of many files, only one of which is your compiled executable file. In addition to the runtime DLLs, you might have special ActiveX controls, data files, and graphic images that your program requires. All these files need to be copied to the appropriate locations on the destination drive. In addition, all Windows components and your program itself may need to be registered in the Windows Registry. As you can see, distributing even the simplest Visual Basic program can be complicated. Luckily, if you use the tools that Visual Basic provides, deployment is not as painful as you might imagine. In this chapter, you look at the how to prepare your program for deployment and then how to use the Application Setup Wizard to do the actual deployment. ■

Working with Version Information

Before you can deploy your application, you must prepare it for distribution. This means working with the App object. The App object is a distinct object with its own set of properties that describes your application. The most commonly used properties of the App object are shown in Table 18.1.

Table 18.1 Commonly Used *App* Object Properties

Property	Description	Remarks
Comments	Returns a string containing comments about the application	Read only at runtime
CompanyName	Returns company or creator	Read only at runtime
EXEName	Returns file name of EXE without extension	Read only
FileDiscription	String that describes the file	Read only at runtime
HelpFile	Specifies the Help file associated with the application	Read and write at runtime
LegalCopyright	Returns copyright notification string	Read only at runtime
LegalTrademarks	Returns trademark information	Read only at runtime
Major	Returns Major version number	Read only at runtime
Minor	Returns Minor version number	Read only at runtime
Path	Returns the directory from which the application starts	Read only at runtime
PrevInstance	Returns a value if an instance of the application is running	Read only at runtime
Product Name	Returns the assigned product name of the application	Read only at runtime
Revision	Returns the revision number of the application	Read only at runtime

You can use these properties to communicate important information about your application to those who will be using it. These properties are set in the Project Properties tabbed dialog box. Figure 18.1 shows the Make tab of the Project Properties dialog box.

You can read the values of these properties at runtime within your VB code (see Listing 18.1). You also can set the value for the version information properties of the App object by right-clicking the compiled EXE file and selecting Properties from the pop-up context menu (see Figure 18.2).

Set App object properties and
select application icons here Set the Minor release number

Set the Major release number Choose native or interpreted compilation and optimization

Here you determine what type
of application to make   Set Revision Number

FIG. 18.1

To access the Project
Properties dialog box,
go to the Project menu
and select
[ProjectName]
Properties.

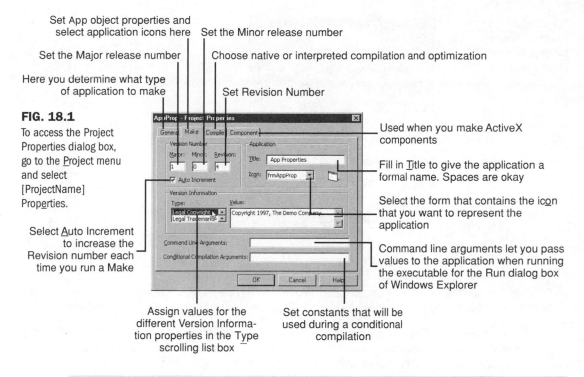

Used when you make ActiveX
components

Fill in Title to give the application a
formal name. Spaces are okay

Select the form that contains the icon
that you want to represent the
application

Select Auto Increment
to increase the
Revision number each
time you run a Make

Command line arguments let you pass
values to the application when running
the executable for the Run dialog box
of Windows Explorer

Assign values for the
different Version Information properties in the Type
scrolling list box

Set constants that will be
used during a conditional
compilation

Part
III

Ch
18

Listing 18.1 18LIST01.TXT—Reading an *App* Object's Properties in Code

```
Private Sub cmdCopyright_Click()
 lblMain.Caption = App.LegalCopyright
End Sub

Private Sub cmdPath_Click()
 lblMain.Caption = App.Path
End Sub

Private Sub cmdProductName_Click()
 lblMain.Caption = App.ProductName
End Sub

Private Sub cmdVersionNum_Click()
 Dim VerNum$

 VerNum$ = CStr(App.Major) & "."
 VerNum$ = VerNum$ & CStr(App.Minor) & "."
 VerNum$ = VerNum$ & CStr(App.Revision)

 lblMain.Caption = VerNum$
End Sub
```

FIG. 18.2
Select the Version
tab to see the version
properties.

Working with the App object's properties is important, because through these properties you and your users can manage multiple releases of your code. Also, using the version properties of the App object, such as LegalCopyright and LegalTrademark, is the way by which users can verify that the program you made really is yours, thus avoiding potential incidents of piracy.

The project AppProp.vbp is program that shows a user created dialog box. On the dialog box there are four buttons that you click to display the values of the various version properties of the App Object. (See Figure 18.3.) The code for the project AppProp.vbp is in the \Chp_18\AppProp directory on the CD-ROM that accompanies this book.

FIG. 18.3
The values of App
object's version
information properties
are embedded within
the binary format of
your Visual Basic
executable. They cannot
be changed at runtime.

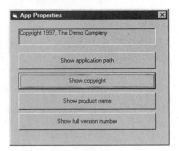

Compiling Your Project

After you set the values for the properties of your project's App object, you are ready to compile your code. Up to this point in your programming activity, your project has been a collection of text files (.FRM and .BAS) and graphic files, which you have run through the Visual Basic IDE. Now it's time to transform these files into an executable file that will run independently of the IDE. This process is called *compiling* your code or *making* an executable. As of Visual Basic 5.0, there are two formats into which you can compile your code—P-Code or Native Code. When you compile your code into P-Code, the resulting executable file runs as interpreted code, just as it did in previous versions of Visual Basic. The code still has to read into the runtime DLLs to get most of the work done. If you compile the code as Native Code, the project files are transformed into more efficient binary code that uses the full capabilities of your computer's processor. This code tends to execute much faster.

However, *Native Code still requires the runtime DLLs.* The only difference is that the DLLs are accessed and used differently by the EXE. A Native code executable file tends to be bigger in size than its P-Code cousin. Thus, if you want to deploy the smallest possible executable file, you should use P-Code—if you want the fastest code possible, you should distribute your application in Native code.

To compile your code into a standard EXE, do the following:

1. Open the project that you want to compile. (In this case, we'll use the project AppProp.vbp.)

2. Select Make [Project Name].exe from the File drop-down menu. This displays the Make Project dialog box (see Figure 18.4).

3. If you want to rename the executable file, you can do so in the File name TextBox.

4. Click the Options button to open the Project Properties tabbed dialog box. Select the Compile tab to choose between P-Code or Native Code compilation (see Figure 18.5).

Part
III

Ch
18

FIG. 18.4

When you compile a project to a standard EXE, Visual Basic automatically defaults the executable file's name to the name of the project. If you want to reset any of the values of the App object's properties, click the Options button to display an abbreviated version of the Project Properties dialog box.

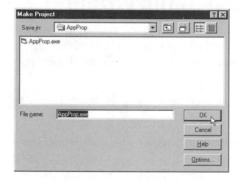

5. Click OK to close the Project Properties dialog box. Click OK on the Make Project dialog box to compile the code.

Completing this process produces an executable file that runs outside the Visual Basic IDE. However, your application is not fully ready for deployment. To deploy the application, you need to run the Application Setup Wizard for the executable to be able to run on a system upon which Visual Basic is *not* installed.

FIG. 18.5

You can select among many options for Native Code compilation. Generally, the faster code option creates a larger file size for the executable.

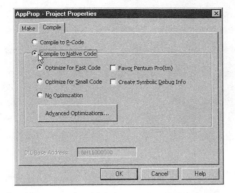

N O T E   Keep in mind that the Make process that you've just done pertains to standard EXE projects. There are many other types of projects that you can make with Visual Basic 5.0, such as ActiveX Controls and ActiveX DLLs to name a few. However, the concern of this chapter is to make stand-alone executables. Subjects such as ActiveX Controls are covered later in this book.

Using the Application Setup Wizard

To have a deployment of your application that will run on any other system, you must have the necessary runtime DLLs, ActiveX files, and other required files installed and registered on the destination system. As you read earlier, you use the Visual Basic Application Setup Wizard to accomplish this.

To create a deployment for your application using the Visual Basic Application Setup Wizard, do the following:

1. Close the Visual Basic IDE and start the Visual Basic Application Setup Wizard from the Start Menu (see Figure 18.6).

2. Read the introduction screen. Then click the Next button to go to the Select Project and Options step (see Figure 18.7).

3. Check the Create a Setup Program option. Click the Browse button to display the "Locate VB application's .VBP file" dialog box (see Figure 18.8).

4. Select the .VBP project file for the application that you want to distribute. Click the Open button on the Locate VB application's *.VBP file dialog box. Then click Next button; the Distribution Method screen appears.

5. Check the Single Directory option if you want to deploy your application on a network drive or create a CD-ROM. (See Figure 18.9.) You can use Floppy Disk to deploy your application on one of more floppy disks. (The number of disks you use is determined by the file size of the all the files combined for your project.) If you want to create a multiple disk directory image (\Disk1, \Disk2, \Disk3, and so on), from which you can burn a CD-ROM or copy each directory onto a respective floppy disk, use the Disk Directories

option. If you use the <u>D</u>isk Directories option, you start by invoking the file setup.exe in the directory \Disk1. For the purposes of this demonstration, you use the <u>S</u>ingle Directory option.

FIG. 18.6
When you installed Visual Basic on your computer, you also installed the Application Setup Wizard.

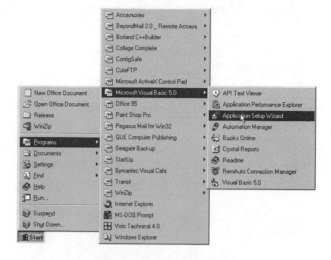

FIG. 18.7
If you are making an ActiveX control, you can choose Create Internet DownLoad Setup. Check the Generate Dependency File check box if you want to keep a list of all the runtime files that your program requires. This list will be a file that has an extension of .DEP, which will be placed in the project's directory.

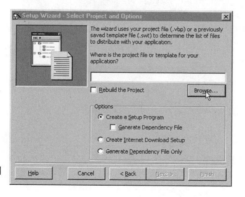

FIG. 18.8
The "Locate VB application's .VBP file" dialog box really is an Open File common dialog box.

FIG. 18.9

You can deploy your application on floppy disks. Or, if you select Single Directory or Disk Directories, you can distribute your application on a network drive or burn the directory(s) on a CD-ROM.

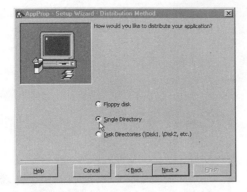

7. Within the Setup Wizard, select the directory you dedicated to be the destination directory for your deployment (see Figure 18.10). Then click the Next button to make the ActiveX Server Components dialog box appear.

FIG. 18.10

You should always have your deployment in a dedicated directory.

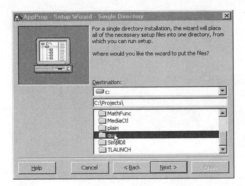

8. If your application used an OLE automation server, you would add it in the ActiveX Server Components dialog box (see Figure 18.11). Click the Next button.

9. Click the Next button in the Confirm Dependencies step of the Setup Wizard (see Figure 18.12).

10. If all the necessary files for your project are listed in the File Summary, click the Next button. If not, click the Add button to add the missing files; then click Next (see Figure 8.13).

11. If you want to keep a record of the setup, click the Save Template button in the final Wizard dialog box (see Figure 8.14). Saving a .SWT setup template file makes this process much faster should you need to repeat it in the future.

12. Click the Finish button.

FIG. 18.11
Many Visual Basic applications use other objects made in Visual Basic. The objects can be on a local drive or elsewhere on a network.

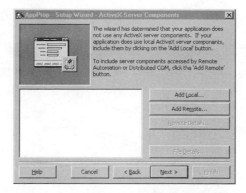

FIG. 18.12
If your application uses ActiveX controls, they will be listed in this step.

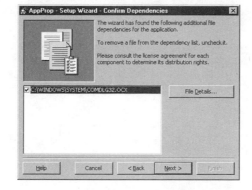

FIG. 18.13
If your application depends on external files (graphics or document files, for example) you add them in this step. Visual Basic has no intrinsic knowledge of such files.

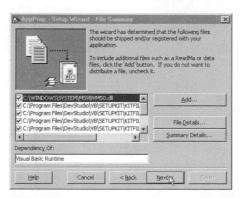

When you click the Finish button, the Application Setup Wizard compresses all the files that are required for a proper deployment of your application. These compressed files are copied into the directory that you determined to be the destination directory during the Setup Wizard process (see Figure 18.15).

FIG. 18.14

This is the last step before the Setup Wizard generates the setup files' configuration.

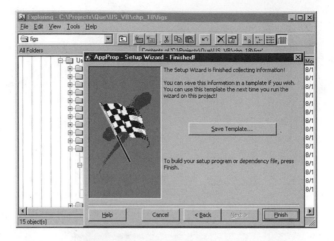

FIG. 18.15

The combined size of all the compressed files for an application's deployment can be large. Even this modest Visual Basic application deployment configuration requires 1.51M of disk space.

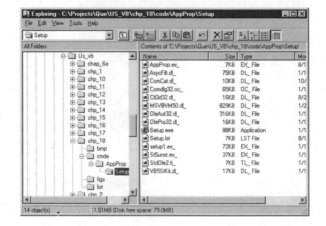

In addition to the compressed files, the Setup Wizard also copies a SETUP.EXE file into the directory. The SETUP.EXE file is the file that your user clicks to invoke the setup process. When clicked, SETUP.EXE runs a setup process that copies your application's files to the user's computer. Files particular to your application are installed in a directory created exclusively for your program by the SETUP.EXE program. ActiveX controls and runtime DLLs are copied to the Windows \System directory. Version checks are performed on all files by the SETUP.EXE program to ensure that you are not overwriting newer files with older ones. In addition to all the file copying, the SETUP.EXE also does all the necessary registrations for your program in the Windows Registry. Finally, an entry for your application is made in the Start Menu.

As you read earlier, you can deploy your application on floppy disks, a network drive, or a CD-ROM. If you plan to distribute on CD-ROM, all you need to do is copy the contents of the setup directory (to which the Application Setup Wizard compressed and copied files) over to your

CD-ROM burning program. Be advised that if you are planning to deploy your application on floppy disks, you should have many formatted, clean disks on hand. VB application deployments eat disks!

Finally, before you deploy your application, check all the files that you are going to distribute for computer viruses. Do this before and after the Setup Wizard does the file compression. After a virus is burned into a CD-ROM, there is no eradicating it, ever! ●

CHAPTER 19

Finding and Fixing Errors

Bugs happen. They always have; they all always will. This is not to say, however, that you should ship code that is buggy. Quite the contrary—your code should be as bug-free as possible.

You can make your code bug-free in two ways: you can prevent them from happening or fix them after they happen. This chapter looks at code-writing techniques that can prevent bugs from happening. You'll also look at methods that help you identify and fix bugs that exist. ■

Using Option Explicit

Learn how to use Option Explicit to avoid typographical errors when working with variables.

Using Breakpoints

Use breakpoints to find bugs while you navigate through your code.

Using Watches

Learn how to check a variable's value at runtime.

Using Step Into and Step Over

Move through your code line-by-line and procedure-by-procedure.

Using Search and Replace

Correct errors in your code on a program-wide scale using the Search and Replace feature of Visual Basic.

Catching Undeclared Variables with *Option Explicit*

As you are coding, after you press Enter, the Visual Basic IDE captures most statement syntax errors you make (see Figure 19.1). When you run your code within the IDE, Visual Basic reports errors such as type mismatches and incomplete code blocks (see Figure 19.2). (This assumes that you have kept the default IDE settings in force. For a more detailed look of the error handling capabilities of the IDE, go to the Options dialog box. You access the dialog box from the Options menu item of the Tools menu.) However, unless you have Option Explicit set, Visual Basic allows your code to run with undeclared variables. The keyword Option Explicit, which you enter in the General section of a form or module, makes it so that all variables in your code must be explicitly declared using one of the following keywords: Public, Private, Dim, or Static.

FIG. 19.1

The Visual Basic IDE catches If statements without the Then keyword as you type. However, it only catches missing End If keywords when you compile the code.

Unwittingly creating a variable due to a typing mistake can lead to disaster. In Listing 19.1, you can see that the programmer made a typing error. She or he originally declared a variable of type Integer, MyNum%, using the Dim keyword. Then she or he inadvertently made a typing mistake, which produced the variable MyNim%. Thus, the code reports the value 0 (zero), as shown in Figure 19.3.

The source code for the examples discussed in this chapter are in the project errors.vbp, in the directory Chp_19\Errors\ on the CD-ROM that comes with this book.

FIG. 19.2
The IDE reports an incomplete Loop block when you compile the code.

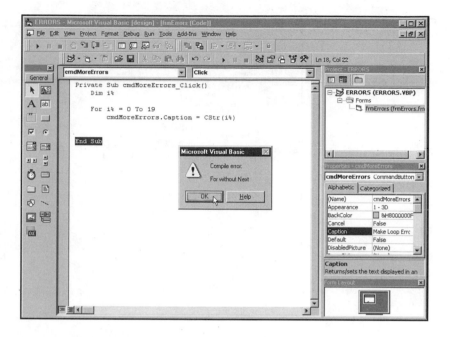

Listing 19.1 19LIST01.TXT—A Bug Caused by a Typing Mistake

```
Private Sub cmdUnWit_Click()
    Dim MyNum%

    MyNum% = 2 + 2

MsgBox CStr(MyNim%)
End Sub
```

FIG. 19.3
Using Option Explicit prevents this from happening.

Without the presence of Option Explicit, the Visual Basic IDE accepted the unwittingly created variable, MyNim%, without a quarrel. And because the default value of any integer upon creation is zero, the logic of the code produces a response that is correct.

Had the programmer used Option Explicit, the IDE would have picked up the typing error when the code was run (see Figure 19.4).

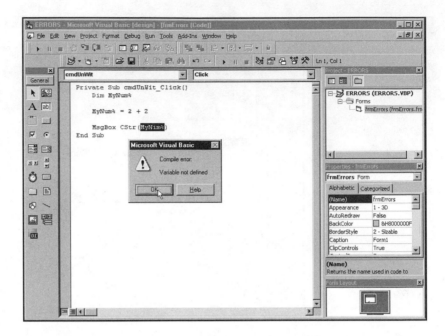

Checking Code Segments with Breakpoints

You can easily stop your Visual Basic code at any point in its execution and examine it with breakpoints. A *breakpoint* is a place in your code at which you stop (break) your code during execution. You can set a breakpoint four ways:

- Click the line of code that you want to break and press the F9 key (see Figure 19.5).
- Click the Breakpoint icon in the Standard Toolbar.
- Toggle the breakpoint from the Debug menu.
- Click in the margin of the Code window.

When you set a breakpoint, you'll notice that the line upon which the break is set turns red (see Figure 19.5). To get your code to break, run the code. When the code breaks, the line upon which you set the break turns yellow. Also, an arrow appears in the left margin of the Code window. This arrow points to the line of code where execution has halted (see Figure 19.6).

If you need to clear all the breakpoints in your code, go to the Debug menu and select Clear All Breakpoints. You can also clear all breakpoints by pressing Ctrl+Shift+F9.

Not all bugs are caused by errors in code syntax. Most bugs are caused by an error in code logic or faulty design. This type of bug is hard to find. You use breakpoints to "narrow down" the region of code where you think a bug is occuring. After you have determined the line of code where you know your bug occurs, you set a breakpoint and look at the erroneous area using Watches.

FIG. 19.5

You toggle breakpoints. The same method you use to set one also clears one.

The Breakpoint icon

Click in the Code window

Set Breakpoint on Debug menu

(Press the F9 Key)

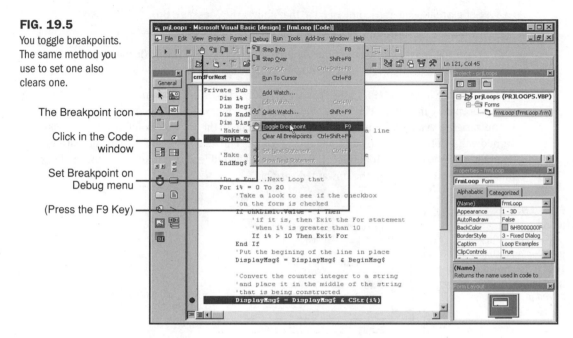

FIG. 19.6

To go to the next breakpoint, press the F5 key.

Arrow points out break

Present breakpoint line

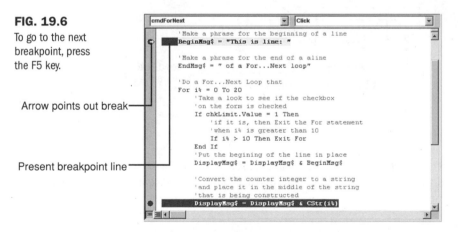

Monitoring Variable Values with Watches

Look again at Listing 19.1 and Figure 19.3. This code has a bug, and the reason is obvious—a typing mistake on the part of the programmer. However, for educational purposes, imagine that you really have no idea why the bug occurred. All you really know is that the Message Box is reporting the wrong answer. This is a good opportunity to use breakpoints and watches.

To set a watch to inspect the value of the variable displayed by the message box, do the following:

1. Set a breakpoint at the line of code that shows the Message Box.
2. Run the code pressing the F5 key.
3. Drag the mouse cursor over the variable that you want to watch (inspect) and let it stay there for a moment. A small window with the value of the variable appears.

As you can see in Figure 19.7, when you watch the variables in question, you can see that there is a discrepancy in values. Thus, you would find that code really did assign the value properly to the variable MyNum% and that the second occurrence of the variable somehow lost the assigned value. Therefore, the addition logic is sound. The next step would be to compare the spelling of the variables. Hopefully, this observation would lead you to discover the spelling mistake and the creation of the unwanted variable.

FIG. 19.7

Holding a mouse cursor over a variable to get the new "Auto Data Tips" pop-up window to appear is called *hovering*.

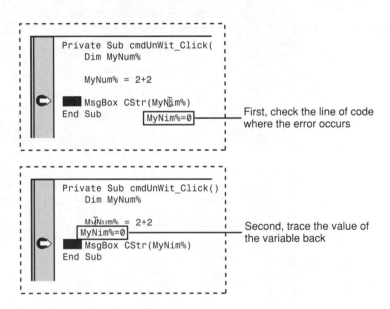

A watch is an extremely powerful debugging tool. It is the fastest way to get at the heart of a problem. And with the hovering Auto Data Tips, which is new to Visual Basic 5.0, using a watch is a simple task.

Monitoring Additional Variables Using Add Watch

At times you will need to watch more than one variable. To do this, you use the Watch window. To add variables to the Watch window, do the following:

1. Set a breakpoint(s) to the variables that you want to add. Press the F5 key.

2. At each breakpoint, highlight the variable that you want to add.

3. Right-click and choose <u>A</u>dd Watch from the pop-up context menu (see Figure 19.8).

FIG. 19.8

You also can access the Add Watch... dialog box from the <u>D</u>ebug menu.

4. Set the proper fields settings in the Add Watch dialog box (see Figure 19.9).

FIG. 19.9

The Add Watch dialog box is a flexible, powerful tool.

Context, the scope of the variable to Watch. You can set this for the Procedure (event procedure or user-defined) within a Form or Module

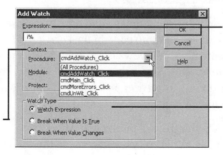

Expression, variable, or statement to Watch

Watch Type, Watch Expression shows the value when you break the code. Break When Value Is True stops the code when the watched expression evaluates to True. Break When Value Changes stops the code when the value of the variable changes

Part
III

Ch
19

5. Click OK in the Add Watch dialog box.

6. To display the Watches window (see Figure 19.10), select Watc<u>h</u> Window from the <u>V</u>iew drop-down menu. This window also appears when you add a watch.

Keeping track of many interdependent variables that are continuously changing can be very hard. The Watch window is an effective tool to use to inspect values in these dynamic situations, particularly with regard to Loops or Arrays.

FIG. 19.10

When in break mode, make sure that you are at a place in your code in which the variables listed in the Watch window are in scope.

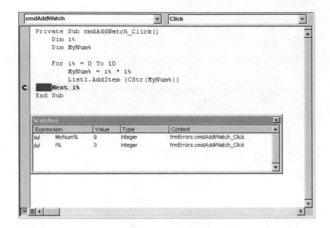

Examining Code Line-by-Line Using *Step Into* and *Step Over*

You "Step" to examine every line of code as it executes in the order that it executes. There are two ways to step—Step Into and Step Over.

When you Step Into code, you move through your code line-by-line. If one line of code happens to be a call to another procedure, either an event procedure or one that is user-defined, you "step into" that procedure (see Figure 19.11).

If you start your code with a Step Into, sometimes you might be surprised to see nothing happen. This is perfectly logical. If you have no code in the Form_Load() event procedure, there is no event to execute. Remember, Windows is an event-driven operating system. Some event must fire for code to execute. The only real default startup code you have is a Form_Initialize(), Form_Load() or Sub Main() procedure. If there is no code behind these events, your program will sit stagnant until an event is fired.

To Step Into some code, is it is better to set a breakpoint where you want to begin to step and then run your code as you normally would. When you come to the breakpoint, simply invoke Step Into to proceed. If you have used Step Into to enter a procedure and you want to quickly exit that procedure, you can Step Out of the procedure by pressing Ctrl+Shift+ F8 or selecting Step Out from the Debug menu.

When you Step Over code, you also move through your code line-by-line. However, when you encounter a line of code that is a call to another procedure, you *do not* enter the called procedure. Rather, you execute that code as if it were solely a single line of code (see Figure 19.12).

You might find it faster and easier to perform these debugging techniques by using the Debug ToolBar (see Figure 19.13).

FIG. 19.11

You can Step Into code by pressing the F8 key or selecting Step Into from the Debug menu.

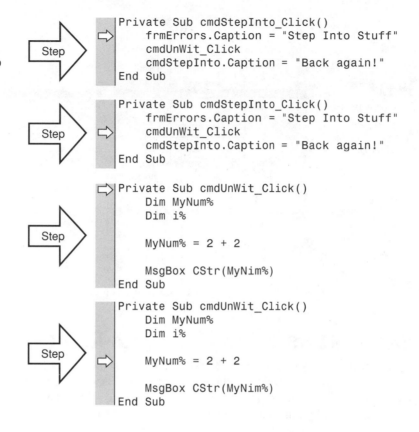

```
Private Sub cmdStepInto_Click()
    frmErrors.Caption = "Step Into Stuff"
    cmdUnWit_Click
    cmdStepInto.Caption = "Back again!"
End Sub
```

```
Private Sub cmdStepInto_Click()
    frmErrors.Caption = "Step Into Stuff"
    cmdUnWit_Click
    cmdStepInto.Caption = "Back again!"
End Sub
```

```
Private Sub cmdUnWit_Click()
    Dim MyNum%
    Dim i%

    MyNum% = 2 + 2

    MsgBox CStr(MyNim%)
End Sub
```

```
Private Sub cmdUnWit_Click()
    Dim MyNum%
    Dim i%

    MyNum% = 2 + 2

    MsgBox CStr(MyNim%)
End Sub
```

Part
III

Ch
19

FIG. 19.12

If you do not want to debug the internal code of an event procedure, such as cmdUnWit_Click(), you Step Over it by pressing Shift+F8.

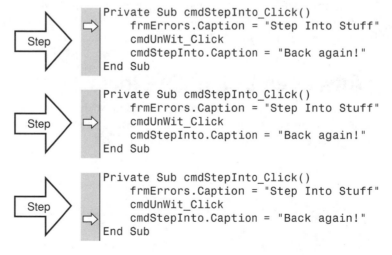

```
Private Sub cmdStepInto_Click()
    frmErrors.Caption = "Step Into Stuff"
    cmdUnWit_Click
    cmdStepInto.Caption = "Back again!"
End Sub
```

```
Private Sub cmdStepInto_Click()
    frmErrors.Caption = "Step Into Stuff"
    cmdUnWit_Click
    cmdStepInto.Caption = "Back again!"
End Sub
```

```
Private Sub cmdStepInto_Click()
    frmErrors.Caption = "Step Into Stuff"
    cmdUnWit_Click
    cmdStepInto.Caption = "Back again!"
End Sub
```

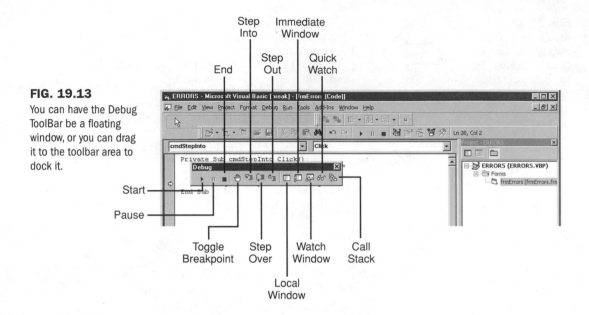

FIG. 19.13
You can have the Debug ToolBar be a floating window, or you can drag it to the toolbar area to dock it.

Stopping at Selected Lines with Run to Cursor

Every time you set a breakpoint it stays in force until you go back into your code and clear it, or clear all the breakpoints by choosing Clear All Breakpoints (Ctrl+Shift+F9) from the Debug menu. Having too many breakpoints makes debugging slow and bothersome. You can make things easier by using Run to Cursor to stop your code at arbitrary points.

You simply click the line of code upon which you want to halt execution and press Ctrl+F8 or select Run to Cursor from the Debug menu. Then press F5 to run your code. The Visual Basic IDE stops execution of your code at the line that you clicked.

Using Advanced Debugging Tools

In addition to being able to watch your code and move through it using the various Step techniques, you can also use the following tools provided with Visual Basic to do advanced debugging. These tools are shown in Figures 19.14 to 19.17.

FIG. 19.14
The Locals window shows all the variables presently in scope and their values. You access the Locals window by selecting Local<u>s</u> Window from the <u>V</u>iew menu.

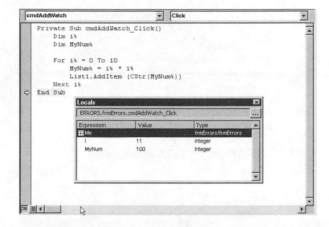

FIG. 19.15
The Immediate window enables you to type in code and run it by pressing Enter.

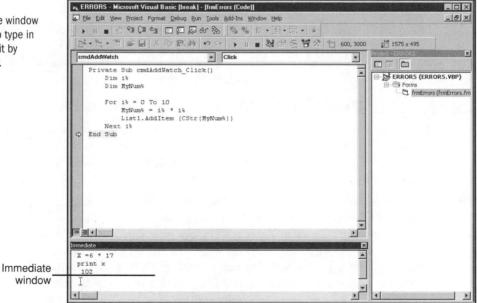

Immediate window ———

Part
III

Ch
19

FIG. 19.16
The Call Stack window shows you all the procedures presently active. This is only functional in break mode.

FIG. 19.17
To show the Quick Watch window, put a break in your code, click a variable, or highlight an expression and select Quick Watch (Shift+ F9) from the Debug Menu.

Invoke Quick Watch ⏤

Highlight a variable ⏤

Set the breakpoint and run the code

Click the Add button to add the variable to the Watch Window

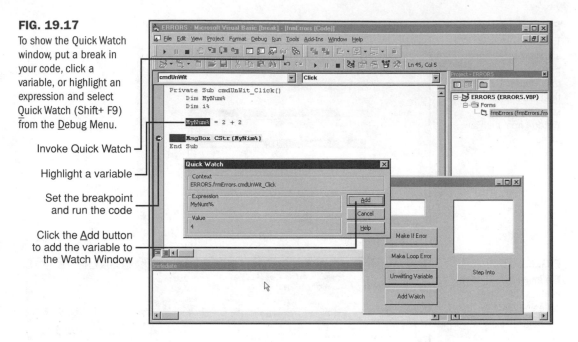

Using *Find* and *Replace*

If you've ever used any type of word processor, at some point you've probably done a Find and Replace. Find and Replace is a technique by which you search a document or portion of a document for a collection of characters and substitute that collection with another—find all occurrences of "Bob" and change them to "Joe," for example.

Find and Replace is a useful debugging tool that enables you to make changes over a large expanse of code with relative ease. For the most part, the code you have seen in this book has not been very big in terms of line count. Thus, finding and fixing something such as the misspelled variable encountered earlier, although a challenge, has not been a difficult task. However, if you have a piece of code that runs more than 10,000 lines (which, by the way, is not unusual for production code), the amount of work that you would have to do to make a change, "x + 2y" to "x * 2y," for example, throughout the code would be considerable. Find and Replace makes things easier.

Find and Replace works much as it does in a word processor. You select a set of characters that you want to locate and then invoke the process.

To Find a set of characters, do the following:

1. Select Find from the Edit menu or press Ctrl+F. This displays the Find dialog box.
2. Enter the word or characters that you want to find in the Find What ComboBox.
3. Click the Find Next button (see Figure 19.18).

FIG. 19.18
The Find dialog box has a good deal of logical search features built in.

Current <u>P</u>rocedure searches the current procedure

Find Whole Word <u>O</u>nly searches for a word not included as part of another word

Direction drop-down list lets you search up or down in the code

Find <u>N</u>ext continues a search

Cancel closes the dialog box

<u>R</u>eplace shows the Replace dialog box

<u>H</u>elp displays the Visual Basic Help text for the dialog box

Current <u>M</u>odule searches the current module

<u>C</u>urrent Project searches the entire project

Searches only highlighted text

Match Ca<u>s</u>e finds words that match inclusive of case sensitivity. For example "MyVar" does not match "myvar"

<u>U</u>se Pattern Matching allows you to search using pattern wild cards

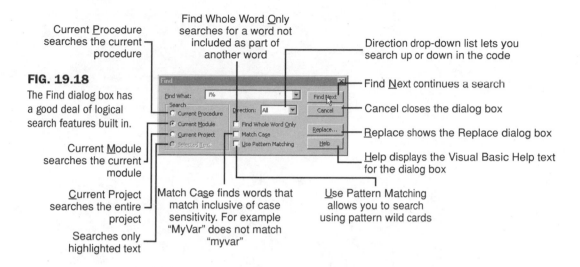

4. To Display the Replace dialog box, click the <u>R</u>eplace button (see Figure 19.19).

▶ **See** Chapter 2, "Customizing and Navigating the Visual Basic Programming Environment," for more information about the Edit menu items, **p. 23**

FIG. 19.19
You can access the Replace dialog box by selecting Replace from the <u>E</u>dit menu or by pressing the Ctrl+H keys.

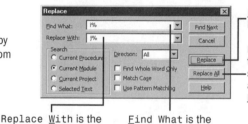

Replace <u>W</u>ith is the word or characters to substitute

<u>F</u>ind What is the word or characters to find

Replace will substitute only the highlighted word

Replace <u>A</u>ll traverses the entire code, the scope of which is determined by the selection of the particular Search option, and replaces all the words entered in the Find What field

Part
III

Ch
19

P A R T IV

Advanced Programming Topics

Working with User-Defined Subs and Functions

You may not be aware of it, but you've been working with Subs and Functions for a while. Event procedures such as Click() and Load() are Subs. And Visual Basic comes with many predefined functions built right into it—LoadPicture() and Len(), for example.

Visual Basic is a *procedural* language. Thus, you have the capability to make blocks of code that can be referred to by a name. After a block of code has a name, it can be *called* and thus executed. In other words, you can write some lines of code, enclose them in a code block, give the block a name, and then call the block when you need it. It's almost like having a program within a program. These little programs that live within larger programs are called Functions if they return a value, and Subs if they do not.

Programmers have used user-defined Subs and *encapsulated* Functions for years. As a matter of fact, a "sub" is a shortened form of "subroutine" that gradually became its own word. They make coding easier, faster, and more *robust*. Also, making your own Subs and Functions puts you on the road to writing code that is *encapsulated* and reusable. ■

Making and Calling a Simple Sub

A Sub is a procedure that executes the lines of code within its block but does not return a value. The syntax for a simple sub is as follows:

```
[Private|Public] Sub SubName()
...lines of code
End Sub
```

Where:

[*Private*|*Public*] are the optional Visual Basic keywords that define the scope of the Sub.

Sub is the Visual Basic keyword that denotes the type of procedure.

SubName is the name that you assign to your Sub.

End Sub are the Visual Basic keywords that denote the end of a code block.

The following code snippet is an example of a simple Sub:

```
Public Sub NoImplement()
     MsgBox "Not Implemented", vbInformation
End Sub
```

When you call this Sub from other areas of your code, the Sub displays a Windows message box with the string "Not Implemented."

This Sub is used in the project TextEdit.VBP from Chapter 13, "Working with Menus." The Sub is inserted in areas of the program where the code is still yet to be written but in which functionality is required so that the programmer doesn't forget that she has some unfinished business.

Listing 20.1 shows the Sub being called by using the Visual Basic Call statement. Using the Call statement is optional. You can call a Sub by using its name only. However, using the Call keyword makes your code more readable. Figure 20.1 shows the result of the call to the Sub NoImplement.

Listing 20.1   20FIG01—Calling a Sub from an Event Procedure

```
Private Sub itmOpen_Click()
     Call NoImplement
End Sub
```

There are two ways to add a Sub to your project. One way is to write the code directly into the General Declarations section of a form or module. The other way is to use the Add Procedure menu item from the Tools menu. To add a Sub to your project by using Add Procedure, do the following:

1. Select Add Procedure from the Tools menu to display the Add Procedure dialog box. Remember that for the Add Procedure menu item to be enabled, you must be in Code window view of the form or module into which you want to add the procedure.

FIG. 20.1

If the programmer needs to change the code for this alert, she does not have to search for every instance of the code. She simply goes to the code block of the Sub to make changes.

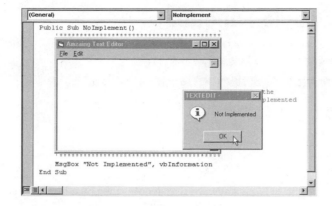

2. Enter the Sub <u>N</u>ame (see Figure 20.2).

FIG. 20.2

The Add Procedure dialog box allows you to create <u>S</u>ubs and <u>F</u>unction for all types of Visual Basic projects as well as <u>P</u>roperty and <u>E</u>vents for ActiveX controls and ActiveX Servers.

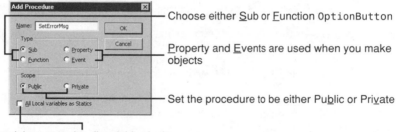

Choose either <u>S</u>ub or <u>F</u>unction OptionButton

<u>P</u>roperty and <u>E</u>vents are used when you make objects

Set the procedure to be either Pu<u>b</u>lic or Pri<u>v</u>ate

Check here to make all variables in the procedure hold their values even when the procedure goes out of scope

3. Click OK to add the Sub's code block to the form or module (see Figure 20.3).

FIG. 20.3

You will find the new Sub in the General section of the form or module.

Navigate to the General section from the Object drop-down ComboBox

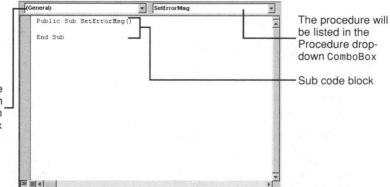

The procedure will be listed in the Procedure drop-down ComboBox

Sub code block

After you create the Sub code block with the Add Procedure dialog box, you simply add the procedure's code within the code block. Do not enter any code for the Sub after the End Sub keywords; this is illegal and generates syntax errors when you compile the code.

Making a Simple Function

A Function is a procedure that executes lines of code and returns a value. The syntax for a declaring a simple Function is as follows:

```
[Private¦Public] Function FunctionName() As DataType
...lines of code
 FunctionName = ReturnValue
End Function
```

Where:

[Private¦Public] is the optional Visual Basic keyword that defines the scope of the Function.

Function is the Visual Basic keyword that denotes the procedure is a Function.

FunctionName is the name that you assign to your Function.

As is the Visual Basic keyword that denotes a data type assignment.

DataType is the data type of the value that the function will return.

ReturnValue is the value that you pass back from the function by assigning it to the function's name. (This is very important!)

End Function are the Visual Basic keywords that denote the end of a code block.

The snippet of code in Listing 20.2 shows a function, GetNumber(), the purpose of which is to return a number defined within the function itself.

(The code for the examples in this chapter is found in the project prjSubs.vbp, in the directory \Chp_20\prjSubs\ on the CD-ROM that comes with this book.)

Listing 20.2   20LIST02.TXT—A Simple Function

```
Public Function GetNumber() As Integer
    Dim a%
    Dim b%
    Dim c%
    'Assign values to some variables
    a% = 7
    b% = 12

    'Add them together
    c% = a% + b%

    'Pass the result out of the function by assigning
    'it to the function name.
    GetNumber = c%
End Function
```

You add a `Function` to your project by using the same two methods that you used to add a `Sub`—either directly into the `General` Declarations section of the form or module or by using the Add Procedure dialog box. However, be advised that you have to manually add a little code when you add a function to your code using the Add Procedure dialog box (see Figure 20.4).

FIG. 20.4
The Add Procedure dialog box adds the code block, but it does not define the data type for the return value nor does it add the function name within the code block so that you can pass values out of the function. You must add these on your own.

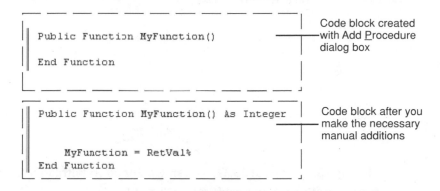

```
Public Function MyFunction()

End Function
```
Code block created with Add Procedure dialog box

```
Public Function MyFunction() As Integer

    MyFunction = RetVal%
End Function
```
Code block after you make the necessary manual additions

Passing Arguments into Subs and Functions

You can enhance the power and versatility of `Subs` and `Functions` by using *arguments*. An argument, also referred to as a *parameter,* is a variable that acts as a placeholder for a value that you will pass "into" the `Sub` or `Function`. You create arguments by placing them within the parentheses of the declaration statement of the `Sub` or `Function`. Listing 20.3 shows the declaration for the function `Foo`. `Foo` has two arguments, one of type `Integer`, and the other of type `String`.

Listing 20.3 20LIST03.TXT—A Function Declaration with Two Arguments

```
Public Function Foo(NumOne As Integer, strName As String) As Integer
```

Using arguments greatly increases the reusability of your code. For example, imagine that in many places of your code you need to figure out the greater of two numbers. Every time you need to do this calculation you could write out the code, line for line. Or, you could write out a function that does this for you and then call the function when you need to do the calculation. The advantage of the latter method is twofold. First, one call will satisfy many needs throughout your code. Second, if you need to enhance this functionality, you don't have to go through your code and make enhancements line by line. You simply go back to the function and make the changes within the function's code block.

Listing 20.4 shows the user-defined function, `GetGreaterNum()`. `GetGreaterNum()` returns the greater of two numbers passed to it.

Part
IV

Ch
20

Listing 20.4   20LIST04.TXT—Using GetGreaterNum()Throughout the Code

```
Public Function GetGreaterNum(NumOne As Integer, NumTwo As Integer) As Integer
    'If the first number is greater than the second
    If NumOne > NumTwo Then
        'return the first number
        GetGreaterNum = NumOne
    Else
        'if not, return the second number
        GetGreaterNum = NumTwo
    End If
End Function
```

Listing 20.5 shows the function `GetGreaterNum()` called from within a `Click()` event procedure.

Listing 20.5   20LIST05.TXT—Using a Function Within an Event ProcedurePrivate Sub cmdGreaterNum_Click()

```
    Dim i%
    Dim j%
    Dim RetVal%

    'Get the input in txtNumOne and convert it to an integer
    i% = CInt(txtNumOne.Text)

    'Get the input in txtNumTwo and convert it to an integer
    j% = CInt(txtNumTwo.Text)

    RetVal% = GetGreaterNum(i%, j%)

    'Take the result from the function, convert it to
    'a string and assign it to the caption of the button.
    cmdGreaterNum.Caption = CStr(RetVal%)
End Sub
```

It's very important when you use `Subs` or `Functions` that the argument's type and order match up. If you have a procedure that has three arguments of type `Integer`, you must pass in three integers. You cannot pass in two `Integers` and a `String`. The compiler will throw an error. For example, if you have a function `Foo()` that is declared as follows:

```
Public Function Foo(iNum as Integer, dAccount as Double) as Double
```

and you call the function using the following line of code:

```
dMyResult = Foo(6, "D56R")
```

This call generates an error. `"D56R"` is of type `String`. The function is expecting the second argument to be of type `Double`. Thus, an error appears.

Also, the argument count must match up. For example, you have a function declared as follows:

```
Public Function Bar(iNum as Integer, dNum as Double, strName as String) as
Integer
```

and you call the function using the following line of code:

```
iMyResult = Bar(6, 7)
```

This call also causes an error. The function expects three arguments. You have passed in only two. Thus, again, an error occurs.

It is possible to make an argument optional by using the Optional keyword before an argument when you declare the function. If this is something you need or want to do, you might want to take a look at the Visual Basic online Help.

Exiting Subs and Functions

Sometimes you'll need to leave a procedure before it finishes. You do this by using the Exit keyword. Listing 20.6 shows the function ExitEarly(), which takes two arguments—an Integer that is used to determine the upper limit of a loop and an Integer that flags the function as to whether a special condition exists that requires the function to be exited early.

Listing 20.6   20LIST06.TXT—The ExitEarly() Function and the Event Procedure that Calls It

```
Public Function ExitEarly(iLimit As Integer, iFlag As Integer) As Integer
    Dim i%
    Dim Limit%

    Dim Flag%


    'Assign the limit argument to a local variable
    Limit% = iLimit

    'Assign the state argument to local variable
    Flag%= iFlag

    'Run a For...Next loop to Limit%
    For i% = 0 To Limit%

        'If the passed in state is one
        If Flag% = 1 Then

            'Check to see if i% equals half the value of
            'the Limit variable
            If i% = Limit% / 2 Then

                'If it does, pass out the value of i%
                'at that point
                ExitEarly = i%
```

Part

IV

Ch

20

continues

Listing 20.6 Continued

```
                    'Terminate the function, there is no reason
                    'to go on
                    Exit Function
            End If
        End If
    Next i%

    'If you made it this far, the flag variable does not
    'equal one, so pass the value of i% out of the function
    'by assigning the value of i% to the function name.
    ExitEarly = i%

End Function
================================================

Private Sub cmdExitEarly_Click()
    Dim i%
    Dim j%

    'Get a value from the TextBox, txtNumOne
    j% = CInt(txtNumOne.Text)

    'Pass the values into the function
    i% = ExitEarly(j%, chkExitEarly.Value)

    'Report the value of i%
    cmdExitEarly.Caption = CStr(i%)
End Sub
```

The function ExitEarly() works by taking the iLimit argument, assigning it to a variable local to the function and then using that local variable to be the upper limit of a For...Next loop. It also takes the iFlag argument and assigns that variable to one that is also local to the function. Then the For...Next loop is run. Within the loop, if the value of the local Flag variable is 1, an If...Then statement checks the value of the counting variable, i%, to see whether it is equal to half the value of the variable Limit. If it is, the value is assigned to the function's name, to be passed back to the call, and the Exit keyword terminates the execution of the function. If the value of the local variable Flag is other than 1, the loop continues until it reaches its limit. Then the value of i% is assigned to the function's name, and control is returned to the calling code.

The function is called from the Click event procedure of a CommandButton, cmdEarlyExit (see Figure 20.5).

Operationally, the user experiences the code by entering a number in the TextBox, txtNumOne (see Figure 20.6). If the user checks the CheckBox, chkExitEarly, half the value entered in TextBox is shown in the Caption of the CommandButton, cmdExitEarly. If not, the Caption will be the value entered in the TextBox plus one. (The increment of one is due to the logic of the For...Next loop.)

FIG. 20.5

One of the nice new features of Visual Basic 5.0 is that the Quick Info window pops up even for user-defined subs and functions.

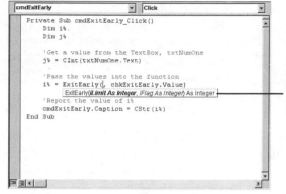

Quick Info window shows the arguments for a function and bolds the argument that is to be entered

FIG. 20.6

The ExitEarly() function is transparent to the user.

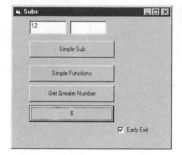

Understanding Scope

In Listing 20.6, you'll notice that both the event procedure, cmdExitEarly_Click(), and the function, ExitEarly() both create a variable, i%, within their respective code blocks by using the Dim statement. These two procedures can create variables with the same name and not cause an error because the *scope* of the created variables is different. It's almost as if they live in different "rooms" in the program. The variable i% in cmdExitEarly_Click() is created when the event procedure is fired; it's valid while the event procedure is running, and it can be "seen" only by the code within the event procedure's block. When the event procedure finishes, the variable is removed from memory. The same is true of the variable i% in ExitEarly(). If for some reason, both were in force at the same time, that would be fine because the scope of each isolates one from the other.

Understanding Encapsulation

You can see in the cmdExitEarly_Click() event procedure shown earlier in Listing 20.6 that the value for the iFlag argument is assigned the setting of the chkExitEarly.Value property and then passed into the function, ExitEarly(). You may be wondering why the value of the CheckBox was not read directly from within the function, ExitEarly(). This is because a

Part IV Ch 20

conscious effort was made to make the function `EarlyExit()` independent of any control or form in the project. If the function had code in it that called chkEarlyExit, if you wanted to use this code in another project, you would have to make sure that a CheckBox named chkEarlyExit existed in the new project. Otherwise, the code would be useless.

However, this is not the case. The function `EarlyExit()` requires only numeric values, being passed as arguments, to be functional. It does not look outside itself for other values. Therefore, the function can be used in a number of different scenarios.

Listing 20.7 shows the function `EarlyExit()` being called from an event procedure `cmdMoreExit_Click()`. The `cmdMoreExit_Click()` event procedure gets the value for the iFlag argument of the `ExitEarly()` function from a local variable, the value of which is based upon the `Value` property of an `OptionButton` control.

Listing 20.7   20LIST07.TXT—Using a Well-Encapsulated Function

```
Private Sub cmdMoreExit_Click()
    Dim i%
    Dim j%
    Dim ExitVal%

    'Get a value from the TextBox, txtNumOne
    j% = CInt(txtNumOne.Text)

    'Set the Value for ExitVal%
    If optEarly.Value = True Then
        ExitVal% = 1
    Else
        ExitVal% = 0
    End If

    'Pass the values into the function
    i% = ExitEarly(j%, ExitVal%)

    'Report the value of i%
    cmdMoreExit.Caption = CStr(i%)
End Sub
```

The event procedures `cmdExitEarly_Click()` and `cmdMoreExit_Click()` get the data to pass to the arguments of function, `ExitEarly()` from completely different sources. However, both get back values appropriate to the respective code (see Figure 20.7). The function `EarlyExit()` displays the same behavior regardless of which control's event procedure is doing the calling and what controls are on the form. This capability of a procedure to hide its inner workings from other code in a program is called *encapsulation*. A well-encapsulated procedure is one that has no external dependencies; the procedure works the same regardless of the other code or elements in the program.

FIG. 20.7
The graphical interface
of frmMain has been
extended to accommo-
date two different ways
of calling the same
function.

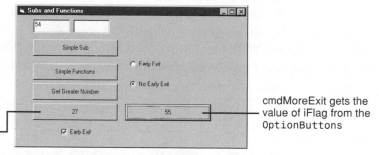

cmdExitEarly gets the
value of iFlag from the
CheckBox

cmdMoreExit gets the
value of iFlag from the
OptionButtons

Making a Procedure Reusable

With all the issue made about encapsulation and the importance of reusable code, the reality is
that the function EarlyExit(), although well-encapsulated, has limited reuse. It lives in the
form, frmMain. If you want to reuse the code in another project, you have to add the entire
form to the new project. In this instance, this requirement is not a very big imposition. But
what if you have a form that has many detailed graphics and ActiveX controls? The new project
might need none of this, and yet to use this sole function, you would have to incur the overhead
of all the extraneous graphics and ActiveX controls. This is far from implementing any concept
of efficient, reusable code.

A better way to make a procedure reusable is to create it within a module. If your procedure is
not dependent on any Visual Basic control and is well-encapsulated, putting it in a module will
offer you a good deal of reuse. Eventually, you will have a library of modules that contain procedures that you will use throughout your programming career.

To put the function EarlyExit() in a module, do the following:

1. Select Add Module from the Project Menu.
2. Select Module from the New tab of the Add Module dialog box (see Figure 20.8).

FIG. 20.8
In addition to being
able to select a new
module from the Add
Module dialog box, you
also can select a new
Add-In module. An Add-
In is a module that
customizes the Visual
Basic IDE.

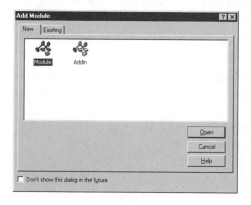

Part
IV
Ch
20

3. Name the module modFunc. Save module to the default file name modFunc.bas.

4. Go to the frmMain Code window. Click the Procedure View icon in the lower left-hand side of the Code window to ensure that the Code window is in Procedure view. Select (General) from the Object box.

5. Select EarlyExit() from the Procedure drop-down CombBox.

6. Press Ctrl+A to select all the code for the procedure ExitEarly() in the Code window (see Figure 20.9).

FIG. 20.9

You can move a procedure to another module using Cut and Paste techniques.

Procedure drop-down combo box

Module file

Form file

Procedure View icon

Full Module View icon

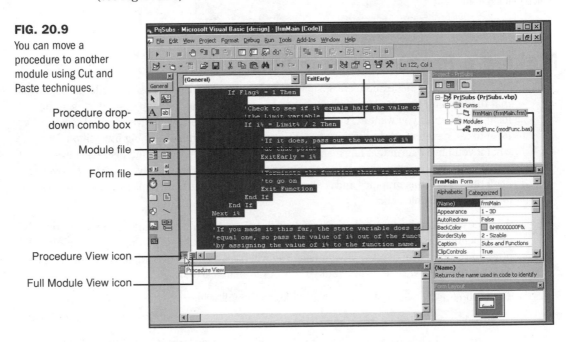

7. Press Ctrl+X to Cut the code of the procedure ExitEarly() to the Clipboard.

8. Select the module modFunc by double-clicking it in the Project Explorer. This brings the General section of the module into the Code window.

9. Click in the Code window.

10. Press Ctrl+V to paste the code from the Clipboard into the General section. EarlyExit() is now listed in the procedure drop-down ComboBox of the modFunc Code window (see Figure 20.10).

11. Save modFunc.bas. The function ExitEarly() has been removed from the form and transferred to the module.

FIG. 20.10

You can navigate to particular forms and modules by double-clicking within the Project Explorer.

File in Code window will be noted in the title bar of the IDE

A module's procedures are listed in the Procedure drop-down ComboBox

The Name property of a module is the only one listed in the Properties window

Double-click a module file in the Project Explorer to bring it into the Code window

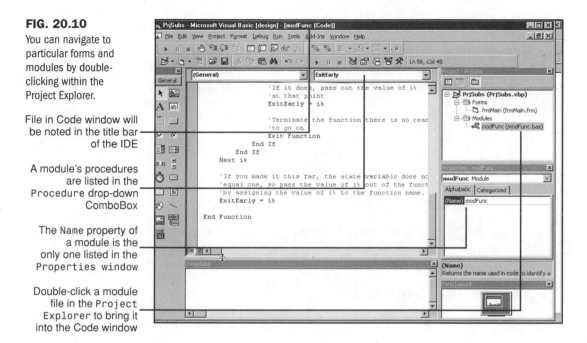

As long as you stay in control of the cutting and pasting process, transferring a procedure from a form to a module is straightforward. If in the future, you require the function EarlyExit() in another project, all you need to do is select Add File (Ctrl+D) from the Project menu to add the module modFunc to the new project. When that is done, the function is accessed like any other function within the project.

Documenting Subs and Functions

Although the function EarlyExit() is functionally adequate, it is difficult to implement from project to project. If another programmer wanted to use it, she would have to take more than a passing glance to figure out what the function was about and how to put it to good use. Proper documentation addresses this deficiency.

All Subs and Functions should have a *header*. A header is a section of commented code that appears at the top of a code block. Usually the header gives a synopsis of the procedure: procedure name, a description of the arguments and return value if any, as well as some remarks as to what the procedure is about with any special instructions. Also in the header is a history of when and who created the code. If any changes are made to the code, a description of the changes and the date of the changes are added to the header. Finally, the header contains the appropriate copyright information.

You should also comment each task within the procedure. This will save time for others who will maintain your code. Commenting your code will save you a lot of effort when it comes to time to revisit the code later.

Part
IV

Ch
20

Listing 20.8 shows the function EarlyExit() documented with a proper header.

Listing 20.8   20LIST08.TXT—A Well-Documented EarlyExit() Function

```
Public Function ExitEarly(iLimit As Integer, iFlag As Integer) As Integer
'*******************************************
'Sub/Function: ExitEarly
'
'Arguments: iLimit   The upper limit of the For..Next Loop
'           iFlag    An integer indicating early exit from
'                    the function. 1 = Exit.
'                    Other values are ignored.
'
'Return: The value of the For...Next loop counter
'
'Remarks:   This function is used to demonstrate the way to use
'           arguments within a function
'
'Programmer: Bob Reselman
'
'History: Created 8/23/97
'
'Copyright 1997, Macmillan Publishing
'*******************************************

Dim i%       'Counter variable
Dim Limit%   'Internal variable for the upper limit of the
             'For...Next loop
Dim Flag%    'Internal variable for the exit flag

'Assign the limit argument to a local variable
Limit% = iLimit

'Assign the state argument to local variable
Flag% = iFlag

'Run a For...Next loop to Limit%
For i% = 0 To Limit%

    'If the passed in state is one
    If Flag% = 1 Then

        'Check to see if i% equals half the value of
        'the Limit variable
        If i% = Limit% / 2 Then

            'If it does, pass out the value of i%
            'at that point
            ExitEarly = i%

            'Terminate the function there is no reason
            'to go on
            Exit Function
        End If
    End If
```

```
    Next i%

    'If you made it this far, the state variable does not
    'equal one, so pass the value of i% out of the function
    'by assigning the value of i% to the function name.
    ExitEarly = i%

End Function
```

Determining Your Entry Point with *Sub Main()*

By default when you start a Visual Basic project, the first form that was created will be the first form that the project loads. This is adequate if you have a one-form project. But what do you do if you have a project with many forms or a project that has no forms at all? For the multiple form problem, you could "chain" Form_Load() event procedures—have one form's Load event procedure Load another form as follows:

```
Private Sub Form_Load()
    Load frmAnotherForm
End Sub
```

This would work for adequately for projects with a limited amount of forms, but it is not the best programming practice, particularly if you have projects that require the presentation of many forms.

For projects that have no forms (there are such projects, particularly in server-side Internet programming using Visual Basic), there's nothing to load. So what do you do for an *entry point* (or starting point) for your program? Visual Basic provides a non-form based entry point for your program—the Sub Main() procedure.

Sub Main() is a special procedure that is reserved by Visual Basic as the startup procedure for any given project. Sub Main() must be declared in a module. There can only be one Sub Main() per project.

To set Sub Main() to be the start up point for a project, do the following:

1. Select [ProjectName] Properties from the end of the Project menu.
2. Select Sub Main from the Startup Object drop-down list in the General tab of the Project Properties tabbed dialog box (see Figure 20.11).
3. Click OK at the bottom of the tabbed dialog box.

After you have defined Sub Main() to be the Startup object for your project, you need to create Sub Main in a module. You can use the Add Procedure dialog box that you've used to create user-defined procedures, or you can enter the declaration manually in the General section of your chosen module. Remember, a project can have only one Sub Main()! After you create Sub Main(), you need to fill in some startup code.

Listing 20.9 shows a Sub Main() that displays two forms using the Show method and then displays a message box after all the forms are visible (see Figure 20.12).

Part
IV

Ch
20

FIG. 20.11

You can choose to have
Sub Main() or any
form in your project as
the Startup Object.

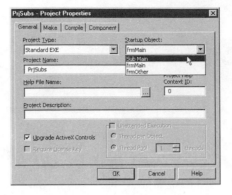

Listing 20.9 20LIST09.TXT—A Simple *Sub Main()*

```
Sub Main()
    'Use the Show method to display both
    'forms upon startup
    frmMain.Show
    frmOther.Show

    'Report that all forms are shown
    MsgBox "Everything shown"
End Sub
```

FIG. 20.12

When using Sub
Main(), remember that
when you unload the
last form, you are not
necessarily going to end
the program.

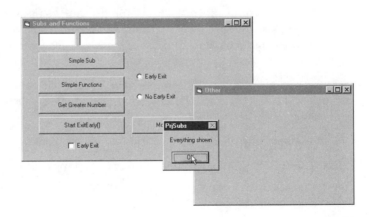

The code for some versions of Sub Main() can be simple. However, some Sub Main() procedures can be complex. Listing 20.10 shows how Sub Main() is used to invoke a comprehensive
startup routine that calls other procedures. This listing is the Sub Main() procedure for the
VBScheduler program that comes on the CD-ROM that accompanies this book.

Listing 20.10 20LIST10.TXT—A More Complex *Sub Main()* that Does More than Load Forms

```
Sub Main()
    'Load the form and let it run the code in the Form_Load event
    'handler
    Load frmMain
    'Intialize the contact list combo box
    Call InitComboAsDb(frmMain.cboName, frmMain.DataMain)
    'Fill the appointment list with today's appoinments
    Call GetDailyAppointments(CDbl(CDate(frmMain.FormDateString())), _
                              frmMain.lstSchedule, _
                              frmMain.DataMain, _
                              gAppointmentDelta%)
    'Show the main form
    frmMain.Show
    'Set the mouse pointer back to an arrow
    frmMain.MousePointer = 0
End Sub
```

CHAPTER 21

Working with Strings and Typecasting

Concatenation

Build strings using the concatenation operator.

Truncation

Obtain substrings using `Left()`, `Right()`, `Mid()`, and `Instr()`.

Data Validation

Validate user input.

Typecasting

Use Visual Basic to do loose and strict typecasting.

Conversion

Learn how to use the Visual Basic conversion functions.

Visual Basic makes working with strings and other data types easy. Whereas in languages such as C or C++ using strings involves the complexities of memory allocation and pointers, the automated nature of Visual Basic removes this complexity for the programmer. Thus, operations such as string concatenation and truncation, which are significant chores in C and C++, are simple in Visual Basic. Visual Basic is a *loosely* typed language. This means that in certain situations one type of data can be used where another type is expected—assigning an integer to the Text property of a TextBox, for instance. However, although loose typing works in most situations, there are times where you must be more strict with your use of data types. To help you address these issues, this chapter takes a look at how to manipulate strings using the intrinsic Visual Basic string functions and how to use the Visual Basic data conversion functions to do typecasting. ■

Concatenating Strings

Concatenating one string to another means combining both strings. You concatenate two strings using the "&" operator, as shown in Listing 21.1.

Listing 21.1 21LIST01.TXT—Simple Concatentation of Two Strings

```
Private Sub cmdBerry_Click()
    Dim strMine As String
    Dim strYours As String
    Dim strResult As String

    strMine = "blue"
    strYours = "berry"
    strResult = strMine & strYours

    cmdBerry.Caption = strResult
End Sub
```

The value of strResult will be "blueberry."

You can also concatenate more than two strings together using the "&" operator. For example, you might want to add a space character between a first name and last name, as shown in Listing 21.2. The result of the code is shown in Figure 21.1.

Listing 21.2 21LIST02.TXT—Concatenating More than Two Strings

```
Private Sub cmdFullName_Click()
    Dim FirstName$
    Dim LastName$
    Dim FullName$

    'Get the first name for the textbox
    FirstName$ = txtFirst.Text

    'Get the last name from another textbox
    LastName$ = txtSecond.Text

    'Concatenate the first and last name, putting
    'a space character between them.
    FullName$ = FirstName$ & " " & LastName$

    'Display the Full Name
    cmdFullName.Caption = FullName$

End Sub
```

FIG. 21.1

You can also use the "+" character to concatenate strings, but that technique is a holdover from earlier versions of Visual Basic.

The code for this section is in the project SmpleStr.VBP, which is in the directory \Chp_21\SmpleStr on the CD-ROM that accompanies this book.

Determining the Length of a String Using *Len()*

You use the Visual Basic Len() function to determine how many characters are in a given string. You will use this function a lot, particularly in conjunction with the other string manipulation functions.

The syntax of the Len() function is:

```
iResult = Len(MyString)
```

Where:

> *iResult* is an integer that contains the number of characters returned by the function.
>
> *Len* is the name of the function.
>
> *MyString* is the string, the length of which you want to determine.

Listing 21.3 shows you how to use Len() function. Figure 21.2 shows the result of the listing in action.

Listing 21.3   21LIST03.TXT—Using the *Len()* Function

```
Private Sub cmdFindLen_Click()
    Dim FindStr$
    Dim iLen As Integer

    'Assign a string to find to the local variable
    FindStr$ = txtFirst.Text

    'Find the length of the string
    iLen = Len(FindStr$)

    'Report the results
    lblResult.Caption = CStr(iLen)

End Sub
```

Part
IV

Ch
21

FIG. 21.2

You can also use the Len() function to find the size (in bytes) of a non-string type variable.

The code for this section is in the project SmpleStr.VBP, which is in the directory \Chp_21\SmpleStr on the CD-ROM that accompanies this book.

Truncating Strings Using *Left()* and *Right()* Functions

You use the Left() and Right() functions to truncate strings. Informally, to *truncate* a string means to "cut off" part of it, to make the string smaller. The Left() function returns a certain amount of characters from the left side of a given string to a *buffer* string. A buffer string is a holding string. The Right() function is similar to the Left() function. But instead of returning characters from the left side of a string, the Right() function returns a given amount of characters from the right side of a string.

The syntax for the Left() and Right() functions is as follows:

```
strResult = Left(MyString, lNumToReturn)
strResult = Right(MyString, lNumToReturn)
```

Where:

> *strResult* is the string returned from the function.
>
> *Left¦Right* is the function name.
>
> *MyString* is the string upon which you want to perform the function.
>
> *lNumToReturn* is a Long that indicates number of characters that you want to return. The least amount of characters you can return is 1. Using 0 (zero) will produce an error.

Listing 21.4 shows you how to use the Left() and Right() functions to truncate a given amount of characters from a string. The result of this code is shown in Figure 21.3.

(The code for the Left() and Right() functions is in the project SmpleStr.VBP, which is in the directory \Chp_21\SmpleStr on the CD-ROM that accompanies this book.)

Listing 21.4 21LIST04.TXT—Using the *Left()* and *Right()* Functions

```
Private Sub cmdLeft_Click()
    Dim NumToTrunc& 'Number of characters to return
    Dim Buffer$  'string buffer
    Dim strMain As String 'string to truncate
```

```
        'Convert the numeral for the number of
        'characters to truncate to a number
        NumToTrunc& = CDbl(txtSecond.Text)

        'Get the string to truncate
        strMain = txtFirst.Text

        'Truncate the string using the Left() function
        Buffer$ = Left(strMain, NumToTrunc&)

        'Display the results
        lblResult.Caption = Buffer$
    End Sub

    Private Sub cmdRight_Click()
        Dim NumToTrunc& 'Number of characters to return
        Dim Buffer$  'string buffer
        Dim strMain As String 'string to truncate

        'Convert the numeral for the number of
        'characters to truncate to a number
        NumToTrunc& = CDbl(txtSecond.Text)

        'Get the string to truncate
        strMain = txtFirst.Text

        'Truncate the string using the Right() function
        Buffer$ = Right(strMain, NumToTrunc%)

        'Display the results
        lblResult.Caption = Buffer$
    End Sub
```

FIG. 21.3

The Left() function returns a given number of characters from the left side of a string. The Right() function returns a given number of characters from the right side of a string.

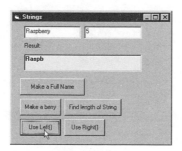

The code for this section is in the project SmpleStr.VBP, which is in the directory \Chp_21\SmpleStr on the CD-ROM that accompanies this book.

Part

IV

Ch

21

Changing a String's Case Using *UCase()* and *LCase()*

The UCase() and LCase() functions affect the case of a given string or character. The UCase() function returns a string in which all the characters are set to uppercase. The LCase() function returns a string in which all the characters are set to lowercase. The syntax for the UCase() and LCase() functions is as follows:

```
strResult = UCase(MyString)
strResult = LCase(MyString)
```

Where:

strResult is the string returned from the function.

UCase¦LCase is the function name.

MyString is the string to set to uppercase (or lowercase).

Listing 21.5 shows you how to use the UCase() and LCase() functions to set a given string to uppercase and lowercase. Figure 21.4 shows the code example in action.

Listing 21.5 21LIST05.TXT—Using the *UCase()* and *LCase()* Functions

```
Private Sub cmdUpper_Click()
    Dim Buffer$
    'Assign the characters in the first textbox
    'to the buffer variable
    Buffer$ = txtFirst.Text

    'Set all the characters in the buffer to
    'upper case and display the result
    lblResult.Caption = UCase(Buffer$)
End Sub

Private Sub cmdLower_Click()
    Dim Buffer$
    'Assign the characters in the first textbox
    'to the buffer variable
    Buffer$ = txtFirst.Text

    'Set all the characters in the buffer to
    'lower case and display the result
    lblResult.Caption = LCase(Buffer$)
End Sub
```

FIG. 21.4

UCase() and LCase() are closely related functions.

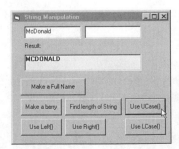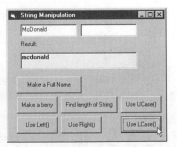

The code for this section is in the project SmpleStr.VBP, which is in the directory \Chp_21\SmpleStr on the CD-ROM that accompanies this book.

Returning Characters from Inside a String Using *Mid()*

The `Mid()` function returns a string of a given number of characters from a specified location in another string. For example, if you want to return the string "Allen" from the string "Edgar Allen Poe," you use the `Mid()` function.

The syntax for the `Mid()` function is as follows:

```
strResult = Mid(MyString, lStartPosition, lLength)
```

Where:

> *strResult* is the string returned from the function.
>
> *Mid* is the function name.
>
> *MyString* is the string from which to extract the return string.
>
> *lStartPosition* is a value of type `Long` that reflects the position upon which the characters to extract begin. If this number is larger than the size of the of MyString, the return will be an empty string (""). This number cannot be less than 1.
>
> *lLength* is a value of type `Long` that reflects the number of characters to return from MyString. The argument is optional. If you do not specify a length, `Mid()` returns all the characters starting from the position determined by `lStartPosition` to the end of the string `MyString`. For example, in the following:
>
> MyString = "Edgar Allen Poe",
>
> strResult = Mid(MyString, 5,5)
>
> the value of `strResult` is "r All". Whereas in the example:
>
> MyString = "Edgar Allen Poe",
>
> strResult = Mid(MyString, 5)
>
> the value of `strResult` is "r Allen Poe".

Listing 21.6 shows you how to use the `Mid()` function to extract a substring from a string. The result of the code is shown in Figure 21.5.

Listing 21.6   21LIST06.TXT—Using the *Mid()* function

```
Private Sub cmdSimpleMid_Click()
    Dim Buffer$      'String Buffer
    Dim MyString$    'The string upon which to perform
                     'the Mid() function
```

continues

Part

IV

Ch

21

Listing 21.6   Continued

```
    Dim StartPos&  'The starting position of the Mid()
                   'function

    Dim ReturnSize& 'Size of the string to return

    'REMEMBER: The "&" data type suffix declares
    'a variable of type, LONG.

    'Assign the text in the first textbox to the
    'MyString variable
    MyString$ = txtFirst.Text

    'Convert the numeral in the second textbox to a
    'LONG and assign it to the starting position
    'variable.
    StartPos& = CLng(txtSecond.Text)

    'Convert the numeral in the third textbox to a
    'LONG and assign it to the return size variable.
    ReturnSize& = CLng(txtThird.Text)

    'Run the Mid() function and assign the result to
    'the buffer variable.
    Buffer$ = Mid(MyString$, StartPos&, ReturnSize&)

    'Display the result in a textbox.
    txtHold.Text = Buffer$
End Sub
```

FIG. 21.5

Remember, the space character occupies a character position.

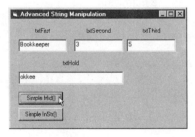

The source code for the Mid() function examples used here is in the project AdvStr.vbp, in the directory, Chp_21\advncstr\ on the CD-ROM that accompanies this book.

The Mid() function is both powerful and tricky to master. It takes some practice to get accustomed to using it. Following are a few helpful things to remember:

The value of the start position variable must be at least 1.

Characters in strings start with "1," unlike array indices, which start at "0."

The space character (" ")is treated as any other character.

If you don't specify a return size variable for the return string, the `Mid()` function returns all characters from the value of the start position variable to the end of the string.

The code for this section is in the project AdvncStr.VBP, which is in the directory \Chp_21\AdvncStr on the CD-ROM that accompanies this book.

Searching for Characters Within a String Using *InStr()*

The `InStr()` function is used to determine whether a character or string exists within another string. If it does, the function returns a `Long` that reflects the position of the located string. For example, if you want to know whether the decimal character "." is in a string, "123.345," you would use the `Instr()` function.

The syntax for the `InStr()` function is:

```
lResult = InStr(iStartPos, strBeingSearched, strLookedFor, iCompare)
```

Where:

lResult is the returned `Long` value that indicates the position of the first found instance of the `strLookedFor` string in the string `strBeingSearched`.

InStr is the function name.

iStartPos is the number that indicates from where to start looking. This argument is optional. If you omit it, the function starts searching at the beginning of the string `strBeingSearched`.

strBeingSearched is the string into which the function searches for the substring `strLookedFor`.

strLookedFor is the string or character for which you are searching.

iCompare is the number that indicates how to look for the string `strLookedFor`. If you omit this argument or set it to 0 (zero), `Instr()` does a case-sensitive search. If you include `iCompare` using the value 1, the search will be non-case sensitive.

Listing 21.7 shows you how to use the `Instr()` function. Figure 21.6 shows the code in action.

Listing 21.7 21LIST07.TXT—Using the *InStr()* Function

```
Private Sub cmdInStr_Click()
    Dim lResult As Long
    Dim strToLookIn As String
    Dim strToLookFor As String
    Dim lStartPos As Long

    'Assign the value for the string in which you are
    'going to look for your character or string.
    strToLookIn = txtFirst.Text
```

continues

Listing 21.7 Continued

```
'Get the string you want to look for from the
'TextBox
strToLookFor = txtSecond.Text

'If the TextBox is not empty, get the starting
'position for the search
If txtThird.Text <> "" Then
    lStartPos = CLng(txtThird.Text)
Else
    'If it is empty , set the starting position to
    'the first character
    lStartPos = 1
End If
lResult = InStr(lStartPos, strToLookIn, strToLookFor)

'Display the answer
txtHold.Text = CStr(lResult)
End Sub
```

FIG. 21.6

The InStr() function reports back the position of the *first* occurrence of a given character or string. If you want to search for other occurrences, you must reset the function's iStartPos argument.

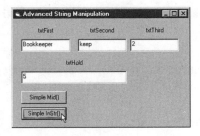

The code for this section is in the project AdvncStr.VBP, which is in the directory \Chp_21\advncstr on the CD-ROM that accompanies this book.

Making String Parsing Functions

Now that you have an overview of the fundamentals of string manipulation using the Len(), Left(), Right(), Mid(), and InStr() functions, you are going to drill down a bit and put what you've learned to more detailed use.

String parsing, the activity of stripping and manipulating strings, is a common activity among programmers. One of the most common parsing requirements that programmers encounter is to retrieve the first-name string and the last-name string from a full-name string. You'll now study a set of user-defined functions that do this. These functions are called GetFirstName() and GetLastName(). GetFirstName() returns the first name from the full name. GetLastName() returns the last name from the full name. Both functions take one argument—a string indicating the full name.

These functions are designed around a central conceptual principle (and assumption)—that within a full-name string, the first name is separated from the last name by a space character (" ") and that if you know the location of the space character in the full-name string, you can strip out the first-name characters and the last-name characters.

Figure 21.7 illustrates logic of determining the first-name and last-name strings from a full-name string. Listing 21.8 shows the code for the functions GetFirstName() and GetLastName().

FIG. 21.7

The most important thing that you need to know to parse names from a string is the position of the space characters.

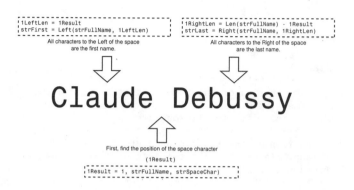

Listing 21.8   21LIST08.TXT—Using *GetFirstName()* and *GetLastName()* to Use String Functions to Do Parsing

```
Public Function GetFirstName(strFullName As String) As String
'*****************************************
'Sub/Function: GetFirstName
'
'Arguments: strFullName  A string representing a full name
'                        to validate
'
'Return:                 A string containing the First Name if the
'                        Full Name string is valid. If the Full Name
'                        string is invalid, the function returns the
'                        string, "ERROR"
'
'Remarks:                A valid string has only one space character
'
'Programmer: Bob Reselman
'
'History: Created 8/23/97
'
'Copyright 1997, Macmillan Publishing
'*****************************************
    Dim lSpacePos As Long         'Position of space character
                                  'in a string
    Dim strSpaceChar As String    'Space character
    Dim strFirstName As String    'Buffer for First Name string
    Dim lResult As Long           'Result variable
    Dim lLeftLen As Long          'Number of characters in First
```

continues

Listing 21.8   Continued

```
                                'Name
    '_*_*_*_*_*_*_*_*_*_*_*_*_*_*_*_*_*_*_*_*_*_*
    'Use the IsValid function to make sure that the
    'Full Name string has only one space character in it.
    If IsValid(strFullName) = False Then
        'If it doesn't, return the error string
        GetFirstName = "Error"
        'And exit the function
        Exit Function
    End If
    '_*_*_*_*_*_*_*_*_*_*_*_*_*_*_*_*_*_*_*_*_*_*
    'Define space character
    strSpaceChar = " "
    '_*_*_*_*_*_*_*_*_*_*_*_*_*_*_*_*_*_*_*_*_*_*
    'Find the position of the space character within the
    'full name string.
    lResult = InStr(1, strFullName, strSpaceChar)
    '_*_*_*_*_*_*_*_*_*_*_*_*_*_*_*_*_*_*_*_*_*_*
    'The position of the space character is also
    'the length to extract for the left side (First Name)
    lLeftLen = lResult
    '_*_*_*_*_*_*_*_*_*_*_*_*_*_*_*_*_*_*_*_*_*_*
    'Extract the First Name and assign it to the
    'First Name variable
    strFirstName = Left(strFullName, lLeftLen)
    '_*_*_*_*_*_*_*_*_*_*_*_*_*_*_*_*_*_*_*_*_*_*
    'Return the value of the first name
    GetFirstName = strFirstName
End Function

Public Function GetLastName(strFullName As String) As String
'*****************************************
'Sub/Function: GetLastName
'
'Arguments: strFullName   A string representing a full name
'                         to validate
'
'Return:                  A string containing the Last Name if the
'                         Full Name string is valid. If the Full Name
'                         string is invalid, the function returns the
'                         string, "ERROR"
'
'Remarks:                 A valid string has only one space character
'
'Programmer: Bob Reselman
'
'History: Created 8/23/97
'
'Copyright 1997, Macmillan Publishing
'*****************************************
    Dim lSpacePos As Long       'Position of space character
                                'in a string
    Dim strSpaceChar As String  'Space character
```

```
Dim strLastName As String    'Buffer for Last Name string
Dim lResult As Long          'Result variable
Dim lRightLen As Long        'Number of characters in Last
                             'Name
'-*-*-*-*-*-*-*-*-*-*-*-*-*-*-*-*-*-*-*-*-*
'Use the IsValid function to make sure that the
'Full Name string has only one space character in it.
If IsValid(strFullName) = False Then
    'If it doesn't, return the error string
    GetLastName = "Error"
    'And exit the function
    Exit Function
End If
'-*-*-*-*-*-*-*-*-*-*-*-*-*-*-*-*-*-*-*-*-*
'Define space character
strSpaceChar = " "
'-*-*-*-*-*-*-*-*-*-*-*-*-*-*-*-*-*-*-*-*-*
'Find the position of the space character
lResult = InStr(1, strFullName, strSpaceChar)
'-*-*-*-*-*-*-*-*-*-*-*-*-*-*-*-*-*-*-*-*-*
'Define the number of characters to be be extracted from the right
'of the space character, (Last Name).
'If you subtract the position of the space character for the total
'number of characers in the Full Name string, this will yield the
'number of characters to extract from the right hand side of the
'Full Name string. Also, this technique avoids including the space
'character itself by accident.
lRightLen = Len(strFullName) - lResult
'-*-*-*-*-*-*-*-*-*-*-*-*-*-*-*-*-*-*-*-*-*
'Extract the right side of the Full Name string and assign
'it to the Last Name Buffer
strLastName = Right(strFullName, lRightLen)
'-*-*-*-*-*-*-*-*-*-*-*-*-*-*-*-*-*-*-*-*-*
'Return the value of the Last Name string out of the function
GetLastName = strLastName
End Function
```

You might have a Full Name that contains a Middle Name or Middle Initial, or a Last Name that is made up of two strings, "Van Beethoven," for example. In this case, the function would not be valid. You will build a *validation* function, IsValid() to determine whether the string can be parsed into a First Name and Last Name.

Figure 21.8 illustrates the logic for the user-defined function IsValid(), and Listing 21.9 shows the code for the function.

FIG. 21.8
Loops are an excellent way to traverse a string, provided you know the length of the string.

Ludwig Von Beethoven

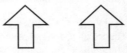

If the string has more than one space character or no space character, then the string is NOT valid.

```
For i% = 1 To NumOfChars%
    PresentChar$ = Mid$(strFullName, i%, 1)
    If PresentChar$ = SpaceChar$ Then
        NumOfSpaces% = NumOfSpaces% + 1
    End If
Next i%

If NumOfSpaces% = 1 Then
    IsValid = True
Else
    IsValid = False
End If
```

Listing 21.9 21LIST09.TXT—The *IsValid()* Function Test to Verify Only One Space Character per String

```
Public Function IsValid(strFullName) As Boolean
'******************************************
'Sub/Function: IsValid
'
'Arguments: strFullName   A string representing a full name
'                         to validate
'
'Return:                  True, if the string has only 1 space
'                         character
'
'Remarks:                 This function is used to determine if
'                         more than one space character exists
'                         in a string.
'
'Programmer: Bob Reselman
'
'History: Created 8/23/97
'
'Copyright 1997, Macmillan Publishing
'******************************************

    Dim NumOfSpaces%     'Hold the count of the number of
                         'spaces in a string
    Dim NumOfChars%      'Number of characters in string
    Dim i%               'Counter variable
    Dim SpaceChar$       'The space character
    Dim PresentChar$     'A buffer to hold one character to
                         'examine
    '-*-*-*-*-*-*-*-*-*-*-*-*-*-*-*-*-*-*-*-*
    'Define the space character
```

```
        SpaceChar$ = " "
        '.*.*.*.*.*.*.*.*.*.*.*.*.*.*.*.*.*.*.*.*.*.*
        'Find out how many characters are in the full name
        NumOfChars% = Len(strFullName)
        '.*.*.*.*.*.*.*.*.*.*.*.*.*.*.*.*.*.*.*.*.*.*
        'Loop through the entire string, strFullName
        For i% = 1 To NumOfChars%
            'Look at each character one at a time
            PresentChar$ = Mid$(strFullName, i%, 1)
            'If the character that you are inspecting is a
            'space....
            If PresentChar$ = SpaceChar$ Then
                '...Increment the space counter variable by 1
                NumOfSpaces% = NumOfSpaces% + 1
            End If
        Next i%
        '.*.*.*.*.*.*.*.*.*.*.*.*.*.*.*.*.*.*.*.*.*.*
        'if there is only one space in the Full Name string...
        If NumOfSpaces% = 1 Then
            '...return TRUE
            IsValid = True
        Else
            'If not, return false
            IsValid = False
        End If
End Function
```

If you want to see this code in action, go to the project AdvncStr.VBP, which is in the directory \Chp_21\AdvncStr on the CD-ROM that accompanies this book. When you run the code, you will see buttons for the GetFirstName() and GetLastName() functions as well as one to test the IsValid() function. Enter a full name in the TextBox, txtHold, and then click the buttons to see the results.

Controlling Data Type Using Typecasting

When you typecast a variable, you transform its value from one type to another. As you read earlier, Visual Basic is so highly automated that it hides many of the mundane chores of typecasting from you. Consider the code in Listing 21.10.

Listing 21.10   21LIST10.TXT—Automatic Typecasting in Visual Basic

```
Private Sub cmdAutoType_Click()
    txtFirst.Text = 5
End Sub
```

Part

IV

Ch

21

The data type that the Text property expects is a String, but it is being assigned an Integer. However, it works! Automatically, Visual Basic is taking the integer 5 and converting it to a String type. You would have to do a lot of work to get this code to work in a more *type safe* language such as C++.

Now consider the code in Listing 21.11 and the related illustration of the listing in Figure 21.9.

Listing 21.11   21LIST11.TXT—A Potential Error

```
Private Sub cmdError_Click()


    lblResult.Caption = txtFirst.Text + txtSecond.Text
End Sub
```

FIG. 21.9

Concatenating string variables yields a different result than adding integers.

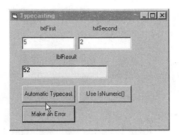

You'll notice that the automated nature of Visual Basic has now broken down. If you type 5 and 2 in the TextBoxes, the result is the string "52", not the integer 7. VB will only convert the "5" to an integer if you try to add it to a value or variable of type Integer; the + operator works just like & for strings.

Thus, thus to ensure that integer addition does indeed happen as you plan, you must convert at least one of the TextBox's Text values to an integer using the CInt() function.

For example, in the following code snippet, if txtFirst.Text and txtSecond.Text hold numeric strings, the value of lblResult's Caption property will be the result of integer addition.

```
lblResult.Caption = CInt(txtFirst.Text) + txtSecond.Text
```

Letting Visual Basic do most of the work with regard to data types might serve you well, but as you can see from the preceding example, getting control of data types and typecasting is a skill that you need to have over the long term.

Validating Data Using *IsNumeric()*

As your programs become more reliant upon valid user input, you need to have a way to address the issue of users inputting text strings when you need them to enter numeric strings. Visual Basic has a built-in function that will help. The function is IsNumeric(). IsNumeric() checks a string to see whether it "looks" like a number. If a string looks like a number, IsNumeric()returns True; otherwise, it returns False. The syntax for IsNumeric() is as follows:

bResult = IsNumeric(MyString)

Where

bResult is a return value of type Boolean.

IsNumeric is the function name.

MyString is the string that you want to check.

Listing 21.12 shows you code that uses IsNumeric to check whether user input can be assigned to variables of type Integer.

Listing 21.12   21LIST12.TXT—Using *IsNumeric* to Validate User Input

```
Private Sub cmdIsNumeric_Click()
    Dim Answer%
    Dim x%
    Dim y%

    If IsNumeric(txtFirst.Text) = True Then
        x% = CInt(txtFirst.Text)
    Else
        MsgBox "Type Error", vbCritical
        Exit Sub
    End If

    If IsNumeric(txtSecond.Text) = True Then
        y% = CInt(txtSecond.Text)
    Else
        MsgBox "Type Error", vbCritical
        Exit Sub
    End If

    Answer% = x% + y%

    lblResult.Caption = CStr(Answer%)
End Sub
```

Changing Data Types Using the Conversion Functions

Throughout this book you have seen the functions CStr() and CInt() used liberally with no real explanation. Let's cover them and their related functions now.

These functions are conversion functions. A *conversion function* transforms a value from one data type into another. In Visual Basic, you typecast using the conversion functions.

Experienced Visual Basic programmers try to impose as much type safety upon their code as they can. Thus, among seasoned programmers, it is not unusual to find the value of an object's property typecast before it is applied to a variable (see Listing 21.12). Of course, before you try to convert a value from one type to another, make sure that the value is appropriate to the type. For example, the following would be erroneous:

```
MyString$ = "Batman"
i% - CInt("Batman")

i% = MyString$
```

Making sure that data type conversion is possible is where validation functions such as IsNumeric(), IsValue(), and IsDate() come in handy. (For a detailed discussion of these functions, read Visual Basic's online help.)

Table 21.1 shows the type conversion functions and provides a discussion and example of each function.

Table 21.1   Type Conversion Functions

Function	Comments	Example
CBool	Converts a value to a Boolean	CBool(-1)
CByte	Converts a value between 0–255 to a Byte	Cbyte(254)
CCur	Converts a value to a Currency data type	CCur("$23.98")
CDate	Converts a date expression to a Date data type	CDate("July 4, 1776")
CDbl	Converts a value to a Double	CDbl(MyInt%)
CDec	Used only with variants	N/A
CInt	Converts a value to an Integer	CInt("4")
CLng	Converts a value to a Long	CLng(Form1.hWnd)
CSng	Converts a value to a Single	CSng("23.1")
CVar	Converts a value to a Variant	CVar(Text1.Text)
CStr	Converts a value to a String	CStr(MyInt%)

CHAPTER 22

Working with Control Arrays

In Visual Basic, you can have an array of Integers or some other data type. You also can have an array of controls. Control arrays are a distinctive feature of Visual Basic that brings efficiency and power to the language. You can use them to create a common event procedure that is shared among all the controls in the control array. You also can use them to add and remove controls and forms to your program dynamically at runtime. Learning to use control arrays is not difficult. This chapter shows you all you need to know to work effectively with them. ■

Design time control arrays

Learn how to make control arrays using the Cut and Paste methods.

Runtime control arrays

Make control arrays on-the-fly using the Load statement.

Common event procedures

Write one event procedure that addresses the actions of many controls.

Frame control

Learn how to use the Frame control to group other controls.

VScroll and HScroll controls

Use the standard scroll bar controls.

Create and destroy controls dynamically

Learn how to use For...Next loops to make and destroy controls.

Creating Control Arrays at Design Time

You can make a control array of most Visual Basic controls. For example, you can have an array of CommandButtons, OptionButtons, Timers, or CheckBoxes, to name a few. Remember that it's fine to change the names of your project, objects, and so on from the names that are listed here so that your array is tailored to your needs. The names listed here, though, are used consistently because that is how they appear on the book's CD-ROM.

> **N O T E** If you want to simply follow along, the code for this section is in the project SimplCA.vbp in the directory \Chp_22\SimplCA\ on the CD-ROM that accompanies this book. ■

To make a control array of CommandButtons at design time, do the following.

1. Create a New project. Name the project SimplCA.vbp. Name the default form frmMain. Set the value of the Caption property of frmMain to "Control Array."

2. Add a CommandButton to the form frmMain. Name the CommandButton cmdMyButton. Set the value of the Caption property of cmdMyButton to "My Button." Place the CommandButton in the center of the form.

3. Make sure that the cmdMyButton is selected. Select Copy (Ctrl+C) from the Edit menu. (This copies the CommandButton to the Clipboard.)

4. Select Paste (Ctrl+V) from the Edit menu. You are presented with a dialog box, as shown in Figure 22.1.

5. Click the Yes button.

FIG. 22.1
When you try to Paste a control with the same name as an existing control from the clipboard, you are asked whether you want to create a control array. If you click Yes, you create a control array. If you click No, you simply create a new control.

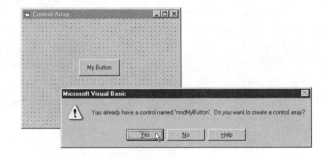

Congratulations, you have just created a control array of two CommandButtons! If you go to the Properties window and display the Object drop-down list, you'll notice that there are now two CommandButtons with the name cmdMyButton, each with its own subscript (see Figure 22.2).

Double-click either CommandButton to take a look at the Click event procedure. You'll notice that it now has an argument called Index (see Figure 22.3). The Index argument is an Integer that indicates the subscript of the control to which the event procedure applies. In a control array, all controls of the array share the same event procedure. The way you differentiate between controls is by the value of Index—0 is the first control, 1 is the second control, 2 is the third, and so on.

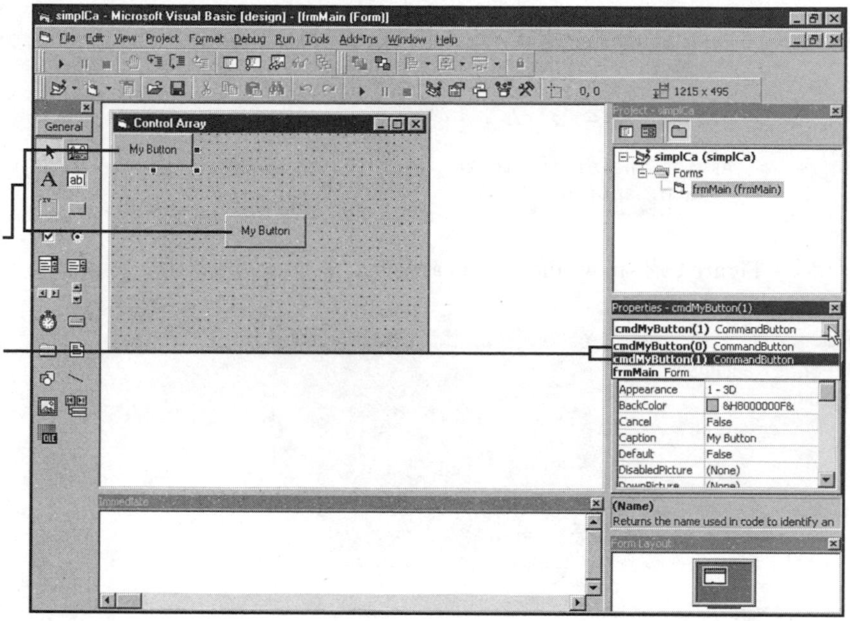

FIG. 22.2

Don't forget that after you make a control array, you must include the subscript with the control's name when referencing it.

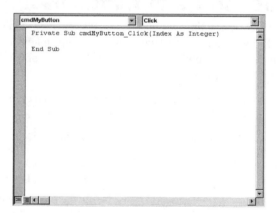

The code in Listing 22.1 displays a string in the title bar of the form frmMain that reports which CommandButton of the control array cmdMyButton() the user clicked. Copying this code to the cmdMyButton_Click(Index as Integer) event procedure can give you a sense of how to work with the Index argument.

FIG. 22.3

With control arrays, Visual Basic automatically passes the value of a control's subscript to the Index argument when you generate a given control's event procedure.

Listing 22.1   22LIST01.PCX—Code that Reports Which Element of the Control Array Fires an Event

```
Dim Msg$
'Make a string that reports which control of
'the control array has fired the event procedure
Msg$ = "You click cmdMyButton(" & CStr(Index)
Msg$ = Msg$ & ")"

'Assign the string to the form's Caption property
frmMain.Caption = Msg$
```

Figure 22.4 shows the code in action.

FIG. 22.4

The Index argument in action.

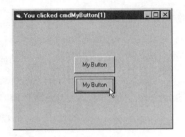

Extending Control Arrays at Runtime

Making a control array at design time will suffice if you know how many controls you are going to need in the array. But what do you do if you don't know how many controls you will need in your control array until the program is running? You solve this problem by adding controls to your control array at runtime using the Load statement.

(If you want to follow along, the code for this section is in the project IntDArry.vbp in the directory Chp_22\IntDArry\ on the CD-ROM that accompanies this book.)

To add a control to a control array at runtime, do the following:

1. Create a New project. Name the project IntDArry.vbp. Rename the default form frmDArry. Set the value of the Caption property to "Intro to Dynamic Arrays."

2. Add a CommandButton to the form frmDArry. Name the CommandButton cmdArrayBut. Place the CommandButton in the upper-left corner of the form.

3. Select the CommandButton. In the Properties window, set the value of the Index property to 0 (zero). This is very important. This action creates a control array with one element (see Figure 22.5).

4. Add the code in Listing 22.2 to the Form_Load() event of the form frmDArry.

5. Save and run the code.

FIG. 22.5

A control array must already exist before you can add controls to it with the Load statement.

Listing 22.2   22LIST02.TXT—Code to Create a New *CommandButton* in a Preexisting Control Array

```
'Create a new command button
Load cmdArrayBut(1)

'Move it directly underneath the old one
cmdArrayBut(1).Left = cmdArrayBut(0).Left
cmdArrayBut(1).Top = cmdArrayBut(0).Top + cmdArrayBut(0).Height

'Make the new button visible
cmdArrayBut(1).Visible = True
```

When you run the code, you'll see that the program makes a new CommandButton within the Form_Load() event procedure (see Figure 22.6).

You must do a certain amount of tweaking to get a newly created control to be operational in your program. New controls are an exact duplicate of the first control element of the control array. The values of all the properties except the Index and Visible properties are identical—including the value of the Left and Top properties. Thus, when you create a new control, it will be placed right over the first control in the array. Therefore, for the new control to be able to coexist with other controls in the control array, you must move the control to a new position.

All newly created elements of a control array have a Visible value of False. When you make your new controls at runtime, don't forget to put in a line of code that sets the value of the Visible property to True. Otherwise, you won't be able to see the control.

FIG. 22.6

Don't forget to set the Visible property of a newly created control to True.

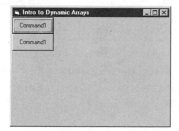

Working with a Common Event Handler

Look at the project Dialer.vbp in the directory \Chp_22\Dialer. This program enables the user to input some numbers into a numeric telephone touch pad to place a call. Also, the user can set whether she or he wants to dial by pulse or tone, and she or he can elect to send a Fax or a simple voice call. This program is a prototype. The Graphical User Interface works, but that's it. No telephonic functionality is built in. That's the nature of prototypes; they are meant to demonstrate an idea only.

This program uses a control array of `CommandButtons` to handle user input (see Figure 22.7). Using a control array greatly simplifies matters. In this project, if you didn't use a control array, you would have 12 event procedures to program—not a very pleasant undertaking. However, when you use a control array, you have only one event procedure to program. You use the `Index` argument within the control array's one event procedure to figure out which control fired the event procedure.

FIG. 22.7
Every element of a control array is listed in the Properties window with its subscript.

Grouping OptionButtons in a Frame control allows you to have sets of options from which to choose

Control array of CommandButtons

Control elements listed in Properties window

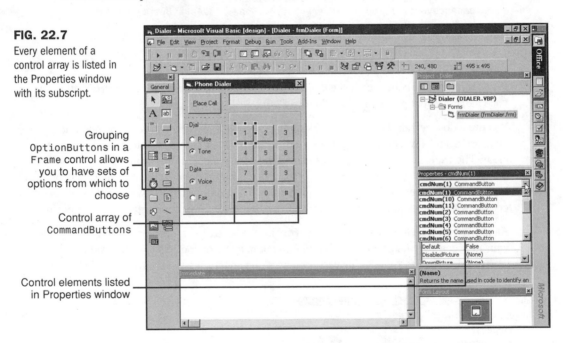

Listing 22.3 shows the code for the `Click()` event procedure of the control array. Notice that the control array's event procedure uses a `Select Case` statement to provide different responses depending on which button has been clicked.

Listing 22.3 22LIST03.TXT—One Event Procedure Does the Work of Twelve

```
Private Sub cmdNum_Click(Index As Integer)
    Dim ReadOut$
    Dim MyChar$
    'Set the string that is presently in the
    'label control to a string variable
    ReadOut$ = lblNumber.Caption

    'Find out which button was clicked by
    'analyzing the Index argument. Depending
    'on which button you push, set the another
    'string variable accordingly.
    Select Case Index
        'This button has the "*" character
        Case 10
            MyChar$ = "*"
        'This button has the "#" character
        Case 11
            MyChar$ = "#"
        'All the buttons have captions that match
        'their index value.
        Case Else
            MyChar$ = CStr(Index)
    End Select

    'Concatenate the new character to the
    'string in the label control.
    ReadOut$ = ReadOut$ & MyChar$

    'Reset the value of the caption of the
    'label control to the concatenated string.
    lblNumber.Caption = ReadOut$
End Sub
```

Grouping Objects with the *Frame* Control

In earlier chapters, you learned that among a group of OptionButtons, only one OptionButton can have a value of True (see Figure 22.8). But as you can see in the project Dialer.vbp shown previously in Figure 22.7, there are times when you will need to have sets of OptionButtons so that you can return many different sets of choices.

You group OptionButtons using a container control such as the Frame control. After a set of OptionButtons are pasted into a Frame, the members of the set are exclusive to one another.

N O T E   Frames are not the only containers. You can also use a PictureBox, for example. ▪

FIG. 22.8

The project NoFrame.vbp demonstrates the shortcomings of ungrouped OptionButtons.

You add a Frame control to a form as you would any other control. After a control is pasted into a Frame, the Frame becomes the container of that control. Thus, all coordinates of the child controls are relative to the Frame. And when you move a Frame, all the controls within the Frame move with it.

There is a trick to using the Frame control. When you add or Paste a control into a Frame, make sure that the frame is selected. If you don't have the Frame selected, the control is really not being added to the Frame. Also, after a control is added or Pasted into a Frame, it cannot be moved out of the Frame except by using the Cut technique (see Figure 22.9).

FIG. 22.9

Make sure that the Frame is selected before you add controls to it.

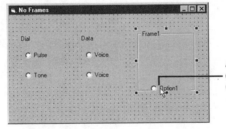

After a control is added to the Frame, it cannot be removed unless you delete or Cut the control

Using the Scroll Bar Controls

The standard scroll bar controls, HScrollBar and VScrollBar, enable you to move through data or a range of values by either clicking the up and down scroll arrows or by moving the scroll bar's scroll box (the small button between the scroll arrows). The scroll bar controls have a few special properties that you should know about. Table 22.1 lists and describes those properties.

Table 22.1   Special Properties for the *HScroll* and *VScroll* Controls

Properties	Description
Min	Sets the lowest possible value of the control when the scroll box is positioned at the topmost or leftmost of the respective scroll bar. The default value is 0.
Max	Sets the highest possible value of the of the control when the scroll box is at the bottom-most or right-most of the respective scroll bar. The default value is 32,767.

Properties	Description
Value	The position of the scroll box relative to the Max and Min properties.
LargeChange	Sets the amount of change of the Value property when the user clicks between the scroll box and scroll arrow.
SmallChange	Sets the amount of change of the Value property when the user clicks the scroll arrow.

(If you want to follow along, the code for this following section is in the project SmpScrll.vbp in the directory \Chp_2\SmpScrll\ on the CD-ROM that accompanies this book.)

To make a form with a VScroll and HScroll control, do the following:

1. Create a New project. Name the project SmpScrll.vbp. Rename the default form frmMain. Set the value of the Caption property to "Simple Scroll Bars."

2. Add a VScroll and HScroll control to the form. Name the VScroll control vscrNS. Name the HScroll control hscrEW.

3. Add two TextBox controls. Name one TextBox txtNS. Name the other txtEW. Set the value of the Text property for both TextBoxes to an empty string (" ") (see Figure 22.10).

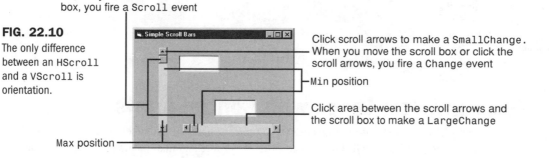

FIG. 22.10
The only difference between an HScroll and a VScroll is orientation.

When you move the scroll box, you fire a Scroll event

Click scroll arrows to make a SmallChange. When you move the scroll box or click the scroll arrows, you fire a Change event

Min position

Click area between the scroll arrows and the scroll box to make a LargeChange

Max position

4. Set the properties for the VScroll and HScroll controls as they are listed in Table 22.2

5. Add the code in Listing 22.4 to the General section of frmMain.

6. Save and run the code.

Table 22.2 Property Settings for Scroll Bar Controls

Property	Setting
Min	0
Max	20
SmallChange	1
LargeChange	2

Listing 22.4   22LIST04.TXT—Change Event Procedures for the *HScroll* and *VScroll* Controls

```
Private Sub hscrEW_Change()
    txtEW.Text = CStr(hscrEW.Value)
End Sub


Private Sub vscrNS_Change()
    txtNS.Text = CStr(vscrNS.Value)
End Sub
```

When you run the code, you'll see that when you click the scroll arrows of the HScroll or VScroll controls, the value of the respective TextBoxes changes by 1, the value of the SmallChange property. If you click the area between the scroll box and the scroll arrow, the amount in the TextBoxes changes by 2, the value of the LargeChange property (see Figure 22.11).

FIG. 22.11

The value of the Max property is set to 20. Therefore, when you move the scroll bars, the values shown in the TextBoxes will never exceed 20.

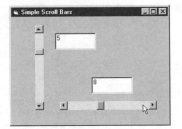

Using *For...Next* Loops with Control Arrays

Using For...Next loops is an efficient way to traverse and manipulate elements in a control array. Listings 22.5 and 22.6 show you two ways to create and manipulate elements in a control array. Listing 22.5 illustrates the old-fashioned way—creating the controls one at a time using the Load statement. Listing 22.6 shows you a way to make the controls using a For...Next loop. Compare the two.

(If you want to follow along, the code for this section is in the project DynCtrl.vbp in the directory \Chp_22\DynCtrl\ on the CD-ROM that accompanies this book.)

Listing 22.5   22LIST05.TXT—Dynamically Making and Manipulating a Control Array One Element at a Time

```
Private Sub cmdMakeArray_Click()
        'Create additional controls in the
        'imgFace control array.
```

```
            Load imgFace(1)
            Load imgFace(2)
            Load imgFace(3)
            Load imgFace(4)

            'Set the top new elements of the control array
            'to the top of the one before it.
            imgFace(1).Top = imgFace(0).Top
            imgFace(2).Top = imgFace(1).Top
            imgFace(3).Top = imgFace(2).Top
            imgFace(4).Top = imgFace(3).Top

            'Set the left starting position of the new
            'control to the left plus the width of the control
            'before it
            imgFace(1).Left = imgFace(0).Left + imgFace(0).Width
            imgFace(2).Left = imgFace(1).Left + imgFace(1).Width
            imgFace(3).Left = imgFace(2).Left + imgFace(2).Width
            imgFace(4).Left = imgFace(3).Left + imgFace(3).Width

            'Set ALL of the controls in the control array
            'and make them visible
            imgFace(0).Visible = True
            imgFace(1).Visible = True
            imgFace(2).Visible = True
            imgFace(3).Visible = True
            imgFace(4).Visible = True
End Sub
```

Listing 22.6 22LIST06.TXT—Using *For...Next* Loops to Make and Manipulate Elements in a Control Array

```
Private Sub cmdLoopArray_Click()
    Dim i%          'Counter variable
    Dim MoreCtrls%  'Number of additional controls
                    'to add to the control array.

    'Set the picture of the first element of the
    'imgFace control array to the picture in the control,
    'imgHappy face.
    imgFace(0).Picture = imgHappy.Picture

    'Set the more controls variable to the amount of
    'additional controls
    MoreControls% = 4

    'Traverse the number of ADDITIONAL controls
    For i = 1 To MoreControls%
        'Create a new control in the array
        Load imgFace(i%)
        'Set the top of the new control to top of the
        'one before it.
```

continues

Listing 22.6   Continued

```
        imgFace(i%).Top = imgFace(i% - 1).Top
        'Set the left starting position of the new
        'control to the left plus the width of the control
        'before it
        imgFace(i%).Left = imgFace(i% - 1).Left + imgFace(i% - 1).Width
    Next i%

    'Traverse ALL of the controls in the control array
    'and make them visible
    For i% = 0 To MoreControls%
        imgFace(i%).Visible = True
    Next i%
    End Sub
```

As you compare the two, you'll notice that everything you can do one at a time, with regard to control array elements, you can do with much more elegance using a For...Next loop. And, the For...Next loop method can control an unknown number of elements in any control array. This gives you versatility and extensibility.

Figure 22.12 shows the project DynCtrl.vbp (in directory \Chp_22\DynCtrl\). The upper portion of the project's form shows an implementation of the code in Listings 22.5 and 22.6. The bottom portion of the form shows a way to use the VScroll control to generate dynamically a varying number of controls in a control array of ImageBoxes.

FIG. 22.12

The number of controls shown is going to be one more than the scroll position because the zero (0) element is the first element in the control array.

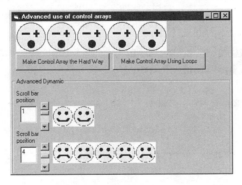

When you study the code in Listing 22.7 closely (which is the Change event procedure for one of the VScroll controls), you'll notice that not only does the code dynamically create new elements of the ImageBox control array using the Load statement, it also dynamically destroys all but the zero value element of the control array using the Unload statement. Be advised that in a real world production environment, unloading and re-creating control array elements each time you need them is a grossly inefficient programming practice. It is done here to demonstrate this Visual Basic feature.

Listing 22.7   22LIST07.TXT—Using a *VScroll* Control and *For...Next* Loops to Create and Destroy Elements of a Control Array

```
Private Sub vscrFirst_Change()
    'This sub removes all the existing elements of
    'the control array, imgFirst(), except for the
    'first one and then creates a new set of elements
    'as determined by the value of the vertical scrollbar
    'position.

    Static NumOfImage%  'Number of images in
                           'ImageBox Control array
    Dim i%  'Counter variable

    'Report the value of the scrollbar position
    'in a TextBox. Don't forget to convert to an integer.
    txtFirst.Text = CStr(vscrFirst.Value)

    'Set the Picture property of the first element of
    'the ImageBox control array to the picture in the
    'happy face image box.
    imgFirst(0).Picture = imgHappy.Picture

    'Unload all pre-existing elements of the ImageBox
    'control array.

    'Make sure the previous value of the Static variable
    'is greater than zero. If the value is zero, you would
    'be trying to unload the zero element control array element.
    'This is bad!
    If NumOfImage% > 0 Then
        'If the number is over zero, there are elements left
        'over from the  last time you used this event
        'procedure.

        '(Remember, a the value of a Static variable holds
        'value after the event procedure goes out of scope.)
        For i% = 1 To NumOfImage%
            'Nuke all the elements of the control array
            Unload imgFirst(i%)
        Next i%
    End If

    'Set a new value for the static variable, NumOfImage%
    'based upon the value of the scroll bar position.
    NumOfImage% = vscrFirst.Value

    'Traverse the intended number of new controls for the
    'control array.
    For i% = 1 To NumOfImage%
        'Make a new ImageBox for the control array
        Load imgFirst(i%)
        'Set the top of the new control to top of the
        'one before it.
```

continues

Listing 22.7   Continued

```
            imgFirst(i%).Top = imgFirst(i% - 1).Top
            'Set the left starting position of the new
            'control to the left plus the width of the control
            'before it
            imgFirst(i%).Left = imgFirst(i% - 1).Left + imgFirst(i% - 1).Width
    Next i%

        'Traverse ALL of the controls in the control array
        'and make them visible
        For i% = 0 To NumOfImage%
            imgFirst(i%).Visible = True
        Next i%
    End Sub
```

There is a word of caution that needs to be mentioned here. If you try to Load a control in a control array using a subscript for a control that already is loaded, you will get an error. If in the DynCtrl.vbp project you click the "Make Control Array the Hard Way" button and then click the "Make Control Array Using Loops" button, an error is generated, as shown in Figure 22.13. This is because the first button's Click event procedure creates a control array, and the second button's Click event procedure tries to create again the same control array using the same subscripts. Be careful when you work with control arrays and For...Next loops.

FIG. 22.13

Using a Load statement on an array element that already exists will cause an error.

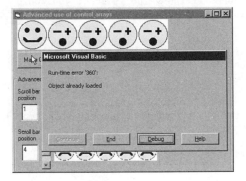

Saving and Retrieving Information

For your program to keep information from session to session, you must be able to store data on the hard drive. Otherwise, when your application terminates, all that program's data in memory will vanish. Likewise, when your program starts, to have any sort of *persistence*, it must be able to retrieve data from the hard disk.

You can save data to and retrieve data from disk in several ways. You can use a binary or text file, you can read from and write to the Windows Registry, or you can use a database. In Chapter 15, "Working with Multiple Forms," you learned how to use the Visual Basic GetSetting() and SaveSetting() functions to read from and write to the Windows Registry. In Chapter 24, "Programming with Databases," you learn how to use a database to perform data persistence. This chapter teaches you to save and retrieve text and graphics to and from a file. ■

Understanding Data and Files

Data lives in computer memory, and a file lives on the hard drive. Your program never works directly with a file on the hard drive. The program asks the operating system to mediate between the hard drive and your program.

You get a "location" of a file on the hard drive by asking the operating system for the *file handle*. You use the `FreeFile` function to get a file handle number from the operating system. After you have a file handle, you use the `Open` statement to assign the handle to the file which you want to write or from which you want to read. When your program "hooks" up a file handle to a file, it can write data to the file using the `Print` (or `Write`) statement or it can read lines of data from a file on disk using the `Line Input` statement. Figure 23.1 illustrates this concept.

FIG. 23.1
Writing to a file is the inverse of reading from a file. You still need a file handle and you need to Open the file.

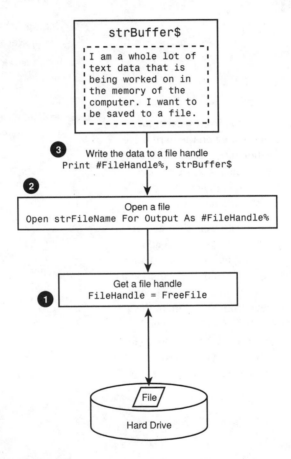

Saving Data Using the *Open* Statement

Look at project AdvTedit.vbp in the directory \Chp_23\AdvTedit\. This program is an enhancement of the simple text editor that you saw previously in Chapter 13, "Working with Menus." In that chapter, you learned how to make a text editor into which you could enter data as well as Cut and Paste it to the Clipboard. However, the Save and Open file features were not implemented. These features have been added in AdvTeditt.vbp.

To use the program, when you want to save data, you click the Open menu item. A common dialog box appears into which you enter a file name and select a location on the hard disk. Then you click the common dialog box's Save button to commit the data to the hard disk (see Figure 23.2).

Part
IV

Ch
23

FIG. 23.2

Using the common dialog box is an easy way to create a file name and location for your data.

Behind the scenes you are using the Open and Print statements. The syntax for the Open statement is as follows:

```
Open FilePath [For Mode] [Access AcessType [LockType] As [#]FileNumber
[Len=CharInBuffer%]
```

Where:

> *Open* is the statement name.
>
> *FilePath* is the exact location of the file to read or save, drive and directory included.
>
> *For* is the keyword that specifies the file mode to follow.
>
> *Mode* is the file access type (see Table 23.1).

Table 23.1 File Modes

Mode	Description
Append	Add data to the end of an existing file. If the file does not exist, it will be created.
Binary	Open a file as pure binary—bit and bytes. If the file does not exist, it will be created.

continues

Table 23.1   Continued

Mode	Description
Input	Open file for reading.
Output	Open file for writing. If the file does not exist, it will be created.
Random	Open file for random access. This is used for simple record storage. If the file does not exist, it will be created.

Access (Optional) is the keyword that specifies access type to follow.

AccessType is the choice of Read, Write, or Read Write.

LockType (Optional) specifies whether others can read the file while your program is working with the file. The values supported are Shared, Lock Read, Lock Write, and Lock Read Write.

As is a keyword that signifies the file handle is about to follow.

is the symbol that denotes the FileNumber integer is a file handle.

FileNumber is the file handle.

Len (Optional) is the a keyword that introduces the record length parameter.

CharInBuffer% is the record length for a file opened for Random access.

You open a file for reading as follows:

```
'Get a free file handle and assign it to the file handle variable
FileHandle% = FreeFile

'Open a file for writing
Open strFileName For Output As #FileHandle%
```

Listing 23.1 shows the event procedure for the <u>S</u>ave menu item. The procedure opens a file using the Open statement and saves the contents of a TextBox to the file using the Print method. After the write takes place, the event procedure closes the file using the Close statement. The Close statement takes the file handle as an argument. It's important to remember to Close a file when you are finished with it. The Close statement frees the file handle from memory.

Listing 23.1   23LIST01.TXT—Saving the *TextBox's* Contents to a File on Disk Using a Common Dialog Box

```
Private Sub itmSave_Click()
    Dim strFileName As String     'String of file to open
    Dim strText As String         'Contents of file
    Dim strFilter As String       'Common Dialog filter string
    Dim strBuffer As String       'String buffer variable
    Dim FileHandle%               'Variable to hold file handle
```

```
'Set the Common Dialog filter
strFilter = "Text (*.txt)¦*.txt¦All Files (*.*)¦*.*"
cdMain.Filter = strFilter

'Open the common dialog in save mode
cdMain.ShowSave

'Make sure the retrieved filename is not a blank string
If cdMain.filename <> "" Then
    'If it is not blank open the file
    strFileName = cdMain.filename

    'Assign a value to the text variable
    strText = txtMain.Text

    'Get a free file handle and assign it to the file handle variable
    FileHandle% = FreeFile

    'Open a file for writing
    Open strFileName For Output As #FileHandle%

    'Set an hour glass cursor just in case it takes a while
    MousePointer = vbHourglass

    'Do the write
    Print #FileHandle%, strText

    'Reset the cursor to the Windows default.
    MousePointer = vbDefault

    'Close the file once you have had your way with it
    Close #FileHandle%
End If

End Sub
```

Retrieving Data Using the *Open* Statement

You retrieve data from disk much the same way you write data to disk. The only difference is that instead of using the Append, Output, Binary, or Random mode, you use the Input mode. Also, instead of using the Print or Write method to write the data, you read the lines of data in the file line-by-line using the Line Input statement.

The syntax for the Line Input statement is as follows:

```
Line Input #FileHandle, strBuffer
```

Where:

> *Line Input* are the keywords for the statement.
>
> # is the character denoting a file handle.

FileHandle is a valid file handle of an open file.

strBuffer is the string into which you put the data retrieved by the statement.

Simple text files are saved to disk in lines. If you were to do some data entry in NotePad and never hit the Enter key, you would have entered one line of code. Every time you strike the enter key, Visual Basic adds the string Chr(13) & Chr(10) (Carriage Return and Line Feed) to the TextBox to mark the end of a line; when you save the file, these characters also are written to the file. Visual Basic has a constant defined for this string, vbCrLf. The Line Input statement reads into a file until it encounters the end-of-line sequence (vbCrLf). Once at the end of a line, the statement takes the characters it finds and sends them to the string buffer argument, discarding the vbCrLf.

To traverse all the lines in the entire file, you use a Do While Loop. You use the Visual Basic EOF() function to determine whether the end of the file has been reached. The EOF() function takes the file handle number as an argument. As long are you are not at the end of the file, the Line Input statement continues reading the lines of the file from within the Do While loop.

Listing 23.2 shows the event procedure for the Open menu item from the AdvTeit.vbp project. This is the menu item upon which the user clicks to open a file into the text editor. The event procedure uses a common dialog box to allow the user to identify a file to open.

▶ **See** Chapter 16, "Using Dialog Boxes," **p. 251**

Listing 23.2   23LIST02.TXT—Using the *Line Input* Statement to Read a Text File

```
Private Sub itmOpen_Click()
    Dim strFileName As String    'String of file to open
    Dim strText As String        'Contents of file
    Dim strFilter As String      'Common Dialog filter string
    Dim strBuffer As String      'String buffer variable
    Dim FileHandle%              'Variable to hold file handle

    'Set the Common Dialog filter
    strFilter = "Text (*.txt)¦*.txt¦All Files (*.*)¦*.*"
    cdMain.Filter = strFilter

    'Open the common dialog
    cdMain.ShowOpen


    'Make sure the retrieved filename is not a blank string
    If cdMain.filename <> "" Then

        'If it is not blank open the file
        strFileName = cdMain.filename

        'Get a free file handle and assign it to the file handle variable
        FileHandle% = FreeFile

        'Open the file
```

```
        Open strFileName For Input As #FileHandle%

        'Make the mouse cursor an hourglass
        MousePointer = vbHourglass

        'Traverse the lines of the file
        Do While Not EOF(FileHandle%) ' Check for end of file.

            'Read a line of the file
            Line Input #FileHandle%, strBuffer     ' Read line of data.

            'Add the line from the output buffer to the text string
            strText = strText & strBuffer & vbCrLf
        Loop

        'Change the mousepointer back to the arrow
        MousePointer = vbDefault

        'Close the file once you have had your way with it
        Close #FileHandle%

        'Assign the retrieved text to the text box
        txtMain.Text = strText

        'Put the file name in the form caption
        frmMain.Caption = "Text Editor- [" & strFileName & "]"
    End If
End Sub
```

Part

IV

Ch

23

You might want to take some time to study the project AdvTEdit.vbp. Many useful programming techniques are in the code that you can use in many situations where you have to accommodate user input and save it to disk.

Manipulating Graphics with *SavePicture()*

In addition to saving and retrieving text from a file, you also can save and retrieve graphics. You use the LoadPicture() function to load a bitmap or icon file from disk and assign it to the Picture property of a PictureBox or Image control. You saw how to use the LoadPicture() function in Chapter 17, "Working With Graphics." The syntax for the LoadPicture() function is as follows:

```
ImageCtrl.Picture = LoadPicture(FilePath)
```

Where:

> *ImageCtrl* is either a PictureBox, Image control, or Form.
>
> *Picture* is the Picture property of that object.
>
> *LoadPicture* is the function name.
>
> *FilePath* is the exact location on disk of the file to load.

You save a picture that has been assigned to a `PictureBox` or `Image` control or Form using the `SavePicture` statement.

The syntax for the `SavePicture` statement is as follows:

`SavePicture Pictue, strFilePath`

Where:

SavePicture is the name of the statement.

Picture is the picture assigned to or embedded in the `Picture` property of a `PictureBox`, `Image` control, or Form.

StrFilePath is the exact location and file name on disk to where you want to save the file.

Listing 23.3 shows the `SavePicture` statement used to save a `Picture` in an `Image` control to a location on disk. The program uses a common dialog box to determine what to name the file and where to store it. The complete code for this program is in project SaveGrfx.vbp in the directory Chp_23\SaveGrfx\ on the CD-ROM that accompanies this book.

Listing 23.3   23LIST03.TXT—Using the *SavePicture* Statement

```
Private Sub cmdImgSave_Click()
    Dim strFilter As String 'common dialog filter
    Dim strFileName As String 'Filename variable

    'Set the CommonDialog filter
    strFilter = "Bitmaps (*.bmp)¦*.bmp"

    'Assign the filter
    cdMain.Filter = strFilter

    'Show the dialog
    cdMain.ShowSave

    'Make sure a value was entered in the
    'common dialog.
    If cdMain.filename <> "" Then
        strFileName = cdMain.filename

        'Save the Picture in the image control
        SavePicture imgMain.Picture, strFileName

        'Tell the user the file's been saved
        MsgBox strFileName & " saved."
    End If
End Sub
```

Also, be advised that the `SavePicture` statement has elementary use. Graphic file formats can be complex. Manipulating them requires advanced programming skills as well as knowledge of the way Windows handles graphical device contexts. If you want to do advanced graphics work in Visual Basic, even if it's just saving graphic files in multiple formats, many third-party ActiveX controls address the special issues and needs of graphics programmers. ●

CHAPTER 24

Programming with Databases

Most professional applications written in Visual Basic are for inputting data into or reading data out of a database. You can use Visual Basic to work with small-scale desktop database formats such as Access MDB files all the way up to large-scale databases such as SQL Server. Regardless of the size of the database, Visual Basic offers a wide range of techniques for programming with them—from the simple to the complex. In this chapter, you look at the fundamental concepts and techniques for database programming with Visual Basic. ■

Flat versus relational databases

Understand the differences between the different types of databases.

Elements of a database

Learn about the different parts of a database.

Data control

See and learn how to use the Visual Basic Data control to work with databases effortlessly.

Data Form Wizard

Use the Visual Basic Data Form Wizard to make forms automatically with bound controls.

Understanding Databases

In simplest terms, a database is a collection of information. The most common example of a database is a phone book, which is a collection of names, addresses, and phone numbers. Each line in a phone book is a *record* that contains the information for a single person or family. A phone book exhibits another characteristic of most databases—the information is presented in a specific order. In the case of the phone book, this is alphabetical order by last name. Computer databases are similar in concept to the phone book. They provide a way to store and retrieve information easily and quickly.

Computers use two basic types of databases—*flat-file* databases and *relational* databases. A phone book is an example of a flat-file database, where a single record stores all the information for each entry, and a single table contains all the records for the database (see Figure 24.1).

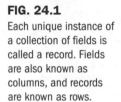

FIG. 24.1

Each unique instance of a collection of fields is called a record. Fields are also known as columns, and records are known as rows.

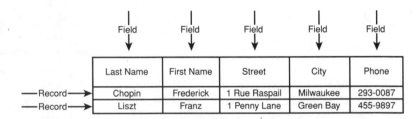

Last Name	First Name	Street	City	Phone
Chopin	Frederick	1 Rue Raspail	Milwaukee	293-0087
Liszt	Franz	1 Penny Lane	Green Bay	455-9897

By contrast, a relational database stores the information in a number of tables that are related by a common field called a *key field*. For instance, you might have a Customer Information table that contains the specifics about customers, and you might have another table called Loans Outstanding that contains information about outstanding loans. Both tables contain a common field called Social Security Number. In a relational database, by keying on the Social Security Number field, you could produce a third table, Average Days to Pay, that is made of data from both the other tables (see Figure 24.2).

Using Database Terminology

Thus far, you have seen a few of the terms, such as *record* and *field*, that are used to refer to the parts of a database. A formal understanding of these terms will help you in the rest of the database discussions. Table 24.1 defines the key parts of a database.

FIG. 24.2
Relational databases
are the most commonly
used types of data-
bases for large-scale
applications.

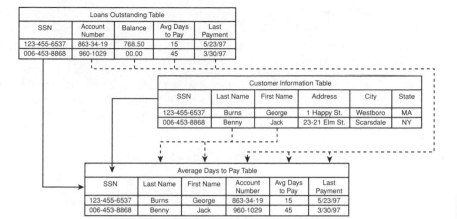

Table 24.1   Elements of a Database

Element	Description
Database	A group of data tables that contain related information.
Table	A group of data records, each containing the same type of information. In the example of the phone book, the book itself is a data table.
Record	A single entry in a table; the entry consists of a number of data fields. In a phone book, a record is one of the single-line entries.
Field	A specific item of data contained in a record. In a phone book, at least four fields can be identified: last name, first name, address, and phone number.
Index	A special type of table that contains the values of a key field or fields and pointers to the location of the actual record. These values and pointers are stored in a specific order and can be used to present the data in the database in that order. For the phone book example, one index might be used to sort the information by last name and first name; another index might be used to sort the information by street address. If you want, you can also create an index to sort the information by phone number.
Query	A command, based on a certain set of conditions or criteria, designed to retrieve a certain group of records from one or more tables or to perform an operation on a table. For example, you would write a query that could show all the students in a class whose last name begins with *S* and who has a grade point average of more than 3.0.
Recordset	A *recordset* is a group of records created from one or more tables in a database. The records in a recordset are typically a subset of all the records in a table. When the recordset is created, both the number of records and the order in which they are presented can be controlled by the query that creates the recordset. The set of records returned by a query is a recordset.

The Microsoft Jet engine provides the means by which Visual Basic interacts with databases. The Jet engine is shared by Visual Basic, Microsoft Access, and other Microsoft products. Don't be mislead by the name "Jet." It has nothing to do with aircraft. It's the tool that you use with Visual Basic to access databases and database functionality.

The Jet engine enables you to work with a wide variety of data types, including several types of text and numeric fields. These different data types allow the developer a great deal of flexibility in designing a database application. Table 24.2 shows all the data types available.

Table 24.2   The Data Types Available with the Jet Engine

Type	Description	Size/Range
Text	Character strings	255 characters maximum
Memo	Long character strings	Up to 1.2 G
Byte	Integer (numeric data)	0 to 255
Integer	Integer (numeric data)	–32,768 to 32,767
Long	Integer (numeric data)	–2,147,483,648 to 2,147,483,647
Counter	Long integer, automatically incremented	
Single	Real (numeric data)	– -3.402823E38 to -1.401298E-45 for negative values and from 1.401298E-45 to 3.402823E38 for positive values
Double	Real (numeric data)	– -1.79769313486232E308 to -4.94065645841247E-324 for negative values and from 4.94065645841247E-324 to 1.79769313486232E308 for positive values
Currency	Real (numeric data)	922,337,203,685,477.5808 to 922,337,203,685,477.5807
Yes/No	Logical/Boolean	
Date	Date and time values	
Binary	Binary data	Up to 1.2 G
OLE	OLE objects	Up to 1.2 G

As your database programming skills develop, you will be interacting with the Jet database engine on an abstract level. For now, the Jet engine will be relatively transparent to you because you will use the Data control to do your database work. The Data control works with the Jet database engine, which in turn works with the database. Whether a database is flat or relational is of marginal importance for the time being. Design time use of the Data control hides most of the inner workings of the database from you.

Working with the *Data* Control

The Data control is a link between the information in your database and the Visual Basic control that you use to display the information. As you set the properties of the Data control, you tell it which database and what part of the database to access. By default, the Data control creates a dynaset-type recordset from one or more of the tables in your database.

The Data control also provides the record navigation functions that your application will need. These buttons, shown in Figure 24.3, enable the user to move to the first or last record in the recordset or to move to a record prior to or following the current record. The design of the buttons makes their use intuitive in that they are similar to the buttons you would find on a VCR or CD player.

FIG. 24.3
The Data control displays the value of the Caption property between the navigation buttons.

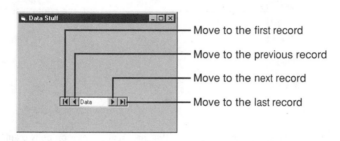

Move to the first record

Move to the previous record

Move to the next record

Move to the last record

Adding the *Data* Control to a Form

To use the Data control, do the following:

(If you want to follow along, the code for this section is in the project DataProj.vbp in the directory \Chp_24\DataProj\ on the CD-ROM that accompanies this book.)

1. Create a new project. Name the project DataProj. Name the default form frmMain.
2. Select the Data control from the Toolbox.
3. Draw the Data control on the form frmMain.
4. Retain the default name of Data control, Data1.
5. Add two TextBox controls to the form. Name one TextBox txtFirst. Name the other txtLast. Position the Data control and TextBox controls as shown in Figure 24.4.
6. Save the project.

Connecting the *Data* Control to Your Database

After the Data control is on your form, you need to make the connection between the Data control and the database information. This is done by setting the properties of the Data control. Although several properties can affect the way a Data control interacts with the database, only two properties are required to establish the link to a Jet database—the DatabaseName and RecordSource properties. Specifying these two properties "connects" a Data control to a specific database and a specific table within the database, respectively. Thus, the Data control is now ready to retrieve, create, and edit information.

FIG. 24.4

You use the Data control to access a database and bind controls on the form to information in the fields of the database.

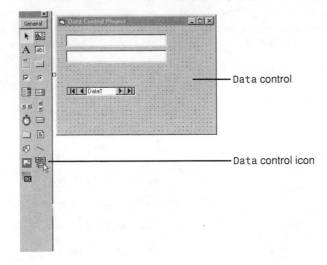

— Data control

— Data control icon

N O T E The DatabaseName property is not the same as the Name property mentioned earlier. The Name property specifies the name of the data control object. This references the object in code. The DatabaseName property specifies the name of the database file that the Data control is accessing.

N O T E Creating a database from scratch in Visual Basic is an advanced skill. Thus, for now, you are going to work with preexisting databases files that were made in the Microsoft Access environment. The demonstration items in this chapter will reference the preexisting Access database file Composer.mdb.

To attach a database and table (recordset) to the Data control, do the following:

1. Select the Data control on the form frmMain in the project DataProj.vbp.
2. Select the DatabaseName property in the Properties window (see Figure 24.5).
3. Select the database Composer.mdb from the DatabaseName dialog box.
4. Select table tblComposers from the RecordSource property drop-down list (see Figure 24.6).
5. Select the TextBox txtFirst on the form frmMain.
6. Select the Data control Data1 from the drop-down list of the TextBox's DataSource property in the Properties window (see Figure 24.7).
7. Select the field FirstName from the TextBox's DataField drop-down list in the Properties window (see Figure 24.8).

FIG. 24.5

When you select the `DatabaseName` property in the Properties window, an ellipsis appears to the right of the value area. Click the ellipsis to open the DatabaseName file dialog box.

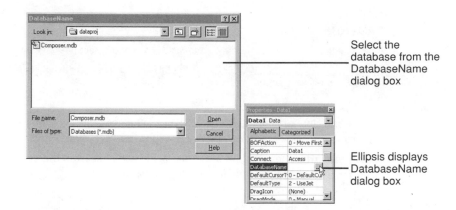

Select the database from the DatabaseName dialog box

Ellipsis displays DatabaseName dialog box

FIG. 24.6

When you assign a database file to the `DatabaseName` property of the `Data` control, the `RecordSource` property drop-down list automatically is populated with all the tables and queries in that database.

FIG. 24.7

The `DataSource` property lists all the `Data` controls on a form.

FIG. 24.8

When you assign a `Data` control to a control's `DataSource` property, all the fields from the table assigned to the `Data` control's `RecordSource` property are displayed in the `DataField` drop-down list.

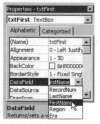

Part

IV

Ch

24

CAUTION

Make sure that you have a table assigned to the `Data` control's `RecordSource` property before you select a value for another control's `DataField`. If you do not have a table assigned to the `RecordSource` property, you will get an error.

8. Assign the `Data` control Data1 to the `DataSource` property of the `TextBox` txtLastName using the same methodology you used for the `TextBox` txtFirstName.

9. In the Properties window, select the field LastName from the `DataField` drop-down list of the `TextBox` txtLastName (see Figure 24.9).

FIG. 24.9

When you assign a table's field to the `TextBox`'s `DataField` property, the contents of that field will be read into that TextBox on a record-by-record basis.

10. Save and run the code (see Figure 24.10).

FIG. 24.10

You can move through the database's table by using the `Data` control's navigation buttons.

In the preceding procedure, you "connected" a database to a `Data` control and selected a `RecordSource` for the `Data` control. Then you assigned that `Data` control to be a `DataSource` for two `TextBoxes`. You *bound* each `TextBox` to a field in the `Data` control's `RecordSource` by selecting a field in the `TextBox`'s `DataField` property drop-down list.

If you wanted to add and bind more `TextBoxes` to the `Data` control, you would follow the process enumerated earlier. You can also bind `Label` controls to a `Data` control as you bound a `TextBox`. Controls such as `CheckBoxes` and `OptionButtons` can also be bound to a `Data` control. However, the type of data of the fields to which the `CheckBox` or `OptionButton` are bound must be Boolean.

Bound controls such as the `TextBox` can also be used to edit the information. To change the information, the user just needs to edit the contents of the control. Then, when the current record is changed or the form is closed, the information in the database is automatically updated to reflect the changed values.

Creating Database-Bound Forms with the Data Form Wizard

Visual Basic provides a tool by which you can automatically make forms that have controls that are bound to a database. The tool is the VB Data Form Wizard. You access this tool through the Add-In menu.

When you install the Visual Basic programming environment on your computer, the VB Data Form Wizard is not installed during that first setup. You must attach it to the Add-In menu separately. To add the VB Data Form Wizard to the Visual Basic IDE, do the following:

(The form that these steps creates is frmWorks, which is part of the project DataProj.vbp in the directory Chp_27\DataProj\.)

Part

IV

Ch

24

1. Select Add-In Manager from the Add-In menu to display the Add-In Manager dialog box (see Figure 24.11).

FIG. 24.11
The VB Data Form Wizard will be added to the Add-In menu after the installation process.

2. Check the VB Data Form Wizard CheckBox in the Add-In Manager dialog box. Click OK (see Figure 24.12).

FIG. 24.12
Visual Basic ships with a host of add-ins.

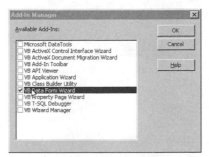

Now that you've attached the VB Data Form Wizard to the Visual Basic IDE, you can use it in all your projects. If you want to remove it in the future, go to the Add-In Manger dialog box and clear the VB Data Form Wizard CheckBox.

You can use the VB Data Form Wizard to create a form for the table tblWorks in the database file COMPOSER.MDB by doing the following:

1. Select the Data Form Wizard menu item from the Add-In menu (see Figure 24.13).

FIG. 24.13

The Add-In Manager attaches add-ins to the Add-In menu.

2. Click the Next button on the Welcome screen (see Figure 24.14).

FIG. 24.14

Check the Skip This Screen in the Future checkbox to get directly to the wizard's main functionality in the future.

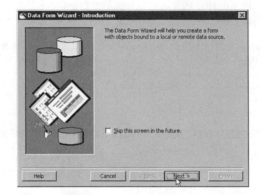

3. Select the Access database format; then click the Next button (see Figure 24.15).

FIG. 24.15

The Jet database engine supports many different types of database formats.

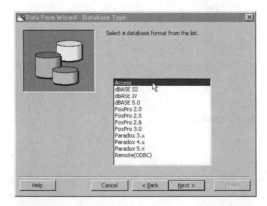

4. Select the database for which you want to make a form by clicking the Browse button. The Access Database dialog box appears. Locate the Composer database; then click the Next button (see Figure 24.16).

FIG. 24.16

You can specify whether you want to view Tables, Queries, or both by using the check boxes on this form.

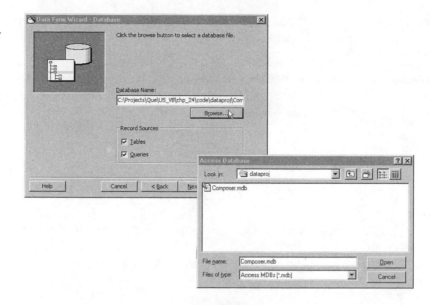

5. Select the Single Record option; then click the Next button (see Figure 24.17).

6. Select the table tblWorks from the Record Source drop-down list (see Figure 24.18).

FIG. 24.17

You select the layout that you want the data form to take by choosing the option that fits your needs.

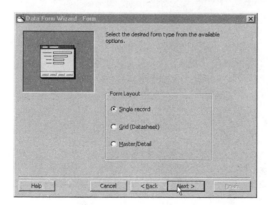

FIG. 24.18
All the tables and queries of the selected database are listed in the Record Source drop-down list. After you select the record source, the fields of the record source will appear in the Available Fields list.

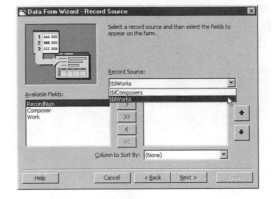

7. Click the Move All Fields to Right button. Click the Next button (see Figure 24.19).

FIG. 24.19
Selecting all the fields makes them appear on the data form. If you only want some of the fields, select them one at a time and click the Move Selected Field to Right button (>). You can remove fields from the data form by clicking the arrow pointing to the left.

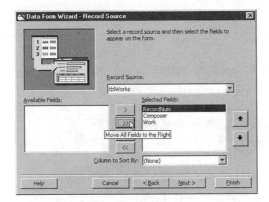

8. Do not uncheck any of the check boxes. Click the Next button (see Figure 24.20).

FIG. 24.20
You can select a limited number of buttons to be on the data form by checking the appropriate check boxes. Click Clear All to clear all check boxes.

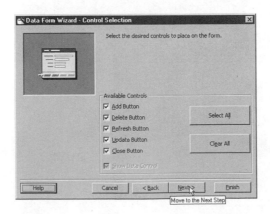

9. Rename the data form frmWorks (see Figure 24.21).

10. Click the Finish button. A final, Data Form Created dialog box appears. Click, OK.

FIG. 24.21

The Data Form Wizard adds the characters "frm" before the RecordSource table or query name to create a default form name. You can change this if you need to. However, the "What do you want to name this form?" field cannot be left blank.

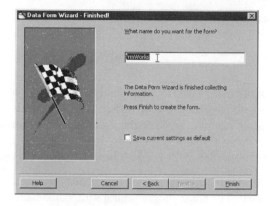

11. Save the code (see Figure 24.22).

FIG. 24.22

The Data Form Wizard will create and size a form with a data control, bound controls, and buttons that enable you to do database actions.

Open the Project Properties dialog box by selecting DataProj Properties from the Project menu.

Select the form, frmWorks from the Startup Object drop-down list (see Figure 24.23).

Run the code (see Figure 24.24).

FIG. 24.23

If you want a newly added form to be the startup form for your application, you must reset the Startup Object.

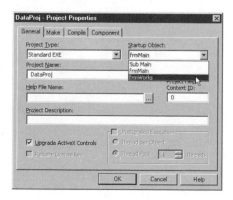

Part IV Ch 24

FIG. 24.24

The data form that the wizard makes enables you to view, edit, add, and delete data from the table assigned to the value of the Data control's RecordSource.

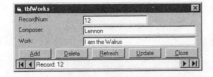

You can use multiple Data controls on a form. Each Data control can be assigned a RecordSource from the same database or from different databases. Also, you can change a Data control's properties at runtime. If you do decide to change properties at runtime, be advised that you will probably have to change more than the Data control's properties. You will also have to change properties of the controls bound to the Data control.

The Data control makes working with databases simple. However, be advised that you have only scratched the surface of database programming with Visual Basic. Database programming is a complete discipline itself. The more complex the data structures and business requirements are, the more complex the programming will become. After a time, you will probably outgrow the Data control in favor of more advanced technologies such as Data Access Objects (DAO) and Remote Data Objects (RDO). Regardless of your future plans, the Data control will serve you well in most aspects of your database programming activity. ●

CHAPTER 25

Adding Help to Your Applications

Help Workshop

Learn about the development system that Visual Basic provides for creating Help files.

Help files

See how Help files are created and the different types of Help documents.

Context-sensitive help

Learn how to make your application use context-sensitive help.

Professionally programmed applications provide online Help. Whether your Visual Basic application is one that is intended for general deployment to a wide variety of users or a specialized corporate application to be used within a limited enterprise, you owe it to your users to provide online documentation that is detailed and understandable. Also, the documentation should be as context-sensitive as possible so that when the user presses the F1 key, she or he arrives at the exact topic in the Help documentation that addresses the particular need at hand. Learning to create useful, appropriate online Help is a profession in itself. This chapter examines what it takes to make a simple Help file particular to your application. Then, you'll learn how to incorporate the Help file into the workings of your application. ■

Installing the Help Workshop

The Microsoft Help Workshop 4.0 is a set of tools, separate from Visual Basic, that you use to create Help files for applications that run under 32-bit Windows operating systems. The Help Workshop is shipped on the same CD-ROM upon which you received your copy of Visual Basic 5.0 in the directory \Tools\Hcw. It ships in a Setup.EXE format. To use the Help Compiler, you must install it from the CD-ROM. To install the Help Workshop on your system, do the following:

1. Go to the directory \Tools\Hcw on the Visual Basic 5.0 CD-ROM.
2. Double-click the file Setup.exe to start the installation process.
3. Follow the directions in the Setup Wizard (see Figure 25.1).

FIG. 25.1

The Help Workshop ships with the Help Compiler, Hotspot Editor, and Dialog Editor as well as all the documentation you need to learn how to use the tools.

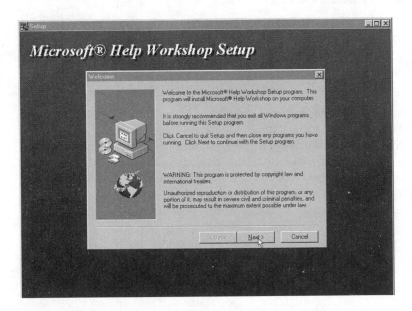

Understanding the Help Workshop

You use the tools in the Help Workshop to make a set of Help files for your application. Generally, the Help files that you make for your application's online Help documentation are a Contents file (.cnt—see Figure 25.2) and associated Help files (.hlp—see Figure 25.3).

A Contents file is similar to a global Table of Contents for your Help documentation. You make the Contents file within the Help Workshop environment (see Figure 25.4).

You create your Help data by using any word processor that supports footnotes and the Rich Text Format (.rtf). Then you "compile" the Rich Text Format files and the Help Project file (.hpj) through the Help compiler to create the Help file (.hlp—see Figure 25.5). Table 25.1 shows the different data and executable files used within this process.

FIG. 25.2

Contents files (.cnt) list the topics of your application's Help documentation in a hierarchy.

FIG. 25.3

A Help file (.hlp) contains topics' text and hypertext.

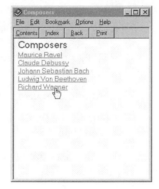

FIG. 25.4

You make Contents files in the Help Workshop.

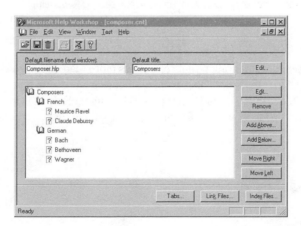

Table 25.1 Parts of the Help Workshop

File	Name	Description
HXW.EXE	Help Workshop	Online documentation workspace
HCRTF.EXE	Help Compiler	Transforms .RTF files into .HLP file
SHED.EXE	Hotspot Editor	Creates hypertext jump regions on bitmaps
DBHE.EXE	Dialog Box Help Editor	Makes context-sensitive Help dialog boxes
HXW.HLP	Help file for Help Workshop	N/A
SHED.HLP	Help file for Hotspot Editor	N/A
DBHE.HLP	Help file for Dialog Box Help Editor	N/A
MyProject.hpj	Help project file	Project-specific data created by Help Workshop
*.RTF	Rich text format files	RTF files that will be transformed into an .HLP file
MyProject.HLP	Help file	Resulting help file made from .RTF file
MyProject.CNT	Contents file	Contents file that is associated with given online Help
MyProject.LOG	Log file	File that lists compilation errors

N O T E Be advised, third-party tools also are available, such as RoboHelp, that automate the creation of both Contents and Help files. These tools work just as well, if not better than, the Help Workshop. ▨

You can have Help documentation that references more than one distinct Help file through a Contents file (see Figure 25.6). This sort of configuration is useful if you have a large program with many different categories of Help topics. Breaking up Help files into many smaller ones makes the development process easier to distribute among many documentation developers.

FIG. 25.5

The production process for a single Help file online Help documentation set.

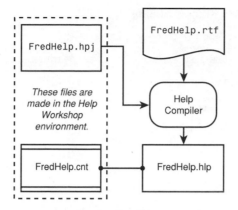

FIG. 25.6

The production process for a multiple Help file online Help documentation set.

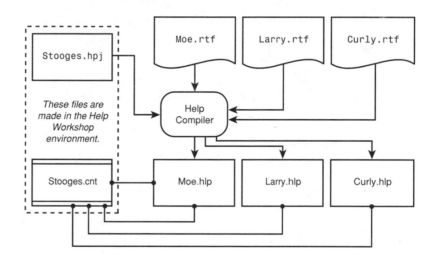

Making a Help File

You make a Help file by using a special footnote markup language in a Rich Text Format (see Figure 25.7). The RTF file is constructed into three sections: the jump text, the topic text, and the footnote tags. The heart of the structure is the topic.

FIG. 25.7

You can use Word to make the RTF files that you will compile into a Help file.

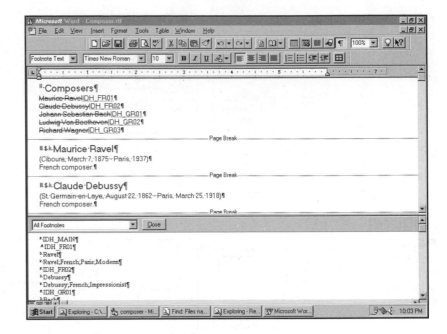

The topic is a section of Rich Text bounded with a page break. The first line of the section is footnoted minimally with the special footnote character "#." You enter the Topic ID of the topic section next to this character in the footnote area of the Rich Text Format file. A Topic ID is a "location address" of the given topic within the RTF file. You also use the characters "$" and "k" as footnote characters at the beginning of each topic section. The "$" character represents a tag for subject. The "k" character is used to denote index keywords that will show up when you look in the Index tab in the Help Topics dialog box. Words entered in the subject footnote will appear in the History window of the Help documentation (see Figure 25.8).

The sections interact by your use of Strikethrough text to indicate that the characters of that text are hypertext—that clicking the text will take you to another Topic section. You follow the Strikethrough text with Hidden character text. The Hidden characters indicate the Topic ID to which the user will be "jumped" when he or she clicks the Strikethrough text. When the user clicks the hypertext, the Help runtime engine (WinHelp.EXE) looks at the Hidden text after the Strikethrough characters for the address of where to jump. Then, after the engine knows the address, it looks up, in the footnote section, the location of that address within the Help file. The engine then goes to the topic at that address and displays the information (see Figure 25.9).

The mechanics of the markup language are difficult to understand at first pass. Also, the nature of this discussion is to give you a sense of how the Help files work. A detailed set of online Help files come with the Help Workshop. You should read them at some length. Also, in the directory Chp_25\Composer\Help\ is the complete Help project upon which this section was based.

FIG. 25.8
Windows Help documentation is made up of many windows.

History window

Topic window

Help Topics dialog box

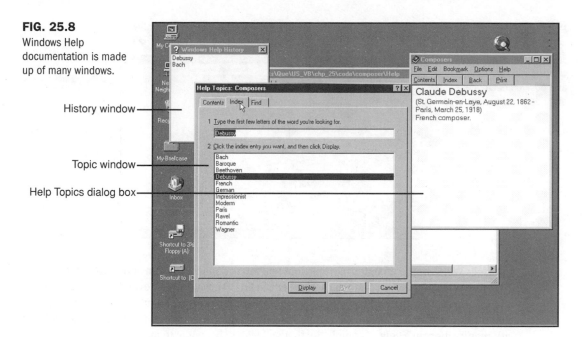

Part
IV
Ch
25

FIG. 25.9
Make sure that there is no space between the Strikethrough text and the Hidden text for the Topic ID. If there is, you cannot make a jump, and you will get an error.

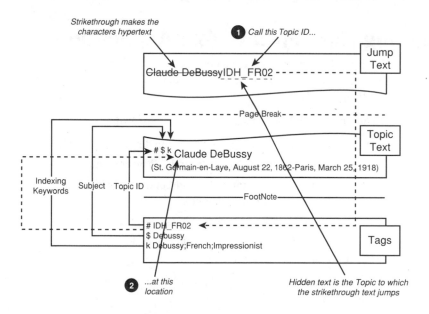

If you open the Help project Composer.HPJ, you will see how to make custom windows for your Help files and associate a Help file with Contents files (see Figure 25.10).

FIG. 25.10
You can make multiple custom Help windows with the Help Workshop and position each one at different locations on the screen.

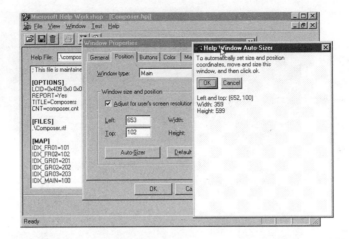

The Help Workshop is an extensive development environment. You can add custom bitmaps to your files and associate certain topics with certain custom windows. It even has a complete macro language built in that allows you to make conditional decisions and use functionality from other programs. You can even access the WinHelp API if you want. This is a powerful tool with many different levels of complexity that will take you a while to master.

Adding Help Files to Your Application

After you have made your Help documentation, you need to integrate it into your program. You associate a Help file to your program at design time from the Project Properties dialog box of the Project menu.

To associate a Help file to a program, do the following:

1. Open the project Composer.vbp in the directory \Chp_25\Composer\.
2. Select composer Properties from the Project menu.
3. Click the ellipsis button to the right of the Help File Name field (see Figure 25.11). This displays the Help File dialog box.
4. Select the Help file Composer.hlp (see Figure 25.12).
5. Click the Open button in the Help File dialog box. Then click OK in the Project Properties dialog box (see Figure 25.13).

To associate a Help file to an application at runtime, use the HelpFile property of the App object as shown in Listing 25.1.

FIG. 25.11

When you associate a Help file with a program, make sure that you maintain an identical directory structure upon deployment. If you don't, the program will not be able to find the Help file.

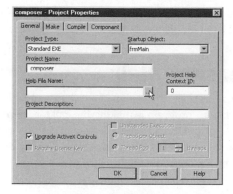

FIG. 25.12

It is best to keep the Help file in the same directory as your application.

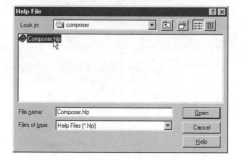

FIG. 25.13

When you associate a Help file to an application using the Project Properties dialog box, if you put the Help file in the same directory as the application, you can truncate the drive and directory path from the location of the file. This eliminates a possible runtime error.

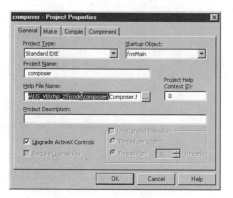

Listing 25.1 25LIST01.TXT—Using the *App* Object to Set an Application's Help File

```
Private Sub Form_Load()
    App.HelpFile = "Composer.hlp"
End Sub
```

After a Help file is associated with an application, if you press the F1 key when your application has the focus, the associated Help file always appears.

Making Context-Sensitive Help

Context-sensitive Help means that your application can call up a specific topic in a Help file based on the area from which your program is making the call for Help. For example, the Help documentation for the Visual Basic IDE has a high degree of context sensitivity. The IDE is automated in such a way that you can access the topic that is directly related to your area of interest by simply pressing the F1 key while the item for which you need help has the focus (see Figure 25.14).

FIG. 25.14

Within the Visual Basic IDE, if you want to get Help for an intrinsic function, put your cursor on the function's keyword and press the F1 key.

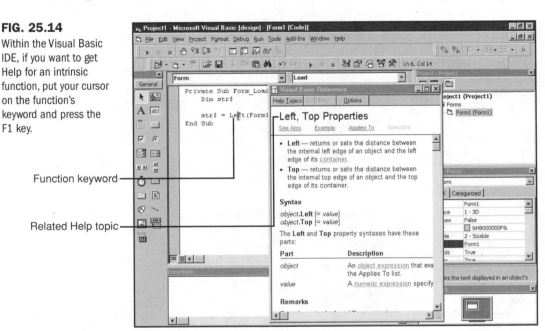

You make your application and your application's Help context-sensitive by assigning a Topic ID's numeric value to the `HelpContextID` property of a given control or object. As you learned earlier, the Topic ID is the string that identifies the location of a given topic within the structure of a Help file. Generally, Topic IDs follow a naming convention that begins with the characters *IDH_*, which loosely stands for *identification for help file*. You follow the underscore character with some additional naming logic. (In the example file, COMPOSER.RTF, French composers start with the characters *FR* followed by serialization numbers, and German composers follow the underscore with the characters *GR*, which also are serialized—GR01, GR02, GR03.) After the Help file has been tagged with Topic IDs, you assign a number that corresponds to a Topic ID's string.

You assign the Topic ID a number in the Map dialog box of the Help Workshop (see Figure 25.15). After the Topic IDs are assigned a unique number, you compile the Help project file. This number assigned to the Topic ID is the value that you will assign to the `HelpContextID` property in your Visual Basic application.

FIG. 25.15

You access the Map dialog box by clicking the Map button of the Help Workshop window.

Again, what you are reading here is an overview. To get a more detailed understanding of this process, take the time to read the Help Workshop's online documentation and study the composer.hpj project.

The Visual Basic project Composer.vbp illustrates assigning a value to the `HelpContextID` property. The project is a control array of five `OptionButtons`. The `HelpContextID` property of each `OptionButton` is assigned a unique value that corresponds to a related Topic ID within the Help file COMPOSER.HLP (see Figure 25.16).

When the user selects a specific `OptionButton` and then presses the F1 key, the Help file, COMPOSER.HLP, automatically opens to the topic related to the `OptionButton` (see Figure 25.17).

In addition to using the `HelpContextID` property to make your program react in a context-sensitive manner when the user presses the F1 key, you can also make message boxes display Help buttons that are context-sensitive. Listing 25.2 shows you how to take advantage of the last two arguments of the `MsgBox()` function, `HelpFile` and `HelpContextID`. Those arguments assign a Help file and topic to the message box. Figure 25.18 shows the listed code in action.

Part
IV
Ch
25

FIG. 25.16
The value for the
`HelpContextID`
is created when you
make the Help file in
the Help Workshop.

OptionButton being
assigned a
HelpContextID value

TopicID is assigned a
numeric value in the
Help Workshop

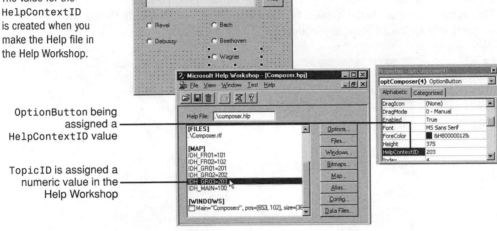

FIG. 25.17
When the user selects
the `OptionButton`
and presses the F1 key,
the appropriate topic
appears in the Help
window.

Listing 25.2   25LIST02.TXT—Assigning Context-Sensitive Help to a Message Box

```
Private Sub cmdAdd_Click()
    Dim i%
    Dim Result%
    Dim Msg$
    'Make a message for the Message Box
    Msg$ = "Strike the Help Button for more help"

    'Display a Message Box with a Help button. Also
    'assign a Help file and Help topic to the Message Box
    Result% = MsgBox(Msg$, vbMsgBoxHelpButton, "Help Demo", _
                App.HelpFile, 100)
```

```
'Traverse all the OptionButtons in the control array
'to find the one that is true. (Count is a property of the
'control array collection that reports the number of items in
'the control array.)
For i% = 0 To optComposer.Count - 1
    If optComposer(i).Value = True Then
        lblComposer.Caption = optComposer(i%).Caption
    End If
Next i%
End Sub
```

FIG. 25.18
Adding Help to a message box greatly increases its effectiveness.

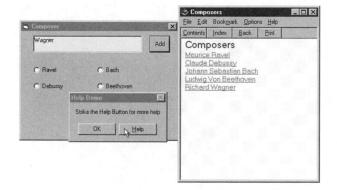

A good prompting scheme notifies a user that not only has an error occurred or decision must be made, but it also provides the user with details about what the issue is about and suggestions about how to resolve the presented issue. By assigning a Help file and `HelpContextID` to a Message Box, you greatly increase the amount of information that you provide to a user at key decision points or when he or she needs to address errors.

You can never offer those using your program too much help. A good, easy-to-use and easy-to-understand Help system will distinguish your program for the better. If you are so inclined, study other programs' Help documentation. Many companies devote a great deal of resources to making quality Help systems, and taking advantage of their efforts will help you in your own endeavors. ●

Appendixes

Glossary

ActiveX   A set of technologies based on Microsoft's Component Object Model (COM) for creating reusable binary objects.

ActiveX code component   A physical file that contains classes from which objects can be defined. ActiveX code components generally have file extensions EXE, DLL, or OCX. Formerly OLE Automation Server.

ActiveX control   An object that can be placed on a form to allow a user to interact with an application. ActiveX controls have events, properties, and methods and can be incorporated into other controls. ActiveX controls have an OCX file extension.

ActiveX document   A Visual Basic application that can be viewed within a container application such as Microsoft Internet Explorer (version 3.0 or later) or Microsoft Office Binder. ActiveX documents do not require HTML code to be viewed or manipulated.

Add-in   A software component that extends the capability of Visual Basic. Some add-ins, such as the Visual Basic Class Builder Utility Add-in, are included with Visual Basic; many more are available from third-party sources. Within the IDE, the Add-In Manager is used to install and remove add-ins.

ANSI   American National Standards Institute. ANSI provides a unique integer code for a character set that includes 256 characters. ANSI includes the 128-character ASCII character set, and also contains international letters, symbols, and fractions.

API (Application Programming Interface)   The API is a set of core Windows functions that allow direct access to many operating system-provided services. The API consists of three main files—user32.dll, gdi32.dll, and kernel32.dll.

Application   One or more software components that perform some action or provide some service; a compiled Visual Basic project. Other examples of applications include Microsoft Visual Basic and Microsoft Word. Also known as program.

Argument   Data sent to a procedure. An argument can be a constant, a variable, or some other expression.

Array   An indexed group of related data. Elements within an array must be of the same data type (for instance, all integers or all strings), and each element has a unique, sequential index number.

ASCII   American Standard Code for Information Interchange. ASCII provides a unique integer code for a character set that includes 128 numbers, letters, and symbols found on a standard U.S. keyboard. A subset of the ANSI character set.

Authentication   The process by which the identity of an ActiveX control is proven to a Web browser. During authentication, the Web browser determines that the control meets a predetermined set of criteria, in essence verifying that the control has not been tampered with and that it will behave in the way the developer of the control originally intended.

Automation server   See *ActiveX code component.*

Bit   The smallest amount of data storage available on a computer. A bit is either 0 or 1.

Boolean   A binary data type; Boolean values are 16-bit (2-byte) true or false values. The Boolean data type does not have a type declaration character.

Bound control   A data-aware control attached to a database through a Data control. At runtime, when the user manipulates the Data control by changing from one row of the database to the next, the bound control changes to display the data found in the columns of the new row. If the user changes the data stored in a row, the new data is saved to the database when the user switches to a new row.

Breakpoint   A specific line within a block of code where program execution automatically stops (during runtime). Breakpoints are user-selectable and are toggled on and off during design time by pressing the F9 key.

Buffer string   A temporary holding location in memory for data that will be parsed or otherwise modified. For example, if an application is to take two string values from a user and then extract a specific section from their sum, each value would be placed in a buffer string. Then these would be concatenated (and placed into another buffer string) before the desired value is parsed from the input data.

Byte   A series of 8 bits. Bytes are the basis for Visual Basic data types; for example, the *single* data type is a 4-byte (32-bit) number.

CAB file   Short for cabinet file. A CAB file is a group of files compressed into one larger file to conserve disk space. CAB files are often used to distribute applications; during installation, the Setup program extracts files from the CAB file and copies them to the appropriate location on the hard disk.

Call   To transfer control of an application to a different procedure. Procedures are called with the Call keyword.

Class   A template used to create user-defined objects. A class defines an object's properties and methods; all instances created from the class use the properties and methods defined by the class.

Class module   A module that defines a class.

Code block   A selection of code; a code block usually consists of all lines necessary to complete a specific task within the application.

COM (Component Object Model)   A standard by which applications can expose objects to the system for use by other applications and conversely a standard by which applications can use objects that have been exposed by other applications.

Compile   To prepare code for execution. In Visual Basic, code can be compiled into either P-code (which results in faster compilation) or native code (which results in faster execution); the type of compilation can be selected from within the Compile tab of the Project Properties dialog box.

Component object   An object that supports automation through exposed properties and methods. Examples of component objects include ActiveX controls, ActiveX documents, and ActiveX code components.

Compressed file   A file that has been modified to take up less space when stored on the hard drive. Generally, compressed files cannot be opened or manipulated until they are uncompressed.

Concatenate   To join together two or more strings in an expression.

Constituent control   Controls that are encapsulated inside another ActiveX control to provide some of its functionality.

Control   An object that can be manipulated, either at design time or at runtime, to present or change data. Controls are manipulated by changing properties during design time and by calling methods or responding to events during runtime.

Control array   An indexed group of similar controls that are of the same type and have the same name. Individual elements within the control array are identified by a unique index number.

Currency   A numeric data type particularly suited to store money data. Currency values are 64-bit (8-byte) integers. The type declaration character for currency values is the at sign (@).

Data member   Private variables of a class. Data members are seen only by the class that defines them.

Date   A numeric data type used to represent dates. Date values are 64-bit (8-byte) floating-point numbers. The Date data type does not have a type declaration character.

DCOM (Distributed Component Object Model)   An extension of COM by which applications can expose objects to computers across a network and conversely an extension by which computers can use objects that have been exposed from across a network.

Decimal   A numeric data type used to specify the number of digits to the right of the decimal point. Decimal values are 96-bit (12-byte) unsigned integers. The Decimal data type must be used in conjunction with a Variant, and does not have a type declaration character.

Deployment   The period when an application is distributed for use by customers or by other applications.

Design time   While creating an application, the time spent creating forms and writing functions. Forms and functions can be altered only during design time. See also *Runtime*.

Destination system   The system on which an application will be installed and used.

Device independence   The concept that software components do not directly control hardware devices. Device-independent software controls hardware by manipulating objects that abstract and expose the functionality of a class of hardware devices.

DLL (Dynamic Link Library)   An executable file that contains a set of functions that can be called by other applications during runtime. DLLs do not generally have a graphical user interface; instead, they are usually accessed by applications without user intervention.

Double   A numerical data type. Double values are 64-bit (8-byte) floating-point numbers. The type declaration character for Double values is the pound sign (#).

Dynamic   A changing object or expression.

Dynaset   A Recordset that can include data from one or more tables from a database. A dynaset can be used to view or modify data contained in the underlying database.

Early binding   A method of using an object by an application. In early binding, objects are defined from a specific class. Early binding is often faster than late binding because the application does not have to interrogate the object at runtime to determine the object's properties and methods.

Element   A single member of an array. Each element of an array is assigned a unique index value, which is used to locate and manipulate specific elements in an array.

Encapsulation   The act of placing code or data in a location, such as a module or control, that is isolated from the rest of an application. Encapsulation hides the internal complexity of an object but still allows the application to use functions contained within it.

Entry point   The starting point in the code of an application. In Visual Basic 5.0, entry points include a `Sub Main` procedure or a `Form Load` event.

Event   A signal fired by the operating system in response to a user action. For example, when a user clicks (and holds down) a mouse button, a `MouseDown` event is sent by the operating system. The active application intercepts this signal and executes the code attached to the `MouseDown` event.

Extensibility   The capability to extend an object's or application's functionality through the use of a programming language or an add-in.

Field   A discrete element of a record in a database; a column in a database. For example, a database of music albums might have many fields including album name, artist name, and album label.

File   A unit of storage on an external storage device such as a hard disk retrievable block of data. Usually stored on a hard drive, files can contain executable programs, word processor documents, or bitmap picture files. In Visual Basic, each form, module, and project is saved as a file.

File handle   A structure that provides access to a file on disk. Also is a number used to identify a file on disk.

Flag   A Boolean variable.

Flat file database   A database file in which each and every record contains all the information required to describe it. Flat file databases often contain redundant information; for example, every record in a flat file database of music albums would require multiple fields to describe the contact information for the artist's fan club. See also *Relational database*.

Focus   The state when an object can receive input from the mouse or keyboard. At any given time, only one object can have focus; this object is usually highlighted with a different color and it contains the text cursor where appropriate.

Form   The basis of an application's graphical user interface. Forms contain objects that allow users to manipulate data and otherwise control an application.

Form Designer   A part of the Visual Basic 5.0 Integrated Development Environment. The Form Designer is used to create an application's graphical user interface by placing objects on forms during design time. At runtime, objects will appear where they have been placed on the forms.

Form Layout window   A part of the Visual Basic 5.0 Integrated Development Environment (MDI version only). The Form Layout window is used to position the forms of an application visually during design time rather than through code. At runtime, forms will appear where they have been placed in the Form Layout window.

Function   A procedure, beginning with `Function functionname()` and ending with `End Function`, that returns a value to the calling procedure when it is complete.

Get A Visual Basic keyword; the part of a Property procedure that gets the value of a property.

Gotcha A detail that can cause problems when overlooked.

GUI (Graphical user interface) A set of forms and objects that enables a user to view and manipulate data and otherwise control an application. A graphical user interface is the part of the application that sits between the user and the underlying procedures of an application.

Header A commented section of code at the beginning of a procedure, usually placed before the Sub or Function statement. The header describes the purpose of the procedure, specifies all variables declared within it, and may additionally contain information identifying the developer who wrote it.

Help Context ID A number that defines a position within a Help file. The Windows Help system uses context IDs to move to new locations within Help files as the user navigates through the Help system.

High-level language A computer language, such as Visual Basic, that can simplify coding by allowing a programmer to write code with highly developed functions and keywords. See also *Low-level language*.

Hovering The act of holding the mouse pointer over an object. For example, a ToolTip may be shown when the pointer hovers over a command button.

HTML (HyperText Markup Language) HTML files are plain text files that include data and instructions for presenting it. When viewed with an Internet Browser, an HTML file may contain text, multiple colors, and graphics. HTML files, which can be linked together via hyperlinks, are the primary method of displaying information on the World Wide Web.

Hyperlinks References between documents that, when selected by the reader, call and display other documents.

IDE (Integrated Development Environment) The IDE includes all the tools necessary to create applications with Visual Basic 5.0, such as the Form Layout window and the Object Browser.

Index A unique number that identifies a single element in an array or a control array.

Index (database) A cross-reference of fields across the tables of a database that enables faster retrieval to specific records in the database.

Inheritance The act of passing property values from a class to objects created by the class.

Initialization The act of setting the value of a variable or expression to a specific "starting" value.

Input box A dialog box, created with the InputBox() statement, that waits for a user to enter text or click a button. When the user closes an input box, a string containing the contents of the text box is returned to the calling procedure.

Instance   A single, individual object created from a class. Also, a variable is an instance of a data type.

Integer   A numerical data type. Integer values are 16-bit (2-byte) numbers. The type declaration character for Integer values is the percent sign (%).

Interpreted language   A language that does not enable compilation to native code. When an application created with an interpreted language is run, the application's code is passed through an interpreter which modifies the code into a form the computer can understand and execute.

Intrinsic control   A control included with Visual Basic, such as the `Label` or `CommandButton` controls. Intrinsic controls cannot be removed from the Toolbox. Also known as standard controls.

Intrinsic function   A predetermined function included with Visual Basic. Examples of intrinsic functions include the type conversion functions such as `CStr()`, which usually converts a numeric expression to a string value.

JScript   The Microsoft implementation of the JavaScript scripting language.

Key field   The field in a database table that uniquely describes each record. For example, the key field in a database table of employees might be the employee number.

Keycode   A constant value that represents a keystroke. Keycodes are sent to the application when a key on the keyboard is pressed and are used to determine which keys are pressed by the user.

Keyword   A word (function, constant, or command) recognized by Visual Basic. Keywords cannot be used to name user-defined structures such as variables or constants (see *Name collision*).

Language independent   Any file, object, or other structure that can be used by any programming language. For example, the Windows API can be used by Visual Basic, C, or Visual C++.

Late binding   A method of using an object by an application. In late binding, objects are defined as `Object`. Late binding is slower than early binding because the application must interrogate the object to determine its properties and methods.

Let   A Visual Basic keyword; the part of a `Property` procedure that assigns a value to a property. Also used to assign a value to a variable, such as "`Let x = 10.`"

Literal statement   Any expression, consisting of ASCII characters and enclosed in quotation marks, that is used literally in a procedure. For example, if the code `MsgBox("This is a button.")` were contained within the `Click` event of a command button, a dialog box containing the text "This is a button." would appear on the screen when the user clicks the button.

Long   A numerical data type. Long (long integer) values are 32-bit (4-byte) numbers. The type declaration character for Long values is the ampersand (&).

Loose typing   Defining and using variables without declaring or following a specific data type. This can lead to type mismatch errors at compile time because expressions or values can encounter data types that they do not support. See also *Strict typing*.

Low-level language   A computer language such as machine language that requires a programmer to write code with lesser developed instructions that the computer can directly understand.

Make   To compile code into a standard application (EXE), dynamic link library (DLL), or ActiveX control (OCX).

Member functions   See *Method*.

Menu bar   The part of Visual Basic IDE located directly below the title bar that allows the user to select functions and commands included with the application. Menu bars can be added to applications created with Visual Basic by using the Menu Bar Editor.

Message box   A dialog box created with the `MsgBox()` statement that provides a message for the user. Message boxes generally include one or more command buttons that enable a user to either clear the dialog box or respond with a yes/no or true/false answer to a query. A message box returns an integer value describing which button was selected.

Method   A procedure associated with a class that manipulates an object. For example, one method of a command button is `SetFocus`, which moves the focus to the command button that invoked the `SetFocus` method.

Module   A block of code saved as a file with the extension BAS. Modules contain declarations and may or may not contain procedures.

Name collision   An error that occurs when different structures are named identically. For example, if a variable is named *string*, a name collision occurs because the word `string` is a Visual Basic keyword. Name collisions also occur if identically named variables are defined within the same scope.

Native code   Binary code that can be directly understood and executed by the computer's processor system. Visual Basic can be set to compile to native code by setting options in the Compile tab of the Project Properties dialog box.

Nesting   The act of including `Loop` or `Select Case` statements within similar statements. For example, a `Do...Loop` can be placed within one case of the `Select Case` statement. Then the repetitive action controlled by the `Do...Loop` executes only if the proper value is passed to the `Select Case` statement.

Object   A discrete combination of code and data, such as a `Listbox` or `CommandButton`, that can be manipulated. Objects contain properties and methods and are defined by a class.

Object Browser   A part of the Visual Basic IDE, the Object Browser enables a programmer to see all the objects (and all the properties of each object) available for use on the system. From the Object Browser, objects can be "turned on" (selected) for use in an application.

Object-oriented programming (OOP) A programming style and a programming language that involves the use of software modules called *objects* to encapsulate data and processing.

OLE Automation Server See *ActiveX code component.*

Option Explicit A Visual Basic keyword; the use of `Option Explicit` forces each variable or expression in an application to be defined with a specific data type through the use of the `Dim`, `Private`, `Public`, `ReDim`, or `Static` keywords. If `Option Explicit` is not used, variables automatically are defined as Variants.

P-Code Pseudo-code; code that cannot be directly understood and executed by the Windows operating system. In Visual Basic, code generally is compiled to P-code at runtime; when creating an executable file, Visual Basic can be forced to compile to P-code by setting the appropriate options in the Compile tab of the Project Properties dialog box.

Parameter A numeric or string value that can be changed to modify an expression.

Parse To use string manipulation functions to change user-inputted string information. For example, the string "Microsoft+Visual&Basic&5.0" might be parsed into company ("Microsoft") and application ("Visual Basic 5.0") strings.

Pattern wildcards Characters such as the asterisk (*) or question mark (?) that cause a query to broaden its result or that allow an expression to restrict inputted data. For example, a database query on all records containing "*ain" would return all records that end in "ain," such as *Spain, train,* and so on.

Persistence The concept of keeping an object's data structure stored in memory or on disk.

Pixel The smallest screen-dependent measure of screen distance. Objects on a form generally are not sized and located using pixels because the number of pixels on a screen varies for different resolutions and for different types of display systems. See *Twip.*

Private A Visual Basic keyword. Variables or procedures defined with the `Private` keyword are available only in the module in which the variable or procedure is defined.

Procedural language A programming language, such as Visual Basic, in which data is manipulated by calling procedures rather than by proceeding line-by-line through all code contained in the application.

Procedure A block of code that can be called from within an application. A procedure might be used to position objects on a form or to calculate information from a set of user data. Different types of procedures include `Functions` and `Subs`.

Program See *Application.*

Project A set of forms and modules that make up an application while it is being developed into an application.

Properties window A part of the Visual Basic IDE. The Properties window enables a developer to view and modify all the properties of a given object during design time. Not available during runtime.

Property   An attribute of an object as defined by a class. For example, one property of a command button is `Caption`, which is the text that appears on the face of the button.

Property procedures   Procedures used to view and modify the properties of an object, such as the `Let` and `Get` statements. The `Get` statement returns a string describing the property (this string appears in the Property window of the Visual Basic 5.0 IDE), and the `Let` statement modifies the value of the property if the new value is of the correct type.

Prototype   An application that simulates the behavior of another, more fully developed application. Visual Basic is often used as a prototyping tool—for example, to develop quickly a possible Graphical User Interface (GUI) for an application before the application is actually developed.

Public   A Visual Basic keyword. Variables defined with the `Public` keyword can be seen by any procedure of any module contained in the application.

Query   A subset of a database that fits specific criteria. For example, a query might be placed on a music album database for all jazz albums. The query would return a recordset that contains only jazz albums and no classical or rock albums.

Record   All the data required to describe one retrievable item in a database; made up of one or more fields; a row in a database. For example, one record in a music album database would contain all the data necessary to describe the album, including artist, label, number of songs, and so on.

Recordset   A set of records from a single database table that meets specific criteria.

Recursion   The process of a procedure calling itself.

Relational database   A database file in which records can include pointers to other tables that contain some of the information required to describe the record. Relational databases can be a more efficient means of storing information; for example, a relational database of music albums would require only one field to describe the contact information for the artist's fan club. This field would hold a pointer to another table containing the fan club information for every artist in the database. See also *Flat file database*.

Robust   A term used to describe an application that can trap and react to errors that occur during execution. For example, a robust calculator application would not crash if the user tried to divide a number by zero. Instead, the user might be provided a dialog box explaining that numbers cannot be divided by zero.

Round   To increase in value to a less precise value. For example, the value 1.652 might be rounded to 2. See also *Truncate*.

Runtime   While creating an application, the time when the code actually is running. Neither forms nor functions can be altered during runtime. See also *Design time*.

Scope   An attribute of a variable or procedure that determines which sections of which modules recognize it. There are three levels of scope: public, module, and procedure. Variables declared with the `Public` keyword can be accessed by any module, whereas variables declared

App
A

within a specific module (with the `Private` keyword) can be used only within that module. Variables declared within a procedure can be used only in that procedure, and they lose their value between calls unless they are declared with the `Static` keyword.

Scroll arrow   The buttons at the top and bottom of a scroll bar that enable the user to move through the data within the object.

Scroll bar   A window element that enables a user to view more available data, when all available data cannot be displayed within an object at one time.

Set   A Visual Basic keyword; the part of a Property procedure that sets a reference to an object. The `Set` statement is used with `Get` and `Let` to view or assign a property's value.

Single   A numerical data type. Single values are 32-bit (4-byte) floating-point numbers. The type declaration character for Single values is the exclamation point (!).

SQL (Structured Query Language)   A set of rules that can control many different types of relational databases, including Microsoft Access and SQL Server databases.

Standard control   See *Intrinsic control.*

Standard EXE   A "traditional" executable application. A standard EXE is a self-contained application that does not expose objects to the system for use by other objects or applications.

Statement   A section of code that fully expresses a single declaration or action.

Static variable   A variable, defined with the `Static` keyword, that does not change its value when sent as an argument between different procedures.

Step   The act of moving through a section of code line-by-line. Stepping, used with a breakpoint, is useful in determining which line is causing a problem in code.

Strict typing   Always declaring and following a specific data type when defining and using variables. This can reduce the number of errors at compile time because expressions or values will encounter only data types that they support. See also *Loose typing.*

String   An alphanumeric data type. String values are either variable-length (up to 2 billion characters) or fixed-length (approximately 64,000 characters); longer strings require more memory. Strings can include numbers, letters, and ASCII symbols. The type declaration character for String values is the dollar sign ($).

Sub   A procedure, beginning with `Sub` *subname()* and ending with `End Sub`, that does not return a value to the calling procedure when it is complete.

Subclassing   The act of modifying the standard behavior of an object provided by Windows.

Subscript (array)   The index value of an element in an array.

Syntax   The specific method by which functions or lines of code are written. Important elements of syntax might include spelling, spacing, and punctuation.

System modal   A window or dialog box that holds control of the entire system until the user responds to it.

Table   The basic mechanism of data storage in a database, made up of tables and rows. In a relational database, multiple tables might be used to store different categories of related information. For example, in a music album database, one table might contain only artist information, whereas others might contain label information or fan club information.

Toolbar   A collection of buttons, contained either in a strip or in a dedicated window, that allows a user to control an application.

Toolbox   A part of the Visual Basic 5.0 Integrated Development Environment. The Toolbox contains the objects and controls that are available for use in an application; objects are dragged from the Toolbox and added to forms during design time.

Traverse   To move through records in a database, elements in an array, or data contained within an object.

Truncate   To shorten or reduce a string value. For example, the value *This is My String* might be truncated to *My String*. See also *Round*.

Twip   A screen-independent measure of screen distance approximately equal to 1/1440 of an inch. Objects on a form should be sized and located using twips rather than pixels so that they appear similarly on different types of display systems.

Type   The attribute of a variable that determines what kind of data it can contain. Different types of data include Integer, Long, Variant, String, and others.

Type declaration character   A character that is added to a variable's name that determines the data type of a variable. A type declaration character is a shorthand method of automatically setting a data type when defining a variable. For example, the type declaration character of the integer data type is the percent sign (%), so an integer variable *x* could automatically be defined with the statement Dim x%.

Type safety   The concept of keeping the data type of a variable or expression correct and consistent. In Visual Basic, type safety can be forced through the use of the Option Explicit keyword.

User control   A subobject of a control. User controls are properties or methods that can be added to an object.

User-defined data types   A data type not intrinsic to Visual Basic, defined using the Type keyword, a list of declared elements, and the End Type keyword. User-defined data types can contain one or more elements of any data type.

Validation   The act of making sure that data is of an appropriate format before it is written to a database.

Variable   A named storage location that contains data and that can be modified during runtime. Variables generally are defined to be a specific data type at design time.

Variant   A data type that can be either numeric or alphanumeric. A variant is automatically created when a variable is not defined to be a specific data type. Variants do not have a type declaration character.

VBA   Visual Basic for Applications. Similar to but a subset of the Visual Basic language, VBA is the programming language included with programs such as Access and Excel.

VBScript   A scripting language, similar to but a subset of the Visual Basic language especially suited to be embedded into HTML files because it must be interpreted by a Web browser. VBScript enables objects to be added to Web pages to accomplish tasks such as password authentication or surveys for data collection.

Visual Basic runtime DLL   One of a set of files required to run an application developed in Visual Basic. Automatically installed with Visual Basic, the runtime DLLs must be copied to any machine on which an application is deployed.

Watch   A variable whose value is tracked during runtime. When a watch is set, it appears in the Watch window (part of the IDE). Watches are updated whenever a breakpoint is reached; thus, changes to values can be seen by placing breakpoints at specific events.

White space   When coding, the space within the code editor that does not contain text, such as blank lines or tab spaces. White space makes it easier to follow the flow of code, especially in more complex structures such as nested loops, within a procedure. ●

What's on the
CD-ROM?

The CD-ROM that accompanies this book provides you
with a useful resource that both supplements and extends
the content of the book. On the CD-ROM, you can find
source code from the book that you can easily copy and
paste into your own applications, two bonus chapters, and
we've also included all of the applications created or used
in the text.

Another exciting part of the CD-ROM is an ample supply
of new, unique, and helpful software, shareware, and
evaluation software we've included. You can use much of
this software in creating your own ActiveX controls, and
other software provides you with Internet, Web, and other
capabilities.

This appendix outlines the basic content and structure of
the CD-ROM, discusses using the contents, and describes
the array of software included. ∎

An Overview of the CD-ROM

As already mentioned, the CD-ROM provides a variety of useful contents. Here's an overview of what you can find:

- Sample code and applications from the book
- Bonus chapters on Objects, Classes, and Creating ActiveX Controls with Visual Basic 5.0.
- VBScheduler personal information manager
- VB Knowledgebase
- Visual Basic Custom Control Edition
- Third-party shareware and demonstration components and programs.

The CD contains several subdirectories located off of the root directory. The directories on the CD-ROM are as follows, with application, code, or chapter-specific subdirectories under each:

Table A.1   Directory Structure on the CD-ROM

Directory	Contents
\CODE	The source code from the book. Each chapter that contains sample files, source code, and so on will be contained in a subdirectory named for the chapter it references
\BONUS_1	Bonus chapter: Working with Objects and Classes
\BONUS_2	Bonus chapter: Making ActiveX Controls
\VBSCHED	VBScheduler personal information manager
\VB_KB	The Visual Basic Knowledgebase
\VBCCE	The Visual Basic Custom Control Edition
\SOFTWARE	Third-party shareware and demonstration software provided for your use and evaluation

Sample Code and Applications

This book contains many code examples in the form of numbered listings that are referenced in the text, as in "see Listing 10.1." These listings are sample code files, provided for example, planning, and reuse purposes. The listing headings direct you to the files on the CD-ROM. For example, consider the following listing heading:

Listing 10.1   10List01.txt—Creating the New *snarfle* Function

This heading indicates that this particular code listing (or example) is included electronically on the CD-ROM. To find it, browse to the `\CODE` subdirectory on the CD and select the file name that matches the one referenced in the listing header from the chapter indicated. In this example, you'd look in the `\CODE\CHP_10\LIST\` subdirectory and open the file, `10List01.TXT`.

Bonus Chapters

This book contains two bonus chapters on the CD-ROM. The first bonus chapter, "Working with Objects and Classes," shows you how to make reusable objects using Visual Basic 5.0. The other bonus chapter, "Making ActiveX Controls," shows you how to make an ActiveX control that you can distribute to other programmers or use in a Web page on the Internet.

VBScheduler

VBScheduler is a personal information manager created by the book's author that is written in Visual Basic 5.0. VBScheduler demonstrates how to write a comprehensive, full featured information manager using only the intrinsic controls. The project comes with complete source code, an associated Access database and a complete Help project with all pertinent files.

Visual Basic Knowledgebase

The Visual Basic Knowldegebase is an online document that contains articles, FAQs, tips and tricks, and other information that help keep you on the cutting edge of Visual Basic programming.

Visual Basic Custom Control Edition

The Visual Basic Custom Control Edition is a subset of the Visual Basic 5.0 programming environment. You use the Visual Basic Custom Control Edition to make your own ActiveX controls in Visual Basic that you can use in your code, distribute to other programmers, or use within a Web page on the Internet.

Third-Party Shareware and Demonstration Software

The CD-ROM comes with a substantial offering of shareware and demonstration software from third-party developers. There are some truly innovative tools on the CD. Everything from industry-specific ActiveX controls to Visual Basic extensions for your site to browsers, viewers, and content creation utilities are included. Be sure to take a few minutes and browse the different toys that are available.

N O T E Most of the products on the CD-ROM are demos or shareware. You may have some difficulty running them on your particular machine. If you do, feel free to contact the vendor. (A vendor would rather have you evaluate their product than ignore it.)

Please note the licensing agreements and obligations for shareware and the purchasing information for registered versions when applicable. ■

Index

Check out Que® Books on the World Wide Web
http://www.quecorp.com

As the biggest software release in computer history, Windows 95 continues to redefine the computer industry. Click here for the latest info on our Windows 95 books

Make computing quick and easy with these products designed exclusively for new and casual users

Examine the latest releases in word processing, spreadsheets, operating systems, and suites

The Internet, The World Wide Web, CompuServe®, America Online®, Prodigy® —it's a world of ever-changing information. Don't get left behind!

Find out about new additions to our site, new bestsellers, and hot topics

In-depth information on high-end topics: find the best reference books for databases, programming, networking, and client/server technologies

A recent addition to Que, Ziff-Davis Press publishes the highly successful *How It Works* and *How to Use* series of books, as well as *PC Learning Labs Teaches* and *PC Magazine* series of book/disc packages

Stay on the cutting edge of Macintosh® technologies and visual communications

Find out which titles are making headlines

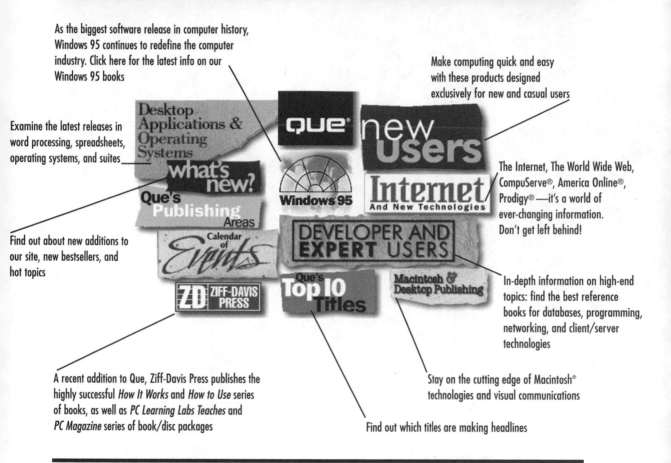

With six separate publishing groups, Que develops products for many specific market segments and areas of computer technology. Explore our Web Site and you'll find information on best-selling titles, newly published titles, upcoming products, authors, and much more.

- Stay informed on the latest industry trends and products available
- Visit our online bookstore for the latest information and editions
- Download software from Que's library of the best shareware and freeware

Complete and Return this Card
for a *FREE* Computer Book Catalog

Thank you for purchasing this book! You have purchased a superior computer book written expressly for your needs. To continue to provide the kind of up-to-date, pertinent coverage you've come to expect from us, we need to hear from you. Please take a minute to complete and return this self-addressed, postage-paid form. In return, we'll send you a free catalog of all our computer books on topics ranging from word processing to programming and the internet.

☐ Mrs. ☐ Ms. ☐ Dr. ☐

Name (first) ☐☐☐☐☐☐☐☐☐☐☐☐ (M.I.) ☐ (last) ☐☐☐☐☐☐☐☐☐☐☐☐☐☐☐☐☐

Address ☐☐☐☐☐☐☐☐☐☐☐☐☐☐☐☐☐☐☐☐☐☐☐☐☐☐☐☐☐☐☐☐

☐☐☐☐☐☐☐☐☐☐☐☐☐☐☐☐☐☐☐☐☐☐☐☐☐☐☐☐☐☐☐☐

City ☐☐☐☐☐☐☐☐☐☐☐☐☐☐ State ☐☐ Zip ☐☐☐☐☐ ☐☐☐☐

Phone ☐☐☐ ☐☐☐ ☐☐☐☐ Fax ☐☐☐ ☐☐☐ ☐☐☐☐

Company Name ☐☐☐☐☐☐☐☐☐☐☐☐☐☐☐☐☐☐☐☐☐☐☐☐☐☐☐☐

E-mail address ☐☐☐☐☐☐☐☐☐☐☐☐☐☐☐☐☐☐☐☐☐☐☐☐☐☐☐☐

1. Please check at least (3) influencing factors for purchasing this book.

Front or back cover information on book .... ☐
Special approach to the content .... ☐
Completeness of content..................................... ☐
Author's reputation .... ☐
Publisher's reputation .... ☐
Book cover design or layout .... ☐
Index or table of contents of book .... ☐
Price of book .... ☐
Special effects, graphics, illustrations .... ☐
Other (Please specify): _____ ☐

2. How did you first learn about this book?

Saw in Macmillan Computer Publishing catalog .... ☐
Recommended by store personnel .... ☐
Saw the book on bookshelf at store .... ☐
Recommended by a friend .... ☐
Received advertisement in the mail .... ☐
Saw an advertisement in: _____ ☐
Read book review in: _____ ☐
Other (Please specify): _____ ☐

3. How many computer books have you purchased in the last six months?

This book only .... ☐   3 to 5 books .... ☐
2 books .... ☐   More than 5 .... ☐

4. Where did you purchase this book?

Bookstore .... ☐
Computer Store .... ☐
Consumer Electronics Store .... ☐
Department Store .... ☐
Office Club .... ☐
Warehouse Club .... ☐
Mail Order .... ☐
Direct from Publisher .... ☐
Internet site .... ☐
Other (Please specify): _____ ☐

5. How long have you been using a computer?

☐ Less than 6 months   ☐ 6 months to a year
☐ 1 to 3 years   ☐ More than 3 years

6. What is your level of experience with personal computers and with the subject of this book?

	With PCs	With subject of book
New	☐	☐
Casual	☐	☐
Accomplished	☐	☐
Expert	☐	☐

Source Code ISBN: 0-7897-1453-1

7. Which of the following best describes your job title?

Administrative Assistant .... ☐
Coordinator .... ☐
Manager/Supervisor .... ☐
Director .... ☐
Vice President .... ☐
President/CEO/COO .... ☐
Lawyer/Doctor/Medical Professional .... ☐
Teacher/Educator/Trainer .... ☐
Engineer/Technician .... ☐
Consultant .... ☐
Not employed/Student/Retired .... ☐
Other (Please specify): _____ ☐

8. Which of the following best describes the area of the company your job title falls under?

Accounting .... ☐
Engineering .... ☐
Manufacturing .... ☐
Operations .... ☐
Marketing .... ☐
Sales .... ☐
Other (Please specify): _____ ☐

9. What is your age?

Under 20 ....
21-29 ....
30-39 ....
40-49 ....
50-59 ....
60-over ....

10. Are you:

Male ....
Female ....

11. Which computer publications do you read regularly? (Please list)

_____
_____
_____
_____
_____
_____
_____
_____
_____
_____

Comments: _____
_____
_____

Fold here and scotch-tape to

‖‚‖‛‖‛‖‛‖‚‖‖‚‖‛‖‚‖‛‖‚‖‖‛‖‛‚‖‚‖‚‖

Licensing Agreement

By opening this package, you are agreeing to be bound by the following:

PRODUCT), the accompanying printed materials, and any copies of the SOFTWARE PRODUCT are owned by Microsoft or its suppliers. The SOFTWARE PRODUCT is protected by copyright laws and international treaty provisions. Therefore, you must treat the SOFTWARE PRODUCT like any other copyrighted material except that you may install the SOFTWARE PRODUCT on a single computer provided you keep the original solely for backup or archival purposes. You may not copy the printed materials accompanying the SOFTWARE PRODUCT.

5. **DUAL-MEDIA SOFTWARE.** You may receive the SOFTWARE PRODUCT in more than one medium. Regardless of the type or size of medium you receive, you may use only one medium that is appropriate for your single computer. You may not use or install the other medium on another computer. You may not loan, rent, lease, or otherwise transfer the other medium to another user, except as part of the permanent transfer (as provided above) of the SOFTWARE PRODUCT.

6. **U.S. GOVERNMENT RESTRICTED RIGHTS.** The SOFTWARE PRODUCT and documentation are provided with RESTRICTED RIGHTS. Use, duplication, or disclosure by the Government is subject to restrictions as set forth in subparagraph (c)(1)(ii) of the Rights in Technical Data and Computer Software clause at DFARS 252.227-7013 or subparagraphs (c)(1) and (2) of the Commercial Computer Software—Restricted Rights at 48 CFR 52.227-19, as applicable. Manufacturer is Microsoft Corporation/One Microsoft Way/Redmond, WA 98052-6399.

7. **EXPORT RESTRICTIONS.** You agree that neither you nor your customers intend to or will, directly or indirectly, export or transmit (i) the SOFTWARE or related documentation and technical data or (ii) your software product as described in Section 1(b) of this License (or any part thereof), or process, or service that is the direct product of the SOFTWARE, to any country to which such export or transmission is restricted by any applicable U.S. regulation or statute, without the prior written consent, if required, of the Bureau of Export Administration of the U.S. Department of Commerce, or such other governmental entity as may have jurisdiction over such export or transmission.

MISCELLANEOUS

If you acquired this product in the United States, this EULA is governed by the laws of the State of Washington.

If you acquired this product in Canada, this EULA is governed by the laws of the Province of Ontario, Canada. Each of the parties hereto irrevocably attorns to the jurisdiction of the courts of the Province of Ontario and further agrees to commence any litigation which may arise hereunder in the courts located in the Judicial District of York, Province of Ontario.

If this product was acquired outside the United States, then local law may apply.

Should you have any questions concerning this EULA, or if you desire to contact Microsoft for any reason, please contact the Microsoft subsidiary serving your country, or write: Microsoft Sales Information Center/One Microsoft Way/Redmond, WA 98052-6399.

LIMITED WARRANTY

and against any claims or lawsuits, including attorney's fees, that arise or result from the use or distribution of your software application product; (E) not permit further distribution of the REDISTRIBUTABLES by your end user. The following **exceptions** apply to subsection (iii)(E), above: (1) you may permit further redistribution of the REDISTRIBUTABLES by your distributors to your end-user customers if your distributors only distribute the REDISTRIBUTABLES in conjunction with, and as part of, your Application and you and your distributors comply with all other terms of this EULA; and (2) you may permit your end users to reproduce and distribute the object code version of the files designated by ".ocx" file extensions ("Controls") only in conjunction with and as a part of an Application and/or Web page that adds significant and primary functionality to the Controls, and such end user complies with all other terms of this EULA.

2. DESCRIPTION OF OTHER RIGHTS AND LIMITATIONS.

   a. **Not for Resale Software.** If the SOFTWARE PRODUCT is labeled "Not for Resale" or "NFR," then, notwithstanding other sections of this EULA, you may not resell, or otherwise transfer for value, the SOFTWARE PRODUCT.

   b. **Limitations on Reverse Engineering, Decompilation, and Disassembly.** You may not reverse engineer, decompile, or disassemble the SOFTWARE PRODUCT, except and only to the extent that such activity is expressly permitted by applicable law notwithstanding this limitation.

   c. **Separation of Components.** The SOFTWARE PRODUCT is licensed as a single product. Its component parts may not be separated for use by more than one user.

   d. **Rental.** You may not rent, lease, or lend the SOFTWARE PRODUCT.

   e. **Support Services.** Microsoft may provide you with support services related to the SOFTWARE PRODUCT ("Support Services"). Use of Support Services is governed by the Microsoft policies and programs described in the user manual, in "online" documentation, and/or in other Microsoft-provided materials. Any supplemental software code provided to you as part of the Support Services shall be considered part of the SOFTWARE PRODUCT and subject to the terms and conditions of this EULA. With respect to technical information you provide to Microsoft as part of the Support Services, Microsoft may use such information for its business purposes, including for product support and development. Microsoft will not utilize such technical information in a form that personally identifies you.

   f. **Software Transfer.** You may permanently transfer all of your rights under this EULA, provided you retain no copies, you transfer all of the SOFTWARE PRODUCT (including all component parts, the media and printed materials, any upgrades, this EULA, and, if applicable, the Certificate of Authenticity), **and** the recipient agrees to the terms of this EULA. If the SOFTWARE PRODUCT is an upgrade, any transfer must include all prior versions of the SOFTWARE PRODUCT.

   g. **Termination.** Without prejudice to any other rights, Microsoft may terminate this EULA if you fail to comply with the terms and conditions of this EULA. In such event, you must destroy all copies of the SOFTWARE PRODUCT and all of its component parts.

3. UPGRADES. If the SOFTWARE PRODUCT is labeled as an upgrade, you must be properly licensed to use a product identified by Microsoft as being eligible for the upgrade in order to use the SOFTWARE PRODUCT. A SOFTWARE PRODUCT labeled as an upgrade replaces and/or supplements the product that formed the basis for your eligibility for the upgrade. You may use the resulting upgraded product only in accordance with the terms of this EULA. If the SOFTWARE PRODUCT is an upgrade of a component of a package of software programs that you licensed as a single product, the SOFTWARE PRODUCT may be used and transferred only as part of that single product package and may not be separated for use on more than one computer.

4. COPYRIGHT. All title and copyrights in and to the SOFTWARE PRODUCT (including but not limited to any images, photographs, animations, video, audio, music, text, and "applets" incorporated into the SOFTWARE

END-USER LICENSE AGREEMENT FOR MICROSOFT SOFTWARE

Microsoft Visual Basic , Control Creation Edition

IMPORTANT—READ CAREFULLY: This Microsoft End-User License Agreement ("EULA") is a legal agreement between you (either an individual or a single entity) and Microsoft Corporation for the Microsoft software product identified above, which includescomputer software and may include associated media, printed materials, and "online" or electronic documentation ("SOFTWARE PRODUCT"). By installing, copying, or otherwise using the SOFTWARE PRODUCT, you agree to be bound by the terms of this EULA. If you do not agree to the terms of this EULA, do not install or use the SOFTWARE PRODUCT; you may, however, return it to your place of purchase for a full refund.

Software PRODUCT LICENSE

The SOFTWARE PRODUCT is protected by copyright laws and international copyright treaties, as well as other intellectual property laws and treaties. The SOFTWARE PRODUCT is licensed, not sold.

1. GRANT OF LICENSE. This EULA grants you the following rights:

    a. **Software Product.** Microsoft grants to you as an individual, a personal, nonexclusive license to make and use copies of the SOFTWARE for the sole purposes of designing, developing, and testing your software product(s) that are designed to operate in conjunction with any Microsoft operating system product. You may install copies of the SOFTWARE on an unlimited number of computers provided that you are the only individual using the SOFTWARE. If you are an entity, Microsoft grants you the right to designate one individual within your organization to have the right to use the SOFTWARE in the manner provided above.

    b. **Electronic Documents.** Solely with respect to electronic documents included with the SOFTWARE, you may make an unlimited number of copies (either in hardcopy or electronic form), provided that such copies shall be used only for internal purposes and are not republished or distributed to any third party.

    c. **Redistributable Components.**

    (i) Sample Code. In addition to the rights granted in Section 1, Microsoft grants you the right to use and modify the source code version of those portions of the SOFTWARE designated as "Sample Code" ("SAMPLE CODE") for the sole purposes of designing, developing, and testing your software product(s), and to reproduce and distribute the SAMPLE CODE, along with any modifications thereof, only in object code form provided that you comply with Section d(iii), below.

    (ii) Redistributable Components. In addition to the rights granted in Section 1, Microsoft grants you a nonexclusive royalty-free right to reproduce and distribute the object code version of any portion of the SOFTWARE listed in the SOFTWARE file REDIST.TXT ("REDISTRIBUTABLE SOFTWARE"), provided you comply with Section d(iii), below.

    (iii) Redistribution Requirements. If you redistribute the SAMPLE CODE or REDISTRIBUTABLE SOFTWARE (collectively, "REDISTRIBUTABLES"), you agree to: (A) distribute the REDISTRIBUTABLES in object code only in conjunction with and as a part of a software application product developed by you that adds significant and primary functionality to the SOFTWARE and that is developed to operate on the Windows or Windows NT environment ("Application"); (B) not use Microsoft's name, logo, or trademarks to market your software application product; (C) include a valid copyright notice on your software product; (D) indemnify, hold harmless, and defend Microsoft from

←